PLAY IN THE AGE OF GOETHE

Introduction

Play in the Age of Goethe and Today

EDGAR LANDGRAF AND ELLIOTT SCHREIBER

IF WE WERE TO take at face value Friedrich Schiller's famous dictum that "the human is truly human only in play," we would have to conclude that no age has ever produced more fully human beings than ours.[1] We are inundated with game play today. Digital devices offer opportunities to play almost anywhere and anytime. No matter what age, gender, or social, cultural, or educational background—we play. The video game industry is bigger than the film and music industries combined, and growing by double-digits each year.[2] Game play has also seeped into nongame settings not just rhetorically, but practically. Patrick Jagoda offers an assessment of the current state of gamification—the use of game mechanics in traditionally nongame activities—which increasingly permeates our economic, social, and cultural life.[3] From marketing to scientific studies to dating sites, games are employed to gather data, sell products and services, and model and affect behavioral patterns, including education. As Donna Haraway presciently attested in "A Cyborg Manifesto," we are "living through a movement from an organic, industrial society to a polymorphous, information system—from all work to all play, a deadly game."[4]

Haraway's statement, including its dire coda, signals how far we are removed from Schiller's identification of play with human fulfillment. Not only have the nature, availability, reach, and social relevance of play changed since the eighteenth century, but the humanism that drives Schiller's argument—itself very much the product of a book culture—is being challenged, in no small part, we suspect, due to the replacement of reading habits by digital gaming. The perceived threat to humanism and humanist values drives much of the vitriol about the potential evils of our contemporary infatuation with game play—and not just by technophobes and geriatric professors of literature. Thinkers of diverse stripes observe that modern game play can foster new forms of social isolation and alienation, and that its addictiveness appears to constitute a threat to the kind of human fulfillment that Schiller associated with play.[5] Politically, too, where Schiller saw the potential of play to help break the circle of tyranny—by allowing subjects to practice how to act responsibly as future free citizens—some contemporary theorists see a game like Candy Crush as a neoliberal training ground for the economization of everything.[6]

To be sure, the movement to "all play" that Haraway perceives as a "deadly game" in "A Cyborg Manifesto" is accompanied by a countermovement that values play more positively. In *When Species Meet*, that is, a little over twenty years after the "Manifesto," Haraway herself promotes an understanding of play that adopts its humanist idealization and makes it the centerpiece of a posthumanist ethos that finds in play the model for the transcending of species-boundaries and the appreciation and enactment of interrelationality.[7] Play apparently transcends the post/humanist divide. Likewise, Jagoda suggests that "play can exceed gamification and its narrow sense of utility in the present" and argues that the "precariousness and uncertainty of play . . . are precisely what make it a critical concept in our moment," one that even holds "the prospect of meaningful social change."[8]

In conjunction with such optimism, it is also worth noting that digital gaming has not entirely superseded other forms of play. Particularly with the proliferation of so-called German-style games, or Eurogames, such as the blockbuster Settlers of Catan, analog gaming has experienced a remarkable global resurgence.[9] This renaissance has occurred in no small measure precisely as a countertrend to digital gaming.[10] In its inaugural issue in 2014, the editors of *Analog Game Studies* point to the humanist values that they see as distinguishing this new wave of board games and role-playing games from their digital counterparts: "Because the impetus is on *invention* as opposed to *industry*, analog games epitomize the potentials of a design ethic which does not pander to over-generalized market demographics."[11] But, as the editors note elsewhere in the same programmatic essay, "the term 'analog' only exists by way of negative comparison to the digital, such that our present-day digital forms of expression produce their analog heritage as a by-product."[12] In other words, the very notion of the analog (e.g., "analog games") can be conceived only in relation to the digital. Digital game play has thus become a ubiquitous frame of reference for all play.

Given the current pervasiveness of digital gaming, and given the tensions and tectonic shifts in the landscape of play in recent decades, it is perhaps small wonder that an intensification of scholarly interest in play has taken place over the last decade. Two interdisciplinary journals devoted to play have been founded, *The American Journal of Play* (in 2008) and *The International Journal of Play* (in 2012); a major resource for play researchers, the two-volume *Handbook of the Study of Play* (2015), was recently published; and numerous collections and monographs have appeared, foremost among them Thomas Henricks's *Play and the Human Condition* (2015).[13] While this renewed attention to play has likely been prompted by very current trends among both children and adults, we contend that it is shaped by a discourse of play that extends back more than two centuries, and to which German letters of the Age of Goethe (roughly the time period between 1770 and 1830) made a decisive contribution. It is here that the parameters are set that continue to guide our debates about what are good rather than bad games, or what constitute good rather than bad practices of play. The decades around 1800 are the formative years for the modern understanding of play and the development of the values with which we continue to assess play, its importance, and its potential reach—the turning point when play is afforded fundamental significance in aesthetics, developmental psychology, pedagogy, and even the sociopolitical arena. This volume sets out to address this pivotal period in the development of modern practices, representations, and theorizations of play. In so doing, we hope to fill an important gap within the discipline of German Studies, as well as within current play research more broadly.

Henricks does, admittedly, acknowledge the legacy of this period, citing Schiller's *On the Aesthetic Education of Man* (1795) as the first modern theory of play.[14] Indeed, Henricks's contributions represent an important instance of the affirmation of humanist values in the study of play.[15] Nevertheless, Henricks and other contemporary play researchers generally neglect to consider the broader discourse of play within which Schiller's theory emerged. It is well known that Schiller draws explicitly on Kant's notion, in the *Critique of Judgment* (1790), of the "free play of imagination and the understanding" that takes place in the perception of beauty.[16] Less well known are the many other significant developments involving play around 1800 in domains such as pedagogy, literature, commerce, and the social life of the rising middle class. In the realm of pedagogy, Johann Heinrich Basedow, Joachim Heinrich Campe, and the so-called Philanthropinist movement built upon the work of John Locke, François Fenélon, and Jean-Jacques Rousseau to make play a pillar of their educational reforms.[17] In contrast to their instrumental use of play for educational and moral ends, Karl Philipp Moritz (*Anton Reiser*) and Johann Wolfgang Goethe (*Wilhelm Meister's Years of Apprenticeship*) developed a notion of imaginative or symbolic play as integral to childhood, as the point of origin of theatrical play, and (according to Goethe in *Poetry and Truth*) as the genesis of storytelling.[18] Toy merchants such as Georg Hieronimus Bestelmeier fed interest in children's educational and imaginative play, producing the first illustrated toy catalogues, thereby enabling direct marketing to consumers.[19] In response to the increased consumption of mass-produced toys, Romantic authors like Jean Paul (*Levana; or, The Doctrine of Education*) and E.T.A. Hoffmann ("Nutcracker and the King of Mice," "The Strange Child") questioned whether commercial toys promote or inhibit the child's imagination. These writers thereby helped define the arena within which the current debate about toys and games for children, from Lego to Halo, takes place.

Beginning in the middle of the eighteenth century, play furthermore assumed an increasingly important role as a medium for the social interactions of middle-class adults. As Dorothea Kühme has documented, society games became centerpieces of familial and social gatherings, as evidenced by the publication of some seventy-four German collections of society games between 1750 and 1850.[20] For the young Friedrich Schleiermacher, theorizing on the basis of his experiences in Henriette Herz's Berlin salon, games in "their more rational forms" serve as models for conceptualizing sociability, that is, "the free play of thoughts and feelings whereby all members mutually stimulate and enliven each other."[21] However, while society games gained favor in middle-class life, games of chance tended to be attacked as decadent, aristocratic pastimes in literary works like August Wilhelm Iffland's *The Player* (*Der Spieler*, 1795).[22] Nonetheless, as Rüdiger Campe argues in *The Game of Probability*, games of chance lie at the basis of the modern understanding of probability (as elaborated in the work of Leibniz, Johann Heinrich Lambert, and other Enlightenment thinkers) and of contingency, whereby the singular is no longer viewed as the necessary, as expressive of divine providence, but as one possibility among others, and hence as something that might be changed, altered, reversed, improved upon if not with the next roll of the dice, then through human intervention.[23]

Following Campe, we can not only link games of chance to the rise of the genre of the novel in the eighteenth and nineteenth centuries but also recognize how the German discourse of play around 1800 proved to be of fundamental importance to the formation of modern selves, society, and culture. Thus, as Christian Moser and Regine Strätling have argued, games of chance underlie the formation of modern subjectivity: "The self that seeks to constitute itself *through play* always simultaneously puts itself *in play*."[24] And as Philipp von Hilgers has shown, games of chance even inform the modern understanding of war. Thus, for Clausewitz, "war resembled less a mechanical system than a card game, in which incalculabilities arise from the mixing of the cards and from the opponents' unanticipatable ways of playing."[25] This modern understanding of war was made possible in no small measure not only by Clausewitz's theory but also by a contemporaneous board game, the Taktisches Kriegs Spiel (Tactical War Game) that was invented by Georg von Reiswitz during the wars of liberation and that was enthusiastically adopted by the Prussian (and later, in the Wilhelmine era, Imperial) military elite as a kind of "war academy."[26]

Of course, play was a central concern of earlier historical periods, as well. Thus, Johan Huizinga, in his classic *Homo Ludens*, declares that "the whole mental attitude of the Renaissance was one of play."[27] A few statistics bear out the validity of Huizinga's bold claim. For instance, Pieter Bruegel the Elder's *Children's Games* (1560) depicts more than 230 children "occupied with 83 different games. The whole city appears to be theirs."[28] The hero of *Gargantua and Pantagruel* (1542) plays 217 games after dinner one evening, suggesting, according to George McClure, "that the sixteenth-century appetite for games could match a giant's boundless capacity for food."[29] Rabelais's first German translator, Fischart, "completed the long list with 372 German card games and dance tunes."[30] It is important to note, however, that game play in the sixteenth and seventeenth centuries was far from universally accepted. As Kelli Wood points out, the papacy in Rome issued over thirty edicts against gambling between 1590 and 1674, that is, during a time period when printed board games proliferated.[31] But the frequency of such attempts to prohibit "sinful" game play—particularly when they involved wagering—only speaks to their popularity across a broad swath of society, from aristocratic leisure culture—where play was a means to combat ennui—to folk festivities. There was, however, neither an especially educational nor a particular humanist dimension attached to such play. The fundamental reevaluation of play—which discovers (or invents) the usefulness of play in pedagogy, aesthetics, and even politics, not to mention Schiller's assessment of play as the most human of human activities—only happens around 1800. It is part of an extensive and nuanced debate about play, about different forms of (game) play, and play's potential social (ab-)

uses which this volume wants to revisit, to add both historical context and theoretical reflection to contemporary concerns and aspirations around play.

We have organized our volume into four parts, each centered on a key concern in the discourse and practice of play in the Age of Goethe: free play, games of chance, children's play, and the play of language. Our collection opens in Part One with two chapters that address the idealist conception of the free play of human faculties that has been fundamental to discussions about play since being formulated by Kant in *The Critique of Judgment*. In the opening chapter, Christian Weber argues that Kant's concept of free play was itself prefigured (and perhaps even made possible) by Goethe's radical innovations within Anacreontic poetry, a subgenre of playful, erotic poetry in German letters that coevolved with modern aesthetic thought. As Weber makes clear, the reevaluation of play as a serious activity cannot be viewed independently of the emergence of an aesthetic discourse that (with Baumgarten's *Aesthetica* from 1758) recognizes the senses and imagination as an autonomous sphere of intuition. This sets the stage for Kant's reinterpretation of aesthetics no longer as merely about sensuous experience but as contributing in its own unique way to the symbolic order that undergirds civil society. In a series of close as well as carefully contextualized readings, Weber teases out the politics (in particular, the sexual politics) of play in poems by Johann Wilhelm Ludwig Gleim, Johann Peter Uz, and Friedrich Gottlieb Klopstock and finally Goethe's "Song Accompanied by a Self-Painted Ribbon" (1775). As Weber shows, Goethe's intervention lies in realizing a free play of the faculties that is the condition of possibility for a free play between the sexes. Twenty years after the publication of Goethe's poem, the political implications of the notion of free play would become one of the central concerns of Schiller's *Aesthetic Letters*, the text that (together with Kant's third *Critique*) is the focus of Samuel Heidepriem's essay. More precisely, Heidepriem is concerned with Paul de Man's scathing critique of the essentializing humanism that de Man locates in Schiller's notion of play, in sharp contrast to Kant's formulation of free play. Heidepriem lucidly distills de Man's argument, positioning it in relation to Jacques Derrida's theory—one of the founding forays of deconstructionist thought—of free versus constrained models of play. Furthermore, Heidepriem challenges de Man's pitting of Kant's conception of play against Schiller's, underscoring Kant's own humanist tendencies, and arguing that both Kant's and Schiller's theories of play are much closer to poststructuralist concerns than de Man suggests.

The two chapters in Part Two focus on games of chance in two key texts of the period, Lessing's Enlightenment play *Nathan the Wise* and Goethe's encyclopedic *Faust* drama. Rather than subject games of chance to a moral critique or cherish them for their entertainment value, both plays recognize games of chance as reflective of the human condition in a world where a profound sense of contingency has come to replace divine providence and necessity. Landgraf's essay explores how Lessing anticipates a notion of "just playing" (Gregory Bateson) that wants to discover the rules of one's own playing whereby the "rules are always changing and always undiscoverable."[32] In *Nathan the Wise*, playing with the rules of the game ("mit dem Spiele spielen") and even "false play"—as Nathan calls the benevolent actions of the father at the heart of the ring parable—are risky but necessary wagers in the Enlightenment's pursuit of religious tolerance, sympathy, and social reciprocity. Nicholas Rennie's contribution expands the opposition between necessity and contingency to encompass two fundamentally different cosmologies that subtend Goethe's *Faust*. As the drama invokes Dante's *Divine Comedy*, the wager between Faust and Mephisto challenges the totalizing gestures of the Renaissance text by initiating an open-ended play of substitution and deferral in a decidedly Derridean sense. While in *Nathan the Wise* the openness of the wager is affirmed as a precondition for the mediation between tradition and contingency, Rennie sees Goethe take a more skeptical stance. The open structure of Faust's wager, which needs to continually postpone and preclude its own resolution, is accompanied by a problematic forgetting that haunts modernity's incessant striving, and that produces a fragmented subjectivity where selfhood and conscience are ungrounded and constantly in play.

Part Three brings together three chapters on children's play in the Age of Goethe, beginning with two essays on Goethe's insights. Elliott Schreiber's essay traces the twentieth-century developmental psychologist Jean Piaget's influential concept of symbolic play back to Goethe's depictions of play in *Wilhelm Meister's Years of Apprenticeship* and *Poetry and Truth*. Piaget, like Goethe, characterizes symbolic play as essentially egocentric. However, where Piaget holds that such play matures into rule-bound, social play during the course of the child's development, Goethe undermines such a teleology by exposing how egocentric, symbolic play continues to drive rule-oriented play. In her contribution, Patricia Anne Simpson points to an even darker current in Goethe's views on play. In particular, Simpson examines Goethe's penchant for two toys popular around 1800: the toy guillotine and the yo-yo. In the process, she reveals what she (following Frederic Jameson) terms the "political unconscious" embedded both in Goethe's writings and in the material culture of the two toys themselves, which bespeak (in more or less apparent ways) anxieties connected to the French Revolution. Simpson thereby brings to light a Goethe who is far more eccentric than the exemplary, monumental figure who was held up as a paragon of both *Bildung* and fatherhood by nineteenth- and twentieth-century pedagogues. Among these was the great nineteenth-century educational reformer, Friedrich Fröbel, the founder of the kindergarten movement, and the subject of Ian McNeely's chapter. McNeely documents how Fröbel synthesized a wide range of current educational views, including those of Rousseau, Pestalozzi, Basedow, Kant, Schiller, and Schleiermacher. According to McNeely, Fröbel's greatest contribution lay in the central importance that he accorded to play in the education of three-to-six-year-olds and in his systematic program to cultivate children's faculties through the introduction of a series of toys or "gifts." McNeely underscores the ambiguity inherent in Fröbel's system of play: on the one hand, Fröbel regards play as having an instrumental function, guiding children toward productive and moral lives as citizens; on the other, the play that Fröbel envisions is autotelic, an end unto itself, and not only for children but also for their teachers. Like Schreiber's and Simpson's essays, then, McNeely's illuminates both the teleological and the antiteleological dimensions of children's play as conceptualized in the Age of Goethe, though the concept of children's play advanced by Fröbel remains distinctly more idealist in its orientation than Goethe's.

We have placed Christiane Frey's contribution as an "interlude" between Part Three and Part Four because its reading of Fichte through Jacobi's lens focuses on the transition from the Enlightenment to the Romantics, whose interest in the play of language is the subject of Part Four. By calling it an interlude, we also wish to highlight her chapter's pragmatic stance, the playful manner in which it approaches Jacobi's critique of Fichte around the simile of a knitted sock (*Strickstrumpf*), a stance that aligns with the ludic performance at the heart of its analysis. Jacobi's simile of the sock not only raises serious epistemic questions about Fichte's speculative reasoning, it also highlights how philosophy conceived as "act-act" or *Thathandlung* is unable to escape its entanglement with play. In this philosophical context, play marks the performative moment within the movement of thought that is speculative reasoning. Furthermore, it provides the enclosure, the warding off (or

Hegung, a term that Jost Trier showed is etymologically related to the word *Spiel*) from the profane that lends Fichte's philosophy the status of a religion. Frey argues that by playing Fichte at his own game, Jacobi's critique reveals how the only way of dealing with Fichte's doctrine of science with the seriousness that it deserves is through play.

Our volume's fourth and final part on the play with language begins with an essay by Michael Powers that, like, McNeely's, examines one of the most influential pedagogical treatises of the first half of the nineteenth century, namely, Jean Paul's *Levana*. Jean Paul's educational theory, too, lays out a teleological model of development that hinges on play, beginning with "theoretical" (or receptive) play, continuing with "practical" (or active) play, and culminating in social play. Powers shows how each of these stages corresponds with a level of linguistic development, running from the preverbal stage to the stage of communicative ability. However, Powers further argues that Jean Paul gestures toward a liminal space between the first two stages that Powers terms "poetic" (in the sense of "poeisis") and that primarily expresses itself as wordplay. Such wordplay both draws and erases the divide between sense and nonsense, meaning and matter, dialogue and monologue, inner and outer. In the process of exploring this liminal space in *Levana* as well as in several other seminal works, Jean Paul, like both Goethe and Fröbel, establishes but also undermines a theory of the developmental trajectory of play, extending it to the acquisition and (poetic) expansion of language. David Martyn's contribution explores the philosophical import that the inability to disentangle seriousness from play has for another highly influential Romantic theory of language, namely that of Schleiermacher. Martyn argues that, both in his lectures on hermeneutics and in his famous essay on translation, Schleiermacher conceptualizes language (in the sense of a particular national language, or "langue," in Saussure's sense of the term) as that which delineates the limits of authorial free play; that is, each national language has its own discrete identity, and works of literary genius are "langual" (or *sprachig*, a term coined by Robert Stockhammer) in that they arise through the interplay between the genius of the author and that of the national language in which they are written. Martyn reveals how, in formulating this theory of authorship, Schleiermacher also invokes another, more pejorative sense of the term "play" in order to rule out of bounds another theory, namely, that of authorship as "metalangual," that is, as transgressing the bounds of any given national language (and indeed the notion of the "langual" as such). Though Schleiermacher attempts to cleanly distinguish between "langual" and "metalangual" theories of authorship, Martyn shows how his use of the key term "play" in the act of differentiating between them creates an unintended slippage. Martyn thereby is able to compellingly argue that as Schleiermacher fails in his attempts to contain, limit, and control play and to separate fully serious from "mere" play, he also fails to establish a notion of original authorship that could secure authorial control outside of and unaffected by the play of language.

In the final essay of Part Four (and of our volume as a whole), Brian Tucker makes clear that wordplay was also a topic of intense interest among the Early Romantic theorists Novalis, August Wilhelm Schlegel, and Friedrich Schlegel, as well as the linguist August Bernhardi. Like Jean Paul, these thinkers associate the capacity for wordplay with childhood, both the childhood of the individual and that of the species. However, in contrast to Jean Paul, these thinkers do not regard wordplay as pushing beyond sense to nonsense, but rather as capable of illuminating deeper meanings and connections inaccessible to language in its ordinary usage among adults. According to the Early Romantics, poetry, through what Friedrich Schlegel terms "musical wit," can offer exemplary instances of such wordplay. Indeed, in the second part of his essay, Tucker shows how two poems by Ludwig Tieck paradigmatically instantiate wordplay and its power to convey insights that would otherwise be ineffable. As Tucker convincingly reveals, the second of these poems does so by playing with a famous poem by Goethe. Tucker's study thereby returns us, with a playful but no less meaningful twist, to Goethe's poetry, this volume's point of departure.

Examining free play, games of chance, children's play, and the play of language around 1800, *Play in the Age of Goethe* fills both a historical and a theoretical gap in current play research. Historically, it offers a rich picture of practices, narratives, and theories of play that shows why this period is often referenced as the starting point of the modern conception of play. Theoretically, our collection brings major thinkers and writers from this period into conversation with a range of influential theorists of the twentieth century, including Bateson, Walter Benjamin, de Man, Derrida, Henricks, Huizinga, Jameson, Piaget, Brian Sutton-Smith, and Trier. Furthermore, in a combined historical and theoretical register, our collection illuminates the antinomies that subtend the discourse of play from the late eighteenth century to the present, and the ways in which these antinomies can also be subverted to produce a more complex understanding of the phenomenon of play. When Schiller asserted that "the human is truly human only in play," he neglected to offer a differentiated understanding of play and of "the human." There is, of course, no simple answer. And this is precisely the point. What play means and what it means in relation to human and nonhuman actors cannot be assessed independently of the ever-changing discourses, practices, and theories of (game) play that help construct and reconstruct the meaning of these terms and their relationship to each other. Our volume hopes to further such a reflective stance and help elucidate some of the main contentions in this relationship, including the question of why play since the Age of Goethe has remained linked so closely with—and yet must also be recognized to supersede changing categories of—the human.

NOTES

1. Friedrich Schiller, *Sämtliche Werke*, ed. Gerhard Fricke and Herbert G. Göpfert (Munich: Hanser, 1962), 5:618.

2. According to a recent article by Tom Wijman in *Newzoo*, the video game industry will grow to 137.9 billion USD in 2018 with mobile revenues accounting for more than 50 percent of the global games market. "Mobile Revenues Account for More than 50% of the Global Games Market as It Reaches $137.9 Billion in 2018," *Newzoo*, April 30, 2018, https://newzoo.com/insights/articles/global-games-market-reaches-137-9-billion-in-2018-mobile-games-take-half/

3. Patrick Jagoda mentions games like Chore Wars which "converts undesirable chores into a game complete with superheroic role-playing" or *Phylo* which invites players "to help researchers with a common problem in comparative genomics." "Gamification and Other Forms of Play," *Boundary 2* 40, no. 2 (2013): 114.

4. Donna Haraway, "A Cyborg Manifesto: Science, Technology, and Socialist-Feminism in the Late 20th Century," *International Handbook of Virtual Learning Environments*, ed. Joel Weiss et al. (Dordrecht, Netherlands: Springer, 2006), 128.

5. See Dana Smith's interesting column, "This Is What Candy Crush Saga Does to Your Brain," *Guardian*, April 1, 2014, https://www.theguardian.com/science/blog/2014/apr/01/candy-crush-saga-app-brain. The World Health Organization recently added "gaming disorder" to the International Classification of Diseases (ICD). See "Gaming Disorder: Online Q&A," September 2018, https://www.who.int/features/qa/gaming-disorder/en/. In addition, the American Academy of Pediatrics (AAP) has warned of "potentially addictive behaviors related to Internet use and gaming," particularly among teens. See Donald Shifrin, Ari Brown, David Hill, Laura Jana, and Susan K. Flinn, "Growing up Digital: Media Research Symposium," American Academy of Pediatrics, October 1, 2015, https://www.aap.org/en-us/Documents/digital_media_symposium_proceedings.pdf. In a recent clinical report, the AAP furthermore notes, "Media (eg, television, video games, and smartphone and tablet applications) use often encourages passivity and the consumption of others' creativity rather than active learning and socially interactive play. Most importantly, immersion in electronic media takes away time from real play, either outdoors or indoors. Real learning happens better in person-to-person exchanges rather than machine-to-person interactions." See Michael Yogman, Andrew Garner, Jeffrey Hutchinson, Kathy Hirsh-Pasek, Roberta Michnick Golinkoff; AAP Committee on Psychosocial Aspects of

Child and Family Health, AAP Council on Communications and Media, "The Power of Play: A Pediatric Role in Enhancing Development in Children," *Pediatrics* 142, no. 3 (September 2018): 8–9, http://pediatrics.aappublications.org/content/pediatrics/142/3/e20182058.full.pdf.

6. This is the argument Patrick Jagoda made in a talk with the title "Gamification (or: Neoliberalism at Your Fingertips)" delivered at the 2018 Society for Literature, Science and the Arts conference in Toronto. Jagoda also noted the positives of game play, its potential to create a sense of contingency, and a sense of alternate worlds and opportunities.

7. "Play is the practice that makes us [Cayenne, her canine, and Donna Haraway] new, that makes us into something that is neither one nor two, that brings us into the open where purposes and functions are given a rest. Strangers in mindful hominid and canid flesh, we play with each other and become significant others to each other. The power of language is purported to be its infinite inventiveness. True enough in a technical sense ('discrete infinity'); however, the inventive potency of play redoes beings in ways that should not be called language but that deserve their own names." Donna Haraway, *When Species Meet* (Minneapolis: University of Minnesota Press, 2007), 237. Play, for Haraway, exceeds language and consciousness as markers of human superiority over animals, though play is not unlike language, as it "rearranges elements into new sequences to create new meanings" (Haraway, *When Species Meet*, 240). She also notes, drawing on Gregory Bateson's analysis of play among animals, how play involves a complex metacommunicative act—"this bite is not a bite"—that Bateson points out is the precondition for more abstract modes of communication, for language, and for social interactions, including empathy, to evolve. For a more detailed discussion of Bateson in relation to the Enlightenment, see Edgar Landgraf's contribution in this volume.

8. Jagoda, "Gamification," 116, 144.

9. Tristan Donovan, *It's All a Game: The History of Board Games from Monopoly to Settlers of Catan* (New York: Thomas Dunne Books, 2017), 237–256.

10. This according to Jonathan Berkowitz, Hasbro Gaming's senior vice president of marketing, quoted in Donavan, *It's All a Game*, 255.

11. Evan Torner, Aaron Trammell, and Emma Leigh Waldron, "Reinventing Analog Game Studies," *Analog Game Studies* 1, no. 1 (August 1, 2014), http://analoggamestudies.org/2014/08/reinventing-analog-game-studies/. Italics in the original.

12. Torner et al., "Reinventing Analog Game Studies."

13. See James E. Johnson, Scott G. Eberle, Thomas S. Hendricks, and David Kuschner, eds., *The Handbook of the Study of Play*, 2 vols. (New York: Rowman & Littlefield, 2015).

14. Thomas Henricks, "Classic Theories of Play," in *The Handbook of the Study of Play*, ed. James E. Johnson et al. (New York: Rowman & Littlefield, 2015), 1:163.

15. See Thomas Henricks, *Play and the Human Condition* (Urbana: University of Illinois Press, 2015). For a critical perspective on Henricks's humanism, see the chapter by Samuel Heidepriem in the present volume.

16. See sec. 9 in Immanuel Kant, *Critique of the Power of Judgment*, ed. Paul Guyer (Cambridge: Cambridge University Press, 2000). Of the recent essays on Kant's concept of free play, see in particular the stimulating article by Thomas Pfau, "The Appearance of *Stimmung*: Play as Virtual Rationality," in *Stimmung: Zur Wiederkehr einer ästhetischen Kategorie*, ed. Anna-Katharina Gisbertz (Munich: Fink, 2011), 95–111. Pfau situates Kant's

ideas at the beginning of a line of thought on play that courses through the writings of Schiller and Goethe, as well as the work of more recent thinkers such as F.J.J. Buytendijk, Eugen Fink, Hans-Georg Gadamer, and Arnold Gehlen.

17. On the influence of Locke's pedagogy of play upon Basedow, see Jürgen Overhoff, ". . . aber mit Lust!," *Die Zeit*, April 10, 2003, http://www.zeit.de/2003/16/A-Basedow.

18. See the chapter by Elliott Schreiber in the present volume. On Moritz's critique of Philanthropinist pedagogy, as well as his concept of *Spielraum* or "play-space," see also Elliott Schreiber, *The Topography of Modernity: Karl Philipp Moritz and the Space of Autonomy* (Ithaca, NY: Cornell University Press and Cornell University Library, 2012). The classic study of Goethe's notion of play is Wolfgang Kayser, "Goethe und das Spiel," in *Kunst und Spiel: Fünf Goethe-Studien* (Göttingen: Vandenhoeck & Ruprecht, 1961). Kayser focuses on Goethe's reverence for play, suggesting that—unlike Schiller, who ultimately instrumentalizes play for the purpose of (political) education—Goethe finds in play a form of freedom from the constraints imposed by reality that enables a heightened state of attentiveness and absorption, a "surrender of our [everyday] existence in order to exist." Kayser, "Goethe und das Spiel," 39. Positioning Goethe in the *teatro del mundo* tradition, Kayser argues that play at its heart contains a religious quality, as it has the power to transform all earthly and transient things into something that "permanently references something higher, essential [*Eigentliches*]." Kayser, "Goethe und das Spiel," 46. Our translation.

19. See Thomas Strauss, *Frühe Spielwelten zur Belehrung und Unterhaltung: Die Spielwarenkataloge von Peter Friedrich Catel (1747–1791) und Georg Hieronimus Bestelmeier (1764–1829)* (Hochwald: Librum, 2015).

20. Dorothea Kühme, *Bürger und Spiel: Gesellschaftsspiele im deutschen Bürgertum zwischen 1750 und 1850* (Frankfurt am Main: Campus Verlag, 1997), 33.

21. Friedrich Schleiermacher, "Toward a Theory of Sociable Conduct," trans. Jeffrey Hoover, in *Friedrich Schleiermacher's Toward a Theory of Sociable Conduct and Essays on Its Intellectual-Cultural Context*, ed. Ruth Drucilla Richardson (Lewiston: Edwin Mellen, 1995), 25.

22. See Kühme, *Bürger und Spiel*, 56–62.

23. See Rüdiger Campe, *The Game of Probability: Literature and Calculation from Pascal to Kleist*, trans. Ellwood H. Wiggins (Stanford, CA: Stanford University Press, 2012).

24. "Das Selbst, das sich *im Spiel* zu konstituieren sucht, setzt sich zugleich auch immer *aufs Spiel*." Christian Moser and Regine Strätling, "Sich selbst aufs Spiel setzen: Überlegungen zur Einführung," in *Sich selbst aufs Spiel setzen: Spiel als Technik und Medium von Subjektivierung*, ed. Christian Moser and Regine Strätling (Paderborn: Fink, 2016.), 20 (our translation; italics in the original). Moser and Strätling are speaking here not only of games of chance but of the element of chance that they see as inherent in all play.

25. Philipp von Hilgers, *War Games: A History of War on Paper*, trans. Ross Benjamin (Cambridge, MA: MIT Press, 2012), 47.

26. Von Hilgers, *War Games*, 51–56.

27. Johan Huizinga, *Homo Ludens: A Study of the Play-Element in Culture* (New York: Roy, 1950), 180.

28. Cäcilia Bischoff, *Masterpieces of the Picture Gallery: A Brief Guide to the Kunsthistorisches Museum*, cited in *Google Arts & Culture*, accessed June 11, 2019, https://artsandculture.google.com/asset/children%E2%80%99s-games/CQEeZWQPOI2Yjg?hl=en.

29. George McClure, *Parlour Games and the Public Life of Women in Renaissance Italy* (Toronto: University of Toronto Press, 2013), 3.

30. Mikhail Bakhtin, *Rabelais and His World*, trans. Hélène Iswolsky (Bloomington: Indiana University Press, 1984), 231.

31. Kelli Wood, “Chancing It: Print, Play, and Gambling Games in the Sixteenth Century,” *Art History* 42, no. 3 (2019): 450–481. Wood points toward similar bans against ball games and gambling in Florence while also noting how “at the same time that the Medici were commissioning artworks that rhetorically promoted a unified identity of Florence and a spectre of control over the city space through the apparatus of public games like *calcio in levrea*, the populace engaged in transitory activities of play in the street that contributed to community identity and belonging in space.” See Kelli Wood, “‘Balls on Walls, Feet on Streets’: Subversive Play in Grand Ducal Florence,” *Renaissance Studies* 32, no. 3 (2018): 367.

32. Gregory Bateson, “Metalogue: About Games and Being Serious,” in *Steps to an Ecology of Mind: Collected Essays in Anthropology, Psychiatry, Evolution, and Epistemology* (Northvale, NJ: Jason Aronson, 1987), 30.

Part I

Free Play

CHAPTER ONE

Beauty and Erotic Play

Anacreontic Poetry's Transformation of Aesthetic Philosophy

CHRISTIAN P. WEBER

ALEXANDER GOTTLIEB BAUMGARTEN'S publication of the *Aesthetica* (1750/1758) is commonly considered the event—at least from the vantage point of German intellectual history—when the new philosophical discipline of aesthetics came into existence. His definition "aesthetica . . . est scientia cognitionis sensitivae" (sec. 1) was revolutionary for two reasons.[1] Firstly, Baumgarten broke with Platonist idealism and Wolffian rationalism by recognizing that the so-called lower faculties of the mind, that is, the senses and the imagination, constitute an autonomous sphere of intuitions and representations based on intrinsic processes and laws undetermined by the higher cognitive faculties of understanding and reason. Secondly, he acknowledged that sensuous cognition is indeed denser, richer, even truer than the abstractions of logical differentiating and reasoning (e.g., sec. 440). For Baumgarten, beauty thus turned into a matter of perfecting sensuous cognition (sec. 14) so that the contemplating subject can fully appreciate the rich complexity and individuality of an artwork. Inspired by this radical positive reevaluation of the sensible, ensuing theories from Winckelmann to Lessing and Herder contributed to the unraveling of the aisthetic, semiotic, and poietic foundations of the arts in an effort to cultivate the senses and the imagination of their readers and to attune them to the beauty of the world. Forty years later, this young and still unsettled discipline experienced a paradigm shift with the publication of Kant's *Critique of the Power of Judgment* (1790),[2] a shift marked by the introduction of "play" as a crucial aesthetic concept that this chapter sets out to illuminate.

AESTHETIC "FREE PLAY"

Even though Kant acknowledged his indebtedness to Baumgarten for clearing the field for aesthetics, his theory differs so remarkably from his predecessor's that it must be regarded as laying a completely new foundation. Most importantly, Kant locates the aesthetic action no longer within the clearly demarcated field of sensuous perception that Baumgarten so fervently protected against any potential intrusion from the understanding and reason; instead, he places it right on the borderline, in the gray area between the lower and the higher faculties of the mind. For him, aesthetics is not just a matter of sense perception and intuition, but essentially one of judgment, that is, the contemplation and reflection of those representations that defy determination through the application of concepts or the subsumption under ideas. This implies, however, that beauty does not occur in a vacuum of naïve sensual bliss, but always already within the symbolic order of culture and societal civility, which, for Kant, predetermine the conditions of the human existence. Under this pretext he can relate the aesthetic experience to "cognition in general" (*Erkenntnis überhaupt*) and insist on its "universal communicability" (*allgemeine Mitteilungsfähigkeit*) as the common ground that warrants the intersubjectivity of aesthetic experiences even without conceptual understanding (sec. 9; 217).

As the coping mechanisms of the symbolic cultural order (language and ideology) fail to process representations, an alternative cognitive process is set into motion that Kant describes as a "free play" (*freies Spiel*) between the "lower" imagination and the "upper" understanding. Kant himself does not further qualify the nature of this "play," but he calls it "free" for mainly two reasons: firstly, the breakdown of conceptual cognition severs the bond between the schema (provided by the imagination as a signified synthetized from manifold sensible intuitions) and the word (provided by the understanding as an arbitrary signifier) and thus releases the imagination from its subservient function to the conceptual understanding, thereby reawakening its originally creative potential.[3] In his *Anthropology*, Kant labels this liberated "productive" imagination also "poetic" (*dichtend*), which relates "play" to poetry.[4] We may infer, then, that the imagination becomes productive by utilizing the words from the ruined concepts as material for a new round of schematizing by creating metaphors and—when pursuing the poetic articulation of an "aesthetic idea"—also symbols.[5] Hence, secondly, the play is "free" in that it unfolds in a medium detached from the real without a preset outcome. It creates imagined alternative realities within the realm of fiction.

Kant defines beauty as the feeling that results from the "state of mind" (*Gemütszustand*) of this free play. The universal communicability of this aesthetic dynamic he sees represented best by the poetry that the play of reflective judgment brings about, and he ranks poetry as the art form of greatest aesthetic value for three reasons: firstly, it "expands the mind [*Gemüt*] by setting the imagination free" and "thus elevates itself aesthetically to the level of ideas"; secondly, it "strengthens the mind by letting it feel its capacity to consider and judge nature, as appearance, freely, self-actively, and independently of determination by nature"—to the effect that the poetic mind is capable of utilizing not just words but also the appearance of nature, "as it were as the schema of the supersensible [*gleichsam zum Schema des Übersinnlichen*]"; thirdly, it is the most truthful art form: "[Poetry] plays with the illusion which it produces at will, yet without thereby being deceitful; for it itself declares its occupation to be mere play" (sec. 53; 326–327). Poetry, as such, is meta-play, that is, play with and about the reflective judgments that constitute the aesthetic experience and contribute to the formation of an individual subject that feels liberated from the physical determination of the body, from the preoccupation of conceptual understanding, and from the burdens of the worldly existence in general. Conversely, this means that the judgment of beauty per se cannot be represented by philosophy because its rationality and discursivity operate in a pre-aesthetic mode. Ultimately, an investigation of the "free play" must be left alone to what it essentially is and what it has become: poesy/poetry.

For this reason, Kant wisely refrained from exploring the nature of this "play" any further, or else he had to resort to poetry himself. Nonetheless, arguably due to its mysteriousness, play has become a most consequential term in the history of aesthetics—from its famous totalizing dictum by Schiller ("the human is truly human only in play") to attempts of ontologizing play by Nietzsche, Heidegger, and Derrida.[6] Taking Kant as their lead, a number of studies set out to investigate the meaning and significance of play in philosophy, yet so far little to no attention has been given to the cultural and, more specifically, poetical contexts that may have inspired Kant's surprising turn to an aesthetic free play and the experience of beauty (or the sublime) as a bridge to connect not just the lower and higher cognitive faculties but also the theoretical understanding and practical reason that were dealt with separately in his two previous *Critiques*.[7] Hence, the present article conducts a genealogical investigation of how play was used not so much within the philosophical discourse but in the poetry of the years from the *Aesthetica* to the *Critique of Judgment*.

As noticed by Gernot Böhme, the various examples employed in the third *Critique* indicate that Kant was very much a "man of the Rococo," a life form greatly appreciative of cultivated playful sociability.[8] Anacreontic poetry, which was fashionable in Germany from the 1740s through the 1770s, abounds with erotic jokes. As I will show in a chronological sequence of selected poems from this period, the jokes turn increasingly licentious as the male lyric voice tends to involve and engage more directly the desired female in an erotic play. My thesis is that the twists and general turn in the relationships between the male and female in the erotic play of Rococo poetry reflect and even prefigure the twists and the paradigm shift that the evolution of aesthetics underwent in the transition period from Baumgarten to Kant.

Moving closer to the third *Critique*'s more imminent conception during the 1770s and 1780s, when Kant aimed at superseding both rationalism and sensualism by shifting to transcendental idealism, the emergence of a new poetry, commonly known as the *Sturm und Drang*, challenged the philosopher. This movement can be characterized as an amalgam of ideas from Spinoza, Leibniz, Shaftesbury, and Shakespeare, culminating in the idea of artistic genius. According to John H. Zammito's reconstruction of the *Critique*'s genesis, Kant conceived his aesthetics also in "defense of reason against what he took to be the dangerous impulses of *Sturm und Drang* irrationalism, especially as carried forward by Johann Gottfried Herder."[9] Even though Zammito may be exaggerating the dispute between the revered philosopher and his favorite student by depicting it as an oedipal rivalry,[10] their dissociation marks a crucial rift within the German Enlightenment during the last third of the eighteenth century.[11] It must be regarded as an ironic twist of historical reason that, of all people, it was Herder's protégé Goethe who reconciled the discrepancy between these two influential figures. After his return from Italy and acquaintance with Schiller, Goethe did not just discover Kantian philosophy and particularly the third *Critique* as initiating a new and "highly pleasant period" of his life, he also realized that "the main ideas of this work were entirely compatible [*ganz analog*] with my way of creating, acting, and thinking so far [*meinem bisherigen Schaffen, Tun und Denken*]."[12] Curiously, this affinity can be registered already in an early work by the young Goethe, his "Song Accompanied by a Self-Painted Ribbon" ("Lied, das ein selbst gemahltes Band begleitete"). This poem appeared first in 1775 but was composed already during the eighteen months (April 1770–August 1771) that he studied in Strasburg, where he enjoyed many formative conversations with Herder. This ostensibly simple yet inscrutably intricate poem marks the culmination point of Rococo sentiments and the turning point toward *Sturm und Drang* aesthetics. At the same time, as we shall see later, it displays a striking prefiguration of Kant's conception of beauty and aesthetic "free play."

POETIC EROTIC PLAY

Before we get to Goethe, we must reconstruct the genealogy of erotic play in Kant's age and turn first to the beginnings of both the Anacreontic and the aesthetic movements, which coevolved in Halle, the center of German Pietism, in the late 1730s and 1740s. Baumgarten taught there at the university until 1740 when he moved to a position at the Viadrina in Frankfurt/Oder. He was succeeded by his student Georg Friedrich Meier, who popularized his predecessor's main ideas on the new discipline of aesthetics by translating them from Latin into German (Kant used Meier's *Rudiments of all Arts and Sciences* [*Anfangsgründe aller schönen Künste und Wissenschaften*], based mainly on Baumgarten's lectures, for his own lectures on this topic in Königsberg).[13] The new appreciation of sensuous cognition in the lectures of both Baumgarten and Meier inspired two generations of students in Halle to write poems about wine, love, and friendship in the cheerful manner of the Greek poet Anacreon:[14] the main figures of the so-called first school of Halle poets were Samuel Gottlob Lange and Jacob Immanuel Pyra, and of the "second school" they were Johann Wilhelm Ludwig Gleim, Johann Peter Uz, Johann Nikolaus Goetz, and Paul Jacob Rudnick. An indication of the close ties between philosophy and poetry is that Meier and Lange coedited a journal with the telling title *The Sociable Man* (*Der Gesellige*), for which the latter crafted a programmatic essay, "On the Anacreontic Ode" (1748). Apart from the traditional bucolic topoi and the common praise of love and wine, Lange names as a "modern" addition to the list of characteristics a gentle application of "subtly mocking jokes" (*feinen spottenden Scherz*).[15] Lange refers here not just to poetry but also to Meier's treatise *On Jokes* (*Gedancken von Schertzen*, 1744), according to which "the joke is a sensuous cognition as well as a sensuous representation of this knowledge," "belongs to the field of aesthetics," and therefore obeys "the rules of beauty."[16] It is composed of both sensuous wit (*sinnlicher Witz*), that is, "the ability to recognize the congruity of things" in terms of their "similarity, identity, and proportion," and sensuous acumen (*sinnliche Scharfsinnigkeit*), that is, "the ability to recognize the differences or the distinction of things" in terms of the same negative categories.[17] According to Meier, a proper joke captures and instantly reveals the paradoxical "oscillation between identity and difference"[18] of wit and acumen: "By means of the joke we must present the audience at once, in one glance, with a very manifold congruence of the things compared. The joke must be a short embodiment of many movements of comparison [*ein kurtzer Inbegriff vieler Vergleichungsstücke*]. It must be, so to speak, similar to an abyss [*einem Abgrunde ähnlich*] in which one sees more and more the longer one peers into it."[19]

Even though Meier does not use the term "play" here, one has only to substitute the words "wit" with "imagination" and "acumen" with "understanding" to realize a structural affinity with Kant's explanation of aesthetic beauty. Moreover, Meier's formula "A joke must contain unequivocally more thoughts than words"[20] foreshadows Kant's notion of the "aesthetic idea," which he defines as a "representation of the imagination that occasions much thinking though without it being possible for any determinate thought, i.e., *concept*, to be adequate to it" (sec. 49; 314). Undeniably, though, crucial differences remain: whereas Meier relates in this context both wit and acumen to sensuous cognition (he distinguishes for both faculties between a sensuous and logical mode of operation), Kant associates only the imagination with the lower faculties of the soul, while he counts the understanding among the higher faculties of the mind. Moreover, as Gabriel Trop points out, Meier remains, by submitting "the aesthetic exercise of the joke to the doctrine of perfectibility of the human senses, . . . ultimately a metaphysician and a rationalist."[21] The early aesthetics of Baumgarten and Meier are thus trapped in a paradox. On the one hand, their efforts to claim an autonomous sphere for sensuous cognition draw a too rigorous line of distinction from the higher cognitive powers, while on the other they import from above the doctrine of perfection as their guiding principle. Kant's aesthetics resolves this contradiction by bringing these antagonistic faculties into play with each other. Yet, by virtue of its attempts to reestablish erotic play between the two sexes, Anacreontic poetry already set a precedent by bringing into play again what had long been separated and alienated.

Play commonly involves more than just one being. This observation is addressed by a programmatic text, Gleim's poem "The Creation of the Woman" ("Die Schöpfung des Weibes," 1758), which reflects on the main and most problematic prerequisite of Anacreontic poetry: the other sex.[22] Before we engage with play in this and other poems, however, we must address the paradoxical status of the woman in poetry in general, since she is represented as the embodiment of play and, at the same time, is played (with) not just by her male counterpart but by the higher authorities of the poet and the patriarchal ideology of society at large. The establishment of middle-class literary circles and the emergence of new aesthetic and poetic discourses in the eighteenth century expanded the playing field for women to partake in literary discussions and—even more so—for the mostly male authors to project their desires onto the female characters and characteristics in their works. Ever since the predominantly negative Christian image of the woman as the demonic, at once seduced and seducing cause of the original sin was largely shattered, philosophers and poets were challenged to reflect on femininity in general, to rethink the role of women in society and how to reintegrate them into the patriarchal structures of their metaphysical/philosophical systems. Consequently, the redrawing of this image became a battleground of conflicting male interests, fantasies, and ideologies.[23]

In the early rationalist phase of Enlightenment, for example, Gottsched established a normative poetics which would allow everyone—without social and gender discrimination—to partake in the production of poetry, if only the contributor adheres to the universal laws of reason and the (patriarchally monitored) rules of his poetics. For Gottsched, the ideal woman was represented by the female scholar who, just like his wife Adelgunde Kulmus (better known as "Gottschedin"), writes literature in agreement with the model set by him.[24] Against this image and the rigid order of the rationalist, male-dominated regime of his age, Gleim felt the urge to inject some play and fun that he associates with the female.[25] "Jove," the poem begins, "observes the first man / How lonesome he is and how seriously he speculates / Over the origin of all things" (I:2–4). Bored from watching just the man brooding over his endless monologues, Jove announces to the circle of gods a solution: "There shall be a woman / A neat little thing for pleasure / That may joke and speak with him" (II:12–14). No sooner said than done:

> She suddenly appeared with a man's complexion,
> But more tender and not quite as old,
> With her nifty eyes she spotted soon
> The thinking being tucked in a corner of his room;
> She hopped swiftly onto him and kissed the man,
> And speaks: A fool you are, just look at me!
> I have been made to play with thee.
>
> (III:15–21)

By transferring the story of creating the woman from the biblical to the mythological context, Gleim reverses the story of the fall of man. According to this rewriting, a sprite Eve is no longer the origin of all evil, but instead the solution to the malady of obsessive metaphysical speculation and sensuous neglect that has befallen the male half of mankind. Eve speaks words of wisdom by simply reminding Adam that the purpose of life lies not only in reflecting about things but in interacting with them as well as with other humans. By insisting on her right to play, she sets out to transgress eighteenth-century gendered dichotomies between the rational male and the emotional female.

For play to occur, certain conditions must be met and rules established within a well-defined playing field set apart from the norms of reality.[26] In this spirit, Gleim counters the criticism of moral indecency against Anacreontic poets in the prefaces to his edition of "Jocular Songs" ("Scherzhafte Lieder"): "Never infer from the poets' writings their morals. You fool yourselves, because these poets are writing only to show off their wit [*Witz*], even though their virtue may appear suspect. They do not present themselves as they are but as the genre of poetry demands; and they are fondest of a poetic system which allows them to be witty."[27] Gleim thus detaches the erotic play of Anacreontic poetry from the social norms of his time by placing it—herein following Baumgarten—within a clearly circumscribed, autonomous aesthetic sphere that shall remain free from any attempt of metaphysical, theological, or ideological intrusion.[28] This explains the return to mythology (which is rather indistinct, neither clearly Greek nor Roman, but a playful amalgam of both) and to the bucolic settings of the idyllic tradition, which provide the necessary fictional foil of contrast to distinguish it from the present conditions of real life.

In the fictional world different rules apply and different possibilities emerge that can be played out poetically. As Wolfgang Iser argued, already the bucolic poetry of Theocritus and Virgil employed the topoi and figures of the idyll not for mimetic purposes but as arbitrary signs for the representation of an artificial, alternative world.[29] In the same vein, the figure of the shepherd serves the Rococo poet as a mask to stage potentialities, and Anacreontic poetry functions as an "ecstatic" medium to articulate latent emotions, desires, and visions.[30] The mask is a limitation, behind which the person can hide and withhold certain aspects of his personality, yet at the same time an extension of the person, a medium to display experiments with identity and deviance from the cultural norms. Mask and person engage in a "permanent exchange of constructive and deconstructive impulses" that emerges from their "play of difference."[31] Consequently, the strict distinction that Lange and Gleim drew between the life depicted in their poems and their personal lives is, in fact, more fluid than they claimed or wanted to admit in public. Anacreontic poetry initiates a fictional play oscillating between the expression of an individual imaginary and the reflection of societal conditions and moral inhibitions of the real. Matthias Luserke characterizes the Rococo accordingly as a "great machinery of sublimation, installed for no other purpose than to let desire speak."[32] At the same time the poet, as in the case of Gleim, experienced a "fantasy of sexual failure, almost amounting to the fear of castration," when confronted with a woman of flesh and blood.[33]

The intricacy and wide range of societal, psychological, and poetical implications in the building of a theoretical scaffold around the scandal of erotic play adumbrate the complexity of the supposedly naïve relationships displayed in Rococo poems. The interpretations of the following three poems, milestones in the evolution of erotic play that reaches its climax with the poetry of the *Sturm und Drang*, reveal how difficult it proved for men to accept a woman's offer to play with her. These poems stage in an increasingly reflective manner scenes of inner conflict in a male lyrical subject torn by the decision to either follow his passion and submit himself to the sensuous/sensual attraction of female beauty or to resist and obey the societal and moral demands on his understanding and reason. (This conflict later gains philosophical prominence in Schiller's aesthetics in terms of "inclination" and "duty.") Even though the negotiations between sensuous and moral cognition are hardly acted or played out by the figures in the poems themselves, their configuration sets in motion the imagination of the observing/reading subject, who engages in a reflective judgment about the aesthetical and moral ambiguity of the presented situation. In this regard, the (latently) erotic play of the poetic figures and the conflicting fancies and thoughts that they provoke in the onlooker prefigure the free play of the cognitive faculties in terms of the Kantian aesthetics.

CONFIGURATIONS OF REFLECTION IN UZ'S "A PAINTING"

In "A Painting" ("Ein Gemälde," 1755), at the climax of the Anacreontic fashion, Johann Peter Uz illustrates the great difficulties the sexes have in interacting with each other.[34] By utilizing the pictorial representation of Anacreontic scenery as the template for an ekphratic description and poetic speculation, he also creates medial tension that stimulates the reader to reflect on the status quo of what is represented and the state of representation in general.[35] The first lines bring at once the discrepancy between the real and the imaginary, that is, the illusory of this fictional world to the reader's attention: "Look! What a tableau! / The flowers on these fields / Blossoming in nature's lap / They are not, o Phyllis! of a real May?" (I:1–4). By openly displaying the mediality and artificiality of the Anacreontic genre, Uz is able to intersect the reflection about the representation of the sexes in the poem with metapoetic reflections about the relationship between poetry and the visual arts and about the conditions (limitations and possibilities) of writing Anacreontic poetry as such. Creating an even greater distance to the real lifeworld and widening the poetic playing field allow the poet some more flexibility within the existing moral code and more liberality with depicting erotic episodes. In the poet's eyes and imagination, the shepherdess is no longer an innocent and naïve maiden, but a woman who stages her female desire before the scenery of an erotically charged landscape:

> She lies, only barely covered,
> Elongated on a bed of flowers.
> With her curls plays
> Zephyr, who cools her down;
> And her white bosom,
> Ripe already for crafty lust,
> Reveals itself under the veil
> And surges up in her sleep.
> (II:9–16)

Not only does Zephyr play with her curls, but conversely, the shepherdess exploits him for her own cunning (dis)play with a shepherd, who, approaching her "with his eyes wide open" (III:19), appears to be quite receptive to her charms:

> How his cheeks glow!
> His body bends down clumsily,
> Clinging on to his staff
> In an awkward position,
> Toward the sleeping beauty.
> (III:20–24)

Unfortunately for him, however, his clumsy and awkwardly leaning position corresponds not at all with the overlong erected staff that he is clinging onto as shown on the picture. Although he shows a physical reaction with the blushing of his cheeks, it falls way short of the intended (and natural) response to engage in an erotic play with the pretending "sleeping beauty." At least, that is how the poetic speaker resolves the tension of this situation that remains rather indecisive in the painting:

> The savage feels a heart!
> Was it a jest of love
> That drove him to this beauty
> As a witness of her might?
> His mind is already more advanced;
> And, fully turned around,
> He'll return to his sheep,
> After he saw her asleep.
>
> (IV:25–32)

At this turning point, the ekphratic description turns more than before into speculation, interpretation, and judgmental reflection (even reflective judgment). This stanza basically contains and performs what poetry can add to the pictorial template and to painting in general. Firstly, it extends the pregnant moment psychologically (but also aesthetically and morally) by staging an internal conflict between the shepherd's "heart" (*Herz*) and "mind" (*Verstand*). What is he going to do? Shall he follow the passion of his senses or the morals of his reason? These may be questions the onlooker of the picture and the reader of the poem ask themselves, which contribute to its aesthetic quality in the Kantian sense of reflective judgment. But the critical situation is soon decided, secondly, by the lyrical speaker, who obviously prefers rationality and therefore extends the decisive moment temporally by envisioning the shepherd returning to his sheep. However, this does not quite do it for the reader yet. As the lyrical speaker marveled about the "jest of love" (*der Liebe Scherz* [*sic*!]), the reader lingers over this putative decision and marvels about the possibility of a joke that the poet may have played on him. Is it really ultima ratio to turn around and return to the herd when the shepherd could have won the embrace of a beautiful woman instead? This last stanza contains certainly some ironic markers by the poet that put into question for readers whether the shepherd's turning-off is the only good solution: the ending sounds far too laconic for an intricate situation such as this one; the language is charged with far too much sensuality, eroticism, and sexual allusion to make this solution fulfilling; finally, the term "fully turned around" (*ganz umgewandt*; IV:30) stands out as an awkward phrase in its topographical meaning of "turned around" 180 degrees. In this phrase the lingering inner conflict continues to resound by evoking two linguistic associations with opposing psychological values: the first association is *ganz unverwandt*, which translates as "steadfastly," while the other, *ganz umgewand*[*el*]*t*, expresses the exact opposite, meaning "completely transformed." Since the latter is truer to the literal topographical meaning, I regard it the stronger of both interpretative options, which would imply that the impact of the aesthetic experience of female beauty has had a longer-lasting effect on the shepherd's soul. And this may well be the effect that the poet intended to have on his readers: to question whether rationalist abstinence, particularly in inviting situations such as this one, is always the solution.

Accordingly, one does find in the erotic poetry of the late Rococo (which lasted well into the nineteenth century) shepherds who do not turn around but engage with the sleeping women. An example for this is the poem "The Sleeping Woman" ("Die Schläferin") that was published anonymously in a collection of sexually quite explicit poems from 1792.[36] Here Thyrsis, tormented by his repressed passion, eventually gives in to his desire, sneaks into the bed of the targeted beauty, and "breaks this flower" while she continues sleeping. One would expect the sleeping woman to express outrage over her rape, but the (rather tasteless and morally unacceptable) joke is that, to the contrary, her only concern is with Thyrsis not waking her and missing out on the pleasure of this lust.

AMBIGUITY OF EROTIC PLAY IN KLOPSTOCK'S "THE ROSY RIBBON"

A less outrageous case of a similar situation is represented in an ode by Klopstock that was originally conceived as an intimate dedication poem to his fiancée Meta (called "Cidli" in Anacreontic fashion) in 1752 and anonymously published under the title "The Sleeping Girl" ("Das schlafende Mädchen") in 1769, though it is better-known under its later title "The Rosy Ribbon" ("Das Rosenband"; since 1798).[37] It has been considered "*the* bourgeoise-sentimental love poem par excellence."[38] The poem performs the transformation of the male lyrical subject and his female object of desire into a couple (hence the personal dedication), a union mirrored by the eponymous metaphor that blends together natural beauty (*Rosen*) and civilizing force (*Band*; translating it as "ribbon" or "garland" does not do fully justice to the latent violence inherent in the German word related to the English "bond"). In this regard, one may doubt whether the ode really enacts the transition from gallant *plaisir*, which enacted love according to well-defined rules and therefore remained largely nonbinding play as in most of the Anacreontic poems, to love coded as passionate and intimate *amour* that resists disciplinary force, rejects moral impositions, and transcends societal divisions.[39] I will leave this question undecided for now, since, as we shall see, the text can be interpreted from different angles as four conflicting events that prevent a definite conclusion. In any case, even though it carries over the common theme of "shepherd contemplating a sleeping beauty," Klopstock's ode differs significantly from the previous Anacreontic poems by avoiding any mythological decorum (except for its last word) and inventing a completely new poetic language of simulated oral intimacy and symbolic immanence that set a new standard for German poetry from Goethe to the Romantics.[40] Moreover, the desiring male has become identical now with the lyrical speaker; he is no longer a dull shepherd who just leans clumsily on his staff, but a man with enough chutzpah and craftiness to utilize the rose ribbons as means for erotic play.

According to a letter that Klopstock wrote to Meta (October 31, 1752), the poem was inspired by a dream: "You lay there sleeping, and I wanted to wake you softly; then in a whim I decided to use your long shepherd's staff so that you wouldn't awake too early, meaning too close to me; but then I found right next to me one of your bonneteonds [velvet ribbons], which I tied to the lower end of the staff to hassle you gently with it. As I was doing this, you suddenly awoke so sweetly; then you embraced me wildly, wildly, and you wouldn't stop clinging on to me."[41] One of the main Anacreontic requisites, the shepherd's staff (which commonly is associated with the shepherd, but here, curiously, belongs to the sleeping girl), is transformed into a means of communication by incorporating female attributes, the velvet ribbons. Klopstock seems to emancipate himself from the dilemma of Anacreontic poetry—characterized by the male figures' inability to communicate and share their desire with a female due to the internalization of rational norms (as exemplified in the poem by Uz), which can result in phantasies of rape (as exemplified by Thyrsis in the previous poem)—through self-castration, that is, by *playing* an effeminate role. Consequently, the woman assumes the opposite role. Meta's exaggerated, almost violent behavior in the dream can be interpreted as a reaction to women's long endurance of neglect as equal partners in social engagements and erotic/sexual play; her wild embraces seem to express the joy of relief about having found a playmate finally, reminiscent of fairy tale endings when the prince kisses the girl to release her from a hundred years of slumber. The playful switching of gender roles in poetry amounts, then, to a device (as simple as it is ingenious) to overcome the rigidity of gender differences and may present for the sexes the only way to find their way back to one another.

The poem completes the symbolical transformation of the shepherd's staff into rosy ribbons (symbolizing the refraction and feminization of the penis), by means of which the simultaneously desired and feared carnal passion is further sublimated and the *sensual-erotic event* turned into a *media event*. In fact, the media of the rosy ribbons themselves are sublimated as they seem to dissolve with the poem's progression: In the first stanza, the lyrical subject utilizes their material quality to "bind" (I:2) the slumbering girl. In the third stanza, the ribbons are utilized in a nonmaterial manner as an acoustic means to further increase the indistinctness of the subject's oral, nonverbal communication ("lisping," III:7) through their "rustling" (III:8). By the fourth and final stanza, they have become obsolete as the speaker receives in return for his play a melting gaze from the girl. As this gaze is reciprocated, it substitutes the rosy ribbons and creates an atmosphere of nonmaterial, immediate understanding that culminates in the dissolution of the difference between male and female: "around *us* it became Elysium" (IV:12).

The medial metamorphosis of the "rosy ribbons"—from their initial use in a mild case of violation to their appropriation as a medium of acoustic manipulation until their final dissolution in the mutual gaze—continues with their rematerialization in form of the poem "Das Rosenband." (Note the shift from plural rose ribbons to the singular of the title.) With the publication of the poem as an all-comprehensive total medium, Klopstock wishes to reach a larger audience that he hopes to awaken from its moral slumber. He thereby turns the intimate message of the genesis of his love relationship to Meta, to whom the poem was initially addressed ("An Cidli"), into a model for how to overcome the gender-reinforced sexual division and potentially all societal partitions. Although the term "Elysium" may signal the return to an imagined golden age in the past, its anachronism contains nonetheless a utopian element by proposing a mystical and aesthetic revision of the mythical foundation of Western culture toward the formation of a more equal civil society.

The lyrical subject performs his play with the rosy ribbons under the conditions of nonverbal communication ("lisping . . . speechlessly"; III:7) and nonconceptual cognition, which give the poem the appeal of a *mystical event*. The stanzas show a progression from her nonsentient slumber (I:3) via his sentient nescience (II:3) into a state of perceptual awakening and instantaneous recognition (IV) that recalls and ultimately revises the biblical myth of Adam and Eve's fall from grace: "Then the eyes of both of them were opened" (Gen. 3:7a)—with the reversed roles that the lyrical speaker (Eve) teases through his play with the rosy ribbons the girl (Adam) to open her eyes and look into his. The figures of the ode do not recognize their shameful nakedness and marked difference, but instead realize their belonging-togetherness. It emerges a new form of sensual and sensuous understanding as an antidote to the conventional form of conceptual understanding that, according to Hamann's *Aesthetica in nuce*, is a direct effect and consequence of man's fall from grace.[42] "Elysium" thus signals (in accordance with the mythological meaning of this chronotype as a resting place of the dead) the return to a prerational *unio mystica* of souls without bodily consciousness of sexual differentiation, as was the state of existence before the fall.[43]

At the same time, as was mentioned earlier, "Elysium" is also a utopian time-space that embraces both man and woman and that, in turn, is generated by the specularity of their mutual glance. As a neutral third it guarantees their equality: "around us *it* became Elysium." The lovers create around them an autonomous sphere with the potential of growing therein into something greater than just their two existences combined. I call this the *aesthetic event*, which differs from the mystical event by its future-oriented potentiality. The promise of continued becoming is embodied in one crucial element that the allegorical exegesis of the poem as a mystical revision of the Fall myth has so far elided: the snake. In "Das Rosenband," the "lisping" and "rustling" of the rosy ribbons certainly evoke associations with this hissing animal winding through leaves. By making an appearance in the first and third stanzas, the rosy ribbons tie the poem together; and with its many repetitions, parallelisms, chiasms, vocal correspondences, and phonetic resonances across lines and stanzas, the poem creates an intricate structure of "laterally reversed identity" and "reciprocal dependency" that mimics the snakelike performance with which the rosy ribbons have bonded man and woman together.[44] The rosy ribbons and even more so the poem "Das Rosenband" serve as exemplary models for what poetic play can accomplish.

According to Hogarth's influential essay *The Analysis of Beauty* (1753), published the year after Klopstock composed his "Rosenband," the waving line of beauty and the serpentine line of grace "give play to the imagination, and delight the eye."[45] There are astonishingly many coincidences between Klopstock's poem and Hogarth's theory. To begin with, Hogarth's ambition, like Baumgarten's and Klopstock's, is to cultivate sensuous cognition: he wants to "teach us to *see with our own eyes*" and gain "a perfect knowledge of the elegant and beautiful in artificial, as well as natural forms," for which "pompous terms of art, hard names," and "prepossessed . . . dogmatic rules" are obstacles that must be removed.[46] He finds the lines of beauty and grace in almost everything, from legs of chairs to Greek statues, but above all—following suit with the voyeuristic male gazes we have encountered in many poems so far—in the female body. Some of his examples are especially reminiscent of Klopstock's ode and Anacreontic poetry. He notes that a "ribbon, twisted round a stick . . . has been a long-established ornament in the carvings of frames, chimney-pieces, and door-cases; . . . called by the carvers, *the stick and ribbon ornament*," which due to its serpentine feature has a pleasing effect.[47] Notwithstanding, the "most amiable in itself is the flowing curl; and the many waving and contrasted turns of naturally intermingling locks ravish the eye with the pleasure of the pursuit, especially when they are put in motion by a gentle breeze."[48] At this point it is worthwhile to remember that up to Hogarth any academic reflection on the matter of beauty was a matter of pursuing ideals of perfection and moral ideas, but not the pursuit of female beauties for the intermingling play of their locks in "a gentle breeze." Discounting the women's rank and status[49] and the men's desire for the opposite sex (even though a subcurrent of erotic attraction remains present throughout the text which puts a decidedly male imprint on Hogarth's aesthetics), the *Analysis* arrives at an innovative cognitive conception of beauty: "The face indeed will bear a constant view, yet always entertain and keep our curiosity awake, . . . because vast variety of changing circumstances *keeps the eye and the mind in constant play*, in following the numberless turns of expression it is capable of."[50] We have here, I would argue, the formula of an egalitarian and dynamic sensualist aesthetics that presents an important link between the erotic play of Anacreontic poetry and Kant's famous definition of beauty as a free play between the imagination and the understanding, especially since Hogarth's notion of play fulfills Kant's main preconditions for the occurrence of pure aesthetic experiences: elimination of conceptual understanding and disinterest in the object itself.[51]

How does Klopstock fit in here? Does his "Rosenband" prefigure an aesthetic event in agreement with the Kantian conditions of disinterested pleasure and nonconceptual free play? Two points contradict this assessment. First, even though the lyrical speaker explicitly rejects verbal communication and stages with the mutual gaze a spontaneous sensuous (aisthetic) form of understanding, his poetic recapitulation nonetheless culminates in a concept. The appearance of "Elysium" as the poem's final word functions as a category to subsume the entire action and thus as a teleological conclusion.

As a result, the poem does not symbolically present an aesthetic moment but allegorically represents a historical narrative. Second, there is also good reason to doubt the equality in the relation of the two sexes, as my reading of the ode suggested in terms of a mystical event, when it comes to its aesthetical (and moral) assessment.[52] If we apply Kant's definition of beauty as a "free play" to the erotic play of the sexes in this poem, it becomes evident that only the male agent is acting freely (though, as line II:6 indicates, even he does not act with full consciousness), while the female remains passive and reacts only at the end. This disparity extends to the poem itself, which contains only the male speaker's recapitulation of events. For the shared experience of the mutual gaze we get to know only his perspective: "She looked at me; her life hung / With this gaze on my life" (IV:10–11). The reader cannot determine with certainty whether this is a true representation of her feelings or not rather an emotional appropriation by the lyric speaker. In the latter case, the mutual gaze does not resolve the initial violent binding of her body and the deception of her senses by means of the rosy ribbons; the poem would function then as an aestheticized cover-up of violation and manipulation. In any event, the looming shadow of this discrepancy and the inconclusiveness about what kind of event the text represents cast doubt about the ode's poetic integrity, unless its aesthetic ambiguity was meant to set in motion an unresolvable play of the hermeneutic judgment.

THE SPECULAR MOMENT OF CORRESPONDING AESTHETIC JUDGMENTS IN GOETHE'S "SONG ACCOMPANIED BY A SELF-PAINTED RIBBON"

Goethe appears to have reacted sensitively to the aesthetic inadequateness of Klopstock's "Rosy Ribbon" by writing a poem in which the last line articulates the wish for "not a meager rosy ribbon" (*kein schwaches Rosenband*; IV:16). As the title "Song Accompanied by a Self-Painted Ribbon" ("Lied, das ein selbst gemahltes Band begleitete"; 1775, composed in 1771 or 1772) suggests, the poem is not just about a love relationship but also a reflection on the relationship of two different artistic media, poetry and painting.[53] Lessing's essay on *Laocoön*, first printed in 1766, proposed the strict differentiation between painting and poetry based on semiotic criteria. According to his influential art theory, poetry is essentially the temporal succession of speech composed of arbitrary acoustic signs (words) and therefore predestined to present consecutive actions, whereas painting is essentially the spatial arrangement of natural signs (images) geared toward the simultaneous representation of figures and events in one pregnant moment. Therefore, the task of poetry shall be no longer to produce ekphratic descriptions of pictorial and allegorical scenes à la Uz. In contrast to his "A Painting," Goethe keeps the ribbon and the song that the lyrical speaker sends to his beloved apart, with each medium conveying essentially the same message in a different manner. The painted ribbon functions as a symbol of love, but by itself it sends an ambivalent, even conflicting message about the nature of the intended relationship: on the one hand, the ribbon suggests a more binding one, which is reinforced by the (more or less) explicit engagement proposal in the poem's fourth stanza; yet, on the other hand, the playful free drawings on the ribbon evoke the characteristic *je ne sais quoi* sentiment of the Rococo and seem to signify the exact opposite: freedom from obligation.[54] Hence, the accompanying song is necessary to spell out how the mixed messages of the painted ribbon can be reconciled, how the recipient should interpret it.

As an instructive device the accompanying song commands hermeneutic scrutiny. Concerning its formal features, it fully complies with Lessing's semiotic model of poetry by connecting each of the increasingly imaginary events of the four stanzas into the sequence of basically one consecutive and dynamic action. The poem presents itself as an interior monologue of the lyrical speaker in the process of drawing floral ornaments on the eponymous ribbon:

> Little flowers, little leaves
> Scatter for me with gentle hand
> Kind young spring-divinities
> Sprightly on an airy band.
>
> (I:1–4)

The Anacreontic requisites, here the young spring-gods and later Zephyr (II:5), are no longer presented as agents in their own right but as purely allegorical figures in the service of the lyrical speaker who imagines them as models for a more playful and lighter execution of his task. What is most innovative, however, is the poetic strategy of representing an inner monologue which allows the reader to witness not only the production process of the ribbon with the greatest possible intimacy but also the emerging composition of the accompanying poem, since the sung monologue is presented as identical to the poem in front of us. Through the monologue as poem, the speaker can express and communicate his emotions and hopes that have motivated him to draw the ribbon, in which his feelings manifest only implicitly and indirectly through the images on its surface and the gesture of offering it as a gift. In this respect, the song must accompany the ribbon because only both media complementing each other contain the exuberant love message and can convey its richness and pathos to the receiving beloved.

An example for the successful cooperation of both media has already been performed in the making of the painted ribbon, since the characteristic Anacreontic trifling (*tändeln*; here rendered as "sprightly") contributes "airiness" as an essential quality to the ribbon. Anacreontic poetry is thereby reduced to a means to the end of producing the painted ribbon as well as the present poem, which communicates emotion (seemingly) with greater immediacy and more authenticity than an Anacreontic poem was able to. Also, the second stanza misappropriates a classical Anacreontic topos for the transportation of the new media to deliver their delicate message(s):

> Zephyr, take it on your wings,
> Twine it around my beloved's dress;
> So before the mirror she springs
> In all her eager joyousness.
> (II:5–8)

Zephyr is literally turned into a messenger with the order to "entwine" (*schlingen*) the ribbon around her dress and, we can infer, her body. The word *schlingen* evokes associations with snakes (*Schlangen*) reminiscent of Klopstock's ode and the famous Laocoön statue that Lessing selected as the artistic model to develop his semiotics of the arts. Indeed, this stanza illustrates *in nuce* the successful application of Lessing's theory into poetic practice. It combines three consecutive actions from different agents into the continuous flow of one single event and manages—appropriate for the transitional character of this stanza—to shift with ease from real actions (the painting and sending off of the ribbon) to increasingly imaginary, more implied than explicated actions: the entwining of the ribbon around the girl's dress, her discovering it, putting on the dress, and rushing to the mirror in all her excitement. The procedure of these actions culminates in a fourth action:

> Sees herself with roses rife,
> Like a rose herself she is,
> A kiss from you! dear life,
> Will reward abundant bliss.
> (III:9–12)

Here the sender imagines the aesthetic effect of his present on the recipient. In the mirror the girl shall see the image of her youth, joyfulness, and beauty just as the male speaker sees and envisions her, so that the reflection image of the girl adorned "with roses rife" and the aesthetic impression of her ("like a rose herself") that the lyrical subject projected onto the rosy ribbon collapse into one vision. For the girl to recognize the identity of both images—to see how he sees her as a beautiful and desirable woman—is what the lyrical speaker really hopes to accomplish. For inciting this kind of (self)-recognition in her, not for the material gift itself, the sender of the ribbon and poem wants to be rewarded by a kiss, which is an almost natural outcome when the desired specular moment of congruent visions occurs.[55]

If the third stanza has already constructed an intricate situation, the fourth stanza even exceeds it by adding new levels of reflection: first, the song now addresses the beloved directly and presents the true offering, but then it also implicitly addresses someone else with the intertextual reference articulated in the poem's final words:

> Feel then what this heart is feeling,
> Freely offer me your hand,
> Let the band that's us conjoining
> Be no meager rosy band!
> (IV:13–16)

Like in Klopstock's ode and in accordance with the pre-Kantian aesthetics in general, the girl's recognition takes place entirely within the realm of sensuous and sensual cognition. The girl shall neither consider whether the sender of this love message is a good moral person nor take into account any familial or societal circumstances that may impede their relationship.[56] The freedom of her decision to offer him her hand shall be grounded exclusively, so the speaker insinuates, in her feeling—or more precisely: her feeling about his feeling for her. However, one may ask how "free" her decision really is in consideration of the messages she received. By adding the song as a commentary instead of letting the painted ribbon speak for itself, by suggesting that both messages together represent no less than his heart ("*this* heart") as their true meaning and his essential offering, and by anticipating how she may offer hers in return by extending her hand to him, the speaker appears to attempt to manipulate the girl's emotions and thereby limit her freedom to decide. In that regard, Goethe's use of the rosy ribbon seems not to be much better than Klopstock's abuse of it as a device of bondage and deception.

However, what distinguishes the two is that the poetic manipulation by Goethe's speaker is meant to present the girl with a pleasant image of herself to increase her self-esteem. Ultimately it is up to the girl alone whether she really feels the core message, whether she judges her represented image in the poem to accord with her own, and whether she wishes to accept this spectacular gift or not. But before she reaches her conclusion, she should activate the message (by putting on the ribbon, running to the mirror, and seeing herself adorned and adored), feel its real impact, and consider its lasting implications. In other words, she should engage in a reflective judgment in which the sensual, the imaginative, and the implicated more serious practical and moral components of this message all come into play.[57] While the painted ribbon can be received simply as a sensual token of sincere emotion, the poem represents already the intellectual processing of this emotion by the speaker, who, by sending it along with the ribbon, offers it to her *as a model* for such an aesthetic reflective judgment. But, again, only the receiving girl can make (or fail to make) an aesthetic judgment about this poetic play addressed to her.

Ultimately, then, the sender arranged the (mixed) messages of ribbon and poem to test the compatibility of the recipient's aesthetic sensibilities and judgments with his own. If the girl (or any reader of the poem) plays along, feels the messages' core meaning, understands its implications and the essential freedom associated with an engagement that is based on this mutual feeling and understanding alone, she is in correspondence with the sender (poet) on aesthetic terms. If this condition is fulfilled, both can potentially live together in harmony,[58] and the union of their loving companionship will be indeed "no meager rosy ribbon" compared with the one presented by Klopstock, which was founded on the sudden overpowering of a slumbering woman by a sneaky male speaker that allowed for no time of reflection and judgment.

By granting his girl the gift of free reflective judgment, Goethe's poetic erotic play fulfills the decisive criterion to qualify as aesthetic free play in agreement with its characterization in Kant's *Critique of Judgment*. Their agreement reaches even deeper levels. Kant defines aesthetic beauty as an essentially subjective phenomenon and an undetermined "feeling of pleasure" (*Gefühl der Lust*) evoked by a representation that cannot be subsumed under concepts and that stimulates the feeling of the experiencing self and the "feeling of life" (*Lebensgefühl*) in general (sec. 1; 204). Note how Goethe's lyrical speaker calls his girl in III:11 not his dear beloved, but "dear life." And as if Kant had Goethe's poem in mind, he lists as things that stimulate the named feeling the following: "Flowers, free designs [*Zeichnungen*], lines aimlessly intertwined in each other [*in einander geschlungene Züge*]" (sec. 4; 207). Read together they form a rosy ribbon exactly as the one described in Goethe's song that shall entwine (*umschlingen*) the girl's dress to excite her to rush in front of the mirror and to look at herself "in all her eager joyousness" (II:8). But, as mentioned earlier, while the lyrical speaker may have calculated on the effect of his offerings to activate a play of reflective judgment, he could neither enforce it nor determine its outcome. On this, Kant says: "Whether a garment, a house, a flower is beautiful: no one allows himself to be talked into his judgment about that by means of any grounds or fundamental principles. One wants to submit the object to his own eyes, just as if his satisfaction depended on sensation; and yet, if one then calls the object beautiful, one believes oneself to have a universal voice [*glaubt man eine allgemeine Stimme für sich zu haben*], and lays claim to the consent of everyone" (sec. 8; 215–216). In the same manner the girl's aesthetic judgment cannot be determined, not even manipulated by the lyrical voice. The most the loving subject can do he has done with the accompanying song, which basically expresses the "universal voice" of *his* aesthetic judgment while painting the ribbon (and representing in his mind her image during this process). He conveys the song to stimulate *her* to make a corresponding aesthetic judgment about him (the offering of his heart), but with no power to determine the outcome of her judgment.

How the girl received the gift and judged we cannot know. (We know, however, that Goethe separated from the original receiver of the ribbon and accompanying song, Friederike, soon after he had sent them.) But the poem made permanent the fleeting universal voice that accompanied an original aesthetic judgment and experience, and as such it continues to stimulate us to engage in an aesthetic judgment with/about the poem. For as long as its appeal to beauty still resounds within us, Goethe's song about the rosy ribbon will continue to perform its intended effect and unite readers with his lyrical voice.

KANT'S MOMENT OF SELF-REFLECTION

In 1764 Kant's "Observations on the Feeling of the Beautiful and Sublime" ("Beobachtungen über das Gefühl des Schönen und Erhabenen") appeared, which rigorously differentiated between the beautiful and the sublime by associating the former with sensuousness, imagination, and femininity, while the latter with understanding, reason, and masculinity. In this context he linked Anacreontic poetry with the beautiful but judged it disparagingly to be "commonly pretty close to being flaccid or trivial" (*gemeiniglich sehr nahe dem Läppischen*).[59] When it came to a characterization of the beautiful, he resorted to attributes, topoi, and descriptions that he could have taken from a textbook on this type of poetry. He mentions "the prospect on meadows with manifold flowers, valleys with serpentine rivulets and covered by grazing herds, the description of Elysium."[60] In another respect, "the lively sensation of the beautiful" reveals itself "through the shiny cheerfulness of the eyes" and "the moves of a smile."[61] He also found these traits of the beautiful generally in "love between the sexes" (*Geschlechterliebe*).[62] In short, a charming girl in a bucolic landscape represented for Kant the emblematic image of the beautiful. Compared with his later definition of aesthetic beauty in the third *Critique*, lacking most is the notion of free play. The precritical Kant was too analytical, conceptual, and obsessed with drawing lines of distinction between the beautiful gendered as feminine and the sublime gendered as masculine to arrive at more synthetic and dynamic conceptions. Even when analyzing "the influence that one sex can have on the other," he came to the conclusion that the purpose of the loving relationship is to make the man "even more noble/sublime" and the woman "even more beautiful."[63] What made Kant change his general attitude toward aesthetics some thirty-five years later we cannot know for sure, but this article has suggested that a foreshadowing of the new paradigm shift can be found in the erotic scenes of the poems discussed that trigger reflective and, to varying degrees, aesthetic judgments.[64]

Another, ancillary indication that Anacreontic poetry may have impacted Kant's reconceptualization of the aesthetic beauty can be found in the *Critique of Judgment* itself. In the "general remark on the exposition of aesthetic reflective judgments" he considers some types of text "which make play [*tändeln*] with (falsely) so-called noble dispositions, but in fact enervate the heart" (273). He mentions the following: "novels, sentimental plays, shallow moral codes" (273). Even though he characterized these texts with arguably the most Anacreontic attribute—*tändeln* (play, trifle)—he notably omitted Anacreontic poems from this list. Perhaps he no longer regards them as so "trivial" (*läppisch*) as he did before.

APPENDIX: POEMS BY GLEIM, UZ, KLOPSTOCK, AND GOETHE

Die Schöpfung des Weibes

FRIEDRICH WILHELM GLEIM

Am Anfang, als die Welt begann,
Sah Jupiter den ersten Mann,

Wie einsam, wie voll Ernst er sann:
Von wem doch das, was ist, den Ursprung hätte;
Wie er, den Grund von jedem Ding
Zu finden, oft im Winkel gieng,
Und immer mit sich selber redte.

Da sprach er zu der Götter Schaar,
Die um ihn her versammlet war:
Der Mensch vertieft sich ganz und gar,
Wenn ich im Denken ihn nicht unterbreche.
Ich will's. Er sprach: Es werd' ein Weib!
Ein liebes Ding zum Zeitvertreib,
Das mit dem Menschen scherz' und spreche.

Schnell stand es da in Manns Gestalt.
Doch zärtlicher, und nicht so alt,
Mit schlauen Augen, welche bald
Auf's denkende Geschöpf' im Winkel fielen;
Und schnell springt's hin, und küßt den Mann,
Und spricht: Du Närrchen, sieh' mich an!
Ich bin gemacht, mit dir zu spielen.

Ein Gemälde

JOHANN PETER UZ

Sieh! welche Schilderey!
Beblümt kein wahrer May,
Im Schoose der Natur,
O Phyllis! diese Flur?
Ein dick Gebüsch umkränzt
Die Quelle, die hier glänzt:
Am grünen Ufer hin

Schläft eine Schäferinn.
Sie liegt nur leicht bedeckt,
In Blumen hingestreckt,
Mit ihren Locken spielt
Ein Zephyr, der sie kühlt;
Und ihre weiße Brust,
Schon reif zu schlauer Lust,

Verräth sich unterm Flohr,
Und wallt im Schlaf empor.

Sieh diesen Schäfer hier,
Der, unbewegt, nach ihr
Mit weiten Augen sieht:
Wie seine Wange glüht!
Sein Leib hangt ungeschickt,
Auf einen Stab gebückt,
In plumper Stellung hin
Zur holden Schläferinn.

Der Wilde fühlt ein Herz!
Hat ihn der Liebe Scherz,
Als Zeugen ihrer Macht,
Zur Schönen hergebracht?
Er hat schon mehr Verstand;
Und wird ganz umgewandt
Zu seinen Schafen gehn,
Nachdem er sie gesehn.

Das Rosenband

FRIEDRICH GOTTLIEB KLOPSTOCK

Im Frühlingsschatten fand ich sie;
Da band ich sie mit Rosenbändern:
Sie fühlt' es nicht, und schlummerte.

Ich sah sie an; mein Leben hing
Mit diesem Blick an ihrem Leben:
Ich fühlt' es wohl, und wußt' es nicht.

Doch lispelt' ich ihr sprachlos zu,
Und rauschte mit den Rosenbändern:
Da wachte sie vom Schlummer auf.

Sie sah mich an; ihr Leben hing
Mit diesem Blick an meinem Leben,
Und um uns ward's Elysium.

Lied, das ein selbst gemahltes Band begleitete

JOHANN WOLFGANG GOETHE

Kleine Blumen, kleine Blätter
Streuen mir mit leichter Hand
Gute iunge Frühlingsgötter
Tändlend auf ein lüftig Band.

Zephir nimm's auf deine Flügel,
Schlings um meiner Liebe Kleid!
Und sie eilet vor den Spiegel
All in ihrer Munterkeit.

Sieht mit Rosen sich umgeben
Sie, wie eine Rose iung.
Einen Kuß! geliebtes Leben,
Und ich bin belohnt genung.

Fühle was dies Herz empfindet,
Reiche frey mir deine Hand.
Und das Band, das uns verbindet,
Sey kein schwaches Rosenband.

NOTES

1. Alexander Gottlieb Baumgarten, *Ästhetik*, ed. Dagmar Mirbach (Hamburg: Meiner, 2007), 1:10. (Baumgarten laid out the main ideas of his new aesthetics already in his master's thesis *Philosophical Meditations on Some Conditions of Poetry* in 1735.)

2. Immanuel Kant, *Critique of the Power of Judgment*, trans. Paul Guyer and Eric Matthews, ed. Paul Guyer (Cambridge: Cambridge University Press, 2000). All subsequent citations from this work will be according to Guyer's translation with reference to the paragraph and pagination of vol. 5 of the Academy edition as rendered in the margins of Guyer's edition.

3. "Signifier" and "signified" are, of course, not Kant's terms. I decided to apply Saussure's terminology to indicate how closely related Kant's theory of the concept is to the linguist's theory of the sign.

4. Immanuel Kant, *Werkausgabe in zehn Bänden* [=WA], ed. Wilhelm Weischedel (Frankfurt am Main: Suhrkamp, 1974), 12:466.

5. For a more detailed analysis of this correlation cf. Claudia Brodsky, "'Judgment' and the Genesis of What We Lack: 'Schema,' 'Poetry,' and the 'Monogram of the Imagination' in Kant," *Eighteenth Century* 51, no. 3 (2010): 317–340, and Eckart Förster, *Die 25 Jahre der Philosophie* (Frankfurt am Main: Klostermann, 2012), 135–147.

6. Friedrich Schiller, *Sämtliche Werke*, ed. Gerhard Fricke and Herbert G. Göpfert (Munich: Hanser, 1962), 5:618.

7. Cf. Ingeborg Heidemann, *Der Begriff des Spieles und das ästhetische Weltbild in der Philosophie der Gegenwart* (Berlin: De Gruyter, 1968), 115–216; Mihai I. Spariosu, *Dionysus Reborn: Play and the Aesthetic Dimension in Modern Philosophical and Scientific Discourse* (Ithaca, NY: Cornell University Press, 1989), 31–53; Jörg Neuenfeld, *Alles ist Spiel: Zur Geschichte der Auseinandersetzung mit einer Utopie der Moderne* (Würzburg: Königshausen & Neumann, 2005), 16–31; Alexander Wachter, *Das Spiel in der Ästhetik: Zu Kants 'Kritik der Urteilskraft'* (Berlin: De Gruyter, 2006).

8. Gernot Böhme, *Kants "Kritik der Urteilskraft" in neuer Sicht* (Frankfurt am Main: Suhrkamp, 1999), 26.

9. John Zammito, *The Genesis of Kant's "Critique of Judgment"* (Chicago: Chicago University Press, 1992), 35.

10. It is the leitmotif of Zammito's book; cf. Zammito, *Genesis of Kant's "Critique,"* 35–44, 137–142, 178–188, 203–206, 242–247.

11. Another rift, which is basically a symptom of the first, occurred when the so-called Spinoza controversy exploded between Jacobi and Mendelssohn over an alleged Spinoza-friendly response by Lessing that was triggered by Goethe's poem "Prometheus."

12. Johann Wolfgang von Goethe, "Einwirkung der neueren Philosophie," in *Sämtliche Werke: Briefe, Tagebücher und Gespräche* [=FA], ed. Friedmar Apel et al. (Frankfurt am Main: Deutscher Klassiker Verlag, 1985–2013), I.24:444. Conversely, he expressed astonishment in *Conversations with Eckermann* that Kant never took notice of him "even though he [Goethe] pursued by his own impulse [*aus eigener Natur*] a similar path as him [Kant]"; FA II.12:243. (All references to the *Frankfurter Ausgabe* of Goethe's works include the division [*Abteilung*] in Roman numerals followed by the volume and page numbers in Arabic numerals.)

13. The three volumes appeared between 1748 and 1750 even before the first volume of Baumgarten's *Aesthetica* was published.

14. Cf. Theodor Verweyen, "'Halle, die Hochburg des Pietismus, die Wiege der Anakreontik:' Über das Konfliktpotential der anakreontischen Poesie als Kunst der 'sinnlichen Erkenntnis,'" in *Zentren der Aufklärung I: Halle. Aufklärung und Pietismus*, ed. Norbert Hinske (Heidelberg: Schneider, 1989), 209–231.

15. Published in *Frühe Schriften zur ästhetischen Erziehung der Deutschen in drei Teilen, Teil 3: Philosophische Ästhetik—Literaturtheorie—neue deutsche Literatur*, ed. Hans-Joachim Kertscher and Günter Schenk (Halle: Hallescher Verlag, 2002), 117.

16. I cite according to the enlarged second edition of 1754: Georg Friedrich Meier, *Gedancken von Schertzen* (Halle: Hemmerde, 1754), 24–25.

17. Meier, *Gedancken*, 49, 51.

18. The wording of Gabriel Trop, who provided a succinct summary of the main ideas of Meier's important treatise in his book *Poetry as a Way of Life: Aesthetics and Askesis in the German Eighteenth Century* (Evanston, IL: Northwestern University Press, 2015), 226–227.

19. Meier, *Gedancken*, 104, as cited and translated by Trop, *Poetry*, 226.

20. Meier, *Gedancken*, 165: "Bey einem Schertze muß ungleich mehr gedacht, als gesagt werden."

21. Trop, *Poetry*, 226.—As much as I appreciate Trop's reconsideration of Meier's aesthetics, in what follows I argue against his assessment that, "for the most part, Anacreontic

poets such as Gleim and Uz do not base their poetic practices on the doctrines of Meier or Baumgarten" (Trop, *Poetry*).

22. Friedrich Wilhelm Gleim, *Sämmtliche Schriften* (Leipzig: Gräff, 1802), 1:54. Translations of this and the following poems are my own. (They are cited in the text with reference to the stanza in Roman and to lines in Arabic numerals.) The translations cannot render the artistic suppleness of the originals, for which reason the German texts are provided in the appendix at the end of this chapter.

23. Silvia Bovenschen reconstructed the history of this reimagination from Gottsched, Rousseau, Herder, Kant, up to Schiller. Unfortunately, her account left out the crucial contribution of the Anacreontic poets (except for a brief chapter on Anna Louisa Karsch). Silvia Bovenschen, *Die imaginierte Weiblichkeit: Exemplarische Untersuchungen zu kulturgeschichtlichen und literarischen Präsentationsformen des Weiblichen* (Frankfurt am Main: Suhrkamp, 2003).

24. Bovenschen, *Die imaginierte Weiblichkeit*, 92–138.

25. Next to the strong movement of pietism in their own town, the main adversary of the Halle Anacreontic poets was the rationalism and normative rigorism of their neighbor Gottsched in Leipzig. Concerning this controversy, see the afterword in Georg Friedrich Meier, *Frühe Schriften zur ästhetischen Erziehung der Deutschen in drei Teilen, Teil 2: Der "kleine Dichterkrieg" zwischen Halle und Leipzig*, ed. Hans-Joachim Kertscher and Günter Schenk (Halle: Hallescher Verlag, 2000).

26. Cf. the formal criteria of play listed by Johan Huizinga, *Homo Ludens: Vom Ursprung der Kultur im Spiel* (Hamburg: Rowohlt, 1969), 13–20.

27. As cited by Albrecht Koschorke, "Die Verschriftlichung der Liebe und ihre empfindsamen Folgen: Zu Modellen erotischer Autorschaft bei Gleim, Lessing und Klopstock," in *Lesen und Schreiben im 17. und 18. Jahrhundert: Studien zu ihrer Bewertung in Deutschland, England, Frankreich*, ed. Paul Goetsch (Tübingen: Narr, 1994), 256.

28. According to Trop, Anacreontic poetry becomes "unbounded play" under the condition of its autonomy (thereby prefiguring Kant's notion of autonomy aesthetics), which distinguishes it from the Baroque paradigm, where play was subordinated to the pursuit of higher Being, and from the Romantics' embrace of ontological play as a means of ceaseless change and eternal Becoming (cf. *Poetry*, 229–242).

29. Wolfgang Iser, *Das Fiktive und das Imaginäre: Perspektiven literarischer Anthropologie* (Frankfurt am Main: Suhrkamp, 1993), 71.

30. Iser, *Das Fiktive und das Imaginäre*, 137–138. Dorothea Kimmich associated with Anacreontic poetry already characteristics of the *Sturm und Drang*: "The nature of the Rococo displaces the world of the court and installs in its stead a rehearsal stage for playful experimentations with naturalness, that is, new productions of individuality." See Dorothea Kimmich, "Auf der Suche nach dem ganzen Menschen: Die künstlichen Paradiese epikureischen Glücks im Rokoko," in *Anakreontische Aufklärung*, ed. Manfred Beetz and Hans-Joachim Kertscher (Tübingen: Niemeyer, 2005), 86.

31. Iser, *Das Fiktive und das Imaginäre*, 143.

32. Matthias Luserke, "*O vis superba formae!* Über die Basia-Gedichte des Johannes Sekundus (1511–1536) und ihr Nachspiel bei Goethe," in *Literatur und Kultur des Rokoko*, ed. Matthias Luserke, Reiner Marx, and Reiner Wild (Göttingen: Vandenhoek & Rupprecht, 2001), 20–21.

33. On Gleim's failed marriage attempts, see Koschorke, "Verschriftlichung der Liebe," 257.

34. Johann Peter Uz, *Saemmtliche Poetische Werke* (Vienna: von Trattnern, 1769), 1:88–89 (see appendix).

35. Helmut J. Schneider identified as the concrete template for this poem the illustration in a 1717 French edition of Longus's *Daphnis and Chloe*, accessed June 10, 2019, https://archive.org/details/bub_gb_tAh8yo4ROiwC/page/n69. See Helmut J. Schneider, ed., *Idyllen der Deutschen* (Frankfurt am Main: Insel, 1981), 78 and 432.

36. Johann Baptist Edler von Alxinger, ed., *Nuditäten oder Fantasien auf der Venus-Geige*, repr. (Leipzig: Nationales Druckhaus, 1985), 177–179. Cf. Karl Richter, "Die Legitimierung der Sexualität in Gedichten des Rokoko," in *Anakreontische Aufklärung*, ed. Manfred Beetz and Hans-Joachim Kertscher (Tübingen: Niemeyer, 2005), 63–77.

37. Friedrich Gottlieb Klopstock, *Ausgewählte Werke*, ed. Karl August Schleiden (Munich: Hanser, 1962), 74–75 (see appendix).

38. Frauke Berndt, *Poema/Gedicht: Die epistemische Konfiguration der Literatur um 1750* (Berlin: De Gruyter, 2011), 179.

39. Cp. Ulrike Landfester, "Das Zittern der Rose: Versuch über Metapher, Geschlecht und Begehren in der deutschen Liebeslyrik," in *Bündnis und Begehren: Ein Symposium über die Liebe*, ed. Andreas Kraß and Alexandra Tischel (Berlin: Erich Schmidt, 2002), 43.

40. Most of the innovative poetical and rhetorical techniques that contributed to this effect were described by Klaus Weimar and—very meticulously—by Berndt, which dispenses me from conducting another detailed formal analysis of this poem. See Klaus Weimar, "Das Wandeln des Wortlosen in der Sprache des Gedichts," in *Klopstock an der Grenze der Epochen*, ed. Katrin Kohl and Kevin F. Hilliard (Berlin: De Gruyter, 1995), 33–45; and Berndt, *Poema/Gedicht*, 179–232.

41. Cited after Berndt, *Poema/Gedicht*, 192.

42. Cf. Johann Georg Hamann, *Sokratische Denkwürdigkeiten: Aesthetica in nuce*, ed. Sven-Aage Jœrgensen (Stuttgart: Reclam, 1998), 87–89.

43. If the poem is understood as a *sensual-erotic event*, as a foreplay that reaches its climax, the appropriate term here would be coitus instead of "Elysium." See Heinz Schlaffer, *Musa iocosa: Gattungspoetik und Gattungsgeschichte der erotischen Dichtung in Deutschland* (Stuttgart: Metzler, 1971), 86.

44. Weimar, "Wandeln des Wortlosen," 37–38.

45. William Hogarth, *The Analysis of Beauty* (London: John Reeves, 1753), 52. (Hogarth published an edition of his engravings in 1745 which featured already a frontispiece with a serpentine line drawn on a painter's pallet and underwritten "Line of Beauty.")

46. Hogarth, *Analysis of Beauty*, 2, 3.

47. Hogarth, *Analysis of Beauty*, 27.

48. Hogarth, *Analysis of Beauty*, 28.

49. "We shall find not only that ladies of fashion, but that women of every rank, who are said to dress prettily, have known their force, without considering them as Principles." Hogarth, *Analysis of Beauty*, 34.

50. Hogarth, *Analysis of Beauty*, 36 (emphasis added).

51. There remain, of course, great differences between these two conceptions of aesthetic beauty (for one, Hogarth does not think of it in terms of a "reflective judgment"

geared toward "cognition as such"), but the association with Hogarth helps explain Kant's grounding of the aesthetics in pleasure and play. Kant certainly knew Hogarth's *Analysis*, since it was translated into German by Christian Mylius (with Lessing's backing) in 1754. Surprisingly, hardly any literature exists on the influence of Hogarth on Kant; Zammito, *Genesis*, mentions Hogarth not once. A first attempt was made by Tom Huhn, but he dealt with each philosopher in separate chapters rather than considering their interconnections. See Tom Huhn, *Imitation and Society: The Persistence of Mimesis in the Aesthetics of Burke, Hogarth, and Kant* (University Park: Penn State University Press, 2004).

52. Cf. Berndt, *Poema/Gedicht*, 227–229.

53. I cite this poem according to the text of its first appearance in Johann Georg Jacobi's *Iris: Vierteljahrsschrift für Frauenzimmer* 2, no. 1 (January 1775): 46 (see appendix).

54. Landfester, "Zittern der Rose," 46–48, noticed a discrepancy between the "hypertrophic use of Anacreontic imagery" and the roses (on the ribbon) as a metaphor for female sexuality. For her, the attempt to tone down desire in the first three stanzas and the manifestation of the male desire of defloration as articulated in the final stanza remain irreconcilable. For this reason, she regards Goethe's poem a "failed lyrical experiment" (Landfester, "Zittern der Rose," 48). In a similar vein, Berndt, *Poema/Gedicht*, 210, interpreted the poem as the speaker's narcissistic attempt to overcompensate for his castration anxiety, triggered by the female genital (the flowers), through mobilizing a plethora of rhetorical devices. In contrast, my interpretation views the lyrical speaker in a more positive light by reading the poem as a sincere offer and invitation to the girl to engage in a series of (aesthetic) reflections: about her beauty as triggered by his offerings, about himself insofar as the ribbon and the poem are manifestations of his feeling and judgment for/of her, and finally about a possible future together. As we shall see, the discrepancies between the two different media (painting and poetry) and their diverging messages can be reconciled only when both the girl's and the male sender's judgments are in sync. As a consequence, the gender divides and status/class barriers that, incidentally, separated Goethe and the poem's original receiver, his beloved Friederike Brion, would collapse as well.

55. Goethe replaced the word "kiss" (*Kuss*) with "look/gaze" (*Blick*) in later printings since the first edition of his collected poems in 1789. Perhaps the later version expresses the specularity of this moment better; it also seems odd to demand the reward of a kiss for a speaker who is absent (but, however, very present in his imagination). I am using "specular" here according to David E. Wellbery, *The Specular Moment: Goethe's Early Lyric and the Beginnings of Romanticism* (Stanford, CA: Stanford University Press, 1996), esp. 50.

56. The original recipient of this poem along with a couple of painted ribbons was Friederike Brion, as Goethe reports in book 11 of *Dichtung und Wahrheit* (FA I.14:491–547). She was a girl from the countryside whom Goethe wooed while he was studying in Strasbourg; as the final stanza of this poem and the autobiographical report of this episode suggest, Goethe may have proposed marriage, but then did not follow through and broke the girl's heart.

57. According to Schlaffer, *Musa iocosa*, 187, the proposed marital bond ("the band that's us conjoining") in the final stanza functions as a stronger substitute for the "airy band" of the first stanza; thereby, Goethe renounces the playfulness of the erotic genre and replaces it with the sincerity of his new lyrical style. In contrast, my reading of the poem as one aesthetic process (from poetic production to aesthetic judgment and hermeneutic reflection) argues for the essential unity of both bands; consequently, there is also no rupture between

the erotic tradition and Goethe's new lyric. Goethe never dismissed the erotic origin of his poetic production.

58. This theme recurs in a prominent later poem, *Die Metamorphose der Pflanzen*, that ends as follows: "the holy love / Strives toward the highest fruit of a shared ethos [*gleicher Gesinnungen*] / The same outlook on things [*gleicher Ansicht der Dinge*], so that in harmonious intuiting [*harmonischem Anschaun*] / The couple unite and discover the higher realm [*finde die höhere Welt*]" (FA I.1:641).

59. WA II:834.

60. WA II:826.

61. WA II:827.

62. WA II:830.

63. WA II:865–866.

64. Bovenschen, *Die imaginierte Weiblichkeit*, 227–244, also considered the remarkable shift from Kant's early to his later critical aesthetics and esp. the question why he elided the theme of femininity in the latter. According to her, Kant denied women the capability to engage in aesthetic reflective judgments (Bovenschen, *Die imaginierte Weiblichkeit*, 236). I don't see anything in Kant's third *Critique* to support this. To the contrary, the present chapter has shown that Kant's later aesthetics is inherently and implicitly also a theory of gender based on equality. In the free play of the aesthetic reflective judgment, the released imagination equates to the role of the female and the deposed understanding to the role of the male in Anacreontic poetry. When conventional cognition and gender norms collapse in aesthetic experiences, only to be renegotiated in poetic and erotic play, this generates ever-new phenomena and experiences of tremendous beauty.

CHAPTER TWO

Free Play in German Idealism and Poststructuralism

SAMUEL HEIDEPRIEM

WHY BRING GERMAN Idealism and poststructuralism into the study of play? One reason is that they can help address a certain *theory gap* in contemporary play scholarship. Recent publications like Thomas S. Henricks's *Play and the Human Condition* (2015) and the two-volume *Handbook of the Study of Play* (2015) show that we are in a very productive moment for play—as an object of social science.[1] And while thinkers such as Immanuel Kant and Jacques Derrida intensely theorized play and its implications, their approaches, language, and writing styles are quite alien to present-day sociology, psychology, education studies, and similar fields where play is now at home. Given the seeming indifference of German Idealism and poststructuralism to "data" and empiricism, compounded by their density and abstraction, it is easy to understand why today's responsible social scientist would want to keep this sort of thinking at bay.[2] This is to say nothing of the decades-long disciplinary antipathy between continental European philosophy and the "rigorous" human sciences. But theory has good reason to take part in the conversation on play. Take the founding document of poststructuralism, Derrida's 1966 talk "Structure, Sign, and Play in the Discourse of the Human Sciences."[3] If one reads it now, the text gives an overview of the movement's future prerogatives—with special emphasis on play as a category that distinguishes the aging tradition of western metaphysics from new modes of thinking.[4] In the audience for Derrida's presentation was Paul de Man, the second figurehead of poststructuralism, who adopted this angle on play as well.[5]

Another poststructuralist priority was to challenge the legacy of classical humanism in the twentieth and twenty-first centuries. This is a point where the theory gap in play studies makes itself uncomfortably present. For instance, *Play and the Human Condition*—true to its title—investigates play as an element of humanity's "essence," which Henricks defines as a "lifelong quest for self-realization." Apparently, we study play for the same reason we study anything else: "because people wish to understand the world and the extent of human capability."[6] In one quick move, Henricks delineates the "what" and the "why" of play scholarship: play belongs to the self-unfolding essence of humanity; we study it to more clearly grasp the nature of this humanity and its relation to the nonhuman world outside. The presuppositions behind such claims recall the heyday of the enlightened *cogito*. Henricks quite confidently assigns an essence—indeed, a *destiny*—to human beings, with no hesitation at the metaphysical scope of this claim. Are we satisfied with so blithe a preconception of the human—effectively a happily integrated Enlightenment subject, playing its way to fulfillment (and, we can imagine, realizing its dominance over the world)—especially today, when theories of posthumanism and critiques of western anthropocentrism seem to be taking us beyond? These discourses are only becoming more prevalent. Play scholarship might do well to make contact with them, and thereby seize a chance to theorize play outside the confines of established human convention and practice.

The conjuncture of German Idealism and poststructuralism helps us do exactly that, while also reflecting on the legacy of humanism itself. When Derrida and de Man discuss play, I argue, two important conceptions from German Idealism are never far afield: the free play of cognitive faculties from Kant's *Critique of Judgment* (1790), and Friedrich Schiller's famous "play drive" (*Spieltrieb*) from *On the Aesthetic Education of Man* (1795).[7] Sometimes the connection is explicit and programmatic on the poststructuralists' part, sometimes not. Regardless, the dynamics of this reception history allow us to (1) enrich contemporary theories of play by outlining two conceptual forms, *free* and *centered* play, that emerge from the nexus of these four thinkers; (2) consider how poststructuralism's relationship with German Idealism complicates the former's attempt to abandon classical humanism outright. Ultimately, Kant and Schiller may offer a middle path between the antihumanism of Derrida and de Man and its unreflexive opposite in today's social science of play.

CENTERED PLAY

Like Derrida, de Man identifies two types of play: one consistent with poststructuralism, the other beholden to western metaphysics. The occasion for de Man's discussion of play is the lecture "Kant and Schiller," delivered at Cornell in 1983, a panegyric to Kant and a vicious critique of Schiller.[8] The talk begins with de Man's confession that he has not prepared a manuscript to read from, because the Schiller material is simplistic enough for him to improvise about it, which he "wouldn't dare" to do with Kant.[9] In ridiculing Schiller, de Man attempts to present himself in the mode of speaking truth to power. De Man insists that Schillerian rather than Kantian precepts dominate the institutional status quo—the prevailing intellectual and discursive conventions of the late twentieth century "come from Schiller, and not from Kant."[10] De Man makes Kant and Schiller emblematic of larger theoretical tendencies that govern his own time as well. If we follow his analogy, the postwar era has, on the one hand, a Schillerian component—ingrained norms and values, "things as they are"—and a subversive Kantian element as well, of which de Man considers himself and Derrida representatives.[11] For de Man, detailed criticism of Schiller's work should help reveal the mechanics, as well as the underlying values, of the western-metaphysical present. Thus we find de Man attacking Schiller at both a logical level—targeting Schiller's analytical process—and an ontological one corresponding to the foundational principles and commitments behind Schillerian aesthetics.

The famous dictum from letter 15 of the *Aesthetic Education* that "man only plays when he is in the fullest sense of the word a human being, and he is only fully a human being when he plays" exemplifies the kind of rhetorical move de Man finds so objectionable in Schiller. Here it is the chiasmus, a device in which separate items are repeated in reverse order, that Schiller uses to link disparate categories by defining them as reciprocally necessary. In this example, play and humanity are presented as analytically interdependent because, as Schiller says, one is fully human *only* in a state of play and can simultaneously play *only* when fully human. In the preceding paragraph, he makes the same move with the categories *play* and *beauty*: "With beauty man shall only play, and it is with beauty only that he shall play" (15:8). And what is beauty? In a person, it is nothing but the chiastic crossing of the categories *life* and *form*: "his form would have to be life, and his life form. . . . Only when his form lives in our feeling and his life takes on form in our understanding, does he become living form; and this will always be the case whenever we adjudge him beautiful" (15:3).[12]

De Man attacks Schiller's apparent overreliance on the chiasmus: Schiller "invites parody," says de Man, "because he cannot write two sentences which are not symmetrically bound around a chiasmic crossing."[13] Later we will consider how justified this dismissal really is.[14] For the moment, reconstructing de Man's critique: the preponderance of this one recognizable rhetorical form in the *Aesthetic Education* makes Schiller's text "tropological." By this de Man means Schiller's whole argument is structured and driven by a repetitive figure, the trope of the chiasmus. As we just saw, this chiastic device allows Schiller to configure various terms (in this case, play, humanity, beauty, life, and form) in a larger interlocking conceptual formation. The principle that holds them together is interdependency, reciprocity, mutual necessity, or, to mention two ideas de Man emphasizes with respect to Schiller, *equilibrium* and *harmony*. For de Man, these are the two motive pillars of Schiller's play theory, which aims at the dissolution of all conflict, the instatement of a pure harmonious zone of play (*Spielraum*), "the space that you need in order to prevent the dialectical encounter from taking place," by which de Man means an encounter that is generative and productive precisely in its negativity, in the destructive collision it involves.[15] In this reading, Schiller tries to resolve long-standing philosophical antagonisms via the play drive, which operationalizes the "perfect reversibility" of the chiasmus to render opposed categories—for example, freedom and constraint, infinity and limitation—"absolutely symmetrical" so "they will never encounter each other."[16]

In the *Aesthetic Education*, the most pressing antagonism is that between humanity's intellectual and sensible natures, which Schiller embodies in respective internal drives toward form and material (*Formtrieb* and *Stofftrieb*). The cerebral form-drive is preoccupied with subjective agency, abstract ideas, and the thought of eternity, while the sense-drive is tied to physicality, feeling, and the perceptual richness of the present. Schiller introduces the play drive as a third term to reconcile these two, which it does, as we might expect, by inducing a mutual exchange of properties. One example: "The sense-drive wants to be determined, wants to receive its object; the form-drive wants itself to determine, wants to bring forth its object. The play drive, therefore, will endeavour so to receive as if it had itself brought forth, and so to bring forth as the intuitive sense aspires to receive" (14:4). The form-drive insists on active determination, the sense-drive passive reception; the play drive reconciles them by integrating activity and passivity into one operation: to receive an impression as though it had produced it, and symmetrically (chiastically) to act as though it were acted upon. Developing this idea in the next paragraph, Schiller writes,

> The sense-drive excludes from its subject all autonomy and freedom; the form-drive excludes from its subject all dependence and passivity. Exclusion of freedom, however, implies physical necessity, exclusion of passivity moral necessity. Both drives, therefore, exert constraint upon the psyche; the former through the laws of nature, the latter through the laws of reason. The play drive, in consequence, as the one in which both the others act in concert, will exert upon the psyche at once a moral and a physical constraint; it will, therefore, since it annuls all contingency, annul all constraint too, and set man free both physically and morally.
>
> (14:5)

The passage is dense with oppositions: autonomy and freedom versus dependence and passivity; physical versus moral necessity; nature versus reason; contingency versus constraint—all rendered reciprocally necessary, and therefore reconciled, in the work of the play drive. It is easier to understand de Man's incredulity when Schiller proposes the *same* procedure—the reciprocity (*Wechselwirkung*) of play—to overcome a whole field of conflicts, many of which have already been theorized separately over centuries of philosophical discourse. How is it that contingency and constraint, nature and reason, form and sense, body and mind are all reconciled through the *same* rhetorical operation? And even if we set aside the persuasiveness of Schiller's play concept and try to assess without prejudice how it works, we still must confirm de Man's basic observation: the omnipresence of the chiasmus. This does not have to mean the *Aesthetic Education* is analytically weak or strong—perhaps just very consistent. On the other hand, what makes so uniform and prefigured a process *free*? De Man might say the *Aesthetic Education*'s tropological model of play means we are only free to make one choice, because a single motif prescribes and directs the course of Schiller's arguments. According to de Man, play simply follows the dictation of the chiasmus.

Derrida likewise criticizes any model of play predetermined by a given logical function. When distinguishing play concepts in "Structure, Sign, and Play," he ascribes to the first and historically predominant type exactly this sort of prior delimitation: the play of any given structure is circumscribed and fixed by a central, governing principle that "closes off the play which it opens up and makes possible"; the core prerogative is to maintain the coherence of the system while allowing a degree of circulation and movement among its parts, "the play of its elements inside the total form."[17] "System" here refers to any discourse or branch of knowledge or theory (in our case, aesthetic theory). The principle that regulates the play of that system Derrida calls the *center*: it is the element that structures play while not being subject to it, a fixed point that, secure in this way, allows the remaining parts to circulate and exchange. This circulation and exchange proceed within parameters established by the center. Derrida: "The concept of centered structure is in fact the concept of a play based on a fundamental ground, a play constituted on the basis of a fundamental immobility and a reassuring certitude, which itself is beyond the reach of play."[18] To bring back de Man's term, the center is the governing trope of the system. Taking de Man's critique of Schiller as an example: the concept of play in the *Aesthetic Education* is *centered* by and on the structural form of the chiasmus. As long as the chiastic logic of the play drive remains unchallenged, according to de Man, Schiller can conjure away any conceptual opposition he wants. The "fundamental immobility" of the chiasmus assures the integrity and consistency of Schiller's aesthetic system.

And the chiasmus does not even complete the foundation—there is a deeper immobility still. Recall it is only the *logical* target of de Man's critique, which also extends to the basic values underlying Schillerian aesthetics. In truth, it is one enormous value, the same that guides play scholars like Henricks: the human. Schiller is a humanist, by which de Man is not referring to Schiller's preoccupation with human worth and dignity, but instead to the more specific fact that, in the *Aesthetic Education*, "the plea for the possibility of the necessity of this synthesis [of the play drive] is made in the name of an empirical concept, which is that of humanity, of the human, which is used then as a principle of closure. The human, the needs of the human, the necessities of the human are absolute and are not open to critical attack. Because the category of the human is absolute, and because the human would be divided, or would be reduced to nothing if this encounter between the two drives . . . is not allowed to take place, for that reason a synthesis has to be found."[19] In de Man's reading, there is no play drive without the prior needs of the human, an "absolute" category that determines the whole aesthetic system. The human needs its drives reconciled; therefore the play drive is created to fashion a "synthesis" between them. But the entire problematic—as with Henricks—is essentially one internal to the human, concerning only the human and its self-integrity. And as de Man claims further, humanity and its needs form a nexus immune to any critical questioning. It is the immobile Derridean center, directing the movement of the system from a fixed point. In this picture, humanity, from its privileged position (as center), effectively deputizes the play drive to serve its ends. But to keep everything chiastic, continuing with de Man's critique, play must then symmetrically determine what it means to be human: "Humanity, which then has to be itself the composite of those two [form- and sense-] drives, is then equated with a balanced relationship between necessity and freedom, which Schiller calls free play, *Spieltrieb*, and which then becomes the determining principle of the human. The human is determined by the possibility of free play."[20] This, at least, is how de Man reads the famous chiasmus in which we are only fully human when we play, and only play when fully human. It is the formula where aesthetic education's logical and ontological commitments come together.

Looking at the development of Schiller's play drive in this way, it is difficult to defend the social-scientific presumption that play is simply (or always) an anthropological *fact*, whether as part of humanity's "essence" or a self-evident form of human activity. With Schiller, play emerges as a *concept*—rather than an observable property or behavior—in response to specific discursive demands, among them the need to provide a philosophically coherent theory of the human subject. The character of this need and the analytical material available for its resolution—in this case, the system of internal drives and mental powers—are not transhistorical, like Henricks's "self-realizing" player-agent, but firmly embedded in the discourse and period of German Idealism.[21] Schiller's efforts to coordinate logic and ontology through play may testify above all to the intellectual inventiveness needed to address the philosophical challenges of the 1790s. Put another way, it shows how much theoretical work was necessary to *create* a workable model of the human—a category today's play science freely presupposes.

FREE PLAY

Schiller avows the *Aesthetic Education* is based on "Kantian principles" (1:3). In *Signs Taken for Wonders*, published the same year de Man lectured at Cornell, Franco Moretti suggests the scholarly consensus (at least in the early 1980s) takes Schiller at his word: "It is well known," writes Moretti in the introductory essay, "that the letters *On the Aesthetic Education of Man* are largely limited to restating the substance of the *Critique of Judgment* while simplifying it."[22] Obviously de Man does not agree—for him there is a salient, vital opposition between the two books. They define contrary tendencies. Nonetheless, they are linked in a way that is central to de Man's larger argument about the history of philosophy after German Idealism. De Man would likely concede that the *Aesthetic Education* is a kind of reproduction of the third *Critique*; but rather than "restating and simplifying" it, as many of his contemporaries seem to accept, de Man believes Schiller does active damage to Kant. Or more closely to de Man's own account: that a certain transformative power opens up in the *Critique of Judgment*, only then to be restrained in the *Aesthetic Education*. De Man calls Schiller's text a "relapse," a regression behind the revolutionary work whose mantle it claims to carry.[23]

What makes the third *Critique* so radical? In describing the book, de Man continually returns to the language of *occurrence*: the *Critique of Judgment* "was an occurrence, something happened there, something occurred."[24] The claim that the third *Critique* "happened" or "occurred" does not seem significant in the ordinary sense of these terms, but for de Man they designate something exceptional—the vast measure of philosophical history, after all, he consigns to the order of *non-occurrence*. To *not* happen is the norm in philosophy. As de Man writes of Kant's legacy: "in the whole reception of Kant from then until now, nothing has happened, only regression, nothing has happened at all."[25] While on its face this claim seems absurd, de Man means that the historically predominant way of reading Kant, the now-prevalent image we have of his work, is non-occurrent, is opposed to the order of happening. Although this is quite abstract, it is useful to remember that for de Man, the notion of occurrence is opposed to tropology as a model for organizing discursive systems. The tropological principle de Man identifies and criticizes in Schiller prevents its elements from emerging at the level of occurrence or happening that he sees at work in Kant. As we saw, tropes for de Man are effectively mechanisms of consistency and control: they standardize and fix play among constituents of a system; they also work to prevent any ruptures in its basic analytical (or ideological) parameters. De Man defines occurrence as exactly this kind of rupture. Tropes are deployed against occurrences to assimilate them back into the preceding tropological form. This is the gesture de Man sees in Schiller's *Aesthetic Education*, which he claims "reinscribes Kant in the tropological system of aesthetics."[26]

The motif of rupture and occurrence is also pronounced in "Structure, Sign, and Play." The occasion for Derrida's talk is what he calls an "event" (*événement*) in the "history of the concept of structure," the external manifestation of which is a "rupture and a redoubling" of this history.[27] Until this event, he argues, the history of structure was the history of centered systems of play, in which one governing epistemic principle replaced another and each dictated the total discursive field of an age. Though this comparison is not explicit, "Structure, Sign, and Play" suggests these centers succeed each other like sovereigns. Derrida describes the history of the West itself (again, "before the rupture") as a "series of substitutions of center for center, as a linked chain of determinations of the center."[28] He encourages us to imagine a rough progression of epochs in western history in which, for instance, God is the center, then Reason, later Science, or the Market. The point for Derrida is that there has always been some transcendental anchor that cannot be questioned. But he believes this may be changing: Derrida identifies an event that has disrupted this smooth succession of centers, and importantly for us, has brought with it a new conception of play. The event itself, what Derrida calls the "decentering" of thought, results from the combined pressure of Nietzsche, Freud, and Heidegger. For Derrida, each of these thinkers attacks the metaphysics of the center at a different point of sensitivity—Nietzsche's "critique of the concepts of Being and truth"; Freud's "critique of self-presence"; the "Heideggerian destruction of metaphysics, of onto-theology"—and together they open up the possibility of a new direction in thinking about structure.[29]

According to Derrida, part of this new thinking is the idea of a structural system *not* fixed around a center, in which the play of its elements assumes a certain priority or primacy—after the rupture effected by the critique of metaphysics, it is possible to affirm play as such. Play, in this view, is no longer simply an annoyance or contingency to be controlled. In the case of a given system or discourse, once the center is removed, play itself becomes the principle of the system: "This field is in effect that of *play*, that is to say, a field of infinite substitutions only because it is finite. . . . There is something missing from it: a center which arrests and grounds the play of substitutions."[30] Because there is no single center, any number of elements internal to the system can play this role—can be substituted for and *into* the center—without ever exerting the kind of structural control that antecedent centers were supposed to. This is what Derrida calls *supplementarity*: in the traditional model, centers were exchanged in a kind of one-to-one equivalence—Reason and Science, for example, occupied essentially the same structural position that God had—and thus the overall formation could retain its basic parameters. But after the break brought about by Nietzsche, Freud, and Heidegger, each new center brings with it a certain surplus or excess by which it *does not match* the precise structural function of the center preceding it. There is never an even substitution or equivalence between centers, and thus a continual state of play in the rest of the system.[31]

It is, of course, not hard to recognize the structural affinity that ties de Man's argument to Derrida's. After all, they are making formally identical claims about the intellectual history of the West: there is in each (1) a long-standing, entrenched tendency (Derrida: centered thought; de Man: tropology); (2) a rupture in that tendency (Derrida: critique of metaphysics; de Man: *Critique of Judgment*); (3) a new form of thought made possible by that rupture (Derrida: play as such; de Man: reading Kant correctly).[32] The terms align substantively as well: "tropology" and "centering" both refer to fixing the play of a system around an immobile source of authority, and the "rupture"—whether Kant or Nietzsche-Freud-Heidegger—amounts to an unseating of this source, at least from its untouchable position. Finally, the new way of thinking Derrida charts in "Structure, Sign, and Play" is marked by a kind of play that is emancipated from traditional metaphysical commitments—no longer a convenient structuring principle deputized by God, Morality, or Science, play is now free to affirm and enact itself *as play*, "without security."[33] For the first time, play is not secondarily or externally determined from above, but now constructs its own field and operation, and this kind of *free play* is definitive for a radical direction in thought after structuralism. Similarly, de Man, in putting Kant's third *Critique* at the center of his own call for thinking outside the status quo, cannot avoid connecting this thinking to Kant's free play of the faculties, one of the book's conceptual pillars.[34] This is reinforced by the organization of "Kant and Schiller," in which the concept of play is prominent: the finale of de Man's critique of Schiller (and the talk itself) is a concentrated attack on the *Spieltrieb* as an example of backward tropology.[35]

For Derrida and de Man alike, a *new* form of thought involves a *free* form of play. A version of this idea is already present in Kant's third *Critique*, in which the free play of cognitive faculties is essentially a state of mind, a disposition of mental powers freed from familiar limitations. For Kant, these limitations refer to the need for a specific faculty of mind to *legislate* over a given realm of thought and experience. In the *Critique of Pure Reason* (1781), understanding (*Verstand*), the faculty by which we use concepts to grasp nature and experience, assumes the legislative role, meaning the other faculties of imagination (*Einbildungskraft*) and reason (*Vernunft*) take on functions understanding assigns to them; likewise, in the *Critique of Practical Reason* (1787), imagination and understanding are subordinated to the legislative power of reason, with its concept of freedom. These separate configurations, dictated respectively by understanding and reason, yield the first two wings of Kant's critical system: the theoretical laws of nature and the practical laws of morality. As Kant puts it succinctly in the (second, published) introduction to the *Critique of Judgment*: "Legislation through concepts of nature takes place through the understanding, and is theoretical. Legislation through the concept of freedom takes place through reason, and is merely practical" (5:174). In this compact restatement of *Critiques* one and two, Kant sets up the intervention of the third: a configuration of the faculties in which no single power predominates. Rather than assigning a new governing faculty, and thereby retaining the structural trend established in the first two *Critiques*, Kant explores the possibility of a wholly new disposition of faculties: "harmonious play" (20:224).[36] Play has a specific position in the developmental arc of Kant's critical philosophy: we find it where Kant begins to think through what happens when no single mental power exerts total control over the others.[37] Or to use the language of post-structuralism, when Kant no longer fixes the powers of the mind around a center—as understanding and reason had been—he encounters play.

This resonance only grows stronger when we consider the free play of the faculties in more detail. Kant associates this state of play with a reflective, rather than determinative, form of judgment. In the published introduction, Kant defines judgment generally as "the faculty for thinking of the particular as contained under the universal. If the universal (the rule, the principle, the law) is given, then the power of judgment, which subsumes the particular under it . . . is *determining*. . . . If, however, only the particular is given, for which the universal is to be found, then the judgment is merely *reflecting*" (5:179; original emphasis). Judgments of reflection differ from determining judgments in that the latter are fixed by some given "rule, principle, or law," while reflective judgment leaves this position open—reflection must find its own universal. Determining judgment proceeds from a known and stable central concept, and it uses this concept to understand and situate particulars. But reflection has no such anchor. Its path to the universal is necessarily open-ended and meandering. The mind roams in reflective judgment, and its faculties can play. As Kant writes in the first introduction to the *Critique*:

> Every *determining* judgment is *logical* because its predicate is a given objective concept. A merely *reflecting* judgment about a given individual object, however, *can be aesthetic* if (before its comparison with others is seen), the power of judgment, which has no concept ready for the given intuition, holds the imagination (merely in the apprehension of the object) together with the understanding (in the presentation of a concept in general) and perceives a relation of the two faculties of cognition which constitutes the subjective,

> merely sensitive condition of the objective use of the power of judgment in general (namely the agreement of these two faculties with each other).
>
> (20:223–224; original emphasis)

Determining judgment proceeds from a "given objective concept"—a concept that is present, intelligible, available for thought. When we compare an object with a concept that is knowable or "objective" in this way, we make a determining judgment. As the passage shows, determining judgment involves a specific relationship of the faculties: imagination apprehends the object, understanding furnishes a given concept, and determining judgment brings the two (the apprehension and the concept) into relation. This exchange is limited to the specific products of imagination and understanding, not the faculties themselves. But exactly this latter kind of relationship, between the actual faculties—or "cognition in general" ("Erkenntnis überhaupt"), rather than any particular act of cognition (5:217)—is the end of reflective judgment, which combines "mere apprehension" of the imagination with a "general concept" from the understanding. Important to note is that Kant refers to two types of concepts: "given objective" concepts, furnished by the understanding in the context of determining judgments, which give these judgments their rule (i.e., their center); and "general" concepts, which the understanding presents in reflective judgment. General concepts, rather than providing judgment with any particular content, refer instead to the understanding's *capacity* for conceptual presentation; likewise, the imagination is active in reflection in its *capacity* for apprehension, not through any specific apprehension.[38] When Dieter Henrich describes reflective judgment as a "search" for the "appropriate general concept,"[39] he captures the open-ended nature, not only of the process—the interplay of imagination and understanding as capacities—but the goal: conceptualization in its generality.

Continuing this theme, Kant writes in the first introduction that play arises between the imagination and the understanding when their respective *general* powers of apprehension and conceptual presentation are "reciprocally expeditious" (20:224). Similarly, in the published introduction, he claims that in a state of play, "no determinate concept restricts" the faculties to a "particular rule of cognition" (5:217). And as the end of the extended passage above makes clear, this play is hardly a momentary leisure for the mind: it is the subjective condition for the overall objective employment of judgment. "Mutual harmony" is the *fundamental position* of the faculties, from which their other "objective" (i.e., fixed by a determinate concept of the understanding) configurations derive. This is a claim of some consequence: Kant is saying that *play precedes constraint*—it is not its release but enabling condition.[40] Henrich emphasizes this order of priority at several points. Reflective judgment involves a "cooperation" between imagination and understanding, he writes, "that takes places *prior* to the employment of any particular concept."[41] He goes on to say that reflective judgment "compares the state of imagination with the conditions of a possible conceptualization in general," such that "the ascent of reflective judgment from imagination toward understanding necessarily always already takes into account the way in which concepts are generally applied." This for Henrich is "precisely how understanding as such enters the play *prior* to the acquisition of any particular concept."[42]

This helps us understand the appeal of Kant's play theory for poststructuralism. The axes of de Man's critique of tropology and Derrida's critique of centered thought are anticipated in two relevant Kantian distinctions: (1) between faculties in free play versus the fixed "legislative" configurations of the first two *Critiques*; and (2) between reflective and determining forms of judgment, which respectively engage the mind as a capacity or tie it to a given concept. Using three different vocabularies, Kant, de Man, and Derrida are outlining a common conception of play: absent any specific principle of fixity, the mind explores the full range of its capacities. This exploration itself has value, and Kant would go further: it is the condition underlying any specific act of cognition.

But we cannot align Kant's reflective free play and the uncentered play of poststructuralism in this way without confronting the problem of the human. For Derrida and de Man, humanism seems to constitute an unambiguous enemy, the irredeemable "before" of poststructuralism. Their texts do not suggest any opportunity for compromise on this question. Yet there are few more rhapsodic advocates of *der Mensch* and its dignity than Kant. Is this an intractable divide? Is Kant's appeal for poststructuralists limited to his concept of play, and his humanism simply regrettable baggage? What is the actual relationship between humanism and play, in Kant and beyond?

HUMANISM AND PLAY

Derrida calls for a form of thought that "affirms play and tries to pass beyond man and humanism."[43] The implication is that play and humanism are antitheses, and indeed, this is precisely Derrida's conception of the human: "that being who, throughout the history of metaphysics . . . in other words, throughout his entire history—has dreamed of full presence, the reassuring foundation, the origin and the end of play."[44] For Derrida, humanism is the paradigm of the center; it denotes the complete history of arresting play by subordinating it to a governing rule. The human (of humanism) is the agent preoccupied with centering play. Similarly, as we saw, de Man identifies humanity as the master-trope in Schiller. For de Man, this means that Schiller's whole architecture of tropologically constrained play is itself grounded on and oriented by a commitment to humanism. Two centuries later, writes de Man, aesthetic education "is still the basis of our liberal system of humanistic education."[45] This system is the target of de Man's polemic, much like the history of metaphysics is Derrida's—the common element is the human as a foundational category. Derrida and de Man alike direct their critiques at an intellectual and institutional status quo understood as the extension of humanism.

On this count, it is difficult not to think of the second formulation (commonly called the "humanity" formulation) of Kant's categorical imperative, which instructs that humanity must never be treated merely as a means, but always as an end in itself.[46] In this way, Kant's moral philosophy appears to "center" the human, making it a principle that can never be subordinated to another. From the standpoint of Derrida and de Man, this would make Kant part of the problem. But the *Critique of Judgment* complicates this picture. To be sure, Kantian aesthetics has a special place for the "supersensible vocation" (20:255–257) of the human subject, but it is unclear whether this is the same subject Derrida criticizes for dreaming of a "reassuring foundation" and the "end of play." At least in the third *Critique*, the Kantian subject *wants* to play, and it takes no special comfort in any "foundation," insofar as this refers to the certainty of determinate cognition. If we look at the text of the third *Critique*, and especially Kant's theory of play, the human of humanism, as Derrida and de Man conceive it, appears like a kind of bogey, almost a strawman—even if Kant's aesthetic thought is centered on the human, this human is a weak center, not even in control of itself, let alone the total discursive field surrounding it.[47] It is hard to imagine the reflective subject, the subject at play, wielding the kind of metaphysical absolutism Derrida ascribes to classical centers. The humanism Kant articulates in the third *Critique* seems much more sophisticated, imaginative, and open than Derrida and de Man would be likely to admit. And it is possible that the concept of play, which makes Kant's human of the third *Critique* a "weak" center, is precisely what makes Kant's humanism "strong," that is, conceptually strong enough to escape the poststructuralist critique of humanism's dogmatic and normative excesses.

Claire Colebrook has argued that Derrida, along with the whole of what we now think of as late twentieth-century "theory" (poststructuralism, deconstruction, critical theory, etc.), prepared the way for academic humanists to think beyond the tradition of humanism, in which a "transcendental humanity" orchestrates epoch after epoch, and the final judgment on all things comes from a "purposive and historical" human subject.[48] As it happens, *purpose* is exactly what Kant denies the reflective subject of play. The famous formula "purposiveness without purpose" ("Zweckmäßigkeit ohne Zweck") describes the state of the mind in aesthetic reflection.[49] In this condition, the subject experiences the formal capacity for purpose-driven thought and activity, without itself possessing any specific purpose. The distinction is analogous to that between determining and reflective judgments: in one case, there is a concrete, given concept; in the other, the overall power of conceptuality. It is the same with purpose (understood as a particular *Zweck*) and the capacity of purposiveness. This is important because a subject can only dictate an end if it has one. I cannot impose "purposiveness" on someone else (what would this mean?), but I can enforce a definite purpose like "be moral," because I presumably have a specific conception of what morality entails. When Colebrook, drawing on Derrida, describes pernicious humanism as "purposive," she refers to an identifiable doctrine, a set of ends dictated by humanity against its others. But Kant's reflective humanity is defined, not by purposes, but purposive*ness*, and any specification of this general capacity (i.e., into given ends) cannot claim the mantle of "humanity"—it is already too limited. In this way, Kant's concept of humanity has a kind of trap door that prevents it from tyrannizing in the manner of other Derridean centers: lacking, by definition, any substantial, positive metaphysical program, it has nothing to exert on an outside. Any such program would involve a concretization of reflection, an arresting of play that, for this reason, cannot speak in the name of humanity.

This is because, in the third *Critique*, Kant arrives at a conception of humanity only by way of free play. Henry Allison reminds us that, for Kant, to describe play as "free" means it is "not directed by a determinate concept, but is still guided by the general conditions of cognition."[50] Judgments like "the wine is delicious" or "democracy is just" are determinative in that they invariably refer to specific interests, whether of a private individual or a group, and can make no a priori claim to represent the whole species. They also fix the activity of the faculties to a specific rule: of personal enjoyment, political value, and so on. Only aesthetic reflective judgment (the pronouncement of beauty) holds the faculties in free play, and in keeping them *nonspecific* in this way, is capable of being *universally communicated*. This kind of judgment alone "appeals to a subjective condition that is accessible to all," as Allison puts it.[51] For Kant, only the *form of cognition itself* is "valid for everyone"—all we can attribute to humanity as a whole is the basic inner framework of thought itself, never any specific thought.[52] Henrich writes that "the harmonious agreement of the cognitive powers arises . . . from *nothing but* the fundamental constitution" of those powers; therefore "we have the right to assume that [play] is a possible state of every mind whose knowledge is of the same kind as ours."[53] In experiencing the pleasure of this harmonious play, I am linked with a wider community of subjects capable of enjoying it as well. Michel Chaouli identifies an important aspect of this approach to humanism:

> It is the pleasure of feeling (rather than merely of knowing) my link "to every human being," not by way of biological or cultural affiliation or even of a fellow feeling, but by feeling my own readiness to address other human beings, no matter their particulars. These are members not of a community imagined to have been already given by virtue of history or geography or race or whatever other features, but of a community that comes into being with the singular and momentary experience of beauty itself. . . . Humanity appears not as an anthropological or biological or political entity to which I may pledge allegiance or from which I may turn; rather it flares up as something to be claimed in a nameless pleasure. In aesthetic pleasure, I demand humanity.[54]

The human community that coalesces around aesthetic experience is not defined by biology, culture, history, geography, race, politics—all these axes are already too confined. The only universal is the experience of beauty, that is, the free play of the faculties, the form of cognition itself. Following Chaouli, this means that aesthetic humanity, properly conceived, can never be a cover for a specific cultural formation attempting to impose itself on others (as it is for western metaphysics in Derrida). Even though Kant is a European Enlightenment philosopher, the concept of cognitive free play as beauty does not refer to the geographical or historical entity "Europe" or the empirical intellectual program of the Enlightenment. These are "particulars" that cannot denominate the collective entity capable of aesthetic experience. Only this collective is humanity.

Chaouli reminds us of another significant point: humanity, in Kantian aesthetics, is not something "already given," but instead "claimed." In aesthetic experience, we "demand humanity." Rather than being posited as a quality we already possess—usually with reference to history, values, politics—humanity is something we must call upon and invoke ourselves. Humanity *emerges* through the universal communicability of pleasure in cognitive free play, and in this sense, it is a *product* of the power of judgment. In more contemporary terminology, this shows humanity is discursive, constituted, generated in the cognitive processes of human beings. One implication is that this kind of humanity cannot be absolute, cannot anchor history from a transcendental super-position—cannot be a stable master-trope or center, depending as it does on a subjective order that is itself contingent and limited. Of course, it could be objected that all nefarious uses of humanism, whether imperialist, colonialist, Eurocentric, or otherwise, are also created by empirical subjects. Nonetheless, these humanisms invariably refer to themselves (and the specific characteristics they attach to humanity) as absolute, as outside contingency, as simply given and valid. Not so with Kant, who *highlights* the fact that humanity only emerges when subjects employ their powers of judgment reflectively, that is, that any conception of humanity is essentially *produced* rather than given.

This brings us to a second consideration: looking at the *Critique of Judgment*, it is striking how unsure of itself the Kantian subject seems to be, how reliant on heuristics and assumptions just to get its cognitive machinery running. In the first introduction, Kant describes as a "sheer assumption" ("bloße Voraussetzung"; 20:210) the idea that the world of experience conforms to our powers of cognition. Later, Kant says this assumption is necessary for us to grasp nature as a system of empirical laws—that is, laws we can understand (20:216). This bears on the most general task of the power of judgment—to subsume the particular under the universal—because this operation can only take place if we "regard the *aggregate* of particular experiences as a *system* of them; for without this presupposition [*Voraussetzung*] no thoroughly lawlike connection, i.e. empirical unity of these experiences can obtain" (20:203; original emphasis). Kant calls this a "heuristic principle" ("heuristisches Prinzip") for employing the power of judgment (20:205). Judgment, the *one faculty* that can lead us to a conception of universal humanity in the third *Critique*, proceeds heuristically, making "sheer" and "necessary" assumptions just to function. Simply securing enough internal integrity to play its role in Kantian philosophy requires judgment to *invent* a system—the idea of nature and experience as an intelligible network of empirical laws. But Kant is very clear: inventions like this one do not constitute any positive form of knowledge. They fail to furnish any "particular objective law" by which to understand the world of experience, but only a "maxim for the power of judgment," and therefore they can contribute only to "critical" rather than "doctrinal philosophy" (20:205).[55]

The question is whether a subject that must trick itself into thinking can ever be transcendental or absolute in the way poststructuralists criticize. I believe two points suggest this critique does not apply to Kant: first, the process of reflective judgment reveals its subject (especially in its universal form, humanity) as inherently *created* rather than eternally present; second, this subject is internally divided from the start, always observing itself, even as it fashions its own basic cognitive preconditions. This subject is neither necessary nor unified. Compounding these limitations is the fact that the system-inventing, fantasizing subject of the third *Critique* is barred from trying to substantialize its ideas, which can never become constitutive principles of reality. This Kant refers to as "aesthetic pathology" and "fanaticism" or "rapture" ("Schwärmerei").[56] As soon as we insist on an objective, experiential expression of an aesthetic idea (or any idea, which by definition can never be given in experience), we are in this twisted, "pathological," "fanatical" zone. Kant's view of this condition is unequivocally negative. Our ideas are only heuristics for the purposes of our own cognitive integrity. They cannot be dictated onto the world. It is difficult to imagine conceptually a Derridean center operating under this limitation: its ideational contents cannot be exported, but are strictly for its own self-fashioning. What a true center must do is provide the rule for a whole discursive field, but this is the crucial step Kant's reflective subject does not take.

We find similar maneuvers in Schiller. As it happens, Andrzej Warminski, an outspoken de Manian and editor of de Man's *Aesthetic Ideology*, has this to say about the humanism of the aesthetic letters: it is "as though the transcendental concept of humanity, rather than grounding our empirical experience, were itself the product of an empirical experience that is not experienced but rather only claimed, *posited*, as taking place."[57] This should sound familiar. Warminski, like de Man, criticizes Schiller for "empiricizing" what should be transcendental—in this case, for "positing" an empirical engagement of the play drive and designing his aesthetic system around this "transcendental experience," which Warminski considers absurd.[58] He grounds this criticism on Schiller's use of the subjunctive, for example, in introducing the play drive: "*Assuming* that cases [of reciprocity between the drives] *could actually occur in experience*, they would awaken in him a new drive" that reconciles formality and sense (14:3; my emphasis). Here Schiller uses the same verb as Kant (*voraussetzen*) to mark off the assumption behind the play drive. In the next paragraph, as we already saw, the operation of this drive is presented conjecturally: because form wants to produce and sense wants to receive, play must produce *as though* it had received, and vice versa. Here again is the subjunctive: *wie er selbst hervorgebracht hätte* (14:4). This, according to Warminski, is empiricizing: by "positing" (Warminski's translation of *voraussetzen*) play in this way, Schiller suggests it is (or could be) empirically observable, all the while trying to "transcendentalize" it as an a priori commandment of reason.[59] As Schiller writes, also in the fourteenth letter, reciprocity between the drives is "a task enjoined upon us by Reason, a problem which man is only capable of solving completely in the perfect consummation of his existence." This perfect final state refers to the "Idea of his Human Nature ("Idee seiner Menschheit"), hence something Infinite, to which in the course of time he can approximate ever more closely, but without ever being able to reach it" (14:2).

For Warminski, this is the point where Schiller tries to have it both ways, positing play empirically while simultaneously grounding it on transcendental laws of reason, specifically the idea of a consummated humanity. In Warminski's critique, Schiller's conceptual sloppiness results from his commitment to humanism. The human is the center of Schiller's disorganized system. But this is just one (tendentious, polemical) perspective. Another way to read the "transcendental" aspect of Schiller's play drive is that reason gives the subject an impossible demand, much like this faculty does in Kant, and the substance of this demand must be assumed, invoked, "posited" (*vorausgesetzt*) because it can never be given in experience.[60] Already constitutionally split between formal and sense-drives—axiomatic for Schiller and implicit when Kant defines the human as a sensuous subject ("Subjekt als Sinneswesen"; 5:196)—the human now faces the additional pressure, from reason, of resolving its own tension.[61] Thus play and its cognate premise: the idea of a total community, something that only exists as "claimed" (Chaouli), but never present. Humanity is an impossible task, an assumption, in both Schiller and Kant, and the individual subject of this humanity, *der Mensch*, is an essentially divided, conflicted entity. Whether we refer to faculties or drives, the human's inner life is fractious and alienating, with consequences significant enough for Kant and Schiller alike to place this issue at the core of their respective aesthetics.

Nonetheless, Kant and Schiller remain fundamentally humanist in the sense that humanity "centers" their aesthetic systems. In this way, they appear to confirm the pattern Derrida sees at work in the western metaphysical tradition. The case of German Idealism faces us with a different question: what happens when the center is divided? Can the *Mensch* of Kant and Schiller—troubled as it is by internal tension, forced to make assumptions and proceed heuristically at so many crucial points—really perform the metaphysical labor of the medieval God, or Reason in the age of Newton? Can it be sovereign over a discursive field, or is it closer to a ceremonial monarch? If Kant and Schiller give us theories of play that present humanity as a weak metaphysical center—foregrounding as they do the indeterminacy and *created* nature of subjectivity—then when does the critique of metaphysics really begin?

Before Nietzsche, Freud, and Heidegger, there was German Idealist humanism, exposing the weak subjective foundation of metaphysical thought. The theory of play shows this weakness to be programmatic: for Kant and Schiller alike, the subject primarily reflects, only incidentally determines, and always struggles for some contrived mnemonic coherence. Play is fundamental; its "serious" specifications come later. Play haunts them and belies their claims to necessity. Metaphysics, as Derrida and de Man understand it, exemplifies unnecessary seriousness. Significantly, it is only *one* such instance. The metaphysical tradition, however vast and imperious, is a local concentration of a much larger field. This is the field of free play. All of which is a reason to correct the theory gap in play studies: by revealing humanity as a weak center, the connection between German Idealism and poststructuralism indicates a terrain beyond (but also encompassing) contemporary social science, which remains locked in the "strong" pretense of western-metaphysical humanism. Both play and humanity are much more capacious than this tradition suggests. Our thinking should be as well.

NOTES

1. Thomas S. Henricks, *Play and the Human Condition* (Urbana: University of Illinois Press, 2015). James E. Johnson, Scott G. Eberle, Thomas S. Henricks, and David Kuschner, eds., *The Handbook of the Study of Play* (New York: Rowman & Littlefield, 2015).

2. Consider *The Handbook of the Study of Play*, where in the introduction, James E. Johnson presents the volume as the first comprehensive, "interdisciplinary and scholarly" overview of play scholarship. *Handbook*, xi. Nonetheless, the work contains only scattered references to German Idealism, and these are remote historical scene-setting at best, not attempts to engage in detail the concept of play in Kant, Schiller et al. The section on poststructuralism in the chapter "Philosophizing Play," by Wendy Russell and Emily Ryall, is

a quarter-page in length, lists only Foucault, Lyotard, Derrida, and Deleuze by name, and does not cite any of them—only a characterization of them (en masse) by Henricks. *Handbook*, 155.

3. Jacques Derrida, "Structure, Sign, and Play in the Discourse of the Human Sciences," in *Writing and Difference*, trans. Alan Bass (Chicago: University of Chicago Press, 1978 [1967]), 278–294.

4. I have benefited from Oliver Marchart's discussion of "Structure, Sign, and Play" in *Post-Foundational Political Thought: Political Difference in Nancy, Lefort, Badiou and Laclau* (Edinburgh: Edinburgh University Press, 2007). Marchart refers to Derrida's essay as the "locus classicus" of poststructuralism (15).

5. See J. Hillis Miller, "Derrida and de Man: Two Rhetorics of Deconstruction," in *A Companion to Derrida*, ed. Zeynep Direk and Leonard Lawlor (Chichester, West Sussex: Wiley Blackwell, 2014), 345–346. Regarding the label "poststructuralism" versus "deconstruction": in this essay I refer to poststructuralism rather than deconstruction only to reinforce the importance of the concept of structure for my own argument, not to take issue with the term "deconstruction."

6. Henricks, *Play*, 1–5. The whole introduction blends this kind of high metaphysics with the very concrete, observational mode of empirical social science.

7. Immanuel Kant, *Critique of the Power of Judgment*, trans. Paul Guyer and Eric Matthews, ed. Paul Guyer (Cambridge: Cambridge University Press, 2000 [1790]). All citations from Kant give the volume and page number of the *Akademie* edition as referenced in the English translation. Friedrich Schiller, *On the Aesthetic Education of Man in a Series of Letters*, trans. Elizabeth M. Wilkinson and L. A. Willoughby (Oxford: Clarendon, 1982 [1795]). Subsequent in-text citations of Schiller will give the letter and paragraph in parentheses, e.g., (15:9) for "man only plays. . . ."

8. Important to keep in mind is that de Man was not a scholar of Kant or Schiller, and his lecture, while useful for theorizing play, is less so as a critical commentary on German Idealism. At the very least, de Man's aggressive contempt for Schiller makes clear this is not a completely evenhanded analysis.

9. Paul de Man, "Kant and Schiller," in *Aesthetic Ideology*, ed. Andrzej Warminski (Minneapolis: University of Minnesota Press, 1996), 129. De Man does not shrink from ad hominem with his reviled Schiller, calling him variously "childish" and "banal." "Kant and Schiller," 141.

10. De Man goes on: "Whatever writing we do, whatever way we have of talking about art, whatever way we have of teaching, whatever justification we give ourselves for teaching, whatever the standards are and the values by means of which we teach, they are more than ever and profoundly Schillerian." "Kant and Schiller," 142.

11. De Man, "Kant and Schiller," 131.

12. These specific examples from the *Aesthetic Education* are mine, not de Man's, but they illustrate his general complaint that in Schiller, "you'll get [the chiasmus] everywhere." "Kant and Schiller," 137.

13. De Man, "Kant and Schiller," 135.

14. For a defense and contextualization of Schiller's play theory that addresses his alleged overreliance on formula, see Frederick Beiser, *Schiller as Philosopher: A Re-Examination* (Oxford: Clarendon, 2005), 141–144.

15. De Man, "Kant and Schiller," 151.
16. De Man, "Kant and Schiller," 148.
17. Derrida, "Structure, Sign, and Play," 279.
18. Derrida, "Structure, Sign, and Play," 279.
19. De Man, "Kant and Schiller," 150; my emphasis.
20. De Man, "Kant and Schiller," 150.
21. Beiser writes that Schiller uses the term "free play" in a "broader sense" than his predecessors by "applying it to the person as a whole." Schiller's expressly anthropological conception of play, for Beiser, builds especially on the work of Lessing, Kant, and Friedrich Wilhelm von Ramdohr. See *Schiller as Philosopher*, 142–143.
22. Franco Moretti, *Signs Taken for Wonders: Essays in the Sociology of Literary Forms*, trans. Susan Fischer, David Forgacs, and David Miller (New York: Verso, 1983), 31.
23. De Man, "Kant and Schiller," 133.
24. De Man, "Kant and Schiller," 134.
25. De Man, "Kant and Schiller."
26. De Man, "Kant and Schiller."
27. Derrida, "Structure, Sign, and Play," 278.
28. Derrida, "Structure, Sign, and Play," 279.
29. Derrida, "Structure, Sign, and Play," 280.
30. Derrida, "Structure, Sign, and Play," 289; original emphasis.
31. See Derrida, "Structure, Sign, and Play."
32. De Man lays out his preferred, "material" approach to Kant in "Phenomenality and Materiality in Kant," the lecture that immediately preceded "Kant and Schiller" at Cornell, and "Kant's Materialism," a 1981 conference, presentation. Both are collected in *Aesthetic Ideology* (70–90 and 119–128, respectively).
33. Derrida, "Structure, Sign, and Play," 292.
34. As Dieter Henrich argues, the theory of play "provides Kant with the most important resources of his critique of taste and thus of the most innovative part of the *Critique of Judgment*." *Aesthetic Judgment and the Moral Image of the World: Studies in Kant* (Stanford, CA: Stanford University Press, 1992), 54.
35. See de Man, "Kant and Schiller," 150–153.
36. From the "first introduction" to the third *Critique*, which was not published with the first edition of the treatise. The chronologically second introduction (the one first published with the book) I subsequently refer to as the "published" introduction. Paul Guyer and Eric Matthews's translation of Kant's third *Critique* contains both introductions.
37. It is necessary to remember, though, as Henrich points out, that the *Critique of Judgment* attempts to do for aesthetic judgment what the first two *Critiques* did for theoretical and practical reason, namely, ground it on a priori principles. When Kant "rethought the epistemology of the *Critique of Pure Reason*," argues Henrich, "he quickly saw that his epistemological theorems about the relationship between imagination and understanding would allow him to produce an explanation of aesthetic judgment whose sources would not be empirical throughout but rather derived from the explanation of the possibility of our knowledge of objects. Hence the new explanation would have the a priori status of a transcendental insight." *Aesthetic Judgment*, 34. But as we will see, this a priori status does not mean that aesthetic judgment is *legislative* in the same way understanding and reason are in the first two *Critiques*.

38. Michel Chaouli captures this dynamic well in "describing the role of concepts" in aesthetic experience: "Aesthetic experience, while foregoing conceptual *determination*, does involve conceptual *capacities*, and crucially so; concepts do not run the show, but they are and must be in play." *Thinking with Kant's "Critique of Judgment"* (Cambridge, MA: Harvard University Press, 2017), 62; my emphasis. Later Chaouli describes aesthetic experience as "laced with conceptuality." *Thinking with Kant's "Critique of Judgment,"* 62.

39. Henrich, *Aesthetic Judgment*, 42.

40. According to Gilles Deleuze, another postmodernist preoccupied with Kant, this shows the systemic priority of the third *Critique*, which Deleuze claims "does not complete the two others; *it provides them with a basis or makes them possible*. A faculty would never take on a legislative and determining role [as it must in the first two *Critiques*] were not all the faculties together in the first place capable of this free subjective harmony." *Kant's Critical Philosophy*, trans. Hugh Tomlinson and Barbara Habberjam (Minneapolis: University of Minnesota Press, 1984 [1963]), 50; original emphasis.

41. Henrich, *Aesthetic Judgment*, 38; original emphasis.

42. Henrich, *Aesthetic Judgment*, 49–50; original emphasis.

43. Derrida, "Structure, Sign, and Play," 292.

44. Derrida, "Structure, Sign, and Play."

45. De Man, "Kant and Schiller," 150.

46. See Immanuel Kant, *Groundwork of the Metaphysics of Morals*, trans. Mary Gregor (Cambridge: Cambridge University Press, 1998 [1785]), 4:429.

47. I should reiterate that my focus in this article is on Kant's third *Critique*, because this is where the concept of play figures most prominently in Kant and because it is the text at the center of Kant's reception by poststructuralists. It would be beyond the scope of this essay to inquire in more detail how the "weak" human of the third *Critique* relates to the "stronger" conceptions of the human in Kant's moral philosophy, including his second *Critique*.

48. Claire Colebrook, "The Context of Humanism," *New Literary History* 42, no. 4 (Autumn 2011): 717.

49. Kant writes in the third *Critique*: "*Beauty* is the form of the *purposiveness* of an object, insofar as it is perceived in it *without representation of an end* [*Zweck*]," 5:236; original emphasis.

50. Henry Allison, *Kant's Theory of Taste: A Reading of the "Critique of Aesthetic Judgment"* (Cambridge: Cambridge University Press, 2001), 117–118.

51. Allison, *Kant's Theory of Taste*, 111.

52. From the third *Critique*: "This state of a *free play* of the faculties of cognition with a representation through which an object is given must be able to be universally communicated, because cognition, as a determination of the object with which given representations (in whatever subject it may be) should agree, is the only kind of representation that is valid for everyone." 5:217; original emphasis.

53. Henrich, *Aesthetic Judgment*, 54; original emphasis.

54. Chaouli, *Thinking with Kant*, 62.

55. As Allison writes, judgments that are strictly reflective "rest upon a methodological claim to the effect that [their] objects must be investigated *as if* they were products" of a particular causality, "rather than a straightforwardly causal claim that they are, in fact, such products." *Kant's Theory of Taste*, 45.

56. See (20:231–232) for Kant on aesthetic-pathological judgment. Kant discusses *Schwärmerei* on (5:275).

57. Andrzej Warminski, "Returns of the Sublime: Positing and Performative in Kant, Fichte, and Schiller," *MLN* 116, no. 5 (December 2001): 973; original emphasis.

58. Warminski, "Returns of the Sublime," 971.

59. Warminski, "Returns of the Sublime," 973.

60. For a reading of the third *Critique* that brings out the self-dividing nature of reason's demands, see David Martyn, *Sublime Failures: The Ethics of Kant and Sade* (Detroit: Wayne State University Press, 2003), 135–169.

61. The fact that sensibility cannot be simply ignored by the intellectual powers (as it is in Enlightenment discourse proper) suggests that by the time of German Idealism, the absolute subject of reason has already started to break down. In the 1790s, aesthetics distinguishes itself from (wholly rational) science by purposefully engaging the category of sensibility, and thus outlines a form of subjectivity no longer "centered" exclusively on reason. See Beiser, *Schiller as Philosopher*, 128.

Part II

Games of Chance

CHAPTER THREE

"Mit dem Spiele spielen"

Lessing's Play for Tolerance

EDGAR LANDGRAF

SINCE THE EIGHTEENTH CENTURY, much of the literature on play has taken a paradoxical position toward its subject. While it has come to understand and appreciate play as an autonomous doing—play is viewed as a self-contained, self-referential activity, and hence as detached from, if not independent of everyday affairs and "serious" concerns—it continuously wants to instrumentalize play's alleged autonomy. Along with the recognition and appreciation of play's autonomy grows the desire to rob play of its freedom by subjecting it to particular educational, aesthetic, political, or social objectives. From Friedrich Schiller's *Letters on the Aesthetic Education of Men* (1795) to Johan Huizinga's *Homo Ludens* (1944) to Thomas Henricks's *Play and the Human Condition* (2015) we find the argument that "play's escape from the chain of material consequences, in essence its triviality, is the very reason why play is so important,"[1] why, to spell out the paradox more clearly, play is thought to have lasting and by all means material consequences. Schiller offers the period's most prominent example for this logic. By subjecting play to its political program—to break the cycle of tyranny—Schiller dictates the uses and limits of play and thus undermines what motivated the instrumentalization of play in the first place: the assumption of its autonomy.[2] Modernity's fascination with play is haunted by this contradiction. It can cherish play only paradoxically, as useful uselessness, interested disinterestedness, (self-)disciplining freedom, procured autonomy, and hence only by invading, directing, necessitating, or otherwise infringing on play's playfulness.

In the accompanying discussions about the *appropriate* instrumentalization of play around 1800, two principally opposing viewpoints emerged. On one side, we have proponents of what we might call direct interventions into play's autonomy, that is, instances where what is recognized as play's freedom motivates programs that want to restrict, channel, discipline, and limit (game) play,[3] supposedly to maximize its utility and minimize the elements of contingency, indolence, chaos, distraction, and physicality associated with play. A footnote in Kant's lecture *On Pedagogy* is quite telling for this tendency, which is most apparent in the pedagogical discourses of the time and spans the gambit from Philanthropinist approaches—with their focus on corporeal aspects of education, on disciplining and training children for their future role in society—to Kant's own more ambitious, neohumanist ideals, where education targets man as a whole and by extension, humankind.[4] The footnote reveals that no matter how important a role Kant attributes to the "free play of the faculties" in his *Third Critique*, he has no patience for the actual practice of play. Associating game play with childishness, he proclaims that it is "truly remarkable to see how reasonable people are able to sit hours shuffling cards. It shows that it is not easy for adults to stop being children. . . . That is why it is of utmost importance that children learn how to work."[5]

Despite occasional lip service toward the contrary, the emphasis on discipline and on putting immediate restrictions on play is shared in large part by Kant's contemporaries Joachim Heinrich Campe, Johann Bernhard Basedow, and, of course, Schiller. Yet also emerging at the end of the eighteenth century is a different attitude toward play which draws on the particular German concept of *Bildung*. As the latter suggests a more holistic approach toward education, it helps promote a notion of play as "self-activity" (Pestalozzi) that would seem to be less restrictive.[6] If we take Goethe's educational novel *Wilhelm Meister's Apprenticeship* (1796) as a model, we see the concept of play being instrumentalized only indirectly. As for many of the Romantics, Goethe's novel values play as a means of self-formation and self-discovery. Against this backdrop, play is granted greater independence—it is no longer or only gently directed from outside—and a wider variety of play modes are being explored. Goethe's novel is symptomatic in this respect, supplementing play with toys and role play with activities that are inventive (e.g., turning everyday artefacts into toys and theater props) and improvisational (ad hoc, interactive, and context dependent).[7] Play here is conceived in analogy to aesthetics as a medium or training ground for the faculties. As in art, the latter hinges on the recognition of and respect for play's autonomy. At least in the liberal arts, the exposure to "just playing" continues to this day to be seen as indispensable for the formation of a child's or young adult's character, for his or her inner or psychological development.

Against the backdrop of these two broadly sketched tendencies in the instrumentalization of play around 1800, I want to turn to Gotthold Ephraim Lessing's work and in particular to *Nathan the Wise* from 1779, the famous play (*Schauspiel*) about religious tolerance and one of the most important German contributions to Enlightenment thought. Game play, social play, and even wagering ("aufs Spiel setzen") recur with surprising frequency in this central and by all means serious Enlightenment text. Most prominent is the game of chess Saladin plays with his sister Sittah at the beginning of the second act, where no one wants to win. Nathan later suggests this form of disinterested, disinvested game play means "playing with the game" ("mit dem Spiele spielen").[8] The chess game is juxtaposed with Nathan's ring parable, the play within the play, the "fable" (*Märchen*; III.6, p. 231 [9:554]) with which Nathan challenges religious dogmatism, and which relies on the "false play" (III.7, p. 234 [9:558])[9] of a father who does not want to disadvantage any of his three sons in order to make its case for religious tolerance. In the following, I want to examine more closely how Lessing distinguishes different modes of game play, playing, and wagering, and how in his writings playing is cast as central to the promotion and practice of Enlightenment ethics. The staging of scenes of play within the play so prevalent in *Nathan the Wise* and also in the comedy *Minna von Barnhelm* (1767) is an aesthetic device that carries its own ethical and even political effect.[10] Furthermore, Lessing's use of play warrants our attention, as it does not follow neatly any of the two tendencies in the treatment of play I sketched above. Lessing neither adopts the rationalist Enlightenment position that would seek to restrict play for its "proper" instrumentalization nor shares the Romantic use of play as a "self-activity" to promote a child's or learner's internal development. Rather than promoting discipline or a narrative of personal growth, Lessing opts, I hope to show, for a pragmatic approach to playing that finds in play a preferred mode of social interaction. As a social activity, playing in Lessing is linked to an interpretive strategy that diverges from the more restrictive, rule-governed, and less playful instrumentalizations of play typically associated with the Enlightenment, but which is also distinct from the subject-centered appropriations of play and the arts often attributed to the Romantics.

Before turning to the two main scenes that feature play within *Nathan the Wise*, I want to address a couple of less prominent instances where the word "play" appears in Lessing's text and which precede the opposition between the game of chess and the "false play" at the center of the ring parable. The word *Spiel* is used already in the first scene of the first act, as part of an implicit discussion of sympathy, a concept central to Lessing's dramaturgy.[11] The scene has Nathan wondering how the absence of the Templar, who heroically rescued his daughter Recha from a fire, might affect Recha's state of mind. Caught between "hate for men" (*Menschenhass*) and sadness (*Schwermut*), Nathan is afraid that "phantasy" will turn his daughter into a dreamer (*Schwärmer*) "In whom the head plays heart, and then again / The heart must play the head" (I.1, p. 179 [9:489]). Play here (as in several other instances) is used in the theatric sense of acting, of role play. Projected onto his daughter's psychological state, (bad) acting becomes the model for her emotional confusion. The operative term, however, is the word "must," indicating as problematic the loss of command, the inability to separate and control the role that head and heart play. In good Enlightenment fashion, this first mentioning of play underlines not the notion that the heart or emotions play no role when we play or for a play, but that the heart's involvement should not come at the expense of the head. The latter, Recha's case indicates, is less about intellectual confusion as it is about a lack of judgment, the inability to empathize. Recha fails to put herself in the position of the Templar as a way to understanding his situation and his reaction to her.

While this first appearance of the word "play" provides a first hint of the social and ethical dimension Lessing attributes to play (in tune with his aesthetics of sympathy), the second appearance of the word embeds such questions in a larger anthropological and even cosmological context. Indeed, already in the very next scene Lessing moves the discussion of play from Recha's imagined internal quarrel to a matter of divine providence. Nathan raises the possibility of Saladin releasing the Templar because he reminded him of his lost brother. Nathan argues that this story is not impossible to believe (as is suggested by Daya, Recha's ignorant nanny), but nevertheless should be viewed as a miracle (*Wunder*) performed "by Him / Who stern resolves, the most ambitious plans / Of kings—His sport if not His mockery—/ Delights to guide by feeble threads" ("sein Spiel—wenn nicht sein Spott—/ Gern an den schwächsten Fäden lenkt"; I.2, p. 182 [9:494]). The use of the word *Spiel* is ambivalent here. The most feeble of threads on the one hand insinuate proximity to death (the possibility of the threads easily breaking), human vulnerability, and a lack of seriousness. From the divine perspective, our earthly existence appears as a mere puppet theater worthy of derision. On the other hand, however, and staying with the figure of the marionette, the "feeble threads" suggest that the earthly play within which we participate is only loosely regulated, that divine providence does not steer our earthly doings with a heavy hand. The scene thus asserts simultaneously divine control and earthly autonomy, seriousness and playfulness, wonder and ridicule. Human existence is not reducible to either side, the metaphor asserts, but like play entails the continued negotiation of both sides of such dichotomies. Put differently, the ambivalence of Lessing's thread metaphor summons *in nuce* a set of crucial antinomies that lie at the center of *Nathan the Wise* (and more broadly of Lessing's thought), namely, the antinomies between divine providence and human contingency, between predetermination and autonomy, between authority and vulnerability.[12] Accordingly, as both a social and an aesthetic practice, play is neither merely about divine providence nor merely about human contingency (luck), but constitutes a preferred site for the negotiation of these central poles of Lessing's anthropology.[13]

The antinomy between providence and contingency is also important in the two main scenes where Lessing's *Schauspiel* features play, the first being Saladin's and Sittah's chess game. Interestingly, the seemingly pointless and dramatically somewhat boring scene entails three levels of play. First, there is the game of chess that apparently no one wants to win. Second, the game of chess is supplemented by a money wager, which again no one seems to want to win. In fact, the wager is doubly undermined. Sittah tells us that she actually wins more money when she loses, because Saladin likes to console her for her loss by giving her more money than they wagered in the first place. It would be a win-win situation for her, if only the whole money wager was not for naught. As we find out a bit later, Sittah, unbeknownst to Saladin, has not collected any of the money she was promised whether she won or lost. As she knows that Saladin is not solvent, she refuses to collect her winnings to prevent Saladin from incurring further debt. In both cases, then, Lessing signals that winning is not the objective of the games they play, indicating that playing, here, is not the means to an end, but the end itself.

That it is indeed the activity of playing itself that matters is most evident when we look at the third level of play surrounding the chess game. It is what Nathan calls "playing with the game" ("mit dem Spiele spielen"), namely, the meta-play that Sittah and Saladin play around the wager and the game of chess. This meta-play does not just revolve around neither party wanting to win but also is about anticipating and catering to the expectations of the other. The scene starts right away as this meta-play, with Sittah asking Saladin to "take back that move," a command followed by a question about the utility of Saladin's next move: "What good / Is that?" (II.1, p. 199 [9:514]). Throughout the scene, Sittah and Saladin orient their words and actions (the moves on the board) either toward what they think the "opponent" wants them to do or toward what they think would be best for the other person. In other words, neither plays chess to win, but rather they play with the game so as to find out how they can make their opponent win, that is, how they can make their sibling happy. It is an attempt to transform the fickle fortunes of game play and wagering into a certain win for both, to turn an unpredictable chance (*Glück*) into the reliable form of happiness (*Glück*) that derives from seeing one's playing partner enjoy his or her good fortunes (*Glück*).[14]

This kind of social play can be observed quite frequently in Lessing's work. Friedrich Kittler understands the "reciprocal expectations of expectations," although in a quite different context, as the principally new discourse mode of the bourgeois family, which undermines the expectations of the aristocratic suitors in Lessing's tragedies.[15] The strategic play of the nefarious suitors (think of the games a Marwood plays in *Miss Sara Sampson* or Marinelli in *Emilia Galotti*) does not look all that different, of course. They, too, orient their actions toward what they think the other expects them to say or do. In Lessing's bourgeois tragedies, both the communication strategies of the seducers and those of the virtuous daughters are bound to fail (Minna's plan almost fails) as they lead to confusion, misunderstanding, and mistrust, that in the end seems to call for the appearance of a decisive patriarchal voice that asserts clarity and direction.[16]

If we read Sittah's and Saladin's meta-game against the backdrop of these failed communication strategies, we notice a number of differences. First of all, it becomes clear that there is more at stake than Lessing—who we know liked to gamble at the local casino—wanting to expose game play as an idle activity with which the aristocracy hoped to avoid *ennui*. The game of chess instead becomes an opportunity for the siblings to exercise their good intentions and their capacity for empathy. Furthermore, as they start playing with the game itself, a different game starts to unfold, one where the rules of the game are loosened and become negotiable. The meta-game revolves around questions such as "Are you or aren't you allowed to take back a move?" Or "Should I or shouldn't I tell you what my next move will be, or what the consequences of your move will be?" and so on. This kind of playing with the rules is not uncommon when we play games in a private setting. We often discuss options with opponents, allow the partner to take back a move, or place wagers with friends or family we do not necessarily want to win. This "mit dem Spiele spielen" undermines the utilitarian appropriation of the game, a fact that is underlined when Al-Hafi, who clearly misses the whole point of the siblings' interaction, wants to finish the chess game to determine an actual winner. From the perspective of the relationship between Saladin and Sittah, the reciprocity with which they make their actions dependent on what they perceive will benefit the other, suggests a sympathetic mode of social interaction where the rules of the game are engaged strategically and thus become themselves part of the playful activity. As the liberal attitude toward rules allows the game to evolve, it is also what drives the empathetic and supportive behavior with which the two siblings relate to each other. Simply put, not adhering strictly to the rules (and in this sense, improvising) creates a level of intimacy and spontaneity where each playing partner is able to engage and react to the contributions and situational needs of the other.[17]

My "positive" reading of the rule-breaking meta-play might seem undermined by the boredom and blindness of Saladin that puts the game of chess they play overall into a negative light. Yet, the critique of this kind of play, as indicated above, is articulated by Al-Hafi (to whom Nathan responds) and seems out of place as Al-Hafi insists on the seriousness of the game for monetary reasons. The important opposition Lessing creates here (clearly in preparation for the play at religious tolerance that is the ring parable) is one between Al-Hafi's seriousness about the game, where the game finds its purpose outside of itself, in its monetary consequences, and the communicative meta-play which evolves around the game of chess and which finds its purpose in the activity itself, the exercise of a sympathetic discourse which orients itself toward the well-being of the other. When Lessing implicitly attributes this purpose to play, he does not fully escape his time's tendency to instrumentalize play; he does, however, attribute an intrinsic value to play (the particular sociability it fosters) that is different from the appropriations of play for extrinsic purposes, from play's mere use as a means to an end.[18]

What is at stake with this opposition between two different modes of play—serious game play versus the playful play with rules—becomes apparent when we look at the Patriarch's insistence on a stark separation between a hypothetical case that would be "but pastime for the mind" ("nur so / Ein Spiel des Witzes"; IV.2, p. 248 [9:577]) and a real situation which would have to be treated with all seriousness.[19] Unlike Saladin, the Patriarch is precisely not interested in what a hypothetical case—and this is what he calls "nur so / Ein Spiel des Witzes"—could teach and how it might alter the rules of the game (the law). As a consequence, he is also not willing to engage the

Templar's question. Rather than allowing the Templar to present his hypothetical case and respond to it, the Patriarch insists on the clear separation between play and life, a separation that puts Nathan's life in immediate jeopardy. Should the question the Templar raised about the ramifications of a Jew raising a Christian child turn out not to be "but pastime for the mind," no circumstance, the Patriarch insists, could alter his view that the Jew needed to be killed. The Patriarch's lack of empathy peaks when he maintains that the Christian child should rather have been left to die than be saved by a Jew, a view he amplifies by repeating several times his gruesome line, "All one! The Jew must burn" ("Tut nichts, der Jude wird verbrannt"; IV.2, p. 249 [9:578]). The Patriarch's insistence on a rigid separation between fact and fiction and the rigid application of the rule of (Christian) law form the opposite to Saladin's and Sittah's playful playing with the rules and the "false play" that lies at the heart of Nathan's ring parable.

Before turning to the famous parable, I want to distinguish more clearly between the two different modes of play I see competing in Lessing's text. To do so, I will draw on Gregory Bateson, in particular on his "Metalogue: About Games and Being Serious" from 1953 and on his paper "A Theory of Play and Fantasy" first read in 1954. Bateson's metalogues are conversations between a father and a daughter about various "difficult subjects" where the "structure of the conversation as a whole is also relevant to the whole subject," as Bateson defines the genre of the "metalogue" in his short introductory note to their publication in *Steps to an Ecology of Mind* (1972).[20] This reflexivity is certainly on display in the "Metalogue: About Games and Being Serious." It is itself both playful and serious as it discusses the difference—or, more precisely, as the conversation comes to appreciate how difficult it is to maintain the difference—between playing and being serious. Discussing seriousness in terms of adhering to rules, Bateson suggests we draw a distinction between playing a game such as rummy or chess where one follows particular rules and "just playing" (like when children play with blocks). The latter has certain rules, too (don't glue the blocks together), but the rules in "just playing" take on a different stature. Playing in this context is not about what follows from following particular rules, but about discovering the rules of one's own playing. For children playing with blocks this might mean exploring how many blocks I can stack in how many ways on top of and around each other to create buildings, towers, or who knows what. With regard to the conversation about a serious topic between father and daughter, playing means to develop and explore first the linguistic and logical rules that might help one to distinguish between being playful and being serious. Unlike game play, "just playing" thus becomes a reflexive process where in the articulation of the rules, the "rules are always changing and always undiscoverable."[21] Neither the transitoriness of the rule or the statutory nor the moments of confusion, error, chaos (things are constantly becoming muddled, as the metalogue puts it) are negative factors, Bateson notes, but form the precondition for saying and seeing new things. "If we didn't get into muddles, our talks would be like playing rummy without first shuffling the cards," adding a bit later on, "the whole point of the game is that we do get into muddles, and do come out on the other side, and if there were no muddles our 'game' would be like canasta or chess—and that is not how we want it to be" (29).[22]

I want to suggest that we apply Bateson's model of "just playing" to the hermeneutic play that Lessing invokes with his ring parable (and with the drama at large as the parable represents a play within the play that distills and simultaneously reflects on the hermeneutic approach crucial for Lessing's play for tolerance). Nathan calls the parable with which he challenges religious dogmatism a "fable" (*Märchen*) and a little "tale" (*Geschichtchen*; III.6, p. 231 [9:554], and III.7, p. 231 [9:555]). Like the earlier game of chess, it is accompanied by a wager, though this wager is more sinister than one where merely money is at stake. Just before Nathan starts narrating the parable, Saladin marvels about Nathan's wisdom and his desire "Not to hide the truth! To stake / One's all upon it! Life and limb! One's goods / And blood" ("Nie die Wahrheit zu / Verhehlen! Für sie alles auf das Spiel / Zu setzen! Leib und Leben! Gut und Blut!"; III.7, p. 231 [9:555]). To which Nathan replies: "Yes, when it's needful and of use" (III.7, p. 231 [9:555]). The seriousness of the situation is further underlined when Saladin interrupts him in the middle of the parable, challenging Nathan's equivocation of the three major monotheistic religions with the warning, "Don't trifle with me!" ("Spiele nicht mir mir!"; III.7, p. 233 [9:557]). Though the audience / reader by now knows Saladin well enough to see in him no serious threat to Nathan's life, Saladin's stance serves to underline that Nathan's play for tolerance is serious also in the sense that it entails the possibility of existential risks for him (and, in the light of the Patriarch's remarks quoted above, for any defender of religious tolerance).[23]

Within the parable, the word *Spiel* appears twice, namely, with reference to the magic ring's stone, the opal that "shed a hundred colors fair" ("der hundert schöne Farben spielte"; III.7, p. 231 [9:555]); and in the accusation before the judge where Nathan explains that each son would rather accuse one of the brothers than their dear father of "false play."[24] Let's first turn to the second mentioning of play in the ring parable, namely, the father's "false play," his illicit duplication of the original ring, an act of artistic forgery. The forgery makes the authenticity and origin of the ring(s) indecipherable and thus suspends the age-old rule that regulated the traditional handing-down of the ring from generation to generation.[25] The genius of the judge lies in his refusal to reinstate the old rule while also not implementing a new rule. Instead, the judge's advice sends the three brothers out on a quest to live up to the promise of the ring (make yourself liked before others and God). The judge frames this quest as an all but open-ended wager ("in a thousand thousand years"; III:7, p. 235 [9:559]), the third and most important wager in *Nathan the Wise*:

> Let each aspire
> To emulate his father's unbeguiled,
> Unprejudiced affection! Let each strive
> To match the rest in bringing to the fore
> The magic of the opal in his ring!
>
> [Es eifre jeder seiner unbestochnen
> von Vorurteilen freien Liebe nach!
> Es strebe von euch jeder um die Wette,
> Die Kraft des Steins in seinem Ring' an Tag
> Zu legen!]
>
> (III:7, p. 235 [9:559])

Because the resolution of the quest, the goal of their competitive striving, is placed beyond their life span, the success, significance, and meaning of their striving are themselves not transparent. As it is part of a competitive wager with multiple participants, it also is one where the rules (how to outdo the competitors) can be expected to constantly change. From this perspective, the earlier chess game between Saladin and his sister gains further significance. It suggests a model of game play—the kind of "mit dem Spiele spielen"—and the development of strategies that help the other party win. For just as in the chess game Sittah and Saladin were playing, wanting to make the other parties win might mean winning yourself as, presumably, acting in such a manner has the potential to live up to the magic of the ring, that is, make you more liked before others and God. In fact, I would suggest that this is precisely the impact that the chess game has narratively on the ring parable: it adds a dimension to the competitive game between religions that otherwise might go unnoticed. Conceived along these lines, the game of religion becomes reflexive. Entering the competition means to acknowledge that the rules can no longer be presupposed as handed down from the past, but need to be discovered as one plays along. This discovery process is itself not static. The open-endedness of the quest suggests that in the articulation of the rules (how to live up to the magic of the ring), the rules can be expected continually to change. With Bateson we can say that Lessing's ring parable reorients or transforms game play—following the rules of the past—into "just playing," an activity where the rules are muddled and have to be discovered on the go, only to be changed by the process of discovery itself.

The possibility of playing such a game hinges on competitiveness[26] but also on a particular semiotic stance. The representational challenges the ring forgery creates have been the topic of much discussion in the secondary literature on *Nathan the Wise*. Earlier I quoted Robert S. Leventhal who points out how Lessing's choice of the opal was not coincidental, but based on the stone's colorful shine (the first mentioning of the word *Spiel* in the ring parable) which introduces representational ambivalence. Leventhal reads Lessing's ring parable as a "hermeneutic intervention" that "reflects on and questions some of the basic premises of eighteenth century hermeneutic theory: the distinction between the literal-grammatical sense of the text and its figural meaning; the insistence of a fundamental, underlying spirit of the text [*Geist*] distinct from its specific interpretation or use; the emphasis on grammatical explication over application; and finally, the supposed unity and authority of the Western Tradition."[27] Leventhal contends that the parable functions as a performative which "does not represent or prescribe a certain system of values to be followed, but rather carries out or enacts a confrontation or clash of the multiplicity and indeterminacy of historical meaning" (130–131). Representational ambivalence is also at the center of Eva Knodt's seminal study from 1988. Challenging David Wellbery's important book on Lessing's *Laocoön* which had juxtaposed Lessing's aesthetics of mimesis with Herder's aesthetics of expressivity, Knodt argues that Lessing breaks with a "bipolar model of the sign"[28] and the representational mode of thinking associated with Enlightenment aesthetics. In a similar vein, to mention another example, Bernhard Greiner reads Lessing's comedy *Minna von Barnhelm* as being about disturbed sign relations that need to be rectified. When Tellheim pawns the engagement ring in the comedy, he is separating its ideal value from its material value; but once Minna plays the ring back into Tellheim's hands, the symbolic value of the ring, Greiner argues, becomes "ambivalent . . . provoking incorrect interpretations."[29]

I want to build on these observations of Lessing's play with the representational structure of signs, by approaching the semiotic question from an anthropological angle that is more closely tied to the question of play and what we might consider as a semiotic stance specific to play. To do so, I will draw again on Gregory Bateson. Bateson allows us to put Lessing's hermeneutics, which defies the normative stance of religious dogmatism by challenging the rigidity of the underlying representational paradigm, in broader evolutionary and ethical terms. In particular, Bateson's essay "A Theory of Play and Fantasy" offers an interesting perspective on the question of the autonomy of play. In this essay Bateson contemplates the implications of watching two young monkeys who are playfully biting each other. Bateson suggests that the separation of play (the friendly nip) from reality (real biting) presupposes a sophisticated use of semiotics. In play, the action is accompanied by a metastatement that communicates that the bite is not meant as a bite. Bateson summarizes this observation in the memorable line, "The playful nip denotes the bite, but it does not denote what would be denoted by the bite."[30] Bateson sees playing as an evolutionary accomplishment that becomes possible when an organism no longer reacts automatically to a "mood-sign" of another organism and "becomes able to recognize the sign as a signal" (183). What turns the sign into a signal is the ability to read the action as containing this paradoxical metastatement, which he spells out as saying, "These actions in which we now engage do not denote what those actions for which they stand would denote" (184). Bateson sees the ability to read such metastatements and the recognition of the difference between sign and signal not only as a precondition for the invention of language but also for "all the complexities of empathy, identification, projection, and so on," and for the possibility of "communicating at multiple levels of abstraction" (185), denotative, metalinguistic, and metacommunicative.

What is fascinating about Bateson's analysis—and in tune with the significance Lessing attributes to playing—is that he recognizes how the condition for playful (and, we might add, peaceful) interaction between independent actors lies in a particular hermeneutic and communication practice, and not in the assertion of reasonability, the adherence to an external moral code, or a (Kantian) notion of maturity. Following Bateson, not just humans but already animals are able to engage in play, that is, in a mode of social interaction that is organized around the recognition of the arbitrariness of signs and that is able to unite in a more or less competitive setting individual participants in a common activity. Following Bateson, then—and, I contend, this is precisely what Lessing's use of play in *Nathan the Wise* suggests—playing is not so much meant to educate its participants or otherwise serve as an (aesthetic) medium directed toward an external goal, but rather, it is its own purpose. For both Bateson and Lessing, what underlies the cultural significance and seriousness of "just playing" is that it constitutes a form of social organization that steps away from immediate responses to signs but creates a space between sign and signal that invites those who respect this space to enter into a process of social interaction that allows for empathy, identification with the other, projection, and so on. Significantly for Lessing's play for tolerance, the semiotics of play also entail the possibility of role play and role reversals, that is, a distancing from the traditional identity of its players, their religious affiliation and social standing. While entering the competitive play prescribed by the judge, these identities might not disappear, but their coercive force is suspended. In this regard, the transition from the reliance on originality and authenticity toward the competitive play for tolerance introduced by the "false play" of the father initiates a practice of play that mediates between the bonds of tradition and providence on the one hand and human contingency, vulnerability, and interagency on the other hand.

Drawing on Bateson, then, we recognize how Lessing's *Nathan the Wise* is quite removed from the attempt to ground ethics in a universalist maxim or categorical imperative. For Lessing, open rules, even the breaking of rules, are the foundation for a playful hermeneutic practice that forms the basis and precondition for religious tolerance and sympathy. Play in Lessing constitutes not an intermediate sphere, a training ground, for the development of skills that will help an enlightened populace to establish a civil society. Rather, Lessing puts competitiveness and playing with the rules at the heart of what he conceives to be an open (and risky) process of social interchange that continually searches for and rearticulates the rules of the game it plays. Lessing's ring parable suggests that we are not to learn *from* playing, but need to learn *how* to play this game and put into practice its underlying hermeneutic stance. This pragmatic outlook, which attributes an intrinsic social value to play, runs counter to the two tendencies in the (pedagogical) instrumentalization of playing I sketched above and that in the cultural history of the West came to dominate the pedagogical instrumentalization of play. Lessing does little to try to "discipline" game play, nor does he advocate employing play as a "self-activity," as an intermediary stage, a mode of self-fashioning that would prepare individuals for a supposed more serious future life. Instead of wanting to utilize play for the development of the kind of interior, individualist, and therefore also insular qualities that remain much at the center of our Western ideal of *Bildung* as it emerges around 1800, Lessing's conception of playing with the game aims at the practical development and exercise of particular communication and social skills. Lessing's *Nathan the Wise* suggests that playful interaction, the competitive back-and-forth between sympathetic players, is itself the attitude and goal that can assure a civil and tolerant society.

NOTES

1. Thomas S. Henricks, *Play and the Human Condition* (Urbana: University of Illinois Press, 2015), 3–4. Henricks here is summarizing what he identifies as one of Huizinga's main assertions about play.

2. See Andreas Gailus's seminal essay on the disciplinary regiment under which Schiller subsumes play in his *Letters on the Aesthetic Education of Man*, not only banning all contingency from play but also reorganizing "man's affective structure in the interest of a political program that grants freedom to individuals only to the extent that this freedom implements the state's control over society." Andrea Gailus, "Of Beautiful and Dismembered Bodies: Art as Social Discipline in Schiller's *On the Aesthetic Education of Man*," in *Impure Reason: Dialectic of Enlightenment in Germany*, ed. Daniel W. Wilson and Robert C. Holub (Detroit: Wayne State University Press, 1993), 152. For a more extensive elaboration of the specific dichotomies Schiller (and Kant) relates in play, see Sam Heidepriem's contribution in this volume.

3. I will reflect on the difference between playing a game and just playing (with open rules) below, drawing on Gregory Bateson's distinction between the two.

4. See Niklas Luhmann's seminal essay "Theoriesubstitution in der Erziehungswissenschaft: Von der Philanthropie zum Neuhumanismus," in Niklas Luhmann, *Gesellschaftsstruktur und Semantik: Studien zur Wissenssoziologie der modernen Gesellschaft* (Frankfurt am Main: Suhrkamp, 1993), 2:105–194. Luhmann sees Kant not only pushing the education system to aspire toward becoming a science but also as helping advance the change from Philanthropinism to neohumanism.

5. "Es ist wirklich besonders, wenn man sieht, wie vernünftige Menschen oft stundenlang zu sitzen und Karten zu mischen im Stande sind. Da ergiebt es sich, daß Menschen nicht so leicht aufhören Kinder zu sein. . . . Es ist von größter Wichtigkeit, daß Kinder arbeiten lernen." Immanuel Kant, "Über Pädagogik," in *Kant's gesammelte Schriften* (Berlin: De Gruyter, 1923), 9:470–472. Unless indicated otherwise, all translations in this article are mine.

6. For a more detailed summary of how much the most influential pedagogues around 1800, including Campe, Basedow, Pestalozzi, and Friedrich Niethammer, nevertheless wanted to restrict play, see Ian McNeely's contribution in this volume.

7. For a more extensive discussion of improvisation around 1800 and its figuration as a playful and educational activity in Goethe's novel *Wilhelm Meister's Apprenticeship*, see Edgar Landgraf, *Improvisation as Art: Conceptual Challenges, Historical Perspectives* (New York: Continuum, 2011), esp. 42–57.

8. II.9, p. 219 [9:539]. Quotes from Gotthold Ephraim Lessing's works will be referenced by act and scene as well as page numbers for the English translations from *Nathan the Wise, Minna von Barnhelm, and Other Plays and Writings*, ed. Peter Demetz, fwd. Hannah Arendt (New York: Continuum, 1991) followed in parentheses by volume and page numbers of *Werke und Briefe in 12 Bänden*, ed. Wilfried Barner et al. (Frankfurt am Main: Deutscher Klassiker Verlag, 1984).

9. The three sons insist before the judge that they cannot accuse their father "of some false play" ("des falschen Spiels"); as a consequence, they accuse each other of having duplicated the ring. A "false play" with rings is also at the heart of Lessing's comedy *Minna von Barnhelm*. As Fritz Martini noted already in his in-depth study of the comedy from 1974, play in Lessing, including wagering and false play, aims at removing characters—in the comedy the tragically stubborn Major von Tellheim—from "their entanglement in frozen words . . . toward a recognition of the reality of their circumstances." Fritz Martini, *Lustspiele–und das Lustspiel* (Stuttgart: Ernst Klett, 1974), 90. Martini concludes that "in such forms of play, human beings show themselves as masters over their lives, that life is not simply calculable, but includes the irrationality of coincidences" (96).

10. Helmut J. Schneider argues that in classical drama, the play within the play serves as a distancing device that "dispels the sense of tragic seriousness" and points specifically to *Nathan the Wise*, which "enacts, in and through its very dramaturgy, the instatement of the aesthetic medium as a means for establishing a new social ethic for the modern, 'autonomous' individual, an individual to be liberated from the blind force and authority of genealogical—ethnic, religious, feudal, etc.—allegiances." Helmut J. Schneider, "Playing Tragedy: Detaching Tragedy from Itself in Classical Drama from Lessing to Büchner," in *The Play within the Play: The Performance of Meta-theatre and Self-reflection*, ed. Gerhard Fischer and Bernhard Greiner (Amsterdam: Rodopi, 2007), 243. I will expand this argument by analyzing more closely Lessing's implicit discussions of game play, playing's pragmatic dimension, and the underlying hermeneutic stance that Lessing's use of play invokes.

11. For a more extensive discussion of Lessing's concept of sympathy, see Hans-Jürgen Schings, *Der mitleidigste Mensch ist der beste Mensch: Poetik des Mitleids von Lessing bis Büchner* (Munich: Beck, 1980).

12. Helmut J. Schneider explores how Lessing employs economies of voluntary exchange (the giving and receiving of gifts) to implement social relations that both affirm and counter the vulnerability and contingency of our human existence (the coincidence of one's birth as much as the exposure to circumstances beyond our control). In this context, Lessing uses game play, wagering, and even gambling to instill the sense of contingency of our human existence for its equalizing effects, and to promote our reliance on and sympathy for each other. Schneider suggests that the "paradox of being autonomous and dependent . . . leads Lessing already before Schiller and Weimar Classicism, to the constitution of an aesthetic sphere of mediation, symbolized by the ring, as it is gifted, traded, substituted, and ultimately used to deceive." Helmut J. Schneider, "Schenken und Tauschen: Bemerkungen zu einer Grundfigur der Lessingschen Dramatik," in *Streitkultur: Strategien des Überzeugens im Werk Lessings; Referate der Internationalen Lessing-Tagung der Albert-Ludwigs-Universität*

Freiburg und der Lessing Society an der University of Cincinnati, Ohio/USA vom 22. bis 24. Mai 1991 in Freiburg im Breisgau, ed. Wolfram Mauser and Günter Saße (Tübingen: Niemeyer, 1993), 471.

13. My reading challenges Horst Lange's contention that game play and wagering in Lessing ultimately are about an assertion of divine providence, an observation Lange makes in reference to Lessing's comedy *Minna von Barnhelm*. Lange is looking for a proper instrumentalization of gambling, which he views as an utterly meaningless activity which people engage in despite knowing that it threatens "their livelihoods, their social identities, the well-being of their families, and their power." Horst Lange, "Betting on Providence: Gambling in Lessing's *Minna von Barnhelm*," *Colloquia Germanica* 41, no. 1 (2008): 1. Lange suggests that Lessing's support for wagering and gambling propagates blind faith in providence: "Dare to gamble, the play seems to command, for only then do you show true faith in God" (7). While I do not want to ignore the importance of providence in Lessing, attributing such blind reliance on faith to Lessing reduces the complexity of Lessing's anthropology, which emphasizes the contingency of the human condition. It thus ignores how Lessing employs playing as a means to negotiate between necessity and contingency, that is, how Lessing's play with games is also, to quote the cardsharper Riccaut in *Minna von Barnhelm*, a play at "corriger la fortune" (IV.2, p. 49 [6:72]).

14. Peter Giese points out how the German word *Glück* contains five different meanings—in French, *chance*, *bonheur*, *fortune*, *félicité*, and *beatitude*—different meanings with which Lessing consciously plays in *Minna von Barnhelm*. Giese argues that the substitution of the ring in *Minna von Barnhelm* as well as the illicit reproduction of the original ring by the weak father in Nathan's ring parable should both be seen not as intrigues but as gambles with which they risk their fortunes and give themselves a chance. See Peter Giese, "Glück, Fortüne und Happy Ending," *Lessing Yearbook* XVIII (1986): 37.

15. See Friedrich Kittler, "Lessing: 'Erziehung ist Offenbarung,'" in *Dichter—Mutter—Kind* (Munich: Fink, 1991), 39–41.

16. For a more extensive discussion of Lessing's communication strategies with regard to evolving discourses of love in the eighteenth century, see Edgar Landgraf, "Romantic Love and the Enlightenment: From Gallantry and Seduction to Authenticity and Self-Validation," *German Quarterly* 77, no. 1 (Winter 2004): 29–46. Ralf Simon also points out how in Lessing, free speech often takes on a precarious role, leading to what Simon calls "the hell of intersubjectivity." Ralf Simon, "Nathans Argumentationsverfahren: Konsequenzen der Fiktionalisierung von Theorie in Lessings Drama *Nathan der Weise*," *Deutsche Vierteljahrsschrift für Literaturwissenschaft und Geistesgeschichte* 65, no. 4 (December 1991): 611. Analyzing Nathan's communication strategies, Simon recognizes the unresolved tension between Nathan's argumentative dominance and his inability to engage the dogmatists in the play, the Derwisch and the Patriarch, which leaves Nathan isolated and at a distance to the grand family reunion staged at the end of the play. With regard to our focus on the role that playing plays in Lessing's *Nathan the Wise*, the tension lies in Nathan announcing but not participating in the kind of play he prescribes with the ring parable, creating a tension between messenger and message that underlines his role as an outsider inside his own play. As Simon puts it, Nathan figures more like a narrator in a novel than a character in a drama (see 622).

17. In her insightful analysis of the role of gambling in Lessing's *Minna von Barnhelm*, Dorothea von Mücke comes to a similar conclusion, namely, that "gambling in combina-

tion with role play are being used to practice a model of fairness that is based on equality and reciprocity as an important aspect of interpersonal relations in a society." Dorothea von Mücke, "Spiel und Glück in Lessings *Minna von Barnhelm oder das Soldatenglück*," in *Sich Selbst aufs Spiel setzen: Spiel als Technik und Medium von Subjektivierung*, ed. Christian Moser and Regine Strätling (Paderborn: Wilhelm Fink, 2016), 60. While not directly addressing aspects of rule-breaking or meta-play in Lessing, von Mücke sees Lessing oppose Kantian ethics with its strict emphasis on duty with "a model of humaneness and tolerance that opposes rigorism with a technique of the self as a playful treatment of luck as an instrument of de-moralization" (66).

18. In an elucidating study, Elliott Schreiber can show how despite their emphasis on the proper pedagogical instrumentalization of play, a closer reading reveals that Johann Bernhard Basedow and Gottlieb Schummel (and to a lesser degree already John Locke) also recognize an intrinsic value of play, "how play and storytelling instantiate an intrinsic morality, as distinct from the extrinsic morality of games and stories that function merely as means to a moral end." Elliott Schreiber, "The Virtue of Play: Games and Stories for Children in Three Pedagogical Texts of the Enlightenment," *Eighteenth-Century Studies* (forthcoming). With this emphasis on play's intrinsic morality, Schreiber sees Schummel anticipating "by about twenty years the theory of sociability advanced by Romantic philosopher and theologian Friedrich Schleiermacher in 1799." While Schleiermacher, however, still applies "an external standard to games and other sociable gatherings, namely, the measure of rationality," in Schummel "by contrast, free sociability is achieved precisely when the group of children liberate themselves from such a standard" (Schreiber, "Virtue of Play"). Against this historical backdrop, *Nathan the Wise* appears more in line with Schummel than with Schleiermacher, as in Lessing's play it is the liberation from the dogmatic application of rules that underwrites an idealized, that is, tolerant sociability.

19. Morgan's translation unfortunately deletes the reference to play and wit in the German original.

20. Gregory Bateson, *Steps to an Ecology of Mind: Collected Essays in Anthropology, Psychiatry, Evolution, and Epistemology* (Northvale, NJ: Jason Aronson, 1987), 12.

21. Gregory Bateson, "Metalogue: About Games and Being Serious," in *Steps to an Ecology of Mind: Collected Essays in Anthropology, Psychiatry, Evolution, and Epistemology* (Northvale, NJ: Jason Aronson, 1987), 30.

22. Bateson's concept of "mere playing" applies to the game of chess in *Nathan the Wise* at the third level of play indicated above, that is, inasmuch as Saladin and Sittah do not simply follow the rules, but are "playing with the game."

23. On this point, I disagree with Helmut J. Schneider's observation that the play with rings in *Minna von Barnhelm* and in *Nathan the Wise* offers the opportunity "to experience our always already existing ties and dependence on others without existential risk" ("ohne existentielles Risiko"). Schneider, "Schenken und Tauschen," 471. Unlike Schiller, Lessing does not separate game play from the possibility of having existential consequences. In fact, Minna, even more so than Nathan, takes on an existential risk in the game she plays with Tellheim. The actual risks involved in playing games might also help explain better—better than the biographical affinity—Lessing's literary interest in wagers and gambling, which, like the fight for tolerance, entail real risks to one's life and prosperity (risks recognized, for example, in the sympathy Minna feels for the shady and broke gambler Riccaut de la Marlinière).

24. As Robert S. Leventhal pointed out, Lessing's choice of the opal as gem is not coincidental. Following Lessing's discussion of the opal in letter 40 of the *Antiquarische Briefe*, Leventhal notes that the "opal resists precise determination because of its manifold irradiation pattern. It cannot be assigned an absolute 'value' precisely because its very existence depends on its particular positionality and application." Robert S. Leventhal, *The Disciplines of Interpretation: Lessing, Herder, Schlegel and Hermeneutics in Germany, 1750–1800* (Berlin: De Gruyter, 1994), 118. The hermeneutic ambivalence of the ring mirrors the ambivalence the parable creates vis-à-vis the question of the original and hence authentic religion.

25. In a footnote, Beate Allert draws a parallel between the father's duplication of the ring in Lessing's ring parable and Walter Benjamin's thesis about the artwork's loss of aura in the age of its technological reproducibility. See Beate Allert, "Pluralisierung der Ringe oder Ringverlust? Lessings Beitrag zur Metaphorisierung und/oder Politisierung der Sprache," in *Streitkultur: Strategien des Überzeugens im Werk Lessings; Referate der Internationalen Lessing-Tagung der Albert-Ludwigs-Universität Freiburg und der Lessing Society an der University of Cincinnati, Ohio/USA vom 22. bis 24. Mai 1991 in Freiburg im Breisgau*, ed. Wolfram Mauser and Günter Saße (Tübingen: Niemeyer, 1993), 113n3. The reference warrants further contemplation. Like in Benjamin, the duplication of the ring in Lessing's parable also suggests an epochal semiotic shift where the original ring—and origin itself—loses its aura or magic and with it its authoritative, binding, tyrannical (Lessing), and discriminatory power. Unlike Benjamin, however, Lessing seeks to transfer the aura from the origin/father to the competitive behavior of the sons, and thus toward the promises of an open future.

26. Arnold Heidsieck quotes Lessing's dialogue on freemasonry in *Ernst and Falk: Conversations for the Freemasons* where the character Ernst concludes that "mankind can be united only by division, and only kept unified through unceasing division." Arnold Heidsieck, "Lessings Vorstellung von Offenbarung," in *G. E. Lessing: Nathan der Weise / Die Erziehung des Menschengeschlechts* (Strasbourg: PU de Strasbourg, 2000), 139–140. Heidsieck relates Lessing's stance on competitiveness to the Scottish Enlightenment and the moral and political philosophy of Hutcheson and Adam Smith.

27. Leventhal, *Disciplines of Interpretation*, 108–109.

28. Eva Knodt, *"Negative Philosophie" und dialogische Kritik: Zur Struktur poetischer Theorie bei Lessing und Herder* (Tübingen: Niemeyer, 1988), 119.

29. Bernhard Greiner, "Streitkultur des Als Ob: Komödie als transzendentale Bedingung des Streitens in *Minna von Barnhelm*," in *Streitkultur: Strategien des Überzeugens im Werk Lessings; Referate der Internationalen Lessing-Tagung der Albert-Ludwigs-Universität Freiburg und der Lessing Society an der University of Cincinnati, Ohio/USA vom 22. bis 24. Mai 1991 in Freiburg im Breisgau*, ed. Wolfram Mauser and Günter Saße (Tübingen: Niemeyer, 1993), 251.

30. Gregory Bateson, "A Theory of Play and Fantasy," in *Steps to an Ecology of Mind: Collected Essays in Anthropology, Psychiatry, Evolution, and Epistemology* (Northvale, NJ: Jason Aronson, 1987), 186.

CHAPTER FOUR

Play with Memory and Its Topoi

Faust

NICHOLAS RENNIE

GOETHE'S *FAUST* ESTABLISHES at the outset a play between two fundamentally opposed conceptions of the universe and of human life within it.[1] On the one hand, the Prologue in Heaven repeatedly emphasizes the overriding authority of a providential plan, of an overarching theodicy within which every apparently random event is subsumed. Responding to Mephisto's reprise of Satan's role in the Book of Job, the Lord suggests that Faust's salvation may be a foregone conclusion: "Though now he only serves me blindly and ineptly, / I soon shall lead him into clarity" (308–309); and a few lines later: "stand abashed when you must needs admit: / a good man, in his groping intuition, / is well aware of what's his proper course" (327–329).[2] Faust's life may be the object of a wager that he makes with the devil, and of another wager that the devil makes with the Lord, but it would seem that, here, nothing is actually left to chance. In Albert Einstein's oft-cited phrase, "God doesn't play dice with the world."[3] This principle is confirmed by the Archangels in their admiring description of the perfection of the universe at the beginning of the scene: in concert with its "brother spheres," we are told, the sun follows its predetermined—literally: pre-scribed—orbit ("vorgeschrieb'ne Reise"; 245). This seeming determinism belongs to a system within which God's Creation reveals "the splendor of its primal day" (250). These words, recurring as a refrain in the Archangels' final line (270), remind us that random events—and indeed time itself—are excluded from the universe that presents itself here within an encompassing vision (*Anblick*; 247, 267). This vision is itself a *totum simul*, a form of understanding that comprehends all moments in time within a single perception.[4] If all future outcomes are literally evident, within this vision, there would seem to be no room for free play.

On the other hand, the scandal of the Prologue in Heaven resides in the fact that the sublime Miltonian vision with which it opens encourages us to forget that the universe here represented itself appears to be the product of hasty improvisation by a traveling theater group that is under pressure to make a quick profit, and whose success is explicitly tied to a distracted audience's unpredictable whims. We witness this group's last-minute preparations in the immediately preceding Prelude on the Stage, where the troupe's director acknowledges that while contemporary German audiences are hardly used to the best (45), theater is nonetheless forced to compete for their attention against other distractions—magazines (116), for instance, or games of cards (125). The Director's words establish a proximity that in turn implies an equivalence between the latter entertainment and the consumption of stage performances, referring to the spectator who, already during the play (*Schauspiel*), looks forward to the game of cards (*Kartenspiel*) that will occupy him afterward. "Just try to keep your audience distracted," the Director admonishes his Poet and Player (131): it cannot be the goal of theater to repair the fractured experience of a modern public, but rather to accommodate itself to this cultural reality. Theater accordingly compensates through the magnitude of its effects what it lacks in coherence. "Only by mass can you subdue the masses" (95), he declares, adding, "Don't wait because your piece is still in pieces! / Whatever you've concocted is sure to be a hit" (99–100). A successful theater simultaneously creates two strong and opposite effects—of paucity and superfluity. It restricts access to a paying audience, heightening the public's curiosity and desire to the point of desperation, such that "they shove and fight to reach our cash-box / and, as at the bakery-door for bread in time of famine, / they nearly break their necks to get a ticket" (54–56). At the same time, spectator, director, and actor alike are compelled by the lure of immediate gratification in its serial repetition and intensification: "If you just give them more and more, and then still more, / I guarantee you'll never miss the mark" (129–130). However, this need for "more and more, and then still more" is ironically contrasted, in this particular case, by the immediate absence of any completed play to present: even as the spectators wait, "Already in their places, quiet and expectant" (41), the troupe debates its plans at length until the Director impatiently interrupts: "This altercation's gone on long enough, / it's time I saw some action too!" (214–215). Following his own injunction to dazzle the audience with displays of "more," he closes the scene by urging his troupe to find the means to reproduce the entirety of the universe itself—its planets and stars, fire and water, and the creatures of the earth—within the theater's confines:

> So now upon our modest stage act out
> creation in its every aspect,
> and move with all deliberate haste
> from heaven, through the world, to hell!
> (239–242)

What the Archangels thereupon describe in the opening lines of the Prologue is apparently this hurriedly assembled theater apparatus; and while we are never again brought back to the frame of the Prelude, the initial sequence of scenes indicates that everything that follows the Prelude is indeed a play within this play, and thus a creation that may have no higher authority than that of a theater director whose own fate is shaped by unpredictable tastes and market forces. Put differently: whether we decide that the action of Goethe's *Faust* takes place within a stable theodicy, or instead within the unpredictable environment of show business—whether we regard Faust's world as the unchanging (250, 270) Creation of the Lord of the Prologue, or as the slapdash creation of the director of a small and unprepared German theater troupe—depends largely on how seriously we view the Prelude on the Stage as a frame for the remaining drama. The fact that this frame remains open at the end reinforces the notion of this question's final undecidability, yet this undecidability is its own form of conclusion. As countless readings reveal, the text makes it easy, by the end, to forget this beginning and its destabilizing function. Yet no divinity ultimately steps forth, ex machina, as the monitory personification of an overarching knowledge and plan, and thus of a moral or epistemological system that might be said to reestablish itself with conclusive authority. The words of predestination, which the Archangels recognize as inscribed in the fabric of the cosmos, are coopted in advance by a theater culture (and commerce) that knows no such permanence. In a drama thematically structured around the principle of wagering, the signifying power of words comes into, and reveals itself as, play.

As I would like to argue in the following, this tension in *Faust* between order and chaos, predictability and chance, is one that centrally involves memory. Of course, many a scene of comeuppance—the concluding arrival of the Stone Guest in the tale of Don Juan, or indeed the devil's return to claim Faust's soul in numerous versions of that legend—signals the reinstitution of a faculty of memory that not only concludes the action but demonstratively brings play itself, along with its risks and amusements, to a sobering end. Withholding a comparable *memento mori*, Goethe's drama instead suggests the possibility of a structure of meaning and morality that hangs in the balance—a principle neatly captured, say, in the image that opens Woody Allen's 2005 *Matchpoint*, of a tennis ball inconclusively suspended in the air after bouncing up off the net's rim. But my focus here concerns not just the memory that constitutes meaning, and the chance that subverts it, but more specifically the spatial, topic order that underlies the shifting memory dynamics of Goethe's work, as well as the relation between the destabilization of this order, and the possibility of conceiving the play's titular hero as a unified self. I begin by returning to the Prologue in Heaven.

Inasmuch as it does suggest the merging of total knowledge and totalizing vision implied in the concept of the *totum simul*, the *Anblick* proclaimed by the Archangels points to a divine memory that contains all things in time. Comparison with one of Goethe's models for his *Faust* drama, Dante's *Divine Comedy*, illustrates the matter. Frances Yates argues in *The Art of Memory* that Dante's *Inferno* can be thought of as a "memory system" and the *Commedia* in its entirety as a "cosmic order of places" structured to enable us to "hold in memory the scheme of salvation, and the complex network of virtues and vices and their rewards and punishments."[5] Harald Weinrich has further examined what he refers to as this "memory artwork," similarly arguing that it presents a vast and intricately organized topography (or "memory-scape") in which memory contents are archived in the same way that images are deposited in and associated with places or topoi in the rhetorical tradition.[6] Dante, who makes his way through this archive, moving from place to place and from one soul's account to the next, is a "memory-man" who duplicates this archive of moral narratives in his own mind and takes it with him back to the world of mortals. Weinrich points out the importance in the *Commedia* of the concept of *damnatio memoriae*, that punishment by which an individual's history is erased from divine memory. The souls in Purgatory need a living individual to remember and pray for them, to secure their place in the memory of God.[7] If to be forgotten is to be damned, to be remembered is to sustain the hope of redemption.

Indeed, remembrance and forgetting constitute a persistent theme of Dante's poem. A sequence of passages toward the end of *Purgatorio* serves as a direct model for the opening of *Faust II* (A Pleasant Landscape) and also highlights the divergent treatment of memory in the two texts.[8] Faust's lines, composed in *terza rima*, directly reference Dante's transformation in the Garden of Eden near the end of *Purgatorio*, but in so doing highlight this key difference. Having traveled through Hell and ascended the Mountain of Purgatory, Dante reaches the Garden of Eden at its summit. Here he is led to two rivers, the first of which is Lethe (*Purgatorio* XXVIII, 130). Dante is submerged in the waters of Lethe (*Purgatorio* XXXI, 101) as Faust will later be "bathe[d] . . . in the dew of Lethe's waters" (4,629). Dante's forgetting, however, is decisively coupled with recollection. His bathing in Lethe's waters is part of a process of atonement and purification in which he participates attentively, and which requires that he forget his sins in order that the waters of the River Eunoe, from which he will drink at the end of the canticle (*Purgatorio* XXXIII.138), may restore his knowledge of the good: "the ingestion of the waters of these two rivers is essential to the accomplishment of (here) leaving one's sins in oblivion and (there) securing in memory all the good things accomplished in one's mortal life."[9] Moreover, forgetting is not just part of atonement; it itself is another form of remembering, establishing as it does its own traces of the past. Thus, when Dante tells Beatrice that he has no recollection of ever having "estranged" himself from her, she reminds him of the effects of Lethe, adding that the very fact of his having forgotten his sins is proof that he committed them (*Purgatorio* XXXIII.92, 95–99).[10] The Faust of A Pleasant Landscape, by contrast, engages in no equivalent process of atonement or remembering. At the opening of the scene, a sleeping Faust is bathed in Lethe's waters at daybreak after Ariel commands a group of spirits that circle his body to "remove the burning barbs of his remorse, / and purge him of all sense of horror" (4,624–625). He sleeps through the ministrations of the spirits until he awakens to a new day and a new sequence of experiences, unencumbered by the past.[11] As the sun rises, he is refreshed and renewed, and he greets the day in the bucolic surroundings in which he finds himself, concluding in the final lines of the passage with an enthusiastic affirmation of "human striving" (4,725). No memory of his past, and in particular of the Gretchen tragedy that has just concluded with the end of Part I, clouds his thoughts. Directly recalling the *Commedia*, this scene suggests the more clearly that Faust is precisely not a "memory-man" in Dante's mold, but one who will emerge from the catastrophes of Part I unburdened, unscathed, and uninterested in his past.

Remembrance and forgetting only become fully apparent as a shaping theme of the *Commedia* in *Paradiso*, however, and it is here that the contrast with the role of memory in Goethe's *Faust* as a whole likewise becomes entirely evident—in particular in its relation to the principle of a memory text or archive. Recurrently, in the final canticle, Dante calls attention to how little of his experience he can in fact report to his audience, for instance when he opens Canto I by saying of heaven,

> He who comes down from there
> can neither know nor tell what he has seen,
> for, drawing near to its desire,
> so deeply is our intellect immersed
> that memory cannot follow after it.
> (*Paradiso* I.5–9)

After summarizing the debates among commentators regarding the precise nature of the relationship here between memory and intellect, Robert Hollander concludes that "whatever hypothesis one accepts, the result is the same . . . : The vision of God cannot be contained in human memory; rather, we can only claim a memory of having had a memory, now lost."[12] Dante writes that what he can represent in his poem is as nothing—it is this mere trace of a memory. "Nevertheless," he continues,

> as much of the holy kingdom
> as I could store as treasure in my mind
> shall now become the subject of my song.
> (*Paradiso* I.10–12)

Paradiso in particular highlights this principle of a rememorative faculty that labors on through its inevitable failure, and whose achievements pale in comparison to its subject, as we see again in Canto XXIII:

> I was like a man who finds himself awakened
> from a vision that has faded [di visïone oblita] and who strives
> in vain to bring it back to mind.
> (*Paradiso* XXIII.49–51)

This memory-project culminates in Dante's final vision in Canto XXXIII of *Paradiso*, where the things of the universe reveal themselves to his gaze as the pages of a book (*volume*; *Paradiso* XXXIII.86). The final lines of the *Divine Comedy* are marked by Dante's repeated insistence that his mind can only recollect a tiny fraction of what he experienced ("My memory of that moment is more lost . . ." [*Paradiso* XXXIII.94]), and that words, in turn, can reproduce only a tiny fraction of what he has retained:

> Now my words will come far short
> of what I still remember, like a babe's
> who at his mother's breast still wets his tongue.
> (*Paradiso* XXXIII.106–108)

> O how scant is speech, too weak to frame my thoughts.
> Compared to what I still recall my words are faint—
> to call them little is to praise them much.
> (*Paradiso* XXXIII.121–123)

This insistence highlights the role of the character Dante's own power of recollection. It serves also as a final reminder of the scale of the topic system that the poet has developed in the course of his work's 100 cantos, and of the memory labor performed by over 14,000 tightly interlocking verses of *terza rima*—a relatively complex verse form particularly resistant to and unforgiving of any memory lapse. Additionally, it calls attention to the infinitely greater power of that divine memory reflected in the written text of the universe. This memory contains and consolidates a comprehensive "structure" in the Derridean sense, realizing the dream of a totality within which every element signifies God as its ultimate referent and center.[13] If the character of Dante's memory and speech are insufficient to contain and represent this totality, the poet's insistence on this very fact expresses itself in such a way as to reaffirm its reality and authority all the more clearly.[14] What is in question here is not the stability and perfection of the signifying system as such, but the fallible subject's ability to apprehend it. The integrity of this universal moral and epistemological order has its correlate in a fact noticed by the poem's readers: almost nothing happens, in the existences of the souls Dante encounters, that would constitute an "event."[15] The prerequisite for that glimpse of a divine totality ultimately realized by Dante is his prior intensive training in reading that text's signs; whatever difficulties this may present, however, the field of signification is itself not—to invoke the term in opposition to which Derrida defines his concept of structure—either subject to, or accommodating of, "play." If Dante's God is what gives the structure of meaning its stability, in the *Commedia*, to endorse the notion of play within this structure would mean to sacrifice this very God as its center.

By extension, every soul has a clearly articulated moral value (and self) within this world. Meaning and identity are fixed, and no more subject to a "play of substitutions" than is the divine judgment that underwrites them.[16]

The scene that opens the Prologue in Heaven in Goethe's drama clearly evokes a comparable total vision—one that embraces past, present, and future within a single divine gaze. However, this *Anblick* cited at the beginning of the work is quite different from the beautiful "moment" (*Augenblick*) that a blinded Faust will herald near the work's end (11,581). Indeed, the *Augenblick*, which had served as the object of Faust's wager with Mephisto since Part I (1,699), and which accordingly structures the drama's plot overall, stands in a complex relation both to the Archangels' *Anblick* of the Prologue and to the climactic vision that Dante struggles to remember and describe in the final canto of the *Commedia*. The compound term *Augen-Blick* (literally "eye-glance") suggests that the moment that Faust invokes has a visual quality that in some sense subtends the possibility of its "beauty" (1,699; 11,581). The wager's positioning of this experience as a culminating moment at the end of the drama, the notion that transcendent forces (Faust's unearthly companion) will allow it to be realized, and the association of this final moment with the possibility of redemption (to which the Lord of the Prologue had alluded as the telos of Faust's life) all invite comparison to *Paradiso* XXXIII. The parallel brings a fundamental difference into relief, however. Faust, whom Max Kommerell famously called a "virtuoso of forgetting" and whom Franco Moretti describes as a tourist-like figure whose "playing with the world" masks the violence of colonial exploration in metaphors of innocence,[17] is no Dantean figure of recollection. He may pass through 3,000 years of history, but once he has disburdened himself, early on, of the story of his and his father's futile efforts to counter the plague (1,024–1,055), it remains unclear what he retains of his own experiences: he does indeed just pass through.[18] His life is eventful, but—aside from a few spasms of conscience vis-à-vis Gretchen in Part I—bears little or no lasting imprint of his experiences. If the sleeping Faust is weighed down by these memories, he is quickly relieved of them when he is bathed in the dew of the River Lethe in the scene A Pleasant Landscape at the opening of Part II (4,629). As Paul Fleming observes in his reading of Kommerell's and Adorno's analyses of the drama, Faust "at no point reflects upon what has happened and what he has done. . . . There is no pause for thought, no introspection, no taking account of himself, no moment of memory."[19]

My interest here is in the connection between forgetting and chance, between memory and order, and indeed—recalling Derrida's opposition—

between structure and play in the respective signifying systems of the works under consideration. Dante's project entails reconstructing in verse the precisely differentiated, vast memory theater of the Christian moral universe, a system of places whose most nuanced topographical distinctions and whose overarching structures alike correlate to gradations within the hierarchy of virtue and sin. To remember this is to call to mind that eternal order that each sinner at one point forgot.[20] All chance and disorder within this system are such only in appearance: reflecting the moral confusion of mortals, they are in turn balanced and canceled out by the divine justice that responds to each sin with its exact punishment. This is the order that Dante glimpses in the written volume that appears before him in the final Canto, and that the text of the *Divine Comedy* attempts to reconstruct.

The text of Goethe's *Faust* stands under the aegis of the *Augenblick* in an entirely different manner. On the one hand, the text is organized around a wager between Faust and Mephisto that has this "moment" as its object. This is a contract whose terms, Faust is warned, Mephisto will not let slip ("Consider well your words—we'll not forget them" [1,707]), and whose phrasing Faust will himself abruptly recall and cite in his final lines. The principle of recollection thus imposes coherence. It draws the beginning and end of the play together, and the *Augenblick* is ostensibly privileged, unique, and at the same time a citation that reminds us that the wager proposed at the beginning has retained its hold and is now being concluded.

However, as Kommerell and Adorno—and after them, Fleming—argue, *Faust*, and in particular *Faust II*, is structured throughout by the principle of forgetting. Faust is saved, writes Adorno, because he is no longer the Faust who signed the pact. This theater piece delivered "in pieces" ("in Stücken"), like that called for by the Director of the Prelude on the Stage (99), manifests in its form what serves as a general principle—that of the subject's nonidentity.[21] Indeed, the drama is made up of a series of disparate elements; it casts aside its forms with the same lightness and speed with which its main protagonist sheds the memories of his past and his misdeeds. Given its structural position in the drama, Faust's concluding *Augenblick* invites us to expect a moment of vision that might consolidate with evidentiary force a unity of insight and knowledge that the episodic structure in particular of Part II has so far kept from view. This moment is a signifier that flaunts its lack of a signified.[22] I mean this not in the sense that the blind Faust misidentifies the object of his affirmation, rapturously mistaking the digging of his grave for the construction of a new paradise on earth (11,569). Rather, I mean it in the sense that his final apostrophe to the "moment," in its tentative and anticipatory formulation ("to the moment, I *could* say" [11,581]; "*Envisioning* those heights of happiness" ["*Im Vorgefühl* von solchem hohen Glück"; 11,585]—my emphasis), sustains a play of substitution and deferral that had structured the wager from the beginning: where the wager's terms had provided Mephisto the incentive to bring Faust quickly to a moment of gratification, Faust's strategy logically consists in postponing his acknowledgment that any given moment can provide it.[23]

In the closing words of the Prelude on the Stage, the Director calls on his theater troupe to mount a play that takes its audience through heaven, the world, and hell (242), in a loose reversal of Dante's trajectory through hell (and thus through the earth), Purgatory, and heaven. But whereas in Dante's culminating moment of vision the knowledge of the universe appears before him in an open archive, in his "highest moment" ("*höchste*[*r*] *Augenblick*"; 11,586) Faust sees nothing, visually consolidates no knowledge, and instead confirms his dedication to a principle of deferral (which in this work manifests itself as a necessary correlate of "striving") that has informed his life all along. He accordingly rearticulates a principle of play that had been introduced thematically through the bet between Mephisto and the Lord, and then through the wager between Faust and Mephisto. Like the roll of a die, however, his affirmation of a "moment" is a play without memory—it presents a random cypher that as such bears no necessary relation to any other moment, subsequent or prior. The *Augenblick* betrays its apparent singularity: affirming it in its arbitrariness, Faust embraces that collapse of experience that Benjamin will identify in the "process of continually starting all over again" that characterizes the life of gambler and factory worker alike.[24] Put in different terms, as an empty cypher the *Augenblick* promised and yielded by Faust's wager serves as the possibility of infinite substitutions, of "play" understood in a Derridean sense.[25] The moment hazarded by Faust remembers nothing, references nothing, and as such brings the possibility of any definitive, sense-giving structure into crisis.

The drama's formal correlate to this play is its episodic juxtaposition of places and styles, or what Moretti, borrowing from Lévi-Strauss, refers to as a method of playful *bricolage* common to the works of what Moretti terms "modern epic."[26] *Bricolage*, of course, centrally involves memory and the resurrection and adaptation of past forms. But the drama presents ambivalent memory: preservation combines with destruction, distortion, and abandonment. The dizzying sequence of poetic forms that makes up Goethe's text highlights this tension between remembering and forgetting. The play draws on themes and formal structures from a wide range of poetic traditions. As an encyclopedia of the cultural knowledge of the late eighteenth and early nineteenth centuries, it is a memory theater (as this idea was developed in the Renaissance) in which the knowledge and traditions of humankind are put on display.[27] But Goethe's *Faust* always also destabilizes its status as theater (conceived in any manner). The sequence of forms—including *Knittelvers*, *terza rima*, iambic trimeter, and prose monologue—manifests itself as a serial presentation and dismissal of the traditions in which they originate. Moreover, the drama resolutely denies us the topic stability that so clearly characterizes the memory structures of the *Divine Comedy*. As Weinrich points out, Part II takes us through a disorienting series of place-changes that contrast sharply with the carefully structured topologies of the rhetorical tradition.[28] The drama is a play *with* memory: it collects and recollects the forms it cites; but in doing so it also relativizes them as so many possibilities of poetic experimentation that are subject to being replaced and forgotten. The dangerous "innocence" that Moretti calls attention to in the drama's *bricolage* attends what Derrida, in his own reading of Lévi-Strauss, describes as "the affirmation of a world of signs without fault, without truth, and without origin."[29] In the person of the drama's titular hero, this innocence expresses itself in forgetting. Here, memory theater is at the same time anti-memory theater. Goethe's *Faust* foregrounds a principle of play that it reflects in the actions of its main character; and in so doing it ties its own play-with-forms to Faust's colonization and abandonment of the people and things he encounters in his travels.[30]

Goethe's dramatic encyclopedia of literary themes and forms underscores an unease with the memory-man that seems more broadly typical of the ambivalent status of *Gedächtnis*, or memory-as-archive, in the Enlightenment, and that in Part I of Goethe's play finds satirical expression in the figure of the aspiring *poeta doctus* Wagner.[31] In Part II we encounter a nimbler memory-figure, that Homunculus who, recollecting at the opportune moment that it is the time of the classical Walpurgisnight (6,940–941), spirits his companions off to Ancient Greece. With this, he demonstrates a virtuosically precise topic awareness: he not only remembers but, having done so, promptly guides his companions to that exact faraway time and place. But if Homunculus knows and remembers everything and contains all of this knowledge in a vast and unerring topic consciousness, he is also not adapted to life: as he gives up his purely mental existence, at the end of Act II, the disembodied Homunculus fractures his enclosing vial against Galatea's shell. His knowledge also bears fruit in no enduring insight on the part of Faust, but rather only triggers its own sequence of ephemeral experiences in Faust's touristic wanderings. Other characters are similarly incapable of establishing a stable memory structure that would embrace and sustain the work as a whole. Gretchen and the couple Philemon and Baucis, bearers of memory all three, are discarded by Faust, as are, it would seem, the moral worlds to which they belong. And Mephisto, an anachronistic figure who remembers and replays the rituals of the Christian devil, concedes at the end that the rest of the world has forgotten him and the hell that he represents: "Try as you will to terrify the sinful," he says to his assistants as he commands them to bring a hell's maw onto the stage of his showdown with Faust's soul, "they think these things are only lies and figments" (11,654–655). Apparently unequipped to adapt to a changed world, he fails in his only objective and remains empty handed. This is no world for those bound by the traditions, moralities, and contracts of the past.

But if no single form or vision can establish itself with any authority, the playful *bricolage* that makes up the drama presents a predicament of its own. In navigating, and re-creating within his verse, the topic memoryscape of Christian morality, Dante's protagonist establishes a stable framework for his own identity. The poet who in Canto I of *Inferno* had reached a point of crisis after departing from the "straight path" ("la diritta via"; I.3) finds his way back by directing his steps sequentially from "place" to "place" within this structure, by subsequently reassembling this hierarchy of loci in his poem, and by working out the precise logic of this system under the instruction of his guides. This is the order that his final vision represents. By contrast, that floating signifier that is Faust's *Augenblick* refers us, inasmuch as it can be said to point to any referent, to the impossibility of memory understood as a coherent and reliable form of self-contextualization or self-construction. The scholar of the beginning who has tried and rejected all of the different forms and memory systems of available knowledge, as well as the identities that accompany them ("I've studied now, to my regret, / Philosophy, Law, Medicine, / and—what is worst—Theology"; 354–356), is in this sense a nobody, a man without qualities, as his subsequent magical and painless transformation and his later flights across time and space render all the more evident. He is connected to no time or place. And on the other hand, the ambivalent relationship with memory that his figure represents is perhaps what renders him most characteristic of the century in which Goethe first fashioned (or rather refashioned) his character: in fleeing from his study and from the feudal order to which it belongs, Faust escapes also from the places—the topoi—of a rhetorical tradition that in the eighteenth century comes to be treated with increasing ambivalence. He continues to travel among these places, and does so even at breakneck speed. But place is no longer a stable referent in the ways that the *memoria* tradition had conceived, nor can a sequence of places connect memories reliably in the chronological experience of a remembering subject. In Faust's *Augenblick*, the slippage of signification exhibits itself in both temporal and spatial form. Disconnecting meaning and identity from both time and place, that nonevent that is Faust's exultant apostrophe to an empty signifier reveals itself as an event in a different sense. It is radically modern in the sense that it playfully, recklessly prefigures that abandonment of an older *episteme* that will find its theoretical articulations in the century after Goethe's completion of his drama, in the writings of Nietzsche, Freud, and Heidegger.[32]

In the originary scene of systematic memory-construction, Simonides of Ceos restores their identities to the crushed and fragmented remains of an assembly of guests by recalling their locations before the collapse of the hall in which they had been seated.[33] In Goethe's play, by contrast, the sites through which Faust and his companion travel, like that Creation that the Director had called for in the Prelude on the Stage, provide no bearings for the construction of a self. This referential unreliability of place was clearly anticipated in the jarring juxtaposition of scenes at the drama's start: if the Archangels of the Prelude present the constellations—the traditional referents of human exploration—as a vast, perfect, and unchanging frame of reference, the prior scene reminds us that these celestial coordinates are just as likely fake, components of the spectacle of that mock-Creation that the Director had called on his colleagues the Poet and Comic to throw together in order to ensure their theater company's survival for another day. The relevant coordinates of value are not those of an eternal order, but rather those of a show business whose fortunes are liable to shift with every production, and whose hectic efforts are mirrored by the frantic throng that the Director imagines fighting its way to his box office through the theater entrance's "narrow gate of grace" ("*enge Gnadenpforte*"; 52). The very notion of redemption, Goethe's metaphor suggests, is tied to a market that is itself subject to the whims of public taste and that is perhaps as volatile as the speculative economy unleashed by the introduction of paper money in Act I of Part II.

In Simonides as in Dante, a physical environment reduced to rubble provides a particularly effective foil for an overarching order that this chaos only apparently effaces. In the story of Simonides, as recounted by Cicero, Castor and Pollux destroy the hall of the nobleman Scopas, and thereby kill him and his guests, after he slights them publicly. The devastation initially precludes a proper burial of the deceased: "when their friends wanted to bury them but were altogether unable to know them apart as they had been completely crushed, the story goes that Simonides was enabled by his recollection of the place in which each of them had been reclining at table to identify them for separate interment." The topic logic of the *ars memoriae* derives from the poet's insight that "the best aid to clearness of memory consists in orderly arrangement. He [Simonides] inferred that persons desiring to train this faculty must select localities and form mental images of the facts they wish to remember and store those images in the localities."[34] The seeming randomness of the disaster belies the fact that it represents a precise retribution within a moral order enforced by demigods and gods. The poet's mnemonic reconstruction not only reassigns shattered body parts to the individuals to whom they belonged, but in enabling their proper burial also restores the dead to living memory and so points to a larger system of meaning that the building's collapse serves to confirm.[35]

Dante's memory-work similarly highlights the relationship between topographical ruin and the moral order whose perfection it paradoxically represents and upholds. As he picks his way unsteadily down a steep landslide with his companion Virgil, the character Dante learns that the terrain's upheaval was caused by the earthquake that marked the Crucifixion (*Inferno* XII.32–45; cf. Matthew 27:51)—an event referenced again as the two clamber over craggy, broken rocks in *Inferno* XXI.109–114, *Inferno* XXIII.137, and *Inferno* XXIV.22–42. The devastation and chaos of the landscape accordingly express the establishment of order—redemption through Jesus and the gospel of love.[36] Dante not only traverses a topography shaped by this past event, however, but also learns to recognize in the apparent disorder of hell's topography a precisely calibrated instrument of justice. Thus, in the Seventh Circle, it is implied that the depth to which the Violent are each immersed in boiling blood—some visible only down to their eyebrows (*Inferno* XII.103), others to their necks (116), chests (122), or feet (125)—corresponds to the degree of each sinner's crimes; punishment is enforced by centaurs who keep each one in place, "shooting arrows at any soul that rises / higher from the blood than guilt allows" (74–75). Moreover, the moral order is not only expressed and enforced through a static topography: Dante witnesses seismic activity as a confirmation of divine justice in the present. Ascending Purgatory, after having felt "the mountain tremble / as though it might collapse" (*Purgatorio* XX.127–128), Dante is informed in the course of Canto XXI that such frightening tectonic movement in each case announces the resurrection of a penitent shade. Here too, what the poet first experiences as frightening instability reveals itself as the expression of an overarching and unchanging divine order—that same order that will reveal itself to Dante in his culminating vision of the written "volume" in the *Commedia*'s final canto (*Paradiso* XXXIII.86). Places recall this order, just as each place's contours and shifts recall and respond to an individual's penance and sins.

How, then, to compare the topic reconstructions of the poets Simonides and Dante to Faust's travels through the landscapes of Goethe's drama, and in particular to his journey through the spatial and temporal expanses of Part II? For Helmut Schanze, Goethe's text constitutes a "theater of recollection" within which 3,000 years of history are organized and rendered evident ("sinnlich vorgeführt") to the viewer's and reader's senses in a spatiotemporal structure that reveals the topic logic of the rhetorical tradition's mnemotechnics.[37] Thus, in the Classical Walpurgisnight of Act II as in the scene Mountain Gorges of Act V, a structure of memory-places (*Merkorte*) enables the poet to provide a vivid and coherent sensory impression of his subject.[38] The "place" of poetry thus constituted is a "psychological-internal" one centered in the mind of the poet.[39] To understand Goethe's approach to drama in general and to *Faust* in particular is to recognize in his work a unity forged through a mental process whose structure resembles the production phases of a speech as conceived by the rhetorical tradition.[40]

Focusing on *Faust II*, Steffen Schneider comes close to Schanze in identifying Goethe's play as a *Gedächtnisdrama* or *Gedächtnistheater*[41] that displays memory at work, as a process in which figures and forms of knowledge are assigned to "places" in the manner of the rhetorical tradition.[42] But where Schanze sees *Faust* as realizing a semiotic and aesthetic ideal of sensory immediacy, Schneider borrows Foucault's concept of the "archive" to argue instead that *Faust II*, reflecting a development that had become evident in *Wilhelm Meister's Journeyman Years* (*Wilhelm Meisters Wanderjahre*), persistently refers us to shifting discourses rather than to a fixed, nondiscursive reality. Schneider cites as a biographical turning point Goethe's planned history of Italian art, a project guided by the architectural metaphor of culture as a building viewable as a discrete whole, arguing that the project fails as Goethe increasingly recognizes his subject as an amorphous flow of data that resists such organic representation.[43]

This is a key insight into the workings of Goethe's play. The drama does not resurrect a world of stable signification from the rubble in the way that either a Simonides or a Dante restores the dead to memory and life within the worlds and cultural certainties presided over by his respective god. The topic structures that organize *Faust II* do not present the knowledge of the play in the way that a rhetorician's memory raises an imaginary house before her inner eye so as to link its contents in a reliable and comprehensive intuitive whole. Rather, "places" are placeholders that refer to the contents of an archive whose contents have expanded beyond any possibility of totalizing imaginative grasp. The archive, by definition, exceeds any single subject-centered imaginative and recollective effort. Schneider accordingly sees the representation of a modern and problematic form of experience in Goethe's late work, a form of experience that is strikingly referenced, for instance, in the debate between Vulcanists and Neptunists in the Classical Walpurgisnight. The scene displays setting and plot, but the appearance of a spatio-temporal coherence is at odds with the underlying failure to settle the dispute over causes of the earth's motions and shape. As Schneider writes, it is not just that Goethe thematizes contemporary debates in the natural sciences—or, one might add, in philosophy and politics;[44] "rather, he shows us how the disputed status of evidence itself matters for the production of poetic texts, in that what is plain to the eye is sacrificed and given over to the conflict among discourses."[45] Goethe's interest in geology and in contemporary theories of tectonic activity accordingly becomes a way in which he engages with historical changes in the structure of human experience. If in 1784 Goethe describes granite as belonging to an "ur-world" prior to and outside of life and history,[46] by the time of *Faust II* the certainty associated with such an extrahistorical point of reference is lost: the drama's landscape instead highlights irreconcilable discontinuities between experience and knowledge, between evidence and theory.[47] The earlier perspective promises a form of secular redemption from history within a stable and unchanging structure of meaning; the latter refutes such a possibility. In an extended scene whose title, "Classical Walpurgisnight," announces the relentless experimentation with forms and motifs that constitutes it, the ground below provides no stable epistemological counterpoint: it itself and the geological principles that subtend it remain in play.

I have suggested above that in *Faust*, "memory theater is at the same time anti-memory theater." How does this idea accord with Schanze's notion of the play as a "theater of memory" (to quote his subtitle), or Schneider's analysis of *Faust* as it reveals the working of a Foucauldian "archive"? For Schanze, the drama is a memory-work in that it represents Goethe's own integration of a heterogeneous range of subjects and experiences into an organic aesthetic whole, an integration that proceeds—and succeeds—

according to the methods of the rhetorical tradition. Goethe's *Faust* displays the subject in a successful enterprise of self-constitution. Indeed, Schanze maps the stages of rhetorical composition onto Goethe's life as writer of this drama: the text that Goethe finishes writing just before his death organically realizes a "conception" that he had already outlined sixty years earlier.[48] By contrast, Schneider's discussion presumes none of this autonomy and integrative power in the subject, which manifests instead as an "effect of epistemic and social processes that it cannot control."[49] Schneider cites Goethe's remark to Johann Peter Eckermann that *Faust II* contains "almost nothing subjective at all" ("fast gar nichts Subjektives"), and indeed Schneider's study is not overtly interested in the fate of individual selves.[50] However, Schneider does recurrently suggest that the character Faust is a subject caught up in the attempt to integrate himself through recollective labor. The archive does not simply free up the individual memory by promising the ready restoration of forgotten contents; the "memory-work" (*Gedächtnisarbeit*) that it engenders is at once more than the effort of any single character, and yet also an exercise in which characters themselves—and the titular protagonist in particular—participate.[51] Thus, even as he dismisses the common view of Faust as a poet, he argues that Faust himself is not only witness to events but rather engages in artistic acts of "recollective imagination" and "transformative recollection."[52] In this view, the Faust of Part II is indeed caught up in the constant, active processing of contents from the cultural memory, which also means that he perpetually struggles against the expropriation of memory that the logic of the archive entails. The attempt to integrate is also an attempt to reject that which resists integration: Goethe's protagonist, Schneider concludes with a reference to Nietzsche's essay on history, finds himself in a struggle to resist the "haunting of life" by the knowledge that the archive supplies.[53] Without referring to the concept of the archive, Peter Matussek similarly argues that Faust is perpetually beset by a "latent living-on of memories" that exacts from him ever more strenuous acts of repression.[54]

Surely Faust's impatience, in both Part I and Part II, does indeed recurrently signal such acts of repression as Faust hastens from one episode to the next. This is also to say, however, that in adapting the myth of the individual who uses the devil's magic to shed not all but most of his past, Goethe creates a hero whose gamble enables a dissolution of his identity that is never countered by any sustained engagement with the past. In a piece on Dante's *Divina Commedia* and Primo Levi's *Se questo è un uomo* (*Survival in Auschwitz*), Günter Butzer argues that whereas topography and mnemonics correspond to and support each other in constructing an encompassing system of meaning in Dante's work, in Levi's novel the two yield a dissonance that threatens the narrator's ability to reconstruct and represent his experiences.[55] This effort, however, underlies the whole of Levi's project. Goethe's character, by contrast, gives no indication of attempting any sustained reconstruction of his self. The principle of the archive as Schneider presents it is indeed important in illuminating the status and interaction of memory contents in *Faust II*; but the protagonist of Part II is not haunted by memories (his or others') in any way that might provide his character consistency, nor does he struggle to integrate these memories coherently within an identity that he could call his own.[56] He is readily infatuated, but he just as readily forgets. Struck blind by Care, Faust acquires no new insight, instead committing himself abruptly to the creation of an "Eden" (11,569) that will consummate his fame "into eternity" (11,583–584). In the lines that lead to his invocation of his wager with Mephisto ("to the moment, I could say . . ."; 11,581), Faust does not engage in that retrospective self-narration that either sustains itself or attempts to do so by drawing on personal recollections or on the memory contents of the archive; on the contrary, he anchors his identity in perpetual futurity, as something that he "could" affirm as a principle of pure possibility.[57]

The Faust myth was always about an individual who speculated on his life. The wager of Goethe's Faust produces something new: a subjectivity that commits itself insistently to its own fragmentation through a gamble that precludes its own resolution in a definable outcome. The arbitrariness of the particular time and place at which he dies underscores the abandonment of the topic structures that had once held the world together as a meaningful whole. Faust's culminating moment does not reveal him attempting to gaze either into a divine Dantean "volume," or into the Foucauldian "archive" that mediates memory and history in the work. Faust's final words substitute for the *totum simul* a vision that cancels the promise of any recollective act of integration, offering instead the spectacle of a selfhood and conscience that are radically open, ungrounded, and in play.[58]

NOTES

This essay is dedicated in gratitude to two extraordinary and very different teachers, Stanley Corngold and Robert Hollander, who first led me to immerse myself in Goethe's *Faust* and Dante's *Commedia*, respectively.

1. For a more extended discussion of this idea, see Nicholas Rennie, *Speculating on the Moment: The Poetics of Time and Recurrence in Goethe, Leopardi and Nietzsche* (Göttingen: Wallstein, 2005), 17–125.

2. I cite, referring to verse numbers, from Johann Wolfgang von Goethe, *Faust I & II*, ed. David E. Wellbery, trans. Stuart Atkins (Princeton, NJ: Princeton University Press, 2014); Goethe, *Faust-Dichtungen*, ed. Ulrich Gaier, 3 vols. (Stuttgart: Reclam, 1999).

3. William Hermanns, *Einstein and the Poet: In Search of the Cosmic Man* (Brookline Village, MA: Branden, 1983), 58.

4. Paul Ricœur, *Time and Narrative*, trans. Kathleen McLaughlin and David Pellauer, 3 vols. (Chicago: University of Chicago Press, 1990), vol. 1, 160. The phrase *totum simul* comes from Boethius. See Boethius, *The Theological Tractates. The Consolation of Philosophy*, trans. H. F. Stewart, E. K. Rand, and S. J. Tester (Cambridge, MA: Harvard University Press, 1973), 422.

5. Frances Amelia Yates, *The Art of Memory* (Chicago: University of Chicago Press, 1966), 95.

6. Harald Weinrich, *Lethe: The Art and Critique of Forgetting* (Ithaca, NY: Cornell University Press, 2004), 26–27.

7. Weinrich, *Lethe*, 29.

8. Gaier compares the passages from *Faust* and the *Commedia* in his commentary: Goethe, *Faust-Dichtungen*, 2:552–554.

9. Cited from Robert Hollander's commentary to *Purgatorio*, XXXI.91–102 in Dante Alighieri, *Purgatorio*, trans. Jean Hollander and Robert Hollander (London: Doubleday, 2003), 654.

10. See Hollander's commentary to these lines in Dante Alighieri, *Purgatorio*, 698. Translations of quotations from the *Commedia* are taken from this edition of the poem by Jean and Robert Hollander; the Italian is quoted from Dante Alighieri, *La divina commedia*, ed. Giorgio Petrocchi (Turin: Einaudi, 1975).

11. In his comparison of these passages, Gaier concludes that Faust is at this point no longer a moral being ("er ist keine sittliche Persönlichkeit mehr"). Goethe, *Faust-Dichtungen*, 2:553.

12. Dante Alighieri, *Paradiso*, trans. Robert Hollander and Jean Hollander (London: Doubleday, 2007), 14.

13. I am referring, of course, to Derrida's lecture "Structure, Sign, and Play in the Discourse of the Human Sciences." See Jacques Derrida, *Writing and Difference*, trans. Alan Bass (Chicago: University of Chicago Press, 1978), 278–293.

14. This is what Derrida terms the "classical" predicament with regard to the totality of a signifying field, where this totality as such is not in doubt. *Writing and Difference*, 289.

15. Attributing this insight to Philip B. Miller, Hollander observes that "Statius's completion of penance [in *Purgatorio* XX] is the only genuine event that occurs involving a damned or a saved soul in the entire *Commedia*." Dante Alighieri, *Purgatorio*, 425.

16. Derrida, *Writing and Difference*, 289.

17. Max Kommerell, *Geist und Buchstabe der Dichtung: Goethe, Schiller, Kleist, Hölderlin*, 4th ed. (Frankfurt am Main: V. Klostermann, 1956), 95. See also Weinrich, who contrasts Dante as rememberer with Faust the "forgetter." Harald Weinrich, "Dante und Faust," in *Vom Nutzen des Vergessens*, ed. Gary Smith and Hinderk M. Emrich (Berlin: Akademie-Verlag, 1996), 126. Franco Moretti, *Modern Epic: The World-System from Goethe to García Márquez* (London: Verso, 1996), 53.

18. Goethe refers to the 3,000-year "phantasmagoria" of Act III of the play in his letter to Wilhelm von Humboldt of October 22, 1826. He uses similar language in a letter of

the same date to Sulpiz Boisserée. See Johann Wolfgang von Goethe, *Sämtliche Werke: Briefe, Tagebücher und Gespräche* (Frankfurt am Main: Deutscher Klassiker Verlag, 1985), IV.41:203, 209.

19. Paul Fleming, "Forgetting—*Faust*: Adorno and Kommerell," in *Adorno and Literature*, ed. Nigel Mapp (London: Continuum, 2006), 135.

20. Weinrich, *Lethe*, 35–36.

21. "Perhaps Faust is saved because he is no longer the person who signed the pact; perhaps the wisdom of this play, which is a play in pieces, a 'Stück in Stücken,' lies in knowing how little the human being is identical to himself." Theodor W. Adorno, *Notes to Literature*, ed. Rolf Tiedemann, trans. Shierry Weber Nicholsen (New York: Columbia University Press, 1991), 119.

22. Rennie, *Speculating on the Moment*, 37.

23. For a discussion of the ways in which the drama sustains this logic of deferral to its final lines, see Nicholas Rennie, "Hier wird's Eräugnis: Performativität und Ende in Goethes *Faust*." In *Geistiger Handelsverkehr: Komparatistische Aspekte der Goethezeit*, ed. Anne Bohnenkamp and Matías Martínez (Göttingen: Wallstein, 2008), 395–410.

24. Walter Benjamin, *Selected Writings*, Vol. 4, *1938–1940*, ed. Howard Eiland and Michael W. Jennings (Cambridge, MA: Belknap Press, 2003), 331.

25. Derrida, *Writing and Difference*, 289. This play of substitutions is anticipated in Faust's translation from the Bible, where the replacement of terms remains, as Kittler argues with reference to Barthes, unguided by a paradigmatic or syntagmatic consciousness. Friedrich A. Kittler, *Discourse Networks 1800 / 1900*, trans. Michael Metteer and Chris Cullens (Stanford, CA: Stanford University Press, 1990), 12–13.

26. Moretti, *Modern Epic*, 19–22, 41, 55 et passim. Moretti is not the first to recognize the reassembly of existing forms in Goethe's *Faust*. As Neil Flax had noted, for instance, "the work invents at once a new dramaturgy and the theater in which it could be performed. But it invents that theater . . . out of materials that were actually present at that moment." "Goethe's *Faust II* and the Experimental Theater of His Time," *Comparative Literature* 31, no. 2 (1979): 166.

27. See, for instance, the chapter "Renaissance Memory: The Memory Theatre of Giulio Camillo," in Yates, *Art of Memory*, 129–159.

28. Weinrich, "Dante und Faust," 123–124.

29. Derrida, *Writing and Difference*, 292.

30. See Moretti, *Modern Epic*, 22–34; Michael Jaeger, *Fausts Kolonie: Goethes kritische Phänomenologie der Moderne* (Würzburg: Königshausen & Neumann, 2004).

31. See, for instance, Jaumann, "Memoria in der Auseinandersetzung zwischen *érudition* und *science* im 17. Jahrhundert," in *Ars memorativa: Zur kulturgeschichtlichen Bedeutung der Gedächtniskunst 1400–1750*, ed. Jörg Jochen Berns and Wolfgang Neuber (Tübingen: Niemeyer, 1993), 286–296; Regina Freudenfeld, *Gedächtnis-Zeichen: Mnemologie in der deutschen und französischen Aufklärung* (Tübingen: Narr, 1996); Weinrich, *Lethe*; Aleida Assmann, *Erinnerungsräume: Formen und Wandlungen des kulturellen Gedächtnisses* (Munich: C. H. Beck, 1999), 29; Dietmar Till, *Transformationen der Rhetorik: Untersuchungen zum Wandel der Rhetoriktheorie im 17. und 18. Jahrhundert* (Berlin: De Gruyter, 2004); Frank Grunert, "Die Marginalisierung des Gedächtnisses und die Kreativität der Erinnerung: Zur Gedächtnistheorie der deutschen Aufklärungsphilosophie," in *Erinnerung, Gedächtnis, Wissen: Studien zur kulturwissenschaftlichen Gedächtnisforschung*, ed. Günter

Oesterle (Göttingen: Vandenhoeck & Ruprecht, 2005), 29–51; Frank Grunert, "Erinnerung als Kreation: Zur Gedächtnistheorie von Christian Wolff und der Wolff-Schule," in *Christian Wolff und die europäische Aufklärung, Akten des 1. Internationalen Christian-Wolff-Kongresses, Halle (Saale), 4.–8. April 2004*, ed. Jürgen Stolzenberg and Oliver-Pierre Rudolph (Hildesheim: Olms, 2007), 391–404.

32. Derrida, *Writing and Difference*, 280.

33. Marcus Tullius Cicero, *De oratore*, 2nd ed. (Cambridge, MA: Harvard University Press, 1967), 465–467 (bk. 2, sec. 86, pars. 351–353).

34. Cicero, *De oratore*, 467 (bk. 2, sec. 86, par. 353).

35. Stefan Goldmann, "Statt Totenklage Gedächtnis: Zur Erfindung der Mnemotechnik durch Simonides von Keos," *Poetica* 21 (1989): 58.

36. See Hollander's commentary to *Inferno* XII.32 and XII.40–45 in Dante Alighieri, *Inferno*, trans. Robert Hollander and Jean Hollander (New York: Anchor Books, 2002), 229–230.

37. Helmut Schanze, *Goethes Dramatik: Theater der Erinnerung*. Theatron: Studien zur Geschichte und Theorie der dramatischen Künste 4 (Tübingen: Niemeyer, 1989), 181.

38. Schanze, *Goethes Dramatik*, 202, 204–205.

39. Schanze, *Goethes Dramatik*, 187.

40. Schanze, *Goethes Dramatik*, 3–4.

41. Steffen Schneider, *Archivpoetik: Die Funktion des Wissens in Goethes "Faust II"* (Tübingen: Niemeyer, 2005), 74, 231.

42. Schneider, *Archivpoetik*, 38–39, 78, 117.

43. Schneider, *Archivpoetik*, 26–27.

44. Regarding seismic activity as a metaphor for upheaval in the philosophical and political world, in *Faust*, see the commentaries to the Classical Walpurgisnight, for instance, Gaier's in Goethe, *Faust-Dichtungen*, 2:735–821 and 3:259–261. See also Ulrike Zeuch, "Goethes Sinngebung des Erdbebens von Lissabon: Zur Funktion der Seismos-Episode im *Faust II*," in *Das Erdbeben von Lissabon und der Katastrophendiskurs im 18. Jahrhundert*, ed. Gerhard Lauer (Göttingen: Wallstein, 2008), 173–187.

45. "Er führt vielmehr im Drama selbst vor Augen, was die umstrittene Stellung der Evidenz für das Verfertigen poetischer Texte bedeutet, indem der Text selbst die Anschaulichkeit seines Geschehens preisgibt und in den Widerstreit von Diskursen überführt." Schneider, *Archivpoetik*, 144. Here and elsewhere, translations from Schneider's study are my own.

46. Schneider, *Archivpoetik*, 127.

47. Schneider, *Archivpoetik*, 133–135. In a similar vein, while I think Jörn Göres yields important insights in his analysis of Goethe's use of topoi, it would be misleading, at least in the case of *Faust II*, to see in these what he describes as a representation of unchanging "originary relations of being" ("Urverhältnisse des Daseins"). Jörn Göres, "Goethes Verhältnis zur Topik," *Goethe-Jahrbuch* 26 (1964): 144–180.

48. Schanze, *Goethes Dramatik*, 218; cf. the discussion of Goethe's "oldest conception," 28–33.

49. Schneider, *Archivpoetik*, 11.

50. Schneider, *Archivpoetik*, 45, 146.

51. Schneider, *Archivpoetik*, 30–31, 74.

52. Schneider, *Archivpoetik*, 172, 194.

53. Schneider, *Archivpoetik*, 233.

54. Peter Matussek, "*Faust II*—die Tragödie der Gedächtniskultur," in *Peter Stein inszeniert Faust von Johann Wolfgang Goethe: Das Programmbuch Faust I und II*, ed. Roswitha Schieb and Anna Haas (Cologne: DuMont, 2000), 295.

55. Günter Butzer, "Höllenfahrt ohne Auferstehung: Die Unterweltsreise als Narrativ katastrophischen Erinnerns," in *Katastrophe und Gedächtnis*, ed. Thomas Klinkert and Günter Oesterle (Berlin: De Gruyter, 2013), 176.

56. "Although Faust is a work literally invaded by phantasms and ghosts, the uncanny, sinister element plays almost no role in it. This is a singular feature, and deserves further examination." Moretti, *Modern Epic*, 23.

57. Schneider, *Archivpoetik*, 32.

58. For their helpful suggestions regarding earlier versions of this essay, I am grateful to the editors of this volume, and to Alessandro Vettori, in particular regarding my discussion of Dante.

Part III

Children's Play

CHAPTER FIVE

Narcissus at Play

Goethe, Piaget, and the Passage from Egocentric to Social Play

ELLIOTT SCHREIBER

THE PSYCHOLOGIST JEAN PIAGET (1896–1980) advanced one of the most consequential theories of cognitive development in the twentieth century, one that left a lasting impact not only on psychology but also on disciplines ranging from education to philosophy.[1] At the heart of Piaget's developmental narrative is the path from egocentric to social thinking, or what Jürgen Habermas—who draws heavily on Piaget in formulating his theory of communicative action—characterizes as "*the decentration of an egocentric understanding of the world*."[2] Children's play figures prominently in Piaget's developmental account, in particular the form of play that he variously designates as symbolic, imaginative, pretend, or make-believe, and that he regards as "the essential ludic system."[3]

The present chapter investigates the origins around 1800 of the discourse of symbolic play within whose framework Piaget formulated his account. Piaget himself suggests the affinity of his larger project with the ideas of three thinkers of this period: Rousseau's conception of the distinctive mentality of the child; Kant's epistemology; and Hegel's dialectic.[4] In his studies on play more specifically, however, Piaget's frame of reference extends only as far back as the work of James Mark Baldwin, Konrad Lange, and Karl Groos at the turn of the twentieth century. I argue that two narratives of play by Johann Wolfgang von Goethe (the first book of *Wilhelm Meister's Years of Apprenticeship* [*Wilhelm Meisters Lehrjahre*, 1795] and the second book of *Poetry and Truth* [*Dichtung und Wahrheit*, 1811]) were pivotal in forging the notion of symbolic play.[5] This notion was then developed by Jean Paul in *Levana; or, the Doctrine of Education* (1807), and became a central theme of literary fairy tales by Romantic authors such as Ludwig Tieck,

E.T.A. Hoffmann, Clemens Brentano, and Hans Christian Andersen.[6] At the end of the nineteenth century, in *The Play of Man* (*Die Spiele der Menschen*, 1899), Karl Groos drew on numerous observations and depictions of children's play, including Goethe's autobiographical recollections, to formulate a theory of play that foregrounds imaginative play.[7] Piaget, in turn, engaged closely with Groos's writings in constructing what even one of Piaget's sharpest critics, Brian Sutton-Smith, characterizes as "the most conceptually elaborate account of play yet to be presented."[8]

While Goethe's narratives help found this lineage, they also offer vantage points from which the trajectory described by Piaget from egocentric, symbolic play to decentered, social play can be seen in a more complex light. In particular, I argue that Goethe's narratives trace how theater and the fairy tale emerge from symbolic play as forms of social play. In contrast to Piaget's depiction of social play, however, Goethe underscores the persistence of symbolic play and its underlying egocentrism within these forms. At the same time, he explores the opportunities that theatrical play and the fairy tale make possible for disrupting the very egocentrism that they perpetuate. The fairy tale, in particular, enables not only the imaginative transformation that occurs within symbolic play but also the transformation of symbolic play itself into self-reflexive play. Such self-reflexive (or, as I term it, narcissistic) play also produces symbols, but ones that have the distinctive character of meta-symbols, or symbols of the second order. Narcissistic play of this kind does indeed effect a decentration of the player's worldview, enabling a recognition of others' perspectives as distinct from the player's own. Paradoxically, though, this decentration itself remains self-centered. Goethe shows imaginative play to thus be capable of transforming in radical ways, but never of entirely overcoming its inherently egocentric logic.

PIAGET ON PLAY

In his early, foundational study, *Judgment and Reasoning in the Child* (1924), Piaget terms egocentrism "the most characteristic phenomenon" of childhood up to the age of about seven, and maintains that it stems from the child's cognitive constitution.[9] According to Piaget, intelligence consists in adaptation to the world. This occurs when one balances what he views as the two poles of cognition, namely, assimilation and accommodation. Assimilation, as he defines it, involves bringing the phenomena that we encounter into congruence with schemas that we have developed to comprehend the world; accommodation, by contrast, adjusts these schemas to fit the phenomena. Prior to the age of seven, assimilation dominates the child's cognitive process. This results in egocentric thought, or the inability to "adapt oneself to the sayings nor to the view-points of other people," and consequently the tendency to take "one's own immediate perception as something absolute" (228). To the extent that younger children each make their own individual points of view absolute, they lack an awareness that they even have a point of view; in other words, they lack self-consciousness (209).

In *Judgment and Reasoning*, Piaget closely associates the child's egocentric perspective with play, asserting that "for ego-centric thought the supreme law is play" (244). In his most extensive study of play, *Play, Dreams and Imitation in Childhood* (*La Formation du Symbole*, 1945), he continues to regard "assimilation to the ego" as "the principle of all play."[10] But here he distinguishes between three forms of play—practice play, symbolic play, and games with rules—that vary considerably in the manner and degree of their egocentrism. He situates these forms of play within a gradated sequence, ranging from play that revolves around the "direct satisfaction of the ego" to play that reconciles such satisfaction with "the demands of social reciprocity" (168).

In practice play, which originates in infancy, the process of assimilation to the ego occurs at the sensory-motor level. On this plane, the child develops schemas related to her bodily activity, for instance, sucking, looking, and grasping. For infants, according to Piaget, an object is never just an object, but rather an object to be sucked, looked at, grasped, and so on. Such activities become play, as opposed to intelligent adaptation, in the moment that the infant engages in them not in an effort to better comprehend her environment, but rather simply to enjoy the "feeling of virtuosity or power" that accompanies the act of assimilation (89).[11]

Around the age of one, practice play undergoes a transformation into symbolic play. The latter is distinct from the former in that it involves assimilation not on the sensory-motor level, but rather on that of representation, through the child's use of symbols. Symbolic play can take a variety of forms. For instance, the child might use one object to signify something else. Piaget thus remarks on how his daughter Jacqueline, at 1; 9 (3) (or the third day of the ninth month of her first year) "put a shell on the edge of a big box and made it slide down saying: '*Cat on the wall*'" (124). Alternatively, the child might use her own body to signify something else: "At 2; 8 (5) she [Jacqueline] crawled into my room on all fours, saying, '*miaow*'" (125). As the child develops, symbolic play becomes increasingly elaborate; for instance, Piaget discusses how, beginning in her second year, Jacqueline's play with dolls resulted in "the construction of whole scenes" (127–129). Symbolic play, whether in its simpler or more complex forms, involves "the assimilation of any one object to another, since any object can be a make-believe substitute for any other" (166).[12] Because "it freely assimilates things to one another and everything to the ego" (87), symbolic play embodies "egocentric thought in its pure state" (167).[13] As such, it "provides the child with the live, dynamic, individual language indispensable for the expression of his subjective feelings, for which collective language alone is inadequate" (167).

Piaget contends that the nature of symbolic play begins to change between the ages of four and seven: symbolic scenes become more orderly and consistent; the "distorting ludic character" of the symbol diminishes as it tends toward greater verisimilitude; and collective symbolism begins to supplant individual symbolism (135). To illustrate this transformation, he juxtaposes how Jacqueline plays with her younger sister Lucienne before and after Jacqueline turns four. Piaget observes that when Jacqueline, at 3; 11 (26), plays a shop game with Lucienne, she treats her as she would a doll (138). At 4; 5 (13), however, Jacqueline plays very differently, adapting herself to the leads that her sister gives her (139). Piaget cites these and similar examples drawn from observations of his children's play to argue that, beginning at about the age of four, "there is a transition from egocentrism to reciprocity, as a result of a double coordination of inter-individual relationships and in representational correlation" (139).[14] This transition becomes even more pronounced after what Piaget calls "the decisive turning point at the age of seven or eight" (139), as evinced by the evolution of Jacqueline and Lucienne's pretend play into collaborative "plays or theatrical performances" that require "an ever-increasing co-ordination of roles" (140).

The same "decisive turning point" marks the transition from symbolic play generally to games with rules, the subject of the first chapter of Piaget's *The Moral Judgment of the Child* (1932), "The Rules of the Game." The game in question is the game of marbles as played by Swiss schoolboys. As in his discussion of collective symbolism in *Play, Dreams and Imitation*, Piaget focuses on how children's play with marbles evolves from egocentric to social. Until the age of four, children incorporate marbles into their pretend play. From the ages of four to six, they presume there to be common rules for the game that they believe have been prescribed by their elders; however, each child plays marbles largely according to his own idiosyncratic rules, believing these rules to be universal. In other words, "He plays in an individualistic manner with material that is social. Such is egocentrism."[15] But beginning at about age seven, "the desire for mutual understanding" arises (42). As a competitive game with the objective of winning one's opponent's marbles, this game remains egocentric; however, the child's primary interest is now social: "The thing now is not only to fight the other boys but also and primarily to regulate the game with a whole set of systematic rules which will ensure the most complete reciprocity in the methods used" (45–46). Starting at about the age of ten, the way that children play the game undergoes a further significant shift: they not only come to master the complex rules of the game but also become increasingly conscious of their ability to change these rules, and furthermore become aware of reciprocity as the guiding principle by which any such changes should be made and judged (71).

In sum, Piaget's studies of play constitute a developmental narrative centered on the rise and decline of symbolic play. According to this narrative, symbolic play, on the one hand, transforms into collective symbolism, and, on the other, gives way to rule-bound play. In the process, the egocentric point of view of the child becomes socialized as she learns to cooperate with other children to create symbols, to coordinate roles, and to set rules. To be sure, Piaget notes that the child's development is, in individual cases, "not linear in character, and its general direction can only be observed by schematizing the material and ignoring the minor oscillations which render it infinitely complicated."[16] Despite this caveat, his account clearly maps out the "general direction" as well as the various developmental stages in "the passage of egocentrism to cooperation."[17]

SYMBOLIC PLAY AND THEATRICAL PLAY IN BOOK ONE OF *WILHELM MEISTER'S YEARS OF APPRENTICESHIP*

Beginning with François Fenélon's *On the Education of Daughters* (*De l'éducation des filles*, 1687) and John Locke's *Some Thoughts on Education* (1693), and continuing with Rousseau's *Émile* (1762) and the work of the Philanthropinists in Germany, Enlightenment pedagogues accorded a key role to play in their efforts to reform education. In the final quarter of the eighteenth century, however, the didactic instrumentalization of play came under assault. In *The Sorrows of Young Werther* (*Die Leiden des jungen Werthers*, 1774), Goethe's eponymous protagonist voices a radically different vision of children's play and of how adults should relate to it. In his letter of June 29, for instance, Werther describes his exuberant play with Lotte's younger brothers and sisters, contrasting it with the contemptuous reaction of another visitor to the family home, the doctor, whom Werther characterizes as "a dogmatic puppet" ("*eine dogmatische Drahtpuppe*") of Enlightenment rationality.[18] In the wake of Goethe's first novel, two further novels contributed decisively to shifting the discourse of children's play away from didactic play and toward one form of play in particular, namely, imaginative play. The first novel to do so was Karl Philipp Moritz's "psychological novel" *Anton Reiser* (1782–86), which vividly depicts its eponymous hero's make-believe and theatrical play. Moritz's novel was followed by Goethe's *Wilhelm Meister's Years of Apprenticeship* (1795), whose first book distills the new notion of imaginative play into apodictic form: "When children play, they know how to make anything out of any thing: a stick becomes a gun, a little piece of wood a sword, any bundle a doll, and any corner a hut" ("Kinder wissen beim Spiele aus allem alles zu machen: ein Stab wird zur Flinte, ein Stückchen Holz zum Degen, jedes Bündelchen zur Puppe, und jeder Winkel zur Hütte").[19]

The eponymous protagonist of Goethe's novel utters this statement while recounting to his lover, the actress Mariane, the evolution of his passion for the theater. This evolution occurs over several phases; in each of these, theatrical play—or "*das Schauspiel*," the first words of the novel—is intimately connected with symbolic play. Wilhelm's account famously begins with his infatuation with the marionette theater ("Puppenspiel" [FA I.9:362], "Kinderspiel" [FA I.9:364]) that was made one Christmas by a young lieutenant in his father's employ, and presented by Wilhelm's mother as a gift to her children. After seeing two performances, staged by the lieutenant, of the biblical story of Jonathan, Saul, David, and Goliath, Wilhelm steals the script and secretly learns it by heart, imagining himself to be both David and Goliath (FA I.9:371–372). He further recalls how one day he performed the play in front of his mother, using little clumps of wax ("Wachsklümpchen") in place of the marionettes (FA I.9:372), a recollection that prefigures his later assertion that, for children, "every little bundle [*Bündelchen*] becomes a doll/puppet [*Puppe*]" (FA I.9:382). The meta-symbolism of this act—Wilhelm crafts symbols (wax figures) as a substitute for symbols (puppets)—doubly instantiates the process of symbolic substitution that, according to Piaget, lies at the heart of imaginative play.

After impressing his mother with this private performance, Wilhelm is granted permission to put on the marionette show with the lieutenant before an invited audience. A period of mostly solitary imaginative play ensues. When Wilhelm eventually becomes bored with reenacting the original play, he uses the marionettes to represent other characters from the theatrical and operatic repertory: "My imagination brooded over that little world, which soon took on a different shape. . . . King Saul in his black, silken robe now had to play Chaumigrem, Cato, and Darius" (FA I.9:374). He also constructs new decorations for the marionette theater and, inspired by his sisters' play with dolls, fashions new costumes for the puppets (FA I.9:375). Wilhelm thus now revels in producing his own symbols, both by recycling old signifiers (the marionettes) to symbolize something new and by creating entirely new signifiers (new costumes and scenery). In Piaget's words, he delights in freely assimilating one thing to another.

The phase of Wilhelm's largely solitary childhood play gives way to one in his youth that is characterized by collective play. While he thereby follows the path of development envisioned by Piaget, in which children transition from egocentric to social play after the age of seven or eight, the manner in which Wilhelm describes this new phase of his play also calls such a trajectory into question: "The distractions of youth, as my circle of friends began to grow, took their toll on my solitary, quiet pleasures. I was by turns a huntsman, a soldier, and a cavalryman, as our games demanded; but I always had a slight edge over the others because I was able to produce the necessary equipment for them. Thus, the swords were mostly from my workshop" (FA I.9:377). Wilhelm now plays primarily with others, and takes on different roles not solely on a whim, but depending on what is required by each particular play. These roles also have the more social character of trades (huntsman, soldier, cavalryman). Nevertheless, this new period of social play bears a striking resemblance to the previous one. Much as, when playing on his own, he used the marionettes to represent different characters (Chaumigrem, Cato, Darius), so now he himself pretends to occupy one trade after another. Furthermore, Wilhelm underscores his "slight edge over the others" ("einen kleinen Vorzug vor den anderen") in producing the necessary props, such as swords—in other words, in manufacturing the symbols that are the basis for his and his friends' pretend play. This assertion of superiority mirrors the decidedly martial subject matter of their play. In short, rather than diminishing during his youth, as Piaget's theory holds, Wilhelm's capacity for imaginative play, and with it his egocentrism, continues to grow.

Wilhelm relates that he eventually tired of this make-believe play with his friends (FA I.9:377), and that he began to organize theatrical performances with them. Again, this next stage of his play preserves the basic structure of the earlier ones. Indeed, it is precisely in reference to this period of theatrical play in his youth that Wilhelm makes his claim about children's capacity for imaginative play, "When children play, they know how to make anything out of any thing. . . . This is how our private theater developed" (FA I.9:382). Goethe thus shows theatrical performance not only to arise out of symbolic play, but to retain a far closer connection with its origins than one might surmise on the basis of Piaget's account, which includes theatrical play among those forms of creative play that, "while they partly derive from symbolic play, develop in the direction of constructive activity or work"—that is, in the direction of activities that Piaget views as based on properly adaptive thinking rather than on pure assimilation.[20]

Indeed, the continuity between the various phases of Wilhelm's play persists up to the moment in time when he recounts his reminiscences to Mariane. Wilhelm's love for Mariane strongly resembles his imaginative play as a child: "And so it is certain that love, which must first animate rosebushes, myrtle groves, and moonlight, can even give to wood shavings and scraps of paper the appearance of animate beings" (FA I.9:410). Wilhelm's love thus appears to animate lifeless objects, much as when, in his childhood, the puppets "seemed to him to be animate, where he believed that he could animate them through the liveliness of his voice, through the movement of his hands" (FA I.9:364). The narrator highlights this connection between Wilhelm's childhood and his youth two paragraphs earlier, at the outset of the fifteenth chapter: "Happy youth! Happy the times when the need for love first stirs! Man is then like a child who delights for hours in his own echo, who carries the conversation on his own, and who is satisfied with it even when his invisible partner only repeats the final syllables of the words he utters" (FA I.9:409). The narrator here identifies a double echo: youth echoes childhood, for like the child, the youth delights in his own echo, even when conversing with his beloved. To employ a term coined by Piaget to describe how children below the age of seven interact with one another during play, such a conversation unfolds in the form of a "collective monologue." According to Piaget, when the child uses this rhetorical form, he "is not speaking to anyone. He is talking aloud to himself in front of others," who function "simply as a stimulus."[21] This is indeed the case in Wilhelm's conversation with Mariane, in the course of which he narrates his reminiscences, completely oblivious to her sadness (FA I.9:377), or to how, in her boredom, she grows tired and eventually falls asleep (FA I.9:376, 381). That is to say, Wilhelm treats Mariane as though she were a marionette, much as Piaget's daughter Jacqueline treats her sister Lucienne like a doll when they play shop.[22]

While Wilhelm's egocentrism thus persists over the course of both his childhood and his youth, Goethe also reveals that symbolic play—in particular, when performed for an audience as theatrical play—contains inherent risks to the very egocentrism that propels it. Consider Wilhelm's description of his first theatrical performance, the marionette show that he stages with the lieutenant:

> The next day, in a performance for children we had invited, we managed well, except in the heat of the moment I dropped my Jonathan and had to reach down with my hand to pick him up: an accident that interrupted the illusion very much, provoked a lot of laughter, and upset me greatly.
>
> [Den anderen Tag, da eine Gesellschaft Kinder geladen war, hielten wir uns trefflich, außer daß ich in dem Feuer der Aktion meinen Jonathan fallen ließ, und genötigt war, mit der Hand hinunterzugreifen, und ihn zu holen: ein Zufall, der die Illusion sehr unterbrach, ein großes Gelächter verursachte, und mich unsäglich kränkte.]
> (FA I.9:373)

The puppet's chance fall (or *Zu-fall*) interrupts the performance's illusion, a word that, as Johann Huizinga notes, "literally means to be 'in-play' (from *inlusio*, *illudere* or *inludere*)."[23] As Thomas Pfau remarks, this incident "shows how the risk laden element . . . of play may at any moment disrupt the ludic space (*Spielraum*) and, thus, jeopardize the promised transfiguration of a quotidian and dispersed experience into the condensed virtuality of aesthetic form (*Gebilde*)."[24] Transposed from Pfau's Gadamerian idiom into Piaget's terminology, this means that the process of assimilating one thing to another (for instance, an inanimate puppet to a living person) is always in danger of falling short. Moreover, the attempt to restore the illusion can in fact have the opposite effect. Thus, when Wilhelm reaches down with his hand to retrieve the puppet, he only further disrupts the illusion, exposing the power grab, so to speak, that takes place when one attempts "to make anything out of any thing," and eliciting the audience's laughter.[25]

The interruption caused by the puppet's chance fall makes possible a kind of reciprocity in the audience's relationship with the players. For Piaget, as noted above, reciprocal relations are the outcome of "a double coordination of inter-individual relationships and in representational correlation," and mark the end of egocentric, symbolic play.[26] The scene in Goethe's novel, however, envisions a very different sort of reciprocity. To begin with, it encompasses not only players, as in Piaget's model of social play, but also spectators, whose presence Piaget leaves out of consideration. Furthermore, Goethe's notion of reciprocity differs markedly from Piaget's in that it arises not from coordination and cooperation, but rather through an unexpected collision of one point of view—the illusion generated through symbolic play—with another, namely, the consciousness of this illusion *as* illusion, or what Goethe, in another theatrical context, terms "self-conscious illusion" ("selbstbewusste[n] Illusion").[27] A final distinction from Piaget lies in the effect that this reciprocity produces. For, at least in the short term, the collision of perspectives has the effect of strengthening rather than decentering Wilhelm's egocentric point of view. Wilhelm is thus incapable of taking the audience's stance and laughing at himself. And when a similar chain of mishaps occurs during his and his friends' performance of Tasso's *Jerusalem Delivered*, to which the audience similarly responds with laughter, Wilhelm swears to himself "to never dare put on a play without the greatest amount of forethought" ("mich nie, als mit der größten Überlegung, an die Vorstellung eines Stücks zu wagen"; FA I.9:380). That is, Wilhelm vows never to risk staging a play without first attempting to contain the element of risk as much as possible. Taken together, these two scenes lay bare the vulnerability of theatrical play to chance interruption. However, they also underscore its staying power, evident in Wilhelm's determination to safeguard his theatrical play from future disruptions.

According to Pfau, these "instances of performative miscarriage" also have a longer-term, traumatic effect on Wilhelm, one that, years later, makes it possible for him to gradually recognize his "unsuitability for the stage" (575). Pfau maintains that "the narrative's progression appears to hinge on its protagonist's vicarious transition from a realm of symbolic and self-conscious play to a more expansive, ludic conception of life itself," one that is more receptive to contingency (575). Jane K. Brown similarly observes that "Wilhelm breaks emotionally with the stage and turns his attention to selfhood in the world."[28] Brown identifies a moral maturation in Wilhelm's break with theater, as Goethe's protagonist "becomes more attentive to the attitudes of the people around him, more sensitive to the moral implications of his behavior" (98). Such a process of maturation would fit the developmental paradigm conceptualized by Piaget. However, as Brown also remarks, in *Wilhelm Meister* the theater is "not simply a detour to be overcome"; thus, she notes how role play and other forms of theatricality remain an integral part of the novel until the very end (99). Goethe thematizes this persistence of symbolic and theatrical play even more strongly sixteen years later in *Poetry and Truth*, emphasizing their enduring hold on his own life and art. By the same token, his autobiography also shows these forms to be open to greater disruption and transformation than does his bildungsroman, and in ways that further complicate Piaget's notion of the passage from egocentric to social play.

SYMBOLIC PLAY, THEATRICAL PLAY, AND FAIRY TALE IN BOOKS ONE AND TWO OF *POETRY AND TRUTH*

Early in Book One of *Poetry and Truth*, Goethe describes how his paternal grandmother (the adult figure whom he describes as most fostering children's play) presented her grandchildren with a puppet performance on Christmas.[29] Goethe comments on the show's effect on its young audience: "This unexpected performance powerfully attracted our young sensibilities. It made an especially strong impression on the boy, one whose effect continued to resonate long after" ("Dieses unerwartete Schauspiel zog die jungen Gemüter mit Gewalt an sich; besonders auf den Knaben machte es einen sehr starken Eindruck, der in eine große langdauernde Wirkung nachklang").[30] The first book of *Wilhelm Meister*, with its similar depiction of the powerful effect of the puppet show on its protagonist, would seem to be a prominent instance of such a *Nachklang*, or echo. Yet, especially for readers in 1811, who most likely approached the autobiography having read Goethe's bildungsroman, it would have been the former that echoed the latter, in a strange reversal of chronology. Stranger still—and an indication that Goethe's autobiography has moved beyond Wilhelm's echo chamber, where the symbolic play of his childhood repeats itself again and again throughout his youth—the *Nachklang* of *Wilhelm Meister* in *Poetry and Truth* is an echo with a difference.

To be sure, Book One and especially Book Two of Goethe's autobiography do indeed recapitulate *in nuce* several episodes of Wilhelm's account of his symbolic play. Much as in *Wilhelm Meister*, Goethe describes how, after the performance of the puppet show, the puppet theater was eventually handed over to him and his sister "for them to practice and for them to bring to life dramatically" ("zu eigner Übung und dramatischer Belebung"; FA I.14:20). The boy (or "der Knabe," as Goethe refers to his younger self) stages his own puppet shows in his home, though he does so together with his friends from the outset (FA I.14:56). As with Wilhelm, he and his friends begin by memorizing and staging the original show, but grow bored with it, and alter both the costumes and decorations so that they can perform other plays (FA I.9:56–57). And as with Wilhelm and his friends, the boy and his playmates eventually outgrow the puppet theater and turn to manufacturing props for their own playacting (FA I.14:57).

However, as much as Goethe's account of his own play as a child mirrors that given by Wilhelm of his childhood and youth, it also diverges from it in significant ways. One of the most important changes involves the way in which Goethe portrays the disruption of theatrical play. His autobiography shifts the focus from the chance interruption, and the audience's amused reaction to it, to the audience's active disruption during his and his friends' first marionette performances: "In the beginning I made many friends by granting first one boy and then another the special privilege of being a spectator; but the inherent restlessness of children kept them from being patient spectators for long. They disrupted the play, and finally we had to seek out a younger audience, which could, if necessary, be held in check by nurses and maids" (FA I.14:56). Despite being invited individually by the boy, the young audience members, in their restlessness, disrupt the play ("Sie störten das Spiel"). As in the wake of the accidental interruption of the puppet show in *Wilhelm Meister*, Goethe reveals here an emergent reciprocity in the relationship between players and audience, who do not just assume a passive role as "patient spectators." As in the scene in Goethe's novel, this reciprocity does not transpire through coordination and cooperation, as conceived by Piaget, but rather through unexpected disruption. The difference between this disruption and the one described in *Wilhelm Meister*, though, is that here the audience takes a more active role in effecting it; the members of the audience instigate it through their restlessness (*Unruhe*), and do not merely react to the players' own accidental disruption (*Unfall*).[31] Both forms of disturbance elicit a similar response, namely, the attempt to forestall any future disruption—in the boy's case by excluding the older, unruly children and admitting only younger spectators who can be kept in line ("in der Ordnung gehalten") by their caretakers.

A similar power play takes place in Book Two of Goethe's autobiography between the players themselves. Like Wilhelm, who produces swords for his and his playmates' pretend play, the boy manufactures armaments as props: "My playmates also made themselves such armaments and held them to be just as beautiful and good as mine; however, I had not limited myself to *one* person's needs, but could furnish several members of our little army with all sorts of props, and so made myself more and more indispensable to our small circle" (FA I.14:57; original emphasis). Like Wilhelm, the boy extends his sphere of influence over his circle of friends by crafting the symbols that subtend their play. Once again, then, Goethe shows that as collective symbolism arises, the egocentrism of symbolic play doesn't give way to cooperation, as Piaget would have it; rather, it itself gives shape to the social circle. This contrast with Piaget is all the more striking given that the boy's and his friends' playacting occurs after he has turned seven (FA

I.14:53), that is, after he has passed what Piaget terms "the decisive turning point" from egocentric to social play.

However, this scene doesn't merely parallel the corresponding one in *Wilhelm Meister* but also takes it in a new direction. While depicting the hegemony exercised by one individual, Goethe's autobiography shows the social sphere to remain one of conflict: thus, the boy's other companions construct their own props, which they regard as "just as beautiful and good" as his, and Goethe suggests that they perhaps even do so as a pointed rejoinder to his own production. The next sentence of the text underscores the presence of this conflict as well as its consequences: "Not surprisingly, such games led to factions, fights, and blows, and usually met a terrible end in quarrels and ill humor" ("Daß solche Spiele auf Parteiungen, Gefechte und Schläge hinwiesen, und gewöhnlich auch mit Händeln und Verdruß ein schreckliches Ende nahmen, läßt sich denken"; FA I.14:57–58). The word *Spiele* here may be seen as referring both to the friends' arms race and to the theatrical plays that their pretend armaments make possible. These games and plays meet their "terrible end" with the collapse of the distance between signifier and signified: they symbolize but also anticipate (Goethe uses the verb *hinweisen*) "factions, fights, and blows." While, in Wilhelm's case, his and his friends' military games lead to "occasional fights" ("manche Mißheligkeit"), their conflicts are "settled easily enough" ("bald beigelegt"; FA I.9:377). What is new in the equivalent scene in Goethe's autobiography is the emphasis on conflict—on what Sutton-Smith terms the "labile, intentionally contrary aspect of play"—as well as on the risk that such conflict can escalate to the point where it turns into physical violence that destroys play itself.[32]

Goethe's depiction of the audience's unrest during the puppet performances and his allusion to the skirmishes between the players resonate with the theme of conflict that he introduces at the beginning of Book Two of his autobiography, which describes the onset of the Seven Years' War. In the opening paragraphs, he relates how Friedrich II's invasion of Saxony challenged the world to be "not merely . . . spectator, but also . . . judge" (FA I.14:53). As a result, the world "immediately split into two parties," an event that Goethe relates occurred in miniature within his own extended family (FA I.14:53), with the smaller part of the family (including his father as well as the boy himself) taking the side of Friedrich, and the larger part (grouped around his maternal grandfather) taking the Austrian side. Goethe remarks, "The boy had no conception that there could be parties or, indeed, that he himself belonged to a party" (FA I.14:55). The boy's perspective as a seven-year-old child thus jibes with the egocentric viewpoint that Piaget attributes to children below that age: "The child experiences the greatest difficulty in entering into anyone else's point of view. Consequently, his judgment is always absolute, so to speak, and never relative, for a relative judgment involves the simultaneous awareness of at least two personal points of view."[33] Goethe attributes to his younger self just such an absolute viewpoint, one that makes a judgment according to the absolute distinction between right and wrong, just and unjust, calling into question "the justice of public opinion" ("die Gerechtigkeit des Publikums"; FA I.14:55). What he is not yet capable of recognizing is that his own viewpoint is itself just as partisan as the opposing one. Unlike Piaget, however, Goethe once again stresses the continuity of this absolute perspective long beyond early childhood. Indeed, he claims that it lasts well into his adulthood, regarding it as "the germ of my disregard, even of my contempt for the public, a feeling that stayed with me for much of my life and was offset only at a late date by insight and education" ("Keim der Nichtachtung, ja der Verachtung des Publikums, die mir eine ganze Zeit meines Lebens anhing und nur spät durch Einsicht und Bildung ins Gleiche gebracht werden konnte"; FA I.14:56).

The boy's attempt to exert his influence over others (both his fellow players and his audience) through his symbolic play would appear to continue in his telling of fairy tales of his own invention.[34] Within the smaller group of playmates who take his side, he seems to succeed where previously he had failed in establishing a monopoly over the production of symbols: he makes his companions "very happy" with his fairy tales, and they especially love it when he relates tales in the first person ("und besonders liebten sie, wenn ich in eigner Person sprach"; FA I.14:58). Goethe remarks on his narrating of fairy tales as a child:

> If one examines this propensity very closely, one might want to recognize in it the presumptuousness with which the poet imperiously expresses even the most improbable ideas and demands that whatever seems in some way true to him, the inventor, be accepted by everyone as real.
>
> [Betrachtet man diesen Trieb recht genau, so möchte man in ihm diejenige Anmaßung erkennen, womit der Dichter selbst das Unwahrscheinlichste gebieterisch ausspricht, und von einem Jeden fordert, er solle dasjenige für wirklich erkennen, was ihm, dem Erfinder, auf irgend eine Weise als wahr erscheinen konnte.]
>
> (FA I.14:58)

In telling fairy tales, one demands that the audience recognize one's own point of view as true, however improbable it might be; in other words, the storyteller's hubris ("Anmaßung") requires the audience's accommodation (or *Anpassung*). Telling fairy tales, then, would appear to intensify the egocentrism that is the driving force of symbolic play. In short, Goethe points to two potential impacts that symbolic play can have upon others. One is the hegemony that a player (or group of players) can exercise over others, as the boy and his friends do by exerting their control over the young spectators of their puppet show, and as the boy appears to do in recounting his fairy tales to his loyal friends. The second potential impact is conflict, as occurs when the unruly older children in the audience disrupt the puppet shows, and when the boy's fellow players challenge his monopoly over the symbols subtending their play. In neither of these scenarios does egocentric, symbolic play transition into social play in Piaget's sense of cooperative play. The second scenario, though, does open egocentric play to contestation, and hence to a different kind of reciprocity than the one envisioned by Piaget. However, the danger, according to Goethe, is that this act of contestation risks radicalizing the very egocentrism that it disrupts, to the point where individuals resort to physical violence to overpower others, thereby bringing about an end to play.

In Goethe's account of his telling of fairy tales, however, a third possibility also comes to light, if we examine this account carefully, as the text invites us to do: "If one examines this propensity very closely, one *might* want to recognize in it the presumptuousness with which the poet imperiously expresses even the most improbable ideas" (my emphasis). In particular, Goethe's use of the subjunctive in the second clause bears further scrutiny. In other words, one *might* want to see poetic hubris at work in Johann's drive to tell fairy tales, but this might also not be the full story. Indeed, the sentence in the text directly preceding this one supports such caution, for here Goethe recounts how he gradually learned to rework the initial braggadocio of his fairy tales ("Luftgestalten und Windbeuteleien") into "artful representations" ("kunstmäßigen Darstellungen"; FA I.14:58). This artistry, I argue, takes the form of self-reflection: it at once enacts symbolic play, and observes that same play as it is being enacted. As such, it is akin to the "self-conscious illusion" triggered by Wilhelm's interrupted theatrical play, with the significant difference that it is now the player himself who combines both perspectives.

Consider the opening paragraph of "The New Paris" ("Der neue Paris") the tale that Goethe retells as a paradigmatic example ("Bei*spiel*";

my emphasis) of the fairy tales that he related to his loyal circle of young friends (FA I.14:58). This first paragraph comprises a kind of prelude (or "Vorspiel," to use the heading familiar from Goethe's *Faust*) to the main story. The boy, as narrator, here describes a dream that he claims to have had recently during the night before Whitsunday; his description focuses on what is arguably the primary concern of this "boyhood fairy tale" (or "Knabenmärchen," the subtitle that Goethe gives to his tale; FA I.14:59), namely, symbolic play itself.[35] The boy tells his audience that he dreamt that he was standing before a mirror and trying, unsuccessfully, to dress himself in his new summer clothes. A young man bearing three apples of different colors appears, whom the boy, in his role as protagonist, quickly identifies as the god Mercury. When the protagonist wants to grab hold of them, Mercury pulls back, telling him that they are not for him, and instructs him that he is to give them to the three most beautiful young people from the city who, each according to his lot, are to find the brides they wish for. In the course of this dream, the apples undergo a series of transformations. First, right before the protagonist wants to grab hold of them, the narrator notes, "one had to take them to be precious stones which had been given the form of fruits" ("Man mußte sie für Edelsteine halten, denen man die Form von Früchten gegeben"; FA I.14:59). Once Mercury has given the apples to him and left, they appear to have grown larger. The protagonist holds them up against the light and finds them to be completely transparent. The narrator continues: "but very soon they drew themselves up in length and turned into three beautiful, beautiful women as large as moderately sized dolls ("aber gar bald zogen sie sich aufwärts in die Länge und wurden zu drei schönen, schönen Frauenzimmerchen in mäßiger Puppengröße"; FA I.14:60). They glide up along the protagonist's fingers, and when he wants to grab them in order to get hold of at least one of them, they are already floating high up above him, and he is left to watch them float away.

The descriptor "as large as moderately sized dolls" ("in mäßiger Puppengröße") naturally recalls the boy's play with *Puppen* in the chapter's frame narrative. It also brings to mind Wilhelm's claim that children know how to make anything from any thing, such that any little bundle can become a doll (or puppet). In the case of the protagonist's dream, apples can become gemstones, which can in turn transform into three beautiful, doll- or puppet-sized women. This is not the only instance of symbolic play in the dream scenario. After the three women fly away, the protagonist, still holding his hands high in the air, looks at his fingers "as though something were to be seen on them. Then, suddenly, I saw the loveliest girl imaginable dancing around on my fingertips" ("als wäre daran etwas zu sehen gewesen. Aber mit einmal erblickte ich auf meinen Fingerspitzen ein allerliebstes Mädchen herumtanzen"; FA I.14:60). Here, too, a symbolic transformation takes place involving the protagonist's own fingers, which in *Wilhelm Meister* are closely associated with the marionettes.[36] In addition, the earlier appearance of Mercury in the dream can also be read as such a transformation, as right before Mercury makes his entrance, the protagonist, gazing at himself in the mirror, sees the locks of his own hair standing out from his head "like little wings" (FA I.14:59). As the protagonist is well aware—he tells Mercury that he has often seen him pictured in illustrations—a winged hat is one of Mercury's signature symbols (FA I.14:59).

This opening scenario underscores the egocentrism that underlies symbolic play. It expresses itself in the protagonist's repeated gesture of attempting to grasp objects or figures. Thus, the narrator claims of the apples, "One had to take them to be precious stones" ("Man mußte sie für Edelsteine halten"; FA I.14:59). This act of taking one thing to be something else—that is, symbolic play—leads in the next sentence to the protagonist's wish to literally take hold of the gemstones for himself: "I wanted to reach for them" ("Ich wollte darnach greifen"; FA I.14:59). Variations of the same gesture recur throughout the account of this dream, as indicated by the verbs *halten*, *festhalten*, *haschen*, and *zugreifen*. These verbs recall several key occurrences of these and similar words in both the first book of *Wilhelm Meister* and the second book of *Poetry and Truth*: the boy's attempt to keep control of his audience ("in der Ordnung gehalten"); his friends' taking their swords to be just as good and beautiful as the boy's ("hielten sie für eben so schön und gut als die meinigen"); Wilhelm and the lieutenant's manner of comporting themselves well during their puppet show ("wir hielten uns trefflich"); and, most particularly, Wilhelm's gesture of reaching for his fallen puppet ("mit der Hand hinunterzugreifen").

However, again and again, this gesture of holding, grabbing, and assimilating to the self encounters resistance by the other figures, much as the boy's audience and playmates resist his attempts to extend his power over them. Thus, Mercury "draws back" ("zog zurück"; FA I.14:59) when the protagonist wants to grasp the apples, telling him, "You must know that they are not for you" (FA I.14:59). Similarly, the three women draw themselves upward ("zogen sich aufwärts"), and then float up and away from the protagonist's reach (FA I.14:60). The dancing girl, by contrast, remains on the tips of his fingers, thus seemingly immediately within reach: "But because she pleased me so much," recounts the narrator, "I believed that I could finally catch her, and I thought that I would be skilled enough to grab her" ("Da sie mir aber gar so wohl gefiel, glaubte ich sie endlich haschen zu können und dachte geschickt genug zuzugreifen"; FA I.14:60). But in the moment that he tries to seize her, he feels "a blow to his head" and falls down unconscious, after which he awakens from his dream (FA I.14:60). Each act of imaginative play within the dream, then, is marked by a tension between a moment of assimilation and one of disruption, whereby the very figures that the protagonist creates through his symbolic play resist being assimilated.

This alternation between assimilation and disruption recurs in the climactic scene of the fairy tale. The day after he awakens from his dream, the protagonist eventually finds himself inside a circular, walled park. At its center is a garden house where he encounters the three women from his dream as well as the dancing girl, whose name he learns is Alerte. After he listens to their music, dances with Alerte, and feasts on fruit that she serves him, Alerte announces, "Now we want to play" (FA I.14:68). She brings him to another room, which contains a rich collection of toys: "It looked like a Christmas fair in there, except that such costly and fine articles have never been seen in a Christmas booth. There were all kinds of dolls, doll clothes, and doll furniture for kitchens, living rooms, and shops; and there were individual playthings in great numbers" (FA I.14:68). Ironically, given the boy's predilection for *Puppen*, Alerte doesn't choose the dolls, claiming, "I know that that's nothing for you" (FA I.14:68). She also rejects the construction toys, which she says she doesn't find entertaining, and instead selects something "that will please both you and me equally" (FA I.14:68). This turns out to be two sets of toy soldiers on horseback, with which they play a game of war (Amazons versus Greeks) on a drawbridge made of interlocking golden weapons, and using polished agate marbles as ammunition. The game that they play is a "regelmäßige[s] Spiel," that is, a game governed by rules (FA I.14:70); thus, they agree to throw from "a certain distance" and expressly stipulate "that we were not to throw with any greater force than was needed to knock the figures over: for none was to be damaged" (FA I.14:69). However, their battle nevertheless escalates to the point where the protagonist throws the marbles with such force at his opponent's cavalry that several of her figures, including the queen, burst into pieces. Even though the shattered figures reconstitute themselves, come to life, and gallop away, Alerte, deeply upset,

> suddenly jumped up and gave me such a box on the ear that my head rang. I had always heard it said that a girl's ear-boxing must be

> repaid with a rough kiss; therefore I grabbed hold of her by the ears and kissed her repeatedly. She, however, uttered such a piercing scream that I myself was startled and let her go, and this was fortunate, for in that very moment, I don't know what happened to me.
>
> [sprang auf mich los und gab mir eine Ohrfeige, daß mir der Kopf summte. Ich, der ich immer gehört hatte, auf die Ohrfeige eines Mädchens gehöre ein derber Kuß, faßte sie bei den Ohren und küßte sie zu wiederholten Malen. Sie aber tat einen solchen durchdringenden Schrei, der mich selbst erschreckte; ich ließ sie fahren, und das war mein Glück: denn in dem Augenblick wußte ich nicht wie mir geschah.]
>
> (FA I.14:70)

The protagonist awakens from his state of unconsciousness at the foot of a linden tree, where he has been catapulted by the drawbridge that is raised after Alerte's scream.

Despite the fact that Alerte pointedly passes up the opportunity to play with dolls in order to play a game with rules, she and the protagonist never in fact leave the realm of symbolic play behind. Hence, the toy soldiers, especially when they come to life ("auch zugleich völlig lebendig wurden"; FA I.14:69–70), recall the boy's puppets, which, as noted above, were given to him "to bring to life dramatically" ("zu eigner . . . dramatischer Belebung"; FA I.14:20). In this scene, then, symbolic play does not give way to rule-bound play, as Piaget maintains, but rather remains closely enmeshed with it. Nor does the players' egocentrism diminish, as evident in the "great self-satisfaction" ("großer Selbstzufriedenheit") with which they both review their armies before the start of their game (FA I.14:69). Indeed, as their competition escalates beyond the ground rules that they have established, the protagonist's assimilatory desire reaches a violent peak when he grabs hold of Alerte's ears and repeatedly kisses her. In the face of this assault, Alerte is far from passive: she delivers the "piercing scream" that frightens the protagonist, who immediately lets her go. The expression that the narrator uses—"ich ließ sie fahren"—recalls the one used by Wilhelm when he describes how he let his puppet drop ("fallen ließ"). The difference, of course, is that in the case of the fairy tale, it is not chance, but rather Alerte's active intervention that causes the protagonist to release her. In short, the pattern of assimilation and active disruption that we noted in the protagonist's dream recurs at the climax of the fairy tale.[37]

Goethe experiments in "The New Paris" with the possibility of a second-order transformation: that is to say, not only the transformation of one thing into the symbol of another, but the transformation of this symbol into a symbol for what *is* other, for that which resists the process of assimilation to the ego. In this connection, the name Alerte is telling: it is a near anagram of the Latin *altera*, or "other," as in the principle codified in Roman law, *audiatur et altera pars*, or "listen to the other side," the very principle that, as Goethe recalls in Book One of his autobiography, is inscribed on the wall of the Frankfurt Römer in the saying, "One man's speech / Is no man's speech: / One should hear them both equally" ("Eines Manns Rede / Ist keines Manns Rede: / Man soll sie billig hören Beede"; FA I.14:25). The second-order symbol cannot entirely escape the egocentric logic of the first-order symbol; indeed, it can even heighten the protagonist's desire to assimilate the other, as when the protagonist responds to Alerte's ear-boxing by grabbing hold of her ears and kissing her, thereby (temporarily) silencing her. Nevertheless, the second-order symbol makes it possible for the protagonist to conceive of the other as other, and not merely as an object to be assimilated to the self.

In contrast to the first-order symbolic transformation, the second-order transformation entails a high degree of self-consciousness, of attentiveness to the egocentrism of symbolic play. Given its self-reflexiveness, it is perhaps more aptly called narcissism, a term that is intimated in the fairy tale's prelude by virtue of the fact that the protagonist is regarding himself in the mirror, and that later in the fairy tale is explicitly articulated by a bird in the walled garden that calls out, "Narcissus, Narcissus, as clearly as only a schoolboy can pronounce it" (FA I.14:62). Alexander Mathäs has convincingly shown that the foundations of the Freudian discourse of narcissism were laid in the late eighteenth century by German writers such as Goethe, Herder, Schiller, and Moritz.[38] He maintains that within the context of this discourse, "narcissism refers to the creation of an idealized image of the self and the desire to merge with this image" (13). According to Mathäs, Goethe and many other writers of the period attempt to distinguish the search for this "whole, inner Self" (29) "from vain egocentrism" that is coded as feminine (19), leading to "the emergence of a male narcissistic aesthetics that reveals fears of feminine intrusion" (20). In "The New Paris," Goethe does indeed distinguish the egocentrism of the first-order symbolic transformation from the narcissism of the second-order transformation. In addition, his fairy tale certainly expresses a fear of "feminine intrusion" (Alerte's repeated violent blows and her "piercing scream"). However, the self that his fairy tale envisions is precisely not characterized by wholeness; the egocentric self is not disavowed, but rather recognized as an ineluctable part of an internally differentiated, self-observing self. Thus, while Goethe's fairy tale, along with its surrounding frame narrative, partially fit into the larger discourse of narcissism around 1800 that, according to Mathäs, Goethe himself helped to establish, it also subverts that very discourse.

Goethe's fairy tale also fits uncomfortably into the more particular discourse of narcissism that took shape in Romantic literature for and about children. According to Hans-Heino Ewers, the Romantic idealization of the child (which Goethe's *Werther* helped inspire) necessitated a new form of children's literature that no longer sought to educate but rather to entertain its young audience by instantiating the "purposelessness of pure play."[39] Ludwig Tieck, writing in *Fantasies about Art* (*Phantasien über die Kunst*, 1799), was among the first Romantics to promote this new understanding of the child: "We don't know how to accept that these figures [i.e., children] sit with us around the font of life and do nothing other than regard themselves therein."[40] Ewers argues that much of Romantic children's literature (such as the fairy tales of the Brothers Grimm) consequently conceives of itself primarily as "a medium for children's self-contemplation and self-enjoyment."[41] To an extent, Goethe portrays his fairy tale in precisely this manner, as evident in his description of the delight that the boy and his companions take in "those fairy-tale-like, self-contented dreams . . . , in which we—I inventing, and my playmates participating—lost ourselves only too happily" ("jenen märchenhaften, selbstgefälligen Träumen . . . , in die wir uns, ich erfindend und meine Gespielen teilnehmend, nur allzugern verloren"; FA I.14:74). However, Goethe further shows their self-contentment to be disrupted both from without and from within. Much as the puppet performance was disrupted earlier in Book Two by the older audience, so the boy and his friends are "awakened" from their "self-contented dreams" by the other boys, "who took pleasure in attacking us with raw mischief" (FA I.14:74). But even prior to this external disturbance, the companions' "self-contented dreams" are challenged from within the fairy tale itself by the figure of Alerte, in whose name alertness or wakefulness is inscribed; thus, she brings the dream comprising the prelude to an abrupt end when she delivers a blow to the protagonist, the figure with whom the boy's friends identify.[42] "The New Paris," then, does indeed function as "a medium of children's self-contemplation," but it does so not only as a medium of self-enjoyment but also as one of self-critique, challenging the very self-contentment that it fosters.

Book Two of *Poetry and Truth* stands in a similarly complex relation to the discourse of symbolic play as it came to be systematized by Piaget. On the one hand, we have seen how, together with Moritz's *Anton Reiser* and Goethe's own *Wilhelm Meister*, Goethe's autobiography helped originate the notion of egocentric, symbolic play that underpins Piaget's account. Contrary to Piaget's developmental model, however, *Poetry and Truth* reveals that egocentrism doesn't cede to cooperation in social play (such as theatrical play), but instead exerts itself all the more strongly, leading to hegemonic power or to conflict. In this regard, Book Two of Goethe's autobiography more closely anticipates the work of Sutton-Smith, for whom play "begins as a mutation of real conflicts and functions thusly forever afterwards."[43] At the same time, "The New Paris" suggests that the genre of the fairy tale can embody an alternative form of symbolic play, or symbolic play of the second order. In transforming egocentrism into narcissism, it begins to recognize and to push against the limits of its own symbolic play. That is, while freely assimilating "things to one another and everything to the ego,"[44] it keeps trying to listen to the other side, even if it may ultimately be unable to break on through. The path from egocentric to social play in "The New Paris" continually loops back upon itself. These narcissistic twists and turns complicate the sharp dichotomy between the egocentric and the social as drawn by Piaget. In observing its own egocentric play, as well as taking note of how others observe it, Goethe's narcissistic fairy tale makes it possible to conceive of a form of social play that contests egocentric play both from without and from within. Precisely because social play is composed of these acts of contestation, egocentric play remains its indispensable precondition, without which it could never be imagined.

NOTES

I wish to express my thanks to Edgar Landgraf and Fritz Breithaupt for their many helpful comments on earlier drafts of this essay.

1. According to Gareth Mathews and Amy Mullin, "It is . . . the work of Jean Piaget that has been most influential on the way psychologists, educators, and even philosophers have come to think about the cognitive development of children." Gareth Mathews and Amy Mullin, "The Philosophy of Childhood," in *The Stanford Encyclopedia of Philosophy* (Spring 2015 Edition), ed. Edward N. Zalta, https://plato.stanford.edu/archives/spr2015/entries/childhood/.

2. Jürgen Habermas, *The Theory of Communicative Action*, trans. Thomas McCarthy (Boston: Beacon, 1985), 1:69. Original emphasis.

3. Jean Piaget, *Play, Dreams and Imitation in Childhood*, trans. C. Gattegno and F. M. Hodgson (New York: W. W. Norton, 1962), 118. As Thomas Henricks notes, "Piaget offers perhaps the best-known theory of how play exemplifies—and contributes to—personal

development." Thomas Henricks, *Play and the Human Condition* (Urbana: University of Illinois Press, 2015), 91.

4. Jean Piaget, *Judgment and Reasoning in the Child*, trans. Marjorie Warden (Paterson, NJ: Littlefield, Adams, 1964), 199. Piaget refers to Kant as "the father of us all." See Jean Piaget, *Insights and Illusions of Philosophy*, trans. Wolfe Mays (New York: World, 1971), 220, as well as 56–58 for a discussion of Kantian epistemology. Piaget notes "a clear parallel between Hegelian dialectic and psychogenesis," but portrays this congruence as "a pure convergence without influence because, unfortunately, I have not yet read Hegel." Cited in Thomas Kesserling, "The Mind's Staircase Revisited," in *The Cambridge Companion to Piaget*, ed. Ulrich Müller, Jeremy I. M. Carpendale, and Leslie Smith (Cambridge: Cambridge University Press, 2009), 372. See also Piaget's discussion of Hegel in *Insights and Illusions*, 58–59.

5. Throughout this essay, I use the terms "symbolic" and "symbol" as defined by Piaget, not in the sense in which Goethe uses them when he contrasts symbol and allegory.

6. See, for example, Ludwig Tieck's "The Elves" ("Die Elfen," 1812), E.T.A. Hoffmann's "Nutcracker and the King of Mice" ("Nußknacker und Mausekönig," 1816) and "The Strange Child" ("Das fremde Kind," 1817), Clemens Brentano's *Gockel, Hinkel und Gackeleia* (*Gockel, Hinkel and Gackeleia*, 1838), and many of Hans Christian Andersen's tales, including "The Elder-Tree Mother" ("Hyldemoer," 1844).

7. See in particular Karl Groos, *The Play of Man*, trans. with the author's cooperation by Elizabeth L. Baldwin (New York: D. Appleton, 1919), 131–144.

8. Brian Sutton-Smith, "Piaget on Play: A Critique," *Psychological Review*, no. 1 (1966): 104.

9. Piaget, *Judgment and Reasoning*, 201–202. For a fuller overview of Piaget's psychology of play, see Richard De Lisi, "Piaget's Sympathetic but Unromantic Account of Children's Play," in *The Handbook of the Study of Play*, vol. 1, ed. James E. Johnson, Scott G. Eberle, and Thomas S. Henricks (New York: Rowman & Littlefield, 2015).

10. Piaget, *Play, Dreams and Imitation*, 168.

11. Brian Sutton-Smith offers a penetrating critique of Piaget's distinction between play and intelligent activity. In contrast to Piaget, Sutton-Smith argues that "play might well be taken as a very positive illustration of the thinking process because it involves the construction of symbols to create new conceptual domains." Sutton-Smith, "Piaget on Play," 110.

12. Karl Groos uses the term "assimilation" in a strikingly similar way to explicate what he calls "constructive fantasy": "The psychic process which transforms a piece of wood into a doll's milk-bottle, a few chips stuck up into men and trees, a cloud into the greatest variety of faces, animals, etc. . . . —all this is synthetic activity which may quite as well be called assimilation as constructive imagination." Groos, *Play of Man*, 137. I have slightly modified the translation to more closely correspond with the original German.

13. In his essay "The Role of Play in Development" (1933), the Russian developmental psychologist Lev Vygotsky disputes Piaget's assertion of the freedom of symbolic play, an assertion that Vygotsky traces back to Goethe: "Goethe's contention that in play any thing can be anything for a child is incorrect." Lev Vygotsky, "The Role of Play in Development," in *Mind in Society: The Development of Higher Psychological Processes*, ed. Michael Cole et al. (Cambridge, MA: Harvard University Press, 1978), 98. This contention, which I discuss in the next section, is actually made by Goethe's protagonist Wilhelm Meister. However indirectly, Vygotsky appears to be the first to connect Piaget's notion of symbolic play with

Goethe's bildungsroman. Yet, he seems to have been unaware of the ways in which Goethe's writings on play also undercut Piaget's ideas, and to a certain extent prefigure his own, for instance, his observation that imaginative play continues to underlie rule-bound play (95).

14. It is not difficult to see here the appeal of Piaget's theory for Habermas, who echoes Piaget's language when he asserts, "Fundamental to the paradigm of mutual understanding is . . . the performative attitude of participants in interaction, who coordinate their plans for action by coming to an understanding about something in the world." Jürgen Habermas, *The Philosophical Discourse of Modernity: Twelve Lectures*, trans. Frederick G. Lawrence (Cambridge, MA: MIT Press, 1987), 296.

15. Jean Piaget, *The Moral Judgment of the Child*, trans. Marjorie Gabain (New York: Free Press Paperbacks, 1997), 37.

16. Piaget, *Moral Judgment*, 27–28.

17. Jean Piaget, "Response to Brian Sutton-Smith," *Psychological Review* 73, no. 1 (1966): 112.

18. Johann Wolfgang von Goethe, *Sämtliche Werke: Briefe, Tagebücher und Gespräche* [=FA], ed. Friedmar Apel et al. (Frankfurt am Main: Deutscher Klassiker Verlag, 1985–2013), I.8:58. (All references to the *Frankfurter Ausgabe* of Goethe's works include the division (*Abteilung*) in Roman numerals followed by the volume and page numbers in Arabic numerals.) In defense of his noninstructional play with the children, Werther pointedly bypasses the Enlightenment pedagogues, and refers to "the golden words of the teacher of humanity," namely, Jesus: "unless you become like one of them!" Edgar Landgraf cogently argues that Werther's narcissistic "'childishness' challenges eighteenth-century ideas that view the identification with social norms and responsibility as appropriate male behavior." Edgar Landgraf, "*Werther*'s Sentimental Narcissism: Consciousness, Communication, and the Origin of the Modern Psyche," in *The Self as Muse: Narcissism and Creativity in the German Imagination, 1750–1830*, ed. Alexander Mathäs (Lewisburg, PA: Bucknell University Press, 2011), 125.

19. FA I.9:382. I have adapted the translation of *Wilhelm Meister's Years of Apprenticeship* by Eric A. Blackall for purposes of emphasis and accuracy. See Johann Wolfgang von Goethe, *Wilhelm Meister's Apprenticeship*, ed. and trans. Eric A. Blackall in cooperation with Victor Lange, vol. 9 of *Goethe's Collected Works*, edited by Victor Lange, Eric A. Blackall, and Cyrus Hamlin (New York: Suhrkamp, 1983).

20. Piaget, *Play, Dreams, and Imitation*, 112.

21. Jean Piaget, *The Language and Thought of the Child*, trans. Marjorie and Ruth Gabain (London: Routledge, 2002), 18, 8.

22. On the etymological relation between "Marion/Marian" and "marionette," see the entry "marionette" in the *Oxford English Dictionary*, accessed August 3, 2018, http://www.oed.com.libproxy.vassar.edu/view/Entry/114139?redirectedFrom=marionette#eid.

23. Johan Huizinga, *Homo Ludens: A Study of the Play Element in Culture* (New York: Roy, 1950), 11. Cited in Thomas Pfau, "*Bildungsspiele*: Vicissitudes of Socialization in *Wilhelm Meister's Apprenticeship*," *European Romantic Review* 21, no. 5 (October 2010): 574.

24. Pfau, "*Bildungsspiele*," 574.

25. The assertion of power is already suggested in the military symbolism of two of the prime examples of symbolic play cited by Wilhelm: "a stick becomes a gun, a little piece of wood a sword" (FA I.9:28). It is also suggested by the maker of the marionette theater,

a man who is only known by his military grade, lieutenant—that is, literally, one who takes the place of another, just as, in symbolic play, one object (or person) substitutes for another.

26. Piaget, *Play, Dreams and Imitation*, 139.

27. Johann Wolfgang von Goethe, "Frauenrollen auf dem römischen Theater durch Männer gespielt," *Der deutsche Merkur* (November 1778): 100. In this essay, Goethe reflects on the Roman theatrical practice of men playing female roles, a practice that he traces back (phylogenetically) to ancient tradition, and (ontogenetically) to children's propensity for cross-dressing. Even the best actor falls slightly short of his ambition to perfectly imitate women (for example, due to the deepness of his voice). Rather than ruining the performance, however, this bodily recalcitrance instead contributes to the audience's "double pleasure": a delight in the illusion, and a delight in the consciousness of the illusion. In many respects, then, Goethe's description of Wilhelm's interrupted marionette performance resonates with this essay of 1788. Both the essay and the scene in the novel anticipate Romantic irony, particularly the phenomenon that Peter Szondi identifies in Ludwig Tieck's comedies as the "transposition of self-consciousness to the aesthetic realm." Peter Szondi, "Friedrich Schlegel and Romantic Irony, with Some Remarks on Tieck's Comedies," in *On Textual Understanding and Other Essays*, trans. Harvey Mendelsohn (Minneapolis: University of Minnesota Press, 1986), 71.

28. Jane K. Brown, *Goethe's Allegories of Identity* (Philadelphia: University of Pennsylvania Press, 2014), 98.

29. Goethe thus recalls, "We ordinarily spent our free hours with Grandmother, whose spacious quarters afforded us plenty of room for our games" (FA I.14:16). All translations from *Poetry and Truth* are my own, though I have consulted and borrowed from the translation by Robert Heitner. Johann Wolfgang von Goethe, *From My Life: Poetry and Truth; Parts One to Three*, trans. Robert Heitner and ed. Thomas P. Saine and Jeffrey L. Sammons, vol. 4 of *Goethe's Collected Works*, ed. Victor Lange, Eric A. Blackall, and Cyrus Hamlin (New York: Suhrkamp, 1983).

30. FA I.14:20.

31. FA I.9:380.

32. Brian Sutton-Smith, "Play Theory: A Personal Journey and New Thoughts," *American Journal of Play* 1, no. 1 (Summer 2008): 91.

33. Piaget, *Judgment and Reasoning*, 216.

34. In suggesting that the telling of fairy tales constitutes a form of play, Goethe places himself in a tradition that extends back to the sixteenth century. Michele Rak has documented that storytelling—including, increasingly, the telling of fairy tales—was performed in the sixteenth and seventeenth centuries as a literary and theatrical game at courts "from Naples to Paris," and gradually spread throughout society. Michele Rak, "Logic of Fairies," *Romanic Review* 99, no. 3–4 (May–November 2008): 308. The frame narrative of one of the first collections of fairy tales, Giambattista Basile's *The Tale of Tales, or Entertainment for Little Ones* (also known as the *Pentamerone*, 1634–1636), situates its storytelling precisely in the context of the "thousand games" played at court. Giambattista Basile, *The Tale of Tales, or Entertainment for Little Ones*, trans. Nancy L. Canepa (New York: Penguin Books, 2016), 123. Basile's *Pentamerone* was being discovered and adapted in Germany by Clemens Brentano in the years 1805–11, that is to say, immediately prior to and during the composition of the first part of Goethe's *Poetry and Truth*.

35. On the connection between playing and dreaming, see Piaget, *Play, Dreams and Imitation*, 169–212. According to Piaget, "children's dreams are a continuation of symbolic play" (176), albeit with a greater tendency toward "secondary" (or unconscious) symbolism (180).

36. Wilhelm thus recalls imagining as a child "how wonderful it would be if with my own fingers I could bring the figures to life" (FA I.9:18).

37. In an insightful and detailed reading of "The New Paris" within the context of a broader analysis of Goethe's *Poetry and Truth*, Gabriele Blod argues that Goethe underscores that the protagonist's and Alerte's game, with its "collision of selfish wishes" ("Aufeinanderprallen der eigensüchtigen Wünsche"), is emphatically a children's game, and that it is consequently only a "preliminary stage of a more mature form of play" ("eine Vorstufe zu einer reiferen Form des Spiels"). Gabriele Blod, *"Lebensmärchen": Goethes "Dichtung und Wahrheit" als poetischer und poetologischer Text* (Würzburg: Königshausen & Neumann, 2003), 140. However, as I argue in this essay, Goethe's fairy tale (together with the narrative in Book Two in which it is embedded) challenges precisely such a smooth developmental narrative.

38. Alexander Mathäs, *Narcissism and Paranoia in the Age of Goethe* (Newark: University of Delaware Press, 2008), 14. Particularly in illuminating what he terms secondary (i.e., unconscious) symbolism, Piaget engages substantially with Freudian thought, including his theory of narcissism. Piaget, *Play, Dreams and Imitation*, 169–212.

39. Hans-Heino Ewers, introduction to *Kinder- und Jugendliteratur der Romantik: Eine Textsammlung*, ed. Hans-Heino Ewers (Stuttgart: Reclam, 1984), 38. This and subsequent translations of passages from Ewers's introduction are my own.

40. Cited in Ewers, Introduction, 38.

41. Ewers, Introduction, 39. In their preface to the first volume of the *Children's and Household Tales* (*Kinder- und Hausmärchen*), which appeared in 1812, a year after the publication of the first part of Goethe's *Poetry and Truth*, the Brothers Grimm note that their tales "are suffused with the same purity that makes children appear so wondrous and blessed to us: they have the same bluish-white, flawless, shining eyes (that small children so love to grab at)." Jacob Grimm and Wilhelm Grimm, "Preface to Volume I of the First Edition of *Children's Stories and Household Tales*," in *The Annotated Brothers Grimm*, trans. and ed. Maria Tatar (New York: W. W. Norton, 2004), 402. The child recipient of fairy tales, then, sees her or his own gaze reflected back in them.

42. Goethe thus writes of his friends that "they especially loved it when I told stories in the first person, and took great pleasure in the fact that such marvelous things could have happened to me, their playmate" (FA I.14:58).

43. Sutton-Smith, "Play Theory," 122.

44. Piaget, *Play, Dreams and Imitation*, 87.

CHAPTER SIX

Playthings

Goethe's Favorite Toys

PATRICIA ANNE SIMPSON

GOETHE'S LIFE, WORK, and legacy have had an impact on national—and transnational—narratives about toys, play, and human nature. Often elevated as an exemplary figure, Goethe takes center stage in a range of studies that honor his contributions to transatlantic cultural legacies, to education, and to the development of genius. In many ways, transnational portrayals of Goethe as a cultural icon established his exemplarity—yet there are many Goethes, instrumentalized for as many purposes. Alongside his poetic production, Goethe's relationship to play attracted attention in his contemporary context, and in the transatlantic world especially in the early twentieth century. His relationship to play via parenting also reorients Goethe's legacy, creating tension between his purported exemplarity and potential eccentricity.[1] Goethe plays darkly; in his parenting, poetics, and politics, he relies on the repetitive temporalities that perform and destroy in the same gesture. In this chapter, I examine Goethe as a player, parent, and poet, in the context of contemporary theories and practices of play and through the lens of material culture and its predominant theorists. Goethe's complex relationship to toys reveals the darker side to play, one that departs from prevailing notions of play in terms of purpose, pedagogy, and innocent experience; it differs markedly from that of Friedrich Schiller as elaborated in his aesthetic letters. Finally, gendered behaviors and the agency of parental regulation of play connect this analysis with Goethe's family romance. Reliance on material culture and reference to pedagogical theory frame my case-study approach to "favorite toys"—not necessarily the puppet theater of his youth, nor the broken crockery of his autobiography—

that ultimately reveal the historical unconscious, embedded in traumatic histories and narratives, of Goethe's favorite things.

In terms derived from Fredric Jameson's early work, I claim there is a political unconscious not only inscribed in Goethe's literary texts but also evident in material objects. Jameson's purpose, to read literary texts according to the imperative "Always historicize!"[2] advances a Marxist model of interpretation; indeed, material culture gains legitimacy through commodity-based analyses. Goethe's relationship to play further reorients his legacy, creating tension between his seemingly irreconcilable attributes. In different ways, these biographical and textual properties of Goethe and his legacy further inscribe stories about the relationship between generations and geographies, between material culture and migration stories. Toys bear witness to history, shape identity, and do the heavy lifting in mimetic play. Historian Leora Auslander, in her seminal essay "Beyond Words," makes the point with crystalline clarity: material objects are not only "the product of history, they are also active agents in history. In their communicative, performative, emotive, and expressive capacities, they act, have effects in the world."[3] Her claim advances a discourse inaugurated by Arjun Appadurai, whose *Social Life of Things* (1988) broke ground, laying a foundation for the examination of material objects in their social contexts, arguing that objects circulate in "different *regimes of value*."[4] The focus on objects as the agents of history invites a more diversified theoretical framework, for which I invoke Walter Benjamin's work on toys. In his review of Karl Gröber's monumental book, Benjamin elaborates a model of interpretation that accommodates my reading of Goethe the player both as a parent and as a poet. Benjamin writes,

> Last, such a study would have to explore the great law that presides over the rules and rhythms of the entire world of play: the law of repetition. We know that for a child repetition is the soul of play, that nothing gives him greater pleasure than to "Do it again!" The obscure urge to repeat things is scarcely less powerful in play, scarcely less cunning in its workings, than the sexual impulse in love.[5]

> [Endlich hätte eine solche Studie dem großen Gesetz nachzugehen, daß über allen einzelnen Regeln und Rhythmen die ganze Welt der Spiele regiert: dem Gesetze der Wiederholung. Wir wissen, daß sie

> dem Kind die Seele des Spiels ist; daß nichts es mehr beglückt, als "noch einmal." Der dunkle Drang nach Wiederholung ist hier im Spiel kaum minder gewaltig, kaum minder durchtrieben am Werke als in der Liebe der Geschlechtstrieb.][6]

He seeks rapprochement between collective and individual stakeholders in early twentieth-century European play practices. The connection to the Freudian model of repetition in child's play, read through the lens of material culture and mimetic play, provides a framework for understanding the darker side of two favorite toys: the miniature guillotine and the yo-yo. In the former, it behooves us to recall that Goethe himself had a role in deciding executions.[7] Additionally, he chose to experience the battlefield and induce cannon fever, yet, through the approbation of playing with particular toys, he proves capable of dissociating from these memories as traumatic—and these decisions impact parenting. The yo-yo, in contrast, embodies the heart of the poet and partner in a love poem that turns out to reiterate, rather than eschew, bourgeois masculine subjectivity and desire. The metonymic relationships between toys and their historical antecedents, mediated by Goethe's biography as a parent, poet, sexual and conversation partner, and diplomat, ground the argument of this chapter. These "toys" represent significant historical links among trauma, migration, and toys in the *Goethezeit*. To connect these complex relationships, I first outline theories of play that foreground the proximity of pleasure and regulatory responses to performative play, a mode that posits a causal logic between childhood practice and adult behavior. Goethe's multilayered responses to play as performance invite closer examination, for the tensions revealed in his various roles as poet, political operative, son, parent, and not least, cultural icon are central to his transnational legacy, poised between exemplarity and eccentricity.

Play, positioned at the nexus of pedagogy and pleasure, is subject to regulation as it mediates the relationship between mind and body, socially constructed and natural environments, *puer ludens* and *homo ludens*. This contrast inevitably invokes a seminal study of play, Johan Huizinga's *Homo Ludens: A Study of the Play Element in Culture* (1944), which represents one significant scholarly contribution to the categorization of human beings not only as *homo faber*, man the maker, but also man at play.[8] Thomas Henricks draws attention to Huizinga's contribution to an understanding that "civilization, at least in its earliest stages, is performed or played."[9] This expansive view of performative play encompasses the creative impulses associated with poetry, music, and dance. Few studies, Huizinga's included, examine the childhood experiences of play from a historical viewpoint, a condition attributable in part to the reliance on found objects, reconstructions from literature, the visual arts, clothing, the decorative arts, and extant books and diaries.[10] Since the period of European Romanticism, childhood has been subject to more generous treatment—at least in theory and the realm of representation—in partial response to the dominance of middle-class values embedded in religious identity, the protection and privilege of the domestic sphere, and the gendered investment, literal and figurative, in family legacies. Similarly, advocates of childhood as a discrete phase of human development, worthy of cultivation, acknowledge play as central. Jean Paul Friedrich Richter manifests this type of thinking in emphasizing the importance of love, specifically parental love, in raising the young: "Love is more clear to children than understanding and more easily imitated—why not always love?" ("Liebe ist den Kindern deutlicher als Verstand und mimischer—warum nicht immer Liebe?").[11] Virtuoso defenses of childhood innocence tangle with undeniable cruelty and harshness in private and public spheres alike. A probe beneath the surface playlands of psychologically complex nineteenth-century children's literature reveals turbulence and trauma. Antidote to a popularized notion of childhood as sacred and sequestered, Lloyd deMause, embarking on a pioneer path to study the history of childhood in a coalition of professional historians, some with a psychoanalytic frame of reference, introduces the topic with blunt-force trauma: "The history of childhood is a nightmare from which we have only recently begun to awaken. The further back in history one goes, the lower the level of child care, and the more likely children are to be killed, abandoned, beaten, terrorized, and sexually abused. It is our task here to see how much of this childhood history can be recaptured from the evidence that remains to us."[12] The multiple contributors to his edited volume cover topics that include infanticide, castration, swaddling, and breast-feeding; and a time span from antiquity to the late nineteenth century. However, a less expansive approach garners insights into the existence and stakes of competing discourses about childhood innocence and inculcation of guilt prior to the sentimentalization of the young. These debates assume a moral patina about the purpose of play and the objects that accompany or regulate it. Toys, as accessories of the play world, figure prominently in discourses about the historical, ethical, and national stories about the relationship between childhood and adult identities.

PERFORMATIVE PLAY

German-speaking Europe has contributed significantly to the production of practical and theoretical essentials of play in ways that have become so naturalized that we overlook them. Goethe's relationship to play provides insight into that cultural tradition. Since the emergence of guilds and cottage industries, cities and centers such as Nuremberg, Sonneberg, and the Harz Mountains (*Erzgebirge*) have engaged in small-scale and mass manufacturing that dominated the global toy market through World War I.[13] Additionally, a cadre of play theorists create a communicative network attuned to the purpose and pedagogies of play. In 1790, Immanuel Kant, in his *Critique of Judgement*, defined the play act in conjunction with aesthetic judgment, with specific reference to the premise: "play, i.e. an occupation that is agreeable on its own account," in contrast to labor, "which on its own account is disagreeable."[14]

Friedrich Schiller, who in part popularized Kant's philosophies, devotes significant attention to the human aspect of play in his *The Aesthetic Education of Man in a Series of Letters* (*Die ästhetische Erziehung des Menschen, in einer Reihe von Briefen*). In 1794, Schiller engages further with Kant's aesthetics and the French Revolution and its aftermath in his attempt to understand the concept of the play drive in terms of affect / sensuousness and rationality as a totality. In aesthetic play, human beings become human. He writes:

> So the play impulse, in which both combine to function, will compel the mind at once morally and physically; it will therefore, since it annuls all mere chance, annul all compulsion also, and set man free both physically and morally. When we embrace with passion someone who deserves our contempt, we feel painfully the compulsion of Nature. When we are unfriendly disposed toward another who commands our respect, we feel painfully the compulsion of Reason. But as soon as a man has at once enlisted our affection and gained our respect, both the constraint of feeling and the constraint of Nature disappear, and we begin to love him—that is, to play at once with our affection and with our respect.[15]
>
> [Der Spieltrieb also, als in welchem beide verbunden wirken, wird das Gemüth zugleich moralisch und physisch nöthigen; er wird also, weil er alle Zufälligkeit aufhebt, auch alle Nöthigung aufheben und den Menschen sowohl physisch als moralisch in Freiheit

> setzen. Wenn wir Jemand mit Leidenschaft umfassen, der unsrer Verachtung würdig ist, so empfinden wir peinlich die *Nöthigung der Natur*. Wenn wir gegen einen Andern feindlich gesinnt sind, der uns Achtung abnöthigt, so empfinden wir peinlich die *Nöthigung der Vernunft*. So bald er aber zugleich unsre Neigung interessiert und unsre Achtung sich erworben, so verschwindet sowohl der Zwang der Empfindung als der Zwang der Vernunft, und wir fangen an, ihn zu lieben, d. h., zugleich mit unsrer Neigung und mit unsrer Achtung zu spielen.][16]

Between the sensuous and the formal drives, Schiller's play impulse originates. Yet the drive and its reception develop away from actual play. In the Fifteenth Letter, Schiller qualifies the sphere of play drive's influence: "Certainly we must not here call to mind those games that are in vogue in actual life, and which are commonly concerned only with very material objects; but in actual life we should also seek in vain for the Beauty of which we are now speaking. The Beauty we actually meet with is worthy of the play impulse we actually meet with; but with the ideal of Beauty which Reason sets up, an ideal of the play impulse is also presented which Man should have before him in all his games" (*On the Aesthetic Education of Man*, 79). Here, Schiller's explicit and Goethe's implicit theory of human play and games diverge: connections between the aesthetic realm and lightness of play are at stake. The former artist is unconcerned with games currently in vogue; Goethe, as I demonstrate, participates directly and indirectly in toy trends, especially when real and material objects are a factor. Much has been written about Schiller's letters: his writings and interpretation of Kant, along with Kant himself, serve as the source for a plural philosophical legacy that connects play with the aesthetic, which I examine before returning to Goethe's eccentric path.

Herbert Marcuse's *Eros and Civilization* offers an example of this persistent philosophical legacy. Marcuse foregrounds the second half of the eighteenth century as the period in which Kant's philosophy stabilized the definition of the aesthetic.[17] In general terms, the aesthetic, and by extension in my reading, play, is not only connected to a feeling of pleasure and a cognitive faculty; rather, Marcuse concludes, the aesthetic dimension emerges "as its *center*, the medium through which nature becomes susceptible to freedom, necessity to autonomy."[18] From autonomy to nature, play is thought to regulate the experience of being human. Yet Goethe, in the example of his life and work, parents and plays toward different ends. A selective yet holistic model of Goethe at play offers an alternative to Schiller's dominant connection between the aesthetic and the beautiful. In two case studies of his "favorite toys," I will demonstrate the connections between Goethe's investment in history and leisure activities, making legible their embeddedness in the darker side of imaginative, repetitive, and imitative play. The darker side further informs the dissemination of a nationalized reception of an exemplary Goethe, at the expense of his playful eccentricity.

THE GUILLOTINE

Few challenges prove more vexing in contemporary childhood studies than generating reliable data about the correlation among children's toys, play practices, and predispositions to violence. While many acknowledge the connection among play, cognitive and social development, and learned and/or performed gender traits, there is little consensus on the issue of childhood development and a causality factor of toy weapons. A cursory Google search yields mostly questions. For example, *WebMD* asks, do toy guns lead to real-life violence?—the answer, in this instance, is a levelheaded "no."[19] The contemporary German context produces varying results: "killer games really do damage" ("Killerspiele schaden doch") and "Potsdam psychologists conducted numerous studies. The result: There is a direct connection between intensive playing of violent computer games and aggression."[20] High-profile acts of violence or aberrance tend to usher in such studies and headlines, yet the existence of direct cause-effect and/or play-criminal behavior relationship inspires staunch and opposing arguments.

By the same token, social psychologists have conducted extensive studies, concluding that expectations in play supervisors and gender-typed toys can influence children's development in ways different than gender-neutral objects.[21] When we ask a different question about toys, mimetic play, and learned behavior, we get a different answer, one that suggests causality. Even if there is no demonstrable cause-effect relationship among the material objects of mimetic and imaginative play and learned behavior, discourses and controversy persist about the ability of play and its accessories to shape adult agency and identity. Nor are these discourses confined to the present.

The image of the guillotine was certainly familiar from the print press as an instrument of execution and horror (figure 6.1); French prisoners held captive in English prisons carved "models" from bone and other material (figure 6.2).[22] The toy trended in 1793 and 1794, which inspired contempt and dismay in Goethe's mother (figure 6.3), an issue with repercussions for the legacy of Goethe in the world. The materiality of the mechanical toy,

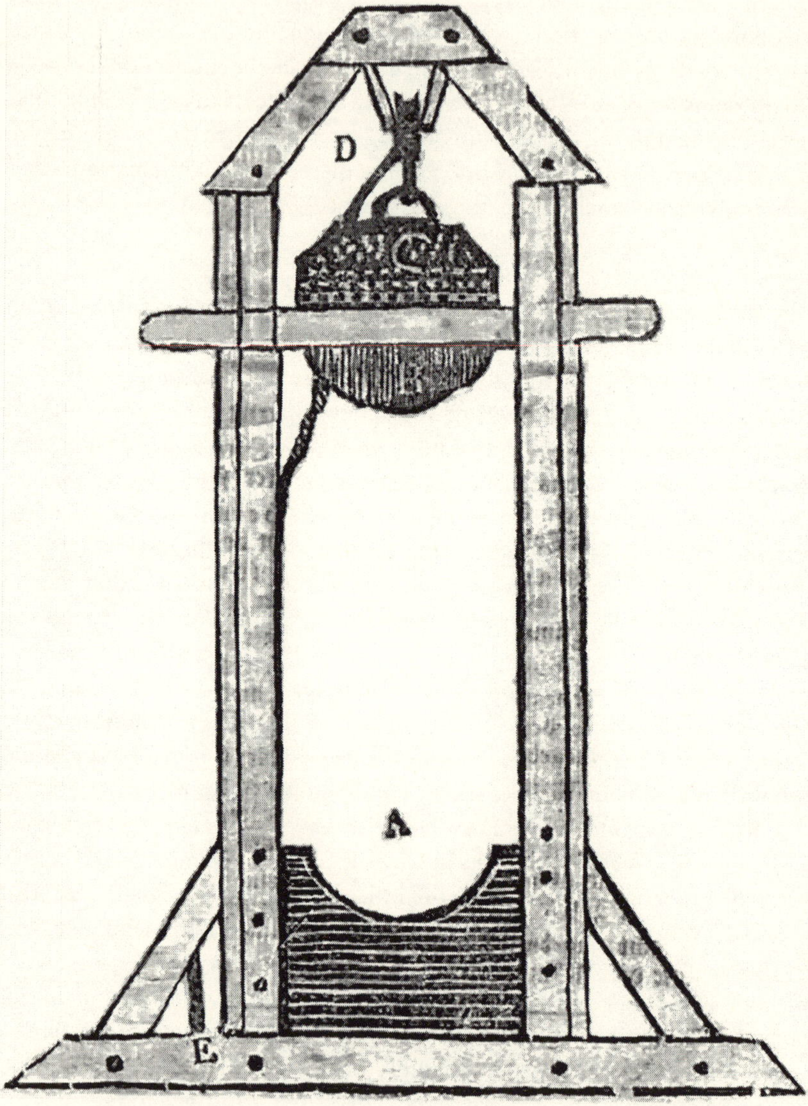

fig. 6.1 Beschreibung der Hinrichtung des Königs von Frankreich Ludwig XVI. . . . (*Description of the Execution of the King of France Louis XVI . . .*) (ca. 1793). Courtesy of Staatsbibliothek zu Berlin. Preußischer Kulturbesitz.

fig. 6.2 Clive L. Lloyd, *Napoleonic and American Prisoners of War, 1756–1816*, plate no. X.

its macabre associations, and its ability to elicit repulsion to this day will be treated more extensively in the following text. Moreover, the intergenerational relationships and tensions in Goethe's prominent family reveal much about the role of paternity in late eighteenth-century German-speaking Europe. Benjamin's contemplation of toys, play, and their political, mate-

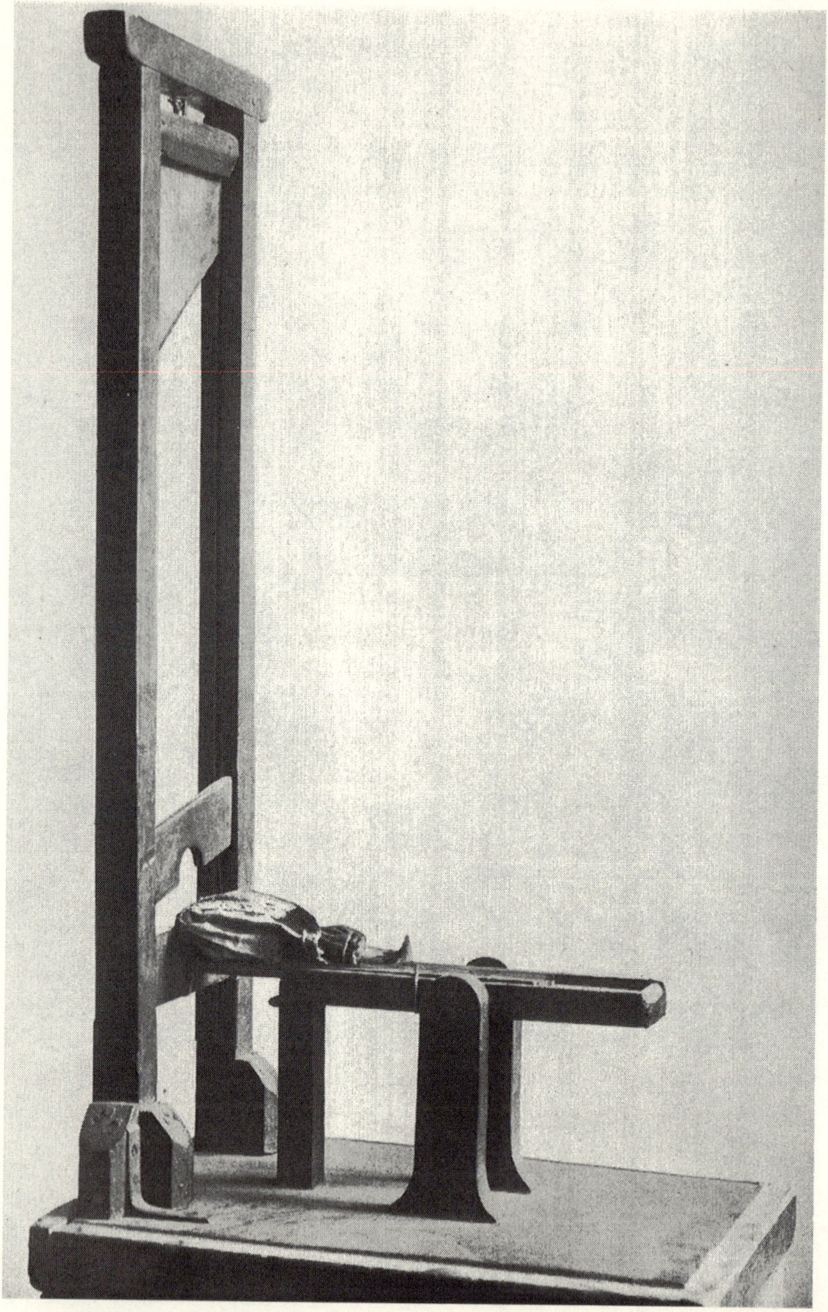

fig. 6.3 Karl Gröber, *Children's Toys of Bygone Days: A History of Playthings of All Peoples from Prehistoric Times to the XIXth Century*, plate no. 153.

rial, and historic associations, though not sustained, nonetheless sheds light on the darker side of play and its connections to a reading of Goethe. In his 1928 essay "The Toy Exhibition at the Märkisches Museum" ("Zur Spielzeugausstellung des Märkischen Museums"), Benjamin acknowledges not only the complexity of play psychology of the child but the therapeutic moments of repetition for adults: "To be sure, play is always liberating. Surrounded by a world of giants, children use play to create a world appropriate to their size. But the adult, who finds himself threatened by the real world and can find no escape, removes its sting by playing with its image in reduced form."[23] In the combined context of Marxist and psychoanalytic interpretations, the toy guillotine's connections to history warrant further exploration, also with the consideration of intersectional identities.

Gender and emerging senses of national identity come to the forefront of the family romance when war and violence are involved. Goethe's mother remained adamant about not supplying war toys in general. As Dagmar von Gersdorff writes in her book about Goethe's grandchildren, the family celebrated Christmas with ritual and fanfare. Frau Aja sent gifts and food from Frankfurt, not available in Weimar—and did much of the baking herself: "The Frankfurt Brenten, which every Christmas Frau Aja had sent promptly to little August along with chestnuts and peppermint cookies, were also unknown in Weimar, though she refused to deliver the cannons Goethe ordered: for war toys, she was unavailable."[24] The cannon, more generically associated with war and bellicosity, held specific meaning for Goethe. He writes about cannon fever in the *Campaign in France* (1792), using his body to slake his curiosity about the battlefield experience.[25] He would not spare August the toy cannon or guillotine. Von Gersdorff further explains that Goethe's love for his son extended to the grandchildren; instead of his mother, Marianne von Willemer provided the pastries and playthings for Walther and Wolfgang, including toy soldiers, though not of tin but of wood with painted cardboard.[26] While war toys and weapons seem to occupy a universal category in male play, their regional, national, historical, and technical attributes reveal particularities that invite closer consideration. The mechanical toy guillotine, in this case, inspires revulsion in Goethe's mother that was shared by twentieth-century historians.

The art historian Karl Gröber articulated the sentiment in his work *Children's Toys of Bygone Days: A History of Playthings of All Peoples from Prehistoric Times to the XIXth Century* (*Kinderspielzeug aus alter Zeit. Eine Geschichte des Spielzeugs* [1928]), echoing the admonitory words of August's grandmother: "Monstrosities, such as every art can show, have not been wanting either; witness the outrageous toy guillotine for beheading doll aristocrats which cropped up fairly often in the French Revolution."[27]

The late eighteenth- and early nineteenth-century European discourse about childhood inscribed a professionalizing household and the roles of its protagonists into a larger social narrative about constructing and cultivating good human beings. Careful selection of toys and their regulation constituted one element of parenting and grandparental practice. The general antipathy toward instruments of war and their potential to model bellicose behavior and inculcate the young and impressionable with detached callousness toward execution indexes a dangerous insensitivity toward human life and historical upheaval, specifically, the violent and existential-political trauma of the French Revolution and Reign of Terror. The paternal desire to amuse the son with a mechanical toy provides evidence that Goethe himself was capable of dissociative play. In some ways, the trivializing of mechanical beheading and capacity for repetition, enabled through wax and the imagination, along with transferring the agency of execution to the playing hand and eye, could function as a distancing and displacing mechanism—a diversion that processes one's own experiences of proximity to death on the battlefield, perhaps, or mourning for lost lives and lifestyles. Goethe and his contemporaries shared varying degrees of knowledge of the Revolution and Terror. In *Faust*, he thematized capital punishment, most memorably in the figure of Gretchen.[28] Beyond the implied readers' appetite for the intimate crime of that imagined infanticide, however, the general public displayed a fascination with the act of beheading.[29] Repetition—and the ability to reattach a wax figure's head, only to repeat the execution indefinitely—incarnates one form of mimesis. The yo-yo, also implicated in the historical trauma of the late eighteenth century, provides a less macabre example.

THE YO-YO

In a significantly different semiotic and behavioral register, the yo-yo informs Goethe's play theory and practice with greater investment in the dynamic of physical and emotional relations between adult interlocutors. Insights into games, play, and Goethe's poetic practice precede my consideration of the yo-yo in the *Venetian Epigrams*. Pierre Bertaux, in his suggestive analysis of Goethe's play drive, devotes a chapter to erotic games. Alighting on the biographical attractions and their motivating, sublimating impulsion into literature, Bertaux situates Goethe's loves from Weimar to Milan. Christiane Vulpius's appearance in the narrative is a game changer. The family constellation re-centers Goethe's play drive and interactions with toys and games. In his classic study of ambiguity in the definitional language of theorizing the "play sphere," Brian Sutton-Smith writes in a generously inclusive way about practices that breach boundaries between the childhood play world and adult enterprises: "Sexual intimates are said to play with each other in innumerable ways, painting each other's bodies, [eating food off of each other, playing hide the thimble in bodily crevices,] and, in general, testing each other with playful impropriety."[30] Sutton-Smith, a play theorist who devoted his work to understanding the cultural significance of play in human life, describes body play in a way that encompasses the intimacies embedded in Goethe's *Roman Elegies* and *Venetian Epigrams*. Immediately, however, the nexus of generative language and erotic pleasure in Goethe's sexualized poetics is invoked: the creative moment gives purpose to play that exceeds Sutton-Smith's theoretical and tactile framework. That moment is recapitulated in Goethe's celebrated verse from the seventh elegy: "Often I even compose my poetry in her embraces, / Counting hexameter beats, tapping them out on her back" ("Oftmals hab ich auch schon in ihren Armen gedichtet / Und des Hexameters Maß leise mit fingernder Hand / Ihr auf den Rücken gezählt").[31] Goethe poetically publicizes the moment of creative and erotic proximity, captured in the "fingering hand." In this image, the body of the poet becomes an instrument of play, metaphorically transforming the bodies into toys. The hand—the noun occurs four times in twenty lines, lightly inflected: "busily thumb" or with a busy hand ("Mit geschäftiger Hand"), "and down over her hip slide my adventuring hand" ("die Hand leite die Hüften hinab"), "with fingers that see" ("mit sehender Hand"), and again tapping the rhythms out "with one hand's fingers" ("mit fingernder Hand")—assumes agency of its own in this process of transfiguration into the nightly play world.[32] In some ways, the poems of the *Elegies* and *Epigrams* cast Italy and the Italian journey and sojourn in general as a type of sex tourism.

Goethe, in *Venetian Epigram* 37, continues his erotic itinerary, introducing the trendy toy that replicates his exploratory sexual adventures. In Benjamin's attention to toys, Goethean wisdom lends authority to solemn words about play. Benjamin quotes Goethe in "Marginal Notes" ("Randbemerkungen"): "And in fact, every profound experience longs to be insatiable, longs for return and repetition until the end of time, and for the reinstatement of an original condition from which it sprang. 'All things would be resolved in a trice / If we could only do them twice.' Children act on this proverb of Goethe's" (120). The impulse to repeat, however, dissolves in the invocation of yo-yos in one epigram. In brief lines about longing, nocturnal loneliness, and the religion of the Nazarene, Goethe alludes to the yo-yo as an accessory of love:

> What an agreeable toy (amusing game)! A disc on a string, I unwind it,
> Casting it out of my hand, and it rewinds in a trice.
> That's how I seem to be casting my heart at this and that beauty:
> But it is never long gone, bounces straight back, as you see.[33]
> (Goethe, *Erotic Poems*, 93)

> [Welch ein lustiges Spiel! Es windet am Faden die Scheibe,
> Die von der Hand entfloh, eilig sich wieder herauf!
> Seht, so schein ich mein Herz bald dieser Schönen, bald jener
> Zuzuwerfen; doch gleich kehrt es im Fluge zurück.]
> (Goethe, *Erotic Poems*, 92)

Browne and Davis identified the object of the epigram and Goethe's probable knowledge of it: "But even as early as 1790, before the full strength of the fad hit Europe generally, Goethe must have been aware of its existence and popularity. The conjugation of Goethe's general propensity for keeping well-informed and the wide-spreadness of the cult of the yo-yo, plus the various literary comments the phenomenon elicited, lead to the inevitable conclusion that Goethe must have known the yo-yo."[34] The yo-yo as a fickle heart that is cast and comes back has been interpreted in various ways, with some scholars suggesting the presence of Goethe's attachment to Christiane and their son as the ultimate destination. Scholars have, however, identified the central role of Christiane's presence in the poems, perhaps the point of return and core of his desire.[35] More generally, scholars have responded varyingly to the *Epigrams*, their reception often situated at the nexus of the biographical, the erotic, and the classical.[36] The playful hand, however, that engages in an affectionate game of "fort / da" with the yo-yo may be performing an erotic legerdemain, but the object itself also recapitulates a momentous historical narrative. The allusion is to Sigmund Freud's game of fetch, in which his toddler grandson tosses an object from his bed, meant for his mother to retrieve, thus asserting control over maternal presence.[37] While Goethe's epigram suggests dalliances of a poetic and sexual nature, the yo-yo arrests the string of fickle and capricious signifiers. Bertaux insists that Christiane plays a different role in the poet's life: she is the only female "with whom Goethe did not play" (100). Play stops.

Benjamin understands the relationship between the child, play, and a dialogue with the nation. His visit to the toy exhibition prompts deep insights into the nature of playful repetition; he connects Goethe's words consciously with play theory and catharsis. Yet there are more sinister connections that exceed the model of Marxist analysis. In his essay on "The Cultural History of Toys" ("Kulturgeschichte des Spielzeuges"), Benjamin observes that children "belong to the nation and the class they come from. This means that their toys cannot bear witness to any autonomous separate existence, but rather are a silent signifying dialogue between them and their nation" ("ein Teil des Volkes und der Klasse, aus der sie kommen. So gibt denn auch ihr Spielzeug nicht von einem autonomen Sonderleben Zeugnis, sondern ist stummer Zeichendialog zwichen ihm und dem Volk") (original 117; translation 116). In the adult world as well, the yo-yo accrues sinister and satirical significance. Here, my focus is extremely narrow; my aim is to probe the real toy story.

In the final images (figures 6.4 and 6.5), we see a series of yo-yo representations in the contexts of criticism and portraiture, including those who ended up on the wrong side of revolutionary politics and practices.[38] According to Chris Goto-Jones, the history of the name varies:

> In fact, the notion that a yo-yo should immediately return to the hand pre-dates the use of the term "yo-yo" in the West. Before Pedro Flores introduced the Filipino practice of looping the string (rather than tying it or otherwise fixing it) around the axel, the yo-yo had been known by a variety of different names: the *bandalore* in France, the *quiz* in England, the *chucki* (an Indian name) during an 18th-century popularity boom in Europe. Historians assume that the yo-yo was known as a *yo-yo* in Asian history, reaching back at least as far as 1000 B.C. in China. In Europe, archaeologists have found twin discs with fixed axels and images that seem to depict people playing with yo-yos as early as 500 B.C. in Greece. This ancient pedigree fuels the myth that the yo-yo is the second oldest toy in history.[39]

Other sources indicate that playing with a yo-yo was a popular pastime, not only among the aristocracy of the late eighteenth and early nineteenth

fig. 6.4 *Emigrant jouant au yoyo* (Emigrant Playing with a Yo-Yo) (1792). Courtesy of Stanford University Libraries and the Bibliotéque Nacionale de France.

fig. 6.5 Beautiful Adeline Playing with Her *Emigran* (ca. 1792). Courtesy of Stanford University Libraries and the Biblioteque Nacionale de France.

centuries: yo-yos "became the favorite toys of famous European conquerors, such as Great Britain's Duke of Wellington and the French Emperor Napoleon Bonaparte."[40]

The nomenclature has a more sinister side. As popular culture scholar and historian of the yo-yo Valerie Oliver observes, the alternate eighteenth-century name of the yo-yo is *l'emigrette*: to leave the country; aristocrats fleeing the perils of French soil took their yo-yos, made of glass and ivory, along with them. The alternate name, *de Coblenz*, embeds the historical narrative into the lives of émigré aristocrats who congregated on the safer side of the Rhine. Noting the yo-yo's role as a stress reliever, Oliver writes, "While being a fashionable toy for the French nobility, those less fortunate are said to have played with their emigrettes to reduce the understandable tension on their one-way trip to the guillotine."[41] In "Marginal Notes," Benjamin acknowledged the links between toys and truths: in these dwell "the transformation of a shattering experience into habit—that is the essence of play" ("Verwandlung der erschütterndesten Erfahrung in Gewohnheit, das ist das Wesen des Spielens"; original 131; translation 120). The migration of the toy across contested European borders, geographical, political, philosophical, and economic, follows a history of privilege, trauma, and seismic shifts in the balance of power.

GOETHE'S EXEMPLARITY

Goethe and his works did not always enjoy a privileged place in the German cultural pantheon. Curiously, around the turn of the century, his transatlantic reception had an elevating effect on his stature—in certain spheres. At the expense of his play-oriented parenting, his willingness to engage in dissociative aesthetic games with violent outcomes, and his more Mephistophelian sensibility—and his positional power, international reception celebrates his genius and exemplarity, particularly with regard to early childhood. A highly influential work, Ellen Key's *The Century of the Child* (1909), inspired a generation of parents and educators on an international scale. A Swedish teacher, suffragist, and writer, Key advocates state support in raising children, instilling moral uprightness through equality in the household, and approaching children as creative and intelligent beings who benefit from disease-free homes and balanced outlooks. In other words, she rejects the practice of raising children in a childhood that is separate, or in contemporary terms, "islanded" from the adult world. With great explanatory force, the concept of "islanding" has productively framed increased attention to childhood as a discrete phase of human existence.[42] By contrast, Key attacks the idea. Homes that produce the best "men and women with the strongest morality" treat children as human beings. She writes, "In a home like this nothing is especially arranged for children; they are regarded not as belonging to one kind of being while parents represent another, but parents gain the respect of their children by being true and natural; they live and conduct themselves in such a way that the children gain an insight into their work, their efforts and, as far as possible into their joys and pains, their mistakes and failures."[43] Throughout her treatise, Key refers liberally to works of literature and philosophy that dominated the German-European tradition, from Goethe to Nietzsche, among a host of others.[44] Her rhetoric is suffused in the canonical teachings of Protestantism, while nuanced when it comes to feminism. Like many of her contemporaries, she espouses cringe-worthy views about hygiene, heredity, and race that leave subsequent generations of readers in a state of profound moral ambivalence vis-à-vis her ostensibly progressive politics on gender equality.

The responsibility of preparing children as individuals for the future is predicated on recognizing the insights of the cultural past. In her chapter on education, for example, she extols Goethe's literary representations of the child: "Goethe showed long ago in his Werther a clear understanding of the significance of individualistic and psychological training, an appreciation which will mark the century of the child. In this work he shows how the future power of will lies hidden in the characteristics of the child, and how along with every fault of the child an uncorrupted germ capable of producing good is enclosed."[45] Key then quotes a passage from *Werther* in which the protagonist vocalizes a secularized version of Christian belief in the innate goodness of children, and she crystallizes all contemporary education into a paraphrase of Goethe: "that almost every fault is but a hard shell enclosing a germ of virtue." Countering the practices of fighting evil with evil, she instead avows allowing nature "quietly and slowly to help itself, taking care only that the surrounding conditions help the work of nature." Succinctly, she concludes, "This is education."[46]

Extending the model of the homology between childhood and nature, Key naturalizes education. Goethe, again, is central to her investigation. In a subsequent discussion of pedagogy and psychology in the Swiss and German traditions, she eschews any sustained consideration of Johann Heinrich Pestalozzi, Johann Bernhard Basedow, and Friedrich Fröbel. Instead, she writes, "I will only mention that the greatest men of Germany, Lessing, Herder, Goethe, Kant and others, took the side of natural training."[47] The expansiveness of Goethe's life and literary productivity enable anyone to find just about anything in his example, a construct to which Key contributes, exploiting the supposition that greatness and natural training are coterminous.

Werther is rarely the model for Goethe on education. Goethe's theories of education, at least as encoded in fiction, have received considerable scholarly and pedagogical attention. In her discussions with Friedrich Fröbel—they met in 1850—Bertha von Marenholtz-Bülow likewise relies on Goethe's greatness and exemplarity and bends him to her purpose. In their discussion of his "School Regions" (*Pädagogische Provinzen*) from the second book of *Wilhelm Meister's Journeyman Years*, von Marenholtz-Bülow and Fröbel note the similarities between the views expressed in fiction and Fröbel's own pedagogical practice: "Goethe, truly, with his seer's glance into the future human development, could not but concur in Fröbel's view, which also embraced humanity in its past, present, and future."[48] This "province" of pedagogy bears resemblance to the actual institution sponsored by Goethe's contemporary, the Pestalozzian reformer Immanuel von Fellenberg, whose son, Wilhelm, the great writer received in Weimar.[49] The idea of graduated work and progressive identificatory codes, such as uniform color, define the method of educating boys to men. In the novel, Wilhelm delivers his son, Felix, to the school. This education involves work. The pedagogical model, which Goethe penned in the early 1820s, represents a moderate yet regulatory approach to shaping masculinity. Many have noted the words inscribed onto Pestalozzi's grave: "Man, Christian, and Citizen. All for others, nothing for himself."[50]

Elsewhere, Goethe reveals a more cutthroat approach to childhood activity. Here one thinks immediately of the hard lessons learned at play in "The New Paris: A Boyhood Fairy Tale" ("Der neue Paris. Knabenmärchen") in the second book of *From My Life: Poetry and Truth* (*Dichtung und Wahrheit*)—"violence is more likely to be banished with violence" ("Force can usually be repelled by force"; the original reads, "Gewalt ist eher mit Gewalt zu vertreiben").[51] While boys at the Fellenberg-influenced school learn through work, in the second example, boys are the presumed players who meet violence with violence, though, importantly, the sentence continues, "but a kindly child, one inclined to love and sympathy, is poorly prepared to defend himself against derision and ill will" ("aber ein gut gesinntes, zur Liebe und Teilnahme geneigtes Kind weiß dem Hohn und dem bösen Willen wenig entgegenzusetzen").[52] Goethe gives us a glimmer of justifying aggression in his childhood incarnation; moreover, in retrospect, he may be speculating on better ways to prepare the well-meaning for encounters with evil and violence in the world. In the realm of play, presumably Christian principles of turning the other cheek, especially to local bullies, simply pale. This counter-model undermines the Christian principles Key mines in Goethe's work.

In particular, Key elevates Goethe as a specimen of holistic education, citing his pedagogical experiences as "ideal, considered apart from some pedantry due to his father's influence." She elaborates:

> At his mother's work-table, he learnt to know the Bible; French he learnt from a theatrical company; English from a language master, in company with his father; Italian, because he heard his sister being taught the language; mathematics from a friend in the household, a study which Goethe applied immediately, first in cardboard diagrams, later in architectural drawings. His essays he prepared in the form of a correspondence in different languages between different relatives, scattered in various parts of the world. Geography he eagerly studied in books of travel in order to be able to give his narrative local colour. He knocked about with his father, learnt to observe different kinds of handwork, and also to try himself small experiments of his own skill.[53]

Her inventory of Goethe's cognitive skills and artisanal abilities acquired and practiced in situ stops short of any acknowledgment of formal training in the visual arts, university legal studies, trips to Italy, and the practice of a profession at court, but Key's point pertains to the cultivation of originality and genius: her Goethe is a paragon.

This version of Goethe the man as exemplary and as an educational theorist benevolent is highly selective and equally assailable. For example, the favorite imaginative activity of his youth, performed with his *Puppentheater*, receives no attention, but this critique distorts Key's project, which involved elevating Goethe as pedagogical model for raising generations to greatness. Goethe provides posterity with moments of equal and greater importance, evidence of churlish behavior or less natural training. One immediately recalls the early passage in *Poetry and Truth* in which he reconstructs his childhood performance for himself and his neighbors, the three brothers von Ochsenstein, the gleeful breaking of crockery that celebrates the unleashed creative and destructive forces of play—the command "Still more!" ("Noch mehr"), to which he responded with enthusiastic fetching of further breakable implements, parallels the repetition compulsion in play; in Goethe's performance, destruction releases creative energy.[54] This indulgence in nihilistic play warrants no mention in Key's citations of Goethean greatness, founded upon a belief in his proximity to nature, but, as Hamlin notes, "toys are not products of nature."[55] But the simultaneous act of creation and destruction shines a light on the construction of Goethe's other favorite toys.

GOETHE'S ECCENTRICITY

Goethe takes play seriously, however, not only as a poet but also as a parent. The legacy of his exemplarity coexists uncomfortably with his eccentricity. We see this in his approaches to play and the acquisition of toys. The legacy of his mother's lament echoes across time and oceans to San Francisco in the era of the Teddy Bear craze. In the *San Francisco Call*, published on February 7, 1910, one headline reads: "Guillotine as Toy for Children in 1793: Goethe's Mother Refused to Buy Machine for Youth." The article recapitulates a discussion of Goethe, his mother's disapproval, and the appetite for toy trends:

> There is a long interval between New Year's day 1793 and that of 1910, both in time and in the character of children's toys, observes the London Globe. Today it is the Teddy bear which delights the small boy. In 1793 the German child was humored with the present on the New Year of a toy guillotine. In 1793 we find Goethe writing to his mother at Frankfort asking her to send to little Augustus this sanguinary machine in miniature. Mme. Goethe was indignant, and wrote to her famous son as follows: "Dear Son—I have only one desire, and that is to give you pleasure. I will execute any command, but to buy so infamous a machine of slaughter I will not in any circumstances. If I could I would arrest the makers and burn such toys by the executioner. Why should children be encouraged to amuse themselves with things so repugnant by putting into their hands this instrument of murder and blood? No, it must not be." Goethe did not dispute the maternal admonition.[56]

The unattributed article I quote above deserves close attention, not only because the author identifies Goethe as a victim of toy trends but also because the piece draws attention to the political and historical resonance in toy production. Goethe as cultural icon figures prominently in the content of the newspaper and in the advocacy of its producers. The connection between the San Francisco publisher John Dietrich Speckels participates in a genealogy of cross-cultural influences with Goethean features. Goethe's cultural presence is more than contingent. Dietrich Spreckels's father, Claus, was among the German Americans in San Francisco who collaborated in efforts to erect the Goethe-Schiller monument in Golden Gate Park. Spreckels the elder acquired and augmented his considerable fortune, inherited by his son, as a sugar magnate. He and his cultural patriots in the Goethe-Schiller Denkmal Gesellschaft of San Francisco began raising money in 1894 for the monument and pedestal; they eventually celebrated its unveiling in 1901.[57] Other monuments followed in immigrant communities across the United States. In this context, familiarity with the vaunted tradition of Goethe's national stature—and statue—as exemplary, interacts with a readership, a comingling of toy traditions, and a call for responsible grandparenting in the face of parental lapses. He himself does not always set the best example. In some ways, he passes on his dedication to fantasy and imaginative play. He encourages, for example, August's interest in the *Puppentheater* he loved so much as a child and an adult. August's occasional letters dutifully document his activity, and he describes a birthday party in a letter dated October 2, 1797:

> In the evening, we performed a shadow play that gave us great pleasure: Hanswurst appeared with his Columbine, a night watchman, a devil, Dr. Faustus, a dragon from Hell, trees, houses, lightening, a magician, a hermit's grove, and finally, a live cat that put out the light. But before the cat played this trick on us, the devil took Hanswurst, Columbine, and Doctor Faust with him into the air. Be well and continue to love me. August Göthe.
>
> [Auf dem Abend spielten wir ein Schattenspiel, das uns viel Vergnügen machte: da kamen ein Hanswurst mit seiner Columbine, ein Nachtwächter, ein Teufel, der Doctor Faust, ein Höllendrache, Bäume, Häuser, Blitze, ein Zauberer, eine Einsiedlergrotte und zuletzt eine lebendige Katze vor, welche das Licht auslöschte. Ehe uns aber die Katze diesen Streich machte, nahm der Teufel den Hanswurst, die Columbine und den Doctor Faust mit sich fort in die Luft. Leben Sie wohl und behalten Sie mich lieb. August Göthe.][58]

Play, theatrics, and magic culminate in the Faust material. The interest in magic will skip a generation for Goethe, who invests quite of bit of energy into outfitting his grandchildren with state-of-the-art *Taschenspielerkasten* (magic kits).[59] He allowed the grandchildren to take magic lessons from a visiting magician, and encouraged their performance before an audience.

Goethe defended his actions with reference to the pedagogical aspect of play to Eckermann: "It is, especially in the presence of a small audience, a wonderful way to practice speaking and gaining physical and mental agility" ("Es ist, besonders in Gegenwart eines kleinen Publikums, ein herrliches Mittel zur Übung in freier Rede und Erlangung einiger körperlichen und geistigen Gewandtheit").[60] Behind the puppet theater and imaginative play associated with performance lurks bellicosity: with the possibility of the opening of "an extension of the theater of war into our area," the puppet theater that Goethe recollects in his autobiography was produced to keep the children at home and engaged in indoor amusements.[61]

However, Key's contemporaries look to Goethe's paternity and play and find his example lacking. Clearly, his was a household name among readers in the first decade of the twentieth century. At that time, a transatlantic audience was sufficiently acquainted with Goethe's rank as international cultural icon to cite him as an authority on play, education, and the consumer habits of parents and grandparents. While he may loom large as a cultural authority and font of frequently arch wisdom about most things, Goethe as a father did not always glean accolades. One famous instance involves his taste in toys. Goethe's playthings—as a father and adult son—pose questions about toys and the nature of cosmopolitan identities in immigration communities. The newspaper story, prompted in part by the popularity of the Teddy Bear, with its presidential political antecedent, quotes Goethe's mother and her incensed and dismayed response to her son's request for a toy guillotine which she was to acquire and send for young August. Before discussing this incident, it is important to note that Goethe had few scruples about acquiring masculinizing playthings for his young son. For example, earlier that same year, Goethe wrote to Christiane from Frankfurt that he was returning to Weimar with shoes for her, an iron, sundries, "also, the saber for the little one is ready" ("auch ist der Säbel für den Kleinen fertig"; August 9, 1793).[62] In his paternal role, Goethe did not oppose toys of war and terror for his son—though later he intervened to prevent August's conscription.

The context of Frau Rath Goethe's original letter provides some further information about her convictions when writing to her son. Beyond the toy-specific diatribe, Elisabeth Goethe forges stronger connections between the mechanical guillotine, historical events, and national identity. In the remainder of the letter, dated December 23, 1793, she provides an account of the local men who inspire feelings of pride in Frankfurt citizenship; they are good Germans with German blood in their veins and uniforms on their backs, prepared "to defend their city in an emergency" ("ihrer Vaterstadt im fall der Noth beyzustehn").[63] She further describes the sacrifices made by locals, the support for the injured, and the voluntary spirit of generosity, winding down with the exclamation, "and you wonder why Frankfurt is becoming so rich" ("nun verwunder mann sich noch daß Franckfurth reich wird").[64] Perhaps most significantly, she signs the letter "Your faithful German mother Goethe" ("deine treue deusche Mutter Goethe"). Of the 414 letters Frau Aja wrote to various interlocutors, this is the only instance of a patriotic variation on a formulaic signature. In fact, in an addendum, she refers to her previous commentary: "I had hardly finished airing my patriotism for the fatherland when your dear letter arrived, and I would like to answer with a few words" ("Kaum hatte ich meinem Vaterländlischen pradiodißmuß Luft gemacht, als dein Lieber Brief ankam, auf den ich mit ein paar Worte noch antworten will").[65]

Both exceptional and exemplary, Goethe represents an emerging model of European masculinity that includes hands-on paternity: the engaged father serves as liaison between the child and the play world. While most of the evidence points to a more focused relationship between fathers and sons, the intervention of male exemplarity in the play sphere effectively inculcates masculinity's attributes into playing children, but also concurrently enables a range of masculinities to become legible in the public sphere. As a corollary, the texts and toys that target the cultivation of masculine traits through imaginative and imitative play prepare the boy reader / player for the seamless transition from imagined to adult citizenship; play embeds political consciousness and historical events into the practices and accessories of play.

CONCLUSION

The two objects of play examined in this chapter function separately, but with shared significance. While play and certain accessories of play assume universal characteristics, their particularities reveal a political unconscious in the social life of material objects. The yo-yo, an object that facilitates an adult and childhood pastime, is present at the site of execution, the last distraction of the condemned, however hygienic and rational and humane the death-delivery-device, the guillotine, was purported to be. The mechanical, miniature, "toy" guillotine and the yo-yo admittedly perform different tasks in Goethe's life and work, respectively, but ultimately they share a certain historical semantics of trauma and migration. Each in its way is representative of the political id that erupted in the aftermath of the French Revolution.

In Goethe's parental life, the guillotine becomes a generational bone of contention, embodying a territorial struggle between himself and his mother, one that recapitulates the attributes of European bourgeois masculinity and its replication through mimetic play. With the repetition of the yo-yo in the realm of the erotic, Goethe as a poetic subject himself segues into a conventional European masculinity, predicated on monogamy, eschewing the to-and-fro of the diverting disc and its pendula movement. Through repetitive play with real objects, Goethe parents toward militarized maleness and partners in respectability. Both objects of play connect and mature the masculine emotional range—always with the possibility of recidivism prompted by the play drive.

With its different backstory, the yo-yo is eroticized; its movements mimicking the arc of affection (and desire) that ultimately returns to the owner, at least as a literary incarnation. In contemporary visual culture and everyday practice, however, the yo-yo is an accessory of distracted play, a pendulous pastime for the politically inconsequential and the uprooted aristocracy waiting for death. Play becomes a metric for gauging Goethe's plural responses to historical trauma and its impact on creativity. For Goethe, the creative impulses of poetry, repetition of wandering desire, and bourgeois masculinity of partnership transfigure the underlying connections to trauma into erotic play. The violence implied and denied in the repeated swipe of the guillotine's blade rehearses a militarized masculinity that depends on dissociative capacities. Goethe's draft of European parental masculinity encompasses both his exemplary and eccentric impulses: to entertain and educate with games of life and death.

NOTES

1. At the Atkins Goethe Conference (State College, PA, October 2017), comments made during a discussion of my presentation on "Frankfurt School Philosophy and the Age of Goethe: Elective Aversions?" shaped my argument in this chapter. In particular, for their interventions in the conversation, I owe thanks to Eva Geulen, who raised the notion of Goethe's eccentricity, and Simon Richter, who pointed to Herbert Marcuse as a potential alternative Frankfurt School model of play. Walter Benjamin's essays on toys and material culture were the focus of my remarks at the roundtable. I am indebted to the editors for their insightful reading of an earlier version of this chapter, which also was shaped by a lively discussion at the Goethe-Museum in Düsseldorf after a public presentation of this research. I thank Dr. Christof Wingertszahn for the invitation and for his response to my lecture.

2. Fredric Jameson, *The Political Unconscious: Narrative as a Socially Symbolic Act* (Ithaca, NY: Cornell University Press, 1981), 9.

3. Leora Auslander, "Beyond Words," *American Historical Review* 10, no. 4 (October 2005): 1017.

4. Arjun Appadurai, introduction to *The Social Life of Things: Commodities in Cultural Perspective*, ed. Arjun Appadurai (Cambridge: Cambridge University Press, 1988), 4.

5. Walter Benjamin, "Marginal Notes on a Monumental Work," in *Selected Writings*, ed. Michael W. Jennings, Howard Eiland, and Gary Smith, trans. Rodney Livingstone et al., vol. 2, *1927–1934* (Cambridge, MA: Harvard University Press, 1999), 120.

6. Walter Benjamin, "Randbemerkungen zu einem Monumentalwerk," in *Gesammelte Schriften*, ed. Rolf Tiedemann and Hermann Schweppenhäuser, vol. 3., ed. Hella Tiedemann-Bartels (Frankfurt am Main: Suhrkamp, 1991), 131.

7. See W. Daniel Wilson, *Das Goethe-Tabu: Protest und Menschenrechte im klassischen Weimar* (Munich: Deutscher Taschenbuchverlag, 1999), for a sustained consideration of this topic.

8. Johan Huizinga, foreword to *Homo Ludens: A Study of the Play Element in Culture* (New York: Roy, 1950), unpaginated.

9. Thomas Henricks, *Play and the Human Condition* (Urbana: University of Illinois Press, 2015), 2.

10. See, for example, the work of Ingeborg Weber-Kellermann, *Die Kindheit: Eine Kulturgeschichte* (Frankfurt am Main: Insel, 1997) and *Die Kindheit: Kleidung und Wohnen, Arbeit und Spiel: Eine Kulturgeschichte* (Frankfurt am Main: Insel, 1979). In the former, Weber-Kellermann provides a narrative of childhood cultures from the Middle Ages through the postwar period, with attention to class difference and intersectionality in children's identities.

11. Gilbert Clarence Kettelkamp, "Jean Paul and His Relationship to the Pedagogical Theories of His Day," abstract (PhD diss., University of Illinois, Urbana, 1941), 6. The author also counts Jean Paul as a "pioneer in giving play" a significant position.

12. Lloyd deMause, "The Evolution of Childhood," in *The History of Childhood*, ed. Lloyd deMause (New York: Psychohistory Press, 1974), 1. The volume, ambitious in its scope to write the history of childhood in the West, originated as a research project under the auspices of the Association for Applied Psychoanalysis. See Lloyd deMause, preface to *The History of Childhood*, ed. Lloyd deMause (New York: Psychohistory Press, 1974), iii.

13. David D. Hamlin, *Work and Play: The Production and Consumption of Toys in Germany, 1870–1914* (Ann Arbor: University of Michigan Press, 2007), esp. chap. 2, "Making the Toys, Making the Industry," 60–102. Though Hamlin focuses on Wilhelmine Germany, his observations about the centrality of these three toy-producing locations obtain.

14. Immanuel Kant, *Critique of Judgement*, trans. and analytical indexes by James Creed Meredith (Oxford: Oxford University Press, 1973), 165.

15. Friedrich Schiller, *On the Aesthetic Education of Man in a Series of Letters*, trans. and intro. Reginald Snell (New Haven, CT: Yale University Press, 1954), 74–75.

16. Friedrich Schiller, *Schillers Sämmtliche Werke* (Stuttgart: J. G. Cotta'sche Buchhandlung, 1879), 4:591.

17. Herbert Marcuse, *Eros and Civilization: A Philosophical Inquiry into Freud* (Boston: Beacon, 1955), 173.

18. Marcuse, *Eros and Civilization*, 174; emphasis in the original.

19. Lisa Zamosky, "Toy Guns: Do They Lead to Real-Life Violence?" *WebMD*, December 1, 2011, https://www.webmd.com/parenting/features/toy-guns-do-they-lead-real-life-violence#1.

20. Parvin Sadigh, "Killerspiele schaden doch," 1. November 2006, 13:00 Uhr Aktualisiert am 18. April 2008, 5:56 Uhr. *ZEIT* online, https://www.zeit.de/online/2006/49/computerspiele-gewalt-psychologie. Translations, unless otherwise noted, are my own.

21. See Rachel Chapman, "A Case Study of Gendered Play in Preschools: How Early Childhood Educators' Perceptions of Gender Influence Children's Play," *Early Childhood Development and Care* 186, no. 8 (2016): 1271–1284. In national print media, see Perri Klass, "Breaking Gender Stereotypes in the Toy Box," *New York Times*, February 5, 2018, https://www.nytimes.com/2018/02/05/well/family/gender-stereotypes-children-toys.html.

22. Clive L. Lloyd, *Napoleonic and American Prisoners of War, 1756–1816* (Woodbridge, Suffolk: Antique Collectors Club, 2007), 16. According to Lloyd, some prisoners of war in England held at depots fared better than others; they had work and some direct access to markets.

23. Walter Benjamin, "The Toy Exhibition at the Märkisches Museum," in *Selected Writings*, ed. Michael W. Jennings, Howard Eiland, and Gary Smith, trans. Rodney Livingstone et al., vol. 2, *1927–1934* (Cambridge MA: Harvard University Press, 1999), 100.

24. Dagmar von Gersdorff, *Goethes Enkel: Walther, Wolfgang und Alma* (Frankfurt am Main: Insel Verlag, 2008), 69.

25. See my *The Erotics of War in German Romanticism* (Lewisburg, PA: Bucknell University Press, 2006), 192, on Goethe's willingness to risk his own safety in order to experience heavy artillery in a way that almost intersects with a Kantian notion of the sublime.

26. See von Gersdorff, *Goethes Enkel*, 69. Alma was not left out; she received a doll.

27. Karl Gröber, *Children's Toys of Bygone Days: A History of Playthings of All Peoples from Prehistoric Times to the XIXth Century*, trans. Philip Hereford (New York: Frederick A. Stokes, 1928), 3.

28. See, for example, Barbara Becker-Cantorino, "Witch and Infanticide: Imaging the Female in *Faust I*," *Goethe Yearbook* 7 (1994): 1–2. Diverging opinions about Goethe's own stance on human rights issues and political decisions funnel around, among other events, the publication of his official writings. See Wilson, *Das Goethe-Tabu*, and his review essay, "Goethe's Writings as Minister of State in Saxe-Weimar and Eisenach," *Goethe Yearbook* 22 (2015): 261–266.

29. See, for example, Kerstin Rehwinkel, "Kopflos, aber lebendig? Konkurrierende Körperkonzepte in der Debatte um den Tod durch Enthauptung im ausgehenden 18. Jahrhundert," in *Körper mit Geschichte: Der menschliche Körper als Ort der Selbst- und Weltdeutung*, ed. Clemens Wischermann and Stefan Haas (Stuttgart: Franz Steiner Verlag, 2000), 151–171.

30. Brian Sutton-Smith, "Play and Ambiguity," in *The Game Design Reader: A Rules of Play Anthology*, ed. Katie Salen and Eric Zimmermann (Cambridge, MA: MIT Press, 2006), 299.

31. Johann Wolfgang von Goethe, *Erotic Poems*, trans. David Luke, intro. Hans Rudolf Vaget (Oxford: Oxford University Press, 1988, 14 (original), 15 (translation).

32. Goethe, *Erotic Poems*, 14 (original), 15 (translation, with my insertions to emphasize repetition of the word "hand").

33. See my modification to the translation in parentheses to emphasize the playfulness of the game, with its underlying seriousness.

34. Richard J. Browne and M. C. Davis, "Goethe and the Yo-Yo," *Modern Language Quarterly* 14, no. 1 (March 1953): 101.

35. See, for example, Ralph Hexter, "Poetic Reclamation and Goethe's *Venetian Epigrams*," *MLN* 96, no. 3 (1981): esp. 534–535.

36. Elisabeth Böhm, "Epoche Machen: Goethes Konstruktion der Weimarer Klassik zwischen 1786 und 1796" (PhD diss., University of Bayreuth, 2010). The dissertation focuses on the origin and publication history, with attention to contemporary politics briefly considered (206). Many focus on the relationship between political upheaval, erotic exploration, and the modernizing of classical form. See, for example, Hans Jürgen Scheuer, *Manier und Urphänomen: Lektüren zur Relation von Erkenntnis und Darstellung in Goethes Poetologie der "geprägten Form"* (Würzburg: Königshausen & Neumann, 1996). Reiner Wild, in *Goethes klassische Lyrik* (Stuttgart: Metzler, 1999), argues that Goethe's classical poetry was "Teil und Ausdruck des 'Projekts Klassik,'" that is, a process, an aesthetic reconciliation between modernity and antiquity; for a reading of the poetics involved in the published (censored) and complete version of the epigrams, see Horst Lange, "Goethe's Strategy of Self-Censorship: The Case of the *Venezianische Epigramme*," *Monatshefte* 91, no. 2 (1999); and for a sustained reading of the site-specific, urban landscape, see Stephan Oswald, *Früchte einer großen Stadt—Goethes "Venezianische Epigramme"* (Heidelberg: Winter 2014).

37. Sigmund Freud, *Beyond the Pleasure Principle*, trans. and ed. James Strachey, vol. 18 of *The Complete Psychological Works of Sigmund Freud* (New York: W. W. Norton, 1976), 14–17.

38. In addition to the images reproduced here, see also the portrayal of an aristocratic child with a bling-encrusted yo-yo, which raises the political and associative significance of the toy, accessed June 30, 2019, https://commons.wikimedia.org/wiki/File:Louis_Charles_of_France2.jpg. I would like to thank Dr. Todd Larkin for assistance with this image.

39. Chris Goto-Jones, "The Secret Life of Yo-Yos," *Atlantic*, April 9, 2015, https://www.theatlantic.com/technology/archive/2015/04/the-yo-yo-effect/389868/.

40. Marjorie L. McClellan, "Hunting for Everyday History Theme 1: Toys and Games," in *Hunting for Everyday History: Local and Regional Organizations* (Wright State University CORE Scholar, 2003), accessed June 7, 2019, https://corescholar.libraries.wright.edu/cgi/viewcontent.cgi?article=1001&context=hunting.

41. Valerie Oliver, "History of the Yo-Yo," Museum of Yo-Yo History, accessed June 7, 2019, yoyomuseum.com/museum_view.php?action=profiles&subaction=yoyo.

42. John R. Gillis "Epilogue: The Islanding of Children—Reshaping the Mythical Landscapes of Childhood," in *Designing Modern Childhood: History, Space and the Material Culture of Children*, ed. Marta Gutman and Ning de Coninck-Smith (New Brunswick, NJ: Rutgers University Press, 2008), 316–330.

43. Ellen Key, *A Century of the Child*, trans. from German version by Frances Maro, reviewed by the author (New York: G. P. Putnam and Sons, Knickerbocker Press, 1909), 198. On eugenics and Key's consideration of Francis Galton's *Hereditary Genius*, see 20–24.

44. See, for example, Key's discussion of the perennial challenges involved in balancing the soul and the body (*Century of the Child*, 6); she refers here to Goethe's call for boldness. On Nietzsche's "superman," see Key, *Century of the Child*, 25–26; on Nietzsche on fidelity, see Key, *Century of the Child*, 35–36. Friedrich A. Kittler makes reference to Key's

influence on pedagogical thought around 1900 in *Discourse Networks*, but not in the context I am establishing for a reading of Goethe.

45. Key, *Century of the Child*, 106.

46. Key, *Century of the Child*, 107. Key is relying on popularized European models of natural education for her interpretation of Goethe and childhood.

47. Key, *Century of the Child*, 184. Later, she advocates teaching history through great works of literature, among them Goethe's *Egmont*. Key, *Century of the Child*, 220.

48. Bertha von Marenholtz-Bülow, *How Kindergarten Came to America: Friedrich Froebel's Radical Vision of Early Childhood Education*, trans. Mrs. Horace Mann (New York: New Press, 2007), 95.

49. Otto Kohlmeyer, *Die Pädagogische Provinz in "Wilhelm Meisters Wanderjahren": Ein Beitrag zur Pädagogik Goethes* (Langensalza: Julius Beltz, 1923), 4.

50. Quoted in Friedrich Fröbel, *The Student's Froebel*, adapted by William H. Herford, intro. Professor M. E. Sadler (London: Sir Isaac Pitman & Sons, 1916), ix.

51. Johann Wolfgang von Goethe, *Dichtung und Wahrheit*, vol. 8 of *Werkausgabe in zehn Bänden* (Cologne: Könemann, 1998), 75. My translation, supplemented by Robert Heitner's translation of Goethe, *From My Life: Poetry and Truth*, Parts One to Three, ed. Thomas P. Saine and Jeffrey L. Sammons, vol. 4 of *Goethe's Collected Works*, ed. Victor Lange, Eric A. Blackall, and Cyrus Hamlin (New York: Suhrkamp, 1983), 61.

52. Goethe, *Dichtung und Wahrheit*, 75; Goethe, *From My Life*, 61.

53. Key, *Century of the Child*, 249.

54. Goethe, *Dichtung und Wahrheit*, 14–15; Goethe, *From My Life*, 22.

55. Hamlin, *Work and Play*, 63.

56. "Guillotine as Toy for Children in 1793: Goethe's Mother Refused to Buy Machine for Youth," *San Francisco Call*, February 7, 1910, 8.

57. *Das Goethe-Schiller Denkmal in San Francisco, California: Erinnerungen an den "Deutschen Tag" der California Midwinter International Exposition 1894, an das "Goethe Schiller Fest" 1895 und an die "Enthüllung des Denkmals im Golden Gate Park 1901"* (San Francisco: C. Leidecker, 1901). An image of Claus Spreckels is included (13).

58. Quoted in Christoph Michel, *Goethe: Sein Leben in Bildern und Texten* (Frankfurt am Main: Insel Verlag, 1998), 281 (my translation).

59. Von Gersdorff, *Goethes Enkel*, 40.

60. Von Gersdorff, *Goethes Enkel*, 41.

61. Goethe, *Dichtung und Wahrheit*, 35; Goethe, *From My Life*, 48.

62. Johann Wolfgang von Goethe, letter to Christiane, *Goethes Ehe in Briefen*, ed. Hans Gerhard Gräf, 2nd ed. (Frankfurt am Main: Rütten & Loening, 1922), 73 (my translation).

63. Catharina Elisabeth Goethe, *Die Briefe der Frau Rath Goethe*, ed. Albert Köster (Frankfurt am Main: Insel, 1969), 321.

64. Goethe, *Die Briefe Frau Rath Goethe*, 321.

65. Goethe, *Die Briefe Frau Rath Goethe*, 322.

CHAPTER SEVEN

Kindergarten and the Pedagogy of Play in the German Educational Revolution

IAN F. MCNEELY

IN 1851, THE AUTHORITIES banned kindergarten in Prussia. The edict announcing the ban cited the dangers of the "socialistic Fröbel system, which is designed to convert the youth to atheism."[1] Friedrich Fröbel (1782–1852) had founded the very first kindergarten in 1840, having spent the previous decades experimenting with various kinds of innovative schools. His "garden for children," a haven for free play for those between three and six years of age, caught on rapidly over the next decade.[2] By 1847, seven Fröbel-inspired kindergartens had opened across Germany, and forty-four new ones cropped up the next year alone.[3] But that same year, 1848, also saw a wave of political revolutions, triggering an outbreak of paranoia that still gripped official Germany three years later. In 1851, the year of the ban, conservative authorities espied a social and religious threat in the unlikeliest of places, kindergarten classrooms, and moved to shutter them as hotbeds of juvenile subversion.

Educated Germans saw through the government's bluff and bluster. The satirical newspaper *Kladderadatsch* mockingly suggested that Prussian officials had become alarmed about coded messages promoting communism in the children's storybook *Slovenly Peter*.[4] (The storybook *was* menacing, but not because of its politics; in the gruesome fashion of the age, it vividly illustrated the consequences of child misbehavior, such as amputation for thumb-suckers and immolation for playing with matches—stern lessons that should have *reassured* conservative authorities.) Fröbel's exasperated aristocratic patroness, Bertha von Marenholtz-Bülow, who had provided material and moral support to the kindergarten movement, privately mocked the official fear of "three-year-old demagogues."[5] It was soon discovered that the bumbling Prussians had confused Friedrich Fröbel with his admittedly more radical nephew Karl, who had recently opened a controversial training academy for female teachers. Even so, Karl Fröbel was, at worst, a feminist, maybe even a socialist, but hardly an atheist.[6] Despite back-channel entreaties from high-placed supporters, efforts to roll back the ban were in vain. Friedrich Fröbel would die a year later.

The repression of the kindergarten is as poignant a symbol of hostility toward educational play as can possibly be imagined. It comports with a clichéd image of nineteenth-century Germany as a land of cheerless, spike-helmeted martinets. Ironically, though, there was no more progressive country than Germany when it came to public education, and no more advanced state than Prussia in making such education available to citizens at government expense. Germany, and Prussia in particular, led the world in providing compulsory elementary education to all school-aged children, and its example spurred other countries, particularly France and the United States, to overhaul their own systems of public schooling.[7] This was also true of secondary and especially tertiary education, owing to the worldwide influence of the German research university. To this day, two German inventions, the kindergarten and the PhD, form the bookends of formal education across the globe. Both were part of an educational revolution that straddled the turn of the century, as a counterpart to political revolution in France and industrial revolution in England. The institutionalization of compulsory public schooling was founded on a new optimism about children's capacity to learn and on a new conviction that through systematic pedagogy that capacity could be made universal. This effected a dramatic remolding of life chances and the life course that has yet to receive due attention from historians and other scholars of the era.[8]

This essay situates Fröbel, heretofore treated as an isolated and admittedly unsystematic thinker, within broader philosophical concerns prevalent during the age of Goethe. Two such concerns, the subjects, respectively, of Kant's first two *Critiques*, informed the prehistory of the kindergarten and other experiments in early childhood education: epistemology (that is, how the child's developing mind perceives the world, learns from it, and ultimately manipulates it) and ethics (how the child can be socialized into ever more mature duties and responsibilities on the path to adulthood). Both came together in theories and practices of play, and through the lens of play we can begin to understand what was truly at stake in Germany's unprecedented investment in human potential through universal education. For despite the Prussian government's paranoid overreaction, Fröbel had fashioned his pedagogy of play from elements already in common currency among mainstream German pedagogues. At the same time, for reasons his forerunners and contemporaries reveal, institutionalized public schooling carefully circumscribed play so as to prepare students for life as well-behaved young adults on the road to maturity.

PLAY IN THE FRÖBELIAN KINDERGARTEN

In retrospect, it is hard for us to imagine what could possibly be controversial about a kindergarten. But it was deeply unsettling to remove three- to six-year-olds from the bosom of the family and entrust them to an experimental community—outside the church, no less. If the Fröbelian kindergarten smacked of socialism, then, this was because it mixed children from different families and social classes together and treated them to a kind of instructional play that looked suspiciously like the avoidance of work. So too, if the Fröbelian kindergarten smacked of atheism, this was because its founder indeed subscribed to a woolly religiosity locating God everywhere in nature, not in the words of the Bible or the ritual of the church. Fröbel was not an atheist but a *pan*theist, technically even a pan*en*theist, viewing God both as suffusing the whole universe and at the same time extending beyond it—both immanent and transcendent.[9]

In their mixture of social nonconformity and avant-garde religiosity, Fröbel's experimental schools—most notably his Universal German Education Institute in Keilhau, which he founded and led between 1817 and 1831—are almost better compared with other nineteenth-century utopian communities rather than regarded as the progenitors of a modern educational institution. Radically, Fröbel's educational communities were founded on the notions that all children are similarly capable of intellectual, moral, and spiritual development; that a school should be a "union of families,"[10] not just a center for children; and that education not only prepared children for productive occupations appropriate to their stations of birth but also nurtured and developed a divine spark within and among them. Play was the great equalizer, the key to it all. As one observer put it, "The pupils live in full equality and freedom amongst themselves, without reference to station, or birth, or dress, nor even the name by which they are called . . . all before the law of play."[11] The kindergarten was a true countercultural movement—and in this sense the Prussian authorities did indeed have cause for concern.

Fröbel's *The Education of Man*, published in 1826, midway through the Keilhau experiment, distilled the theory and practice that later animated the kindergarten. Departing from the Christian doctrine of original sin and, like many pedagogues of his era, placing himself firmly in the tradition of

Rousseau, Fröbel held that all children are born good.[12] Children are endowed with a beneficial natural impulse to what he, following Pestalozzi, called "self-activity"—a healthy, independent instinct to explore the world and to learn and grow by interacting with it, touching it, testing it. Far from tempting children to indolence, distraction, and reckless abandon, play gives free rein to this God-given goodness. It is the "purest, most spiritual activity of humanity" in childhood, forming the "germinal leaves of all later life."[13] Play allows children to devote their attention to whatever objects stimulate their self-activity, instead of having them prescribed by a parent or teacher. Its very spontaneity and serendipity confirm, wherever the child happened to turn, the unity-in-diversity of all Creation, enabling him "to see individual things in their connection with a whole . . . to comprehend [the world] in its extent, its diversity, its integrity."[14] Play, to put it in Kantian terms, mediates between subject and object, the mind and the world, leading the child to "behold his inner life in external phenomena."[15] Evoking a Romantic Neoplatonism promising reunion with a celestial perfection from which we have become alienated on our debased earthly plane, Fröbel even claimed that play helps "all-surveying man . . . rise through ascending degrees of consciousness to perfect insight into the ground, conditions, and goal of his life."[16] This heavenward ascent could also be a literal one: "To climb a new tree is to the boy the discovery of a new world."[17]

Fröbel recognized play as more than merely a means of understanding or internalizing the world, however. As an outwardly directed impulse, it furnishes a means for the child's innate self-activity to apprehend and manipulate the external environment. Play is buoyant, bounding, conquering, acquisitive, physical;[18] it imprints the divine energy inborn in the child onto the matrix of spiritual forces that surround him everywhere. Play develops power, control, and mastery of nature:

> Everything must submit to [the child's] formative instinct; there in the heap of earth he builds a cellar, a cavern, and on it a garden, a bench. Boards, branches of trees, laths, and poles are made into a hut, a house . . . snow . . . stones . . . all this is done in the spirit and tendency of boyhood, in the spirit and tendency of unification and assimilation.
>
> The unifying and, at the same time, self-reliant spirit unites all things that come near and seem adapted to its nature, its wants, and inner status—unites stones and human beings in a common purpose, a common endeavor. And thus each one soon forms for

> himself his own world; for the feeling of his own power implies and soon demands also the possession of his own space and his own material belonging exclusively to him.[19]

Lest this imply an antisocial individualism, conjuring the image of a petty conqueror bestriding his own private rock pile, Fröbel maintained that play also integrates the child into the human, social, moral world. Play instills the "civil and moral virtues,"[20] cultivates "brotherly union,"[21] and develops healthy relationships with others, the basis for all society. Boys at play, through their games, learn nothing less than "justice, moderation, self-control, truthfulness, loyalty, brotherly love, and strict impartiality."[22] Now, this was quite a rosy take on the rough-and-tumble of the boyhood schoolyard. But there, Fröbel discerned nary a trace of bullying, intimidation, or juvenile chest-thumping. To him, the playground offered "encouragement for the weaker, younger, and more delicate [and] fairness to those unfamiliar with the game."[23]

Fröbel's imagery centered on the physical—on schoolyard games and nature walks and "treasuries of unknown stones and plants . . . worms, beetles, spiders, and lizards."[24] But the play instinct is not limited to the actual natural and social worlds. Fictional stories, fables, legends, myths, adventure tales: these, too, stimulated the boy, through his imagination rather than his senses, and widened his horizons just as much as exposure to nature.[25] Through stories, "mind breathes mind; power feels power and absorbs it, expands heart and soul, strengthens the mind, unfolds life in freedom and power." The play of imagination through stories offers a privileged avenue to self-knowledge for the young child. Here, Fröbel departed from Rousseau's *Emile*, who had inveighed against fictional stories, vouchsafing Emile a single novel, *Robinson Crusoe*, about being shipwrecked: coping with solitude. For Fröbel, by contrast, stories draw the child into the selves of others. Unlike play with objects, stories about others' lives provide a "mirror," and "points of comparison with the life [the boy] himself has experienced." In this way, they gratify "the innermost desire and need of a vigorous, genuine boy to understand his own life, to get a knowledge of its nature, its origin and outcome."[26] But like other, more physical, forms of play, stories too act to expand the individual's confidence and power. "Every story [is] a new conquest, a fresh treasure [to] add to his own life for advancement and instruction."[27]

As all of these quotations suggest, play is resolutely boyish and masculine, an expression of vigor, energy, and the impulse to conquer. Even though girls were most certainly included in Fröbel's kindergartens, neither girls per se nor the retiring, nurturing, domestic virtues of nineteenth-century femininity in general occupy a discernible role in his theory of child's play. To be sure, there was something quite progressive about Fröbel's very silence on gender. He could easily have crafted a demure feminine foil to his boyish ideal, just as Rousseau had concocted a Sophie for Emile, but he instead resisted any theoretical differentiation of boys' and girls' forms of play—at least among children of kindergarten age. Moreover, Fröbel recruited both young women and young men to act as kindergarten teachers (and incidentally, the German word *Kindergärtner* refers to the teacher, not the student). For this fact alone, he counts as a male feminist as much as anyone of his time.

Still, in his account of child development, Fröbel subscribed to a division of gender roles that was utterly conventional for the time. Feminine and masculine, the interior world and the exterior world, subjective and objective, heart and head: these were the gendered polarities whose complementarity in the growing child produced unity and wholeness.[28] The balance between the two simply shifted as the child developed. In Fröbel's conception, mothers take the lead when children are infants, singing and playing with them, moving their limbs, developing their physical sensations as they together enacted a "dyadic" emotional bond. But the development of free movement, when the child begins to walk, and becomes an independent agent increasingly separated from the "dyad" of mother and infant, marks the onset of a more masculine phase of play and child development.[29] At the culmination of this stage—around three years old, precisely when kindergarten begins—a firmer guiding hand is required. "A young man is preferable [as a kindergarten teacher], precisely because even a married woman is going to have a difficult time with rambunctious and energetic little boys."[30]

In Fröbel's schools, children, girls and boys, were hardly left to their own devices. Play was instead quite purposive and directed. The forms of play that Fröbel prescribed, his famous "gifts," were highly structured, sequenced, and detailed. Each was meant to impart a practical—but equally important, also a spiritual—lesson, all in a progressive chain of revelations. Thus the first gift was a simple cloth ball, to hone motor skills but also to symbolize the unity of the universe. Further gifts incorporated spheres, cubes, cylinders, blocks, pyramids, sticks, and other basic geometric shapes in various colorful combinations. The fifth gift, for example, was a cube containing twenty-seven smaller cubes, which, when inverted on a table and carefully drawn upward to reveal the contents within, presented a tidy spectacle of unity-in-multiplicity. Reliance on geometry and abstraction was a legacy of Fröbel's early career at the newly established University of Berlin, when he had apprenticed under Christian Samuel Weiss, the founder of modern crystallography. The beauty of crystals inspired Fröbel to see nature and spirituality as one, and the Fröbel gifts that developed out of this early conviction became the most novel and enduring aspect of his system. They lay the basis for a specialized craft knowledge passed along from teacher to teacher and school to school, and later mass-produced in fetchingly illustrated books and wooden mail-order kits as the kindergarten movement spread. Many of Fröbel's acolytes slavishly obeyed his elaborate instructions for use of these playthings and even petitioned him for more detail when it was lacking.[31] Like a modern-day Pythagoras, he had somehow divined an elemental sensory-spiritual lexicon at the intersection of mathematical science and mystical insight. Even if we have long since forgotten about the pseudo-philosophy that once underpinned it, Fröbel's style of play lives on in the primary-colored building blocks, parquet patterns, and Tinkertoys found today in every preschool classroom.

Fröbel's fascination with crystalline forms offers a final clue to his idealized school: their beauty derives from their patterned uniformity and regularity, the harmonious integration and repetition of like elements—and not their uniqueness. For all the emphasis he placed on the spiritual development of the individual, for all his novelty in emphasizing spiritual development as inextricable from sensory and social development, and for all the diversity, multiplicity, and unpredictability of interests he discerned in play, Fröbel gave little thought to identifying, much less cultivating, what makes each particular child special or unique.[32] He was tone-deaf, in short, to what contemporaries called the *Bildung* of the individual. The learning processes he described, whether abstractly, in his theoretical writings, or concretely, through his series of "gifts," apply indiscriminately to all children. Play, in his scheme, externalizes a robust inner activity, but is hardly concerned with its converse: the shaping and molding of a particular inner self or personality through contact with, and experiments in, an external nature and society. Thus, playacting and role play, which invite the child to try on different selves as a means to construct a self of one's own, have no place in his vision. For Fröbel, all happy, healthy boys are interchangeable; psychologically, they are flat and uncomplex. And girls, though again, emphatically a part of his actual schools, are nowhere treated as distinct from (even as inferior to) boys; they are simply untheorized. The great irony of the attack on his system of play by conservative authorities was that for all its countercultural aspects, it was ultimately designed to produce well-adjusted and cheerfully conformist young men: exactly what the Prussian state should have wanted.

PLAY IN PESTALOZZI, KANT, AND SCHLEIERMACHER

What was it about play's indisputable power and efficacy as a means of early childhood learning that for those who rejected Fröbel's unconventional wisdom seemed so subversive? Three theorists of education, Pestalozzi, Kant (himself in dialogue with the so-called Philanthropinists), and Schleiermacher, offer provisional answers to this question. Together they reveal why the kindergarten stood in tension with formal, official education even though both grew out of a common pedagogical ferment.

The Swiss pedagogue Johann Heinrich Pestalozzi (1746–1827) is generally regarded as the central figure in the German educational revolution; he was the inspiration not only for Fröbel's pedagogy of play but to a large extent for the entire reform of primary education in Prussia. Pestalozzi saw himself as the continuator of Rousseau's progressive, naturalistic alternative to traditional book-learning and rote instruction—even naming his son Jean-Jacques. Unlike Rousseau, whose *Emile* was but a thought experiment, Pestalozzi demonstrated that universal education could actually work in practice. He made particular inroads among the poorest and most disadvantaged children, establishing schools in neglected, out-of-the-way Swiss towns like Stans, Burgdorf, and Yverdon, the last of which became an international center for pilgrims attracted to his methods. Among his most prominent advocates were J. G. Fichte, the philosopher and prophet of German national education, who met him personally in 1794, and the educational reformer Wilhelm von Humboldt, who with his colleagues and successors dispatched over a dozen student-teachers to Yverdon between 1805 and 1825 to catalyze the renovation of primary schooling back in Prussia.

Fröbel had spent more than two years with Pestalozzi at Yverdon. Strip away the fuzzy spiritualism and the crystallographically inspired curriculum from Fröbel's system, and what remains derives largely from Pestalozzi. Anticipating Fröbel's sequence of fundamental "gifts," Pestalozzi aimed in his seminal 1801 treatise, *How Gertrude Teaches Her Children*, to distill education down to its simplest elements, then carefully build up the child's mind through a gradual and logical accumulation of those elements. He decried premature attempts to introduce children to words and concepts for which they had no concrete sensory referents, and held even greater scorn for the endless catechizing and brute-force memorization that constituted so much of what passed for schooling in his day. Pestalozzi instead developed what he called an "ABC of apperception," the latter term an imperfect translation of the German word *Anschauung*, which denotes an active form of looking, the ability to grasp a sensory perception and assimilate it into one's overall understanding.[33] Apperception was a clear anticipation of the "self-activity" later echoed in Fröbel. The key to a healthy child's education was to harness this natural, outwardly directed impulse to apprehend the world in such a way as to build up complex ideas from simple perceptions, starting from the very simplest. Such a pedagogy could become painfully literal, such as when Pestalozzi prescribed teaching words one letter at a time—"b . . . ba . . . bat . . . bath . . . bathe . . . bathed"—as if individual letters somehow constituted the irreducible perceptual elements that formed larger concepts. But this was necessary if education were to be rebuilt from scratch.[34]

Where Fröbel was mystical, spiritual, and holistic, Pestalozzi was rational, mechanical, and reductionistic. He held learning to be governed by "physico-mechanical laws" (eleven of them, to be precise) "according to which our minds pick up and keep outer impressions."[35] Pestalozzi had cobbled together his cognitive psychology from ideas ubiquitous during the Enlightenment, by his own admission through trial and error. From Locke, he took the idea that the mind grows from blankness through the progressive assimilation of sensory inputs; from Rousseau, the conviction that the naturalness of sensory stimulation rather than the artificiality of words is the best antidote to educational confusion and societal corruption; and from Kant the insight that the architecture of our minds pre-equips us to sort and sift sensory data and gradually subject them to rational understanding. Number, form, and language: these were the cognitive givens, much like Kantian categories, that organized our experience and inspired the physical "object lessons" that became a staple of Pestalozzi's system.[36] "You want to mechanize education," his detractors claimed, a charge he was only too proud to accept: "I am trying to psychologize the instruction of mankind."[37]

What underlay Pestalozzi's reductionist pedagogy was his commitment to providing even the poorest children with an education, which he counted among the "rights of man in society."[38] Intervening against harried teachers perennially inclined to berate their charges as unimprovable urchins, he sought to demonstrate step by tiny step that even the most underfurnished minds are well suited to build complex understandings from simple ones. The insistence that teaching be painstakingly reconstructed from the standpoint of the child's inherent abilities, rather than the adult's educational goals, was revolutionary for the time—indeed, in Pestalozzi's view, a frontal assault on all prior pedagogy, and a direct continuation of the projects of Locke and Rousseau. Nothing enraged him more than the miseducation caused by the premature indoctrination of abstract concepts through traditional book-learning, a mode of teaching first prized by medieval monks and later promulgated by Protestant reformers and their Jesuit opposite numbers. Here, Pestalozzi's sober treatise took off on a ranting tangent. Abetted by the art of printing, he argued, the "tongue-twisting of our knowledge" had "forsaken the even road of sense-impression." This spawned a century of "wordy babblers" giddily unmoored from concrete reality and "degraded to lies and folly." The ultimate harvest of this speculative frenzy was nothing less than "sansculottism": political upheaval fueled by "a dreamy or rather raving condition of baseless, frantic presumption." Only by reattaching pedagogy to sound moorings, to "sense-impression [as] absolutely the foundation of all knowledge," could the dream of mass education be salvaged from the nightmare of mass revolution in Pestalozzi's troubled era.[39] However radical his methods, Pestalozzi's horror of revolution was what endeared him to leaders of both conservative and liberal stripes active during the Prussian Reform Movement.

Because the stakes were so very high, there was absolutely no room for error in Pestalozzi's educational scheme: literally no "play" in the system. Play, whether in the form of games, exercise, theater, humor, or simple spontaneity, had no role in such a precise, prescribed, and exacting method. Teaching was, to be sure, an art and not a science, but an art whose purpose was to imitate and at most improve upon a preexisting, God-given natural model. "Man becomes man only through the art [of education]," but that art "cannot add a hair's breadth to the spirit of that form through which our race is raised from confused sense-impressions to clear ideas." This was an art grounded in a pre-Romantic, neoclassical aesthetics, one disavowing idiosyncrasy, originality, creativity, or distinctiveness in the pursuit of harmony, balance, sound organization, and, most especially, conformity to a transcendent "prototype" (*Urform*).[40] Such an education consists in aligning the form of the mind with the order of nature, minimizing the slippage that occurs in traditional education when unnatural, artificial concepts are allowed to disrupt their tight coupling. The unmistakable corollary was that there is one and only one right way to educate and be educated. To be sure, Pestalozzi had good reason for such a straitened and uncompromising view of teaching and learning. He sought not so much to liberate the creative energies of individuals of genius but to remedy the defective mental and social development created by the mass poverty and oppression he saw all around him.

Like Fröbel, then, but in a different way, Pestalozzi sought to produce well-adjusted, cookie-cutter pupils: interchangeable, healthy young citizens. Fröbel innovated by ascribing a morally and spiritually elevating power to play, liberating pedagogy from the dryly mechanistic, rationalistic

Enlightenment-era epistemology to which Pestalozzi clung in spite of its deficiencies and long after it had gone out of fashion. But while Fröbel was unusual in tying play so deeply to spirituality, plenty of others had already cast it as means to children's ongoing physical, cognitive, and moral development. By focusing on disciplining the body and molding the will of the young student—to name two other areas where Pestalozzi's pedagogy was notably underdeveloped—they simply ascribed far less ethical value to play than Fröbel later would.

Immanuel Kant (1724–1804) in many ways espoused the conventional wisdom about play that Fröbel would eventually overturn. His remarks on the subject in *On Pedagogy* present us with an almost comical stereotype of Prussian rectitude. Quite conventionally, Kant held play as the frivolous opposite of rewarding work, valuable as a rejuvenating respite from scholastic discipline, perhaps even to exercise the mind somewhat, but hardly a means to cultivate morals. At best, playing games can rise to a form of self-abnegation through which the child "denies himself other needs, and thus learns gradually to impose other and greater privations on himself." Play, when it was allowed, must, however, always have a "purpose and an end," mainly physical toughness: "The more [the child's] body is strengthened and hardened, the safer is he from the disastrous consequences of pampering." Preeminently, this meant gymnastics—but not the kind that instills "affected elegance."[41]

While happy to concede that the child needs and deserves hours of play, Kant hastened to emphasize that "he must also learn to work."[42] Ascribing to work the same qualities Fröbel would ascribe to play—the capacity to engross and absorb the active mind—Kant held that through work, "man must be so fulfilled by the purpose which he has in mind, he becomes oblivious of himself." The purpose of education was to forge such habits of mental focus. "Education must be full of constraint," designed to combat the child's natural instincts, not give expression to them, even for the purpose of channeling and shaping them to productive ends. "The school is a forced culture," where "indiscreet curiosity" must not be indulged lest the child fail to acquire single-mindedness and self-discipline. For all these reasons, "to lead the child to look upon everything as play is very injurious."[43] That might set the child up for a dissipated adulthood, a life squandered at chess, dice, or faro.

Kant's pedagogical writings largely predate the maturation of his Idealist philosophy. Though they were edited and published in 1803, they were drawn from university lectures he first gave in 1776–77, before his three *Critiques*, and then repeated during the decade these canonical works were published (1781–90). In large measure, *On Pedagogy* instead registers the influence of Johann Bernard Basedow (1724–90), whose textbook Kant glossed for his lectures, and who, after Pestalozzi, counts as perhaps the second most important progenitor of educational reform in late Enlightenment Germany.[44] It was Basedow who in 1774 first applied Rousseau's ideas to the design of an experimental school, the hugely influential *Philanthropinum* at Dessau, which styled itself as a progressive, practical, modern alternative to the rigors of traditional Pietist teaching—the conservative pedagogy to which Kant himself had been subjected as a child. Kant supported Basedow's *Philanthropinum* and even led a public fund-raising campaign for it.

It was Basedow, too, who more than anyone else popularized the use of play as an educational technique. With his numerous disciples, some of whom went on to found their own schools and/or author their own treatises, he taxonomized and described the various forms of play in elaborate detail—even if many of these same followers later rebelled at what they, like Kant, saw as Basedow's lax practices.[45] Joachim Heinrich Campe (1746–1818), for example, Basedow's onetime collaborator and later rival, critiqued Basedow for letting children play too much, referring darkly to an epidemic of "play addiction" (particularly through cards, dice, billiards, and the lottery) and its "seductive" effects on the "young soul."[46] Gymnastics, under the pioneering J.C.F. GutsMuths (1759–1839), likewise took a more strenuous, less frivolous form, just as Kant had urged, as part of a widespread cultural movement to harden the masculine body.[47] In due course, a new generation of neohumanist educators led a full-court backlash against the Philanthropinists, defending a rigorous revival of classical learning as an alternative to the flighty, progressive tolerance of juvenile dissipation and the lack of system and rigor among Basedow and his successors. At the core of the neohumanist critique was the "sweetening" of education through play—literally, in an oft-repeated anecdote, through cookies baked in the shape of the ABCs to entice the child into learning how to read. As Friedrich Niethammer (1766–1848) summed up the case, "If you accustom children to playing around [*Spielerei*] in order to sweeten their work, they will play at their work their whole lives." Children must instead be submitted to an unapologetically demanding work ethic: "laboriousness" as a "virtue of the will" made "second nature through practice." The neohumanists' stricter approach would in due course become enshrined in the classical curriculum of the nineteenth-century *Gymnasium*.[48]

Viewed in this light, Kant had clearly staked out a mainstream middle position—supportive of play, but only in limited settings—during the decades that the Philanthropinists had made it a central category of pedagogical discourse and debate. Kant's conceptual distinctions were the only innovative aspect of what was otherwise a casually unoriginal view of play. He treated play as part of "physical culture," not "moral culture," and, at that, what he called "free" physical culture as opposed to "scholastic" physical culture (which, "on the other hand, is a serious affair").[49] This did not mean, in Kant's scheme, that play was merely what we would call physical, that is, bodily. Rather, his distinctions assigned play to the lower as opposed to the higher mental faculties, and among those lower faculties cast free play in a role subordinate to scholastic instruction. Play did serve to stimulate the mind, but only at the quasi-mechanical level of building the child's attention span, memory, imitative capacity, and habituation to following rules—basic functions of well-ordered cognition, and the prerequisites to developing discipline and avoiding "distractions" and bad habits. Even imagination belonged to these lower faculties: a useful capacity, to be sure, but one that must be "governed and brought under rules" rather than "further stretched and strained by fairy-tales"—not to mention novels, of which Kant sternly disapproved.[50]

Such a view of play comports with Kant's larger philosophical project, which reserves all forms of freedom for a higher plane far removed from the sensory, the physical, the concrete—elevated even above the lower and more mechanical mental functions—and which then proceeds to define freedom, counterintuitively, as adherence to universal moral law through the exercise of reason: the categorical imperative. It is not clear in Kant's conception whether the habits of routine mental discipline formed through play can even prepare the learner to exercise this higher moral-rational will. Play, to put it differently, barely belonged to the realm of his first *Critique*, to the sphere of how we come to know the world, much less to the realm of his second, where ethical reason is developed for practice.

To be sure, in his third and final *Critique*, on the power of judgment, Kant did stake out a conceptual space for the playful, the contingent, the creative, the imaginative—what he called the "free play between imagination and understanding." This was the faculty that Friedrich Schiller (1759–1805) explicitly assimilated to education in his *Letters on the Aesthetic Education of Man* (1794). For Schiller, the "play impulse" (*Spieltrieb*) is in fact the very wellspring of human creativity, the bridge between the sensual and the rational, the material and the ideal. Famously, "Man only plays when in the full meaning of the word he is a man, and he is only completely a man when he plays." It is clear in Schiller's treatment, however, that the play impulse arises in the imagination, not in the body; it finds expression in adult works of art, not in childish games; and most importantly, precisely because it is the highest outlet for human freedom, it resists being institutionalized, least of all in a school, lest artistic genius be fettered or constrained in any way.[51] From the perspective of educating children, Kantian aesthetics, even in Schiller's elaboration of it, put a firm lid on play. Idealist philosophy had sundered its multiple meanings, until then productively ambiguous, along every axis—literal and metaphorical, bodily and imaginative, childlike and adult, rule-bound and improvisational. In every instance, those types of play found in the children's schoolyard were consigned to a lower realm.

The liberal Protestant theologian Friedrich Schleiermacher (1768–1834) articulated the fullest contemporary contrast to Fröbel's vision of play. His influential lectures on education were delivered the same year, 1826, that Fröbel's *Education of Man* appeared, and offer the first rigorous treatment of play as part of an Idealist philosophical system.[52] There and in his broader writing and activity—notably his influence on the new University of Berlin, second only to Humboldt's—Schleiermacher cast himself as a pragmatic innovator, a gradualist reformer, the doyen of what one might call the center-left of establishment Prussian pedagogy. As an educational thinker, he was particularly attentive to the layers of *time*: to the succession of individual moments where present distractions are brought to yield before future life goals; to the distinct periods of maturation and schooling from infancy to childhood through career training, whether for the trades or at university; and ultimately to the obligations each generation has to its successor. His was an ethical system deeply concerned with the moral reproduction of society through education, in which play had a confined but critical role.[53]

Schleiermacher built his theory of play in good dialectical fashion on a series of conceptual opposites: play versus seriousness (*Ernst*), present versus future, home versus school. Each term in a pair was mapped onto its two counterparts so as to give these everyday words new and more complex valences. Echoing Schiller, who had defined play as "the extinction of time in time," he contended that "to play is essentially to be purely in the present, the absolute negation of the future."[54] It thus belonged at home, so that seriousness could be pursued at school. "School life is work life, or a life of practice; life at home is a life of play."[55] The subtle middle term in this otherwise banal statement is "practice" (*Übung*)—the effort to become better at a thing that actually takes root in play yet transcends it as the child grows from careless absorption to the purposeful cultivation of a future ability. "Satisfaction in the moment without consideration of the future is, in the life of the child, what we call *play* in the broadest sense; busying oneself with the future, *practice*."[56]

The transition from "play" via "practice" to "seriousness" defined the boundary between one phase of childhood and another. During home life, before school begins, the two are "indifferently" intertwined. Preparation for school requires nimbly disentangling them, coaxing the child toward seriousness through the patient cultivation of mindful repetition and conscious improvement. Each life period must be given its due lest the next one begin on an unstable footing; to impose practice too hastily is to risk impairing the "joy of childhood." But while the shift must be almost imperceptibly gradual, "habituation to order"—order being the principle that "governs public instruction"—"is gradually fixed" as the end result.[57] However strained and devoid of practical detail, Schleiermacher's terminological redefinitions were intended to mark a formal caesura in the life of a child, paralleled in the institutional organization of society: to effect a deliberate and characteristically modern schism from a premodern world where work and play, adults and children, had always been intermixed. At stake was the legitimacy of the school as an age-old institution newly refounded in his own time, one that, starting with the Philanthropinists, had been consciously redesigned to socialize children explicitly for their future roles—and, in Schleiermacher's view, now finally free to focus solely on that purpose.

By these lights, a kindergarten focused on play was not so much preparation for school as a foil to it. Fröbel's pedagogy of play became the first step in a road not taken once Schleiermacher had gently but definitively cast it as unsuitable for later learning. Play's potential as a means to train mind and morals in later life was abandoned before the imperative of molding future adults. Ethics, for Schleiermacher and his followers, trumped epistemology, in stark contrast to Fröbel's vision of moral and mental growth as coequal and inseparable. Schooling, as it first became universal, was defined as the phase in life when childish things are put aside, when play ends and work begins, when the stages of child development were mapped onto an escalating hierarchy of civic and social obligations fixed in successive levels of schooling, primary, secondary, and tertiary. The extinction of play, of spontaneous activity unconcerned with future consequences, became the precondition for individual self-directedness and for adult moral and civic responsibility. Maturation was remolded around age-appropriate milestones—the expectations of three- and six-year-olds, or *Schüler* and *Studenten*—in ways we now take for granted as a consequence of the schooling revolution.

And yet, just as the child transitions only gradually from home to school, so Schleiermacher carved out a space for play at the cusp of adulthood, as a means of easing the individual's entry into wider communities of grownup life in civil society. Regarding young men enrolled in trade schools, he extolled "free activity and play" as a "countervailing power" to the dissolution of a common school spirit after they went their separate occupational ways. Gymnastic exercises he commended as an ideal means of "forgetting one's particular occupation and station" in purposeful enjoyment outside work, so long as gymnastic associations were thoughtfully designed to mitigate "class divisions" while still conforming to "prevailing social norms" of rank and station.[58] Schleiermacher also wrote with special fondness, even indulgence, toward Germany's notoriously undisciplined university students, who lacked the adult oversight their peers enjoyed (or suffered) in English colleges. Against other university reformers, notably Fichte, whose plan for higher learning had envisioned elders presiding in loco parentis at a kind of Platonic barracks, he successfully argued that the very principle of academic freedom required that students be let loose as adults, even if that meant tolerating their boisterous "music and singing," "debauchery," and "cynical disorder" and the irritations of "their own linguistic culture." The "transition to autonomy, the coming into being of life through free choice," the chance to "try out every order and way of life"—the chance to *play*—was part and parcel of university life, an indispensable stage on the road to full maturity.[59]

Except perhaps for Schiller, adult play had been an alien concept to the pedagogues of the German educational revolution. Yet adult play abounded in early nineteenth-century Germany, in the dueling societies and fraternities (*Burschenschaften*) frequented by university students and in the singing, sharpshooting, and gymnastics societies that constituted organized German nationalism. Such a lively associational life, populated by grown men, was a subversive form of adult role-play if there ever was one, a fabricated culture in which subjects of Germany's still-disunited states playacted the part of citizens of a still-imaginary German nation—and with the utmost solemnity and seriousness. Fröbel was himself a committed German nationalist, dating from his early involvement in the volunteer paramilitary Lützower Freikorps, where the gymnastic archnationalist Friedrich Ludwig "*Turnvater*" Jahn had introduced him to his later Keilhau collaborators Heinrich Langethal and Wilhelm Middendorf (who were, in turn, both avid students of Schleiermacher). Until the end of his days, Fröbel equated German national unity with the universal progress of humanity. The cosmopolitan nationalism he espoused was nothing if not a repository for the potent bonds of intergenerational obligation that Schleiermacher in his arid treatise had so earnestly sought to describe.[60]

Fröbel ultimately diverged from his contemporaries by casting play, together with the spiritual growth it uniquely enabled, not as a means to some other educational goal—a productive citizen, a loyal subject, a rationally self-directed individual—but as an end unto itself. Indeed, his most radical aim was *not* in fact to teach children how to play, for in his view they were born with the impulse to do so already. Rather, the whole thrust of Fröbel's writings, his "gifts," his relentless agitation, and his many experimental schools, was to teach *adults* how to play. His most famous dictum, "Come, let us live for our children," is revealingly ambiguous in this regard. *Kommt, lasst uns unsern Kindern leben*: let us live not only *for* our children but also *with* and *through* them. Fröbel spent a career training a cadre of caring professionals—the "kindergarteners" in the German sense of the word—to make their life's work out of play. The kindergarten movement licensed parents and teachers to enjoy their children, and to see in the activity of guiding their play not a falling away from adult responsibility but the very embodiment of it. It should come as no surprise that such a project would conflict with the serious adult experiment in deliberate human development that was the German educational revolution.

NOTES

1. Ludwig von Rönne, *Das Unterrichtswesen des preußischen Staates* (Berlin: Veit, 1855), 1:866–867.

2. Note that in Germany today, the word *Kindergarten* still encompasses a range of preschool ages, not just the year before elementary school proper, as in the United States.

3. Ann Taylor Allen, "Spiritual Motherhood: German Feminists and the Kindergarten Movement," *History of Education Quarterly* 22, no. 3 (Autumn 1982): 327. Allen's *The Transatlantic Kindergarten: Education and Women's Movements in Germany and the United States* (New York: Oxford, 2017) provides the best scholarly history of the kindergarten, with an extensive analysis of its relation to the 1848 Revolution on 36–45.

4. *Kladderadatsch: Humoristisch-satirisches Wochenblatt* no. 36, September 7, 1891, 142.

5. Bertha von Marenholtz-Bülow, *Erinnerungen an Friedrich Fröbel*, vol. 1 of *Gesammelte Beiträge zum Verständniß der Fröbel'schen Erziehungsidee* (Kassel: Georg H. Wigand, 1876), 129–133.

6. For more on Karl Fröbel and his *Hochschule* for women, see Catherine M. Prelinger, *Charity, Challenge, and Change: Religious Dimensions of the Mid-Nineteenth-Century Women's Movement in Germany* (Westport, CT: Greenwood, 1987), 95–100, 127–134, 161–162 (including Friedrich Fröbel's reaction).

7. See, for example, Victor Cousin, *Rapport sur l'état de l'Instruction Publique dans quelques pays de l'Allemagne et particulièrement en Prusse* (Paris: Imprimerie royale, 1832); Horace Mann, *Report of an Educational Tour in Germany, and Parts of Great Britain and Ireland* (London: Simpkin, Marshall, 1846); Henry Geitz, Jürgen Heideking, and Jürgen Herbst,

eds., *German Influences on Education in the United States to 1917* (Cambridge: Cambridge University Press, 1995).

8. David Baker, *The Schooled Society: The Educational Transformation of Global Culture* (Stanford, CA: Stanford University Press, 2014) argues that this scholarly omission extends to the social theory of the modern world generally. But on Germany, see Karl Schleunes, *Schooling and Society: The Politics of Education in Prussia and Bavaria, 1750–1900* (Providence, RI: Berg, 1989).

9. Alfons Rinke, *Friedrich Fröbels philosophische Entwicklung unter dem Einfluß der Romantik* (Langensalza: Hermann Beyer & Söhne, 1935), 106.

10. Friedrich Fröbel, *Die Pädagogik des Kindergartens: Gedanken Friedrich Fröbel's über das Spiel und die Spielgegenstände des Kindes*, vol. 2 of *Friedrich Fröbel's gesammelte pädagogische Schriften*, ed. Wichard Lange (Berlin: Th. Chr. Fr. Enslin, 1862), 122–125; Fröbel, *Friedrich Fröbel's Pedagogics of the Kindergarten*, trans. Josephine Jarvis (New York: D. Appleton, 1895), 160–165. A note on source citations: I have relied extensively on nineteenth-century English translations of key works by Fröbel, Pestalozzi, Kant, and others, both because they provide highly competent renderings of often contorted German prose into an accessible Victorian style and because they thereby give English speakers access to a valuable body of primary materials. In every instance, I have checked the English translation against the German original and made emendations where appropriate. In this note and the notes below, full citations are given in the first instance to both the German original and the English translation, whereas in subsequent instances the page numbers of the English translation are given in square brackets (e.g., 122–125 [160–165]).

11. Christian Zeh, "Bericht über die Fröbelsche Erziehungsanstalt zu Keilhau: An das hochfürstliche Consistorium zu Schwarzburg-Rudolstadt, " *Isis von Oken* 2, no. 7 (1825): 781.

12. Friedrich Fröbel, *Die Menschenerziehung, die Erziehungs-, Unterrichts-, und Lehrkunst, angestrebt in der allgemeinen deutschen Erziehungsanstalt zu Keilhau* (Keilhau: Verlag der allgemeinen deutschen Erziehungsanstalt, 1826), 140–143; Fröbel, *The Education of Man*, trans. W. N. Hailmann (Mineola, NY: Dover, 2005), 119–122. Note that the Keilhau Institute was a forerunner to the 1837 school that in 1840 Fröbel first dubbed a "kindergarten," so strictly speaking the pedagogy of play revealed in Fröbel's *Menschenerziehung* predates the first named kindergarten by ten to fifteen years. Importantly, Fröbel's famous gifts, described later in this chapter, were first developed during this interim period.

13. Fröbel, *Menschenerziehung*, 69–70 [54–55].

14. Fröbel, *Menschenerziehung*, 123 [102–103].

15. Fröbel, *Pädagogik*, 183 [238].

16. Fröbel, *Pädagogik*, 152 [198]; see also 9 [11–12] for similar imagery.

17. Fröbel, *Menschenerziehung*, 123 [103].

18. Fröbel, *Menschenerziehung*, 416 [303].

19. Fröbel, *Menschenerziehung*, 126–127 [106–107].

20. Fröbel, *Menschenerziehung*, 133–134 [114].

21. Fröbel, *Menschenerziehung*, 127 [107].

22. Fröbel, *Menschenerziehung*, 132–133 [113].

23. Fröbel, *Menschenerziehung*, 133–134 [114].

24. Fröbel, *Menschenerziehung*, 125–126 [105].

25. Fröbel, *Menschenerziehung*, 136 [116].

26. Fröbel, *Menschenerziehung*, 418 [305].

27. Fröbel, *Menschenerziehung*, 424 [309].

28. Letter to Amalie Marschner, February 2, 1847, reprinted in Helmut Heiland, *Die Spielpädagogik Friedrich Fröbels*, vol. 5 of *Beiträge zur Fröbelforschung* (Hildesheim: Olms, 1998), 343.

29. Heiland, *Die Spielpädagogik Friedrich Fröbels*, 122, 126 on the *Mutter- und Koselieder.*

30. Letter to Amalie Müller, ca. November 25, 1839, repr. in Heiland, *Die Spielpädagogik Friedrich Fröbels*, 316, with comment on 291.

31. Fröbel, *Pädagogik*, 150 [196].

32. Contrast this with David Hamlin's emphasis on the individualizing effects of commercialized play during the Wilhelmine period in his engaging study of the German toy industry, *Work and Play: The Production and Consumption of Toys in Germany, 1870–1914* (Ann Arbor: University of Michigan Press, 2007), 8–15.

33. (Johann) Heinrich Pestalozzi, *Wie Gertrud ihre Kinder lehrt, ein Versuch den Müttern Anleitung zu geben, ihre Kinder selbst zu unterrichten* (Bern: Heinrich Gess, 1801), 29–30; Pestalozzi, *How Gertrude Teaches Her Children: An Attempt to Help Mothers to Teach Their Own Children and an Account of the Method*, ed. Ebenezer Cooke and trans. Lucy E. Holland and Frances C. Turner (Syracuse, NY: C. W. Bardeen, 1898), 54.

34. Pestalozzi, *How Gertrude*, 174–180, at 180 [153–156, at 156]. The English translation uses the word "gardener" instead of *gebadet*.

35. Pestalozzi, *How Gertrude*, 32–34 [56–57]; also 143–154 [131–139]; and "Die Methode: Eine Denkschrift Pestalozzi's," in *Allgemeine Monatschrift für Erziehung und Unterricht*, ed. J. P. Rossel (Aachen, 1828), 9:71–73 [319–320, in *How Gertrude*].

36. Pestalozzi, *Wie Gertrud*, 158–169 [142–149]. Pestalozzi's emphasis on language probably owes less to Kant than to Herder, who gave more philosophical emphasis to this human capacity.

37. Pestalozzi, *Wie Gertrud*, 32 [57] and Pestalozzi, "Die Methode," 67 [315], respectively.

38. Pestalozzi, *Wie Gertrud*, 201 [169].

39. Pestalozzi, *Wie Gertrud*, 272–282 [220–227], with quotations on 272 [220], 278 [224], 280 [225], 281 [226].

40. Pestalozzi, *Wie Gertrud*, 139–141 [129–130]; for further instances of neoclassical aesthetic tropes, see ibid., 34 [57], 159 [143], 169 [149]; and Pestalozzi, "Die Methode," 73 [321]: "The mechanism of nature as a whole is great and simple. Man! imitate it."

41. Immanuel Kant, *Über Pädagogik*, ed. Friedrich Theodor Rink (Königsberg: Friedrich Nicolovius, 1803), 162.

42. Kant, *Über Pädagogik*, 73 [165].

43. Kant, *Über Pädagogik*, 77 [167–168].

44. Note that Kant gave the lectures at least three other times between 1780 and 1787, apparently only using Basedow's *Methodenbuch* the first time. See Robert B. Louden, "'Not a Slow *Reform*, but a Swift *Revolution*': Kant and Basedow on the Need to Transform Education," in *Kant and Education: Interpretations and Commentary*, ed. Klas Roth and Chris W. Surprenant (New York: Routledge, 2012).

45. Heikki Lempa, "Techniques of Epicurean Masculinity: The Play Method in German Education, 1774–1820," in *Masculinity, Senses, Spirit*, ed. Katherine M. Faull (Lewisburg,

PA: Bucknell University Press, 2011), with useful mentions of Salzmann, Bahrdt, Brandes, and Jahn as well.

46. Johann Heinrich Campe, ed., *Allgemeine Revision des gesammten Schul- und Erziehungswesens* (Hamburg: Bohn, 1785–92), 5:672–695 on *Spielsucht*; also 1:65; 8:95–141, 355–403; 9:395–399. See also Simone Austermann, *Die "Allgemeine Revision": Pädagogische Theorieentwicklung im 18. Jahrhundert* (Bad Heilbrunn: Julius Klinkhardt, 2010), 159–161.

47. Lempa, "Techniques," 95. More broadly, see Teresa Sanislo, "Models of Manliness and Femininity: The Physical Culture of the Enlightenment and Early National Movement in Germany, 1770–1819" (PhD diss., University of Michigan, 2001).

48. Friedrich Immanuel Niethammer, *Der Streit des Philanthropinismus und Humanismus in der Theorie des Erziehungs-Unterrichts unserer Zeit* (Jena: Friedrich Frommann, 1808), 239–249, with quotations at 239, 245, 247, 249.

49. Kant, *Über Pädagogik*, 72–73 [164–165].

50. Kant, *Über Pädagogik*, 81–82, 87 [174, 180–181].

51. Friedrich Schiller, *Über die ästhetische Erziehung des Menschen in einer Reihe von Briefen* (Stuttgart: Reclam, 1965), 57–62 (on *Spieltrieb*), 63 (for quotation); for further evidence on this conception of play in Schiller, see ibid., 114, 122–123.

52. By contrast, Johann Friedrich Herbart (1776–1841), a founder of philosophical pedagogy as a discipline and Kant's own successor at Königsberg, does not seem to have had a theory of play.

53. Heinrich Scherer, *Die Pädagogik als Wissenschaft von Pestalozzi bis zur Gegenwart* (Leipzig: Friedrich Brandstetter, 1907), 2:142–162 is still a valuable treatment.

54. Schiller, *Ästhetische Erziehung*, 57, using the term *aufheben*; Friedrich Schleiermacher, *Erziehungslehre: Aus Schleiermacher's handschriftlichem Nachlasse und nachgeschriebenen Vorlesungen*, in *Friedrich Schleiermacher's Sämmtliche Werke*, Abteilung 3, vol. 9, ed. C. Platz (Berlin: G. Reimer, 1846ff.), 676.

55. Schleiermacher, *Erziehungslehre*, 651; also 676: "In general the state of being a child [*Kindsein*] can be expressed through play, that of becoming a grown-up [*Menschwerden*], through practice."

56. Schleiermacher, *Erziehungslehre*, 77 (emphasis added); also 78 for what follows below.

57. Schleiermacher, *Erziehungslehre*, 312, 316–319, with quotations on 312, 316, 317, 319; see also 368–369.

58. Schleiermacher, *Erziehungslehre*, 556–560.

59. Schleiermacher, *Erziehungslehre*, 566–573; Friedrich Schleiermacher, "Gelegentliche Gedanken über Universitäten im deutschen Sinn: Anhang über eine neu zu errichtende Universität," in *Friedrich Schleiermacher's Sämmtliche Werke*, Abteilung 3, vol. 1, ed. C. Platz (Berlin: G. Reimer, 1846ff.), 608; translated as *Occasional Thoughts on Universities in the German Sense: With an Appendix Regarding a University Soon to Be Established*, trans. Terrence Tice and Edwina Lawler (Lewiston, NY: Edwin Mellen, 1991), 54–55.

60. Among many examples, see Friedrich Fröbel, *Ueber deutsche Erziehung überhaupt, und über das allgemeine Deutsche der Erziehungsanstalt in Keilhau insbesondere* (Rudolstadt: Hofbuchhandlung, 1822). For the Jahn connection, see Alexander Bruno Hanschmann, *Friedrich Fröbel: Die Entwickelung seiner Erziehungsidee in seinem Leben* (Eisenach: J. Bacmeister, 1874), 93–94. "Turnvater" was the nickname given to Jahn to celebrate him as the father of modern German gymnastics (*turnen*).

Interlude

CHAPTER EIGHT

Ich möchte hören,
wie man diesem Strumpfwesen
abstreiten wollte . . .
—F. H. Jacobi

Invective, Eulogy, Play

Jacobi's Sock 1799

CHRISTIANE FREY

YES, AT ISSUE HERE is indeed nothing more than a sock—or to be more precise, Jacobi's simile of the *Strickstrumpf*, the knitted sock, as it is used in his infamous open letter to Fichte of 1799. But before we come to matters of knitting, a few words about why we should be interested in Friedrich Heinrich Jacobi in the context of a volume on play in the Age of Goethe. Why, of all thinkers, Jacobi? Wasn't he the one who initiated one of the most serious and polemical philosophical disputes of the eighteenth century, namely, the so-called pantheism controversy?[1] And was he not the one who emphatically defended the existence of something "real" beyond what can be known? Wouldn't Jacobi seem to be the most earnest of all of the philosophers around 1800, the kind of philosopher who would object to any play in philosophy?[2]

And indeed: in the aforementioned open letter to Fichte, in the section dated March 6, "play" (511/206) is used as a pejorative term in characterizing Fichte's philosophy. Our new "sciences," Jacobi complains—with obvious allusion to Fichte's *Wissenschaftslehre* or "Doctrine of scientific knowledge"—are but mere "plays," games, that is, invented by our minds as a way of "passing the time" (511/206). Science, in the new fashion typified by Fichte, no longer dealt with what Jacobi calls "the truth" in the singular, but rather with mere "truths" (512/207) in the plural. In the sciences the mind now did nothing more than to "organize its lack of knowledge" ("der Geist organisiert nur seine Unwißenheit") without any insight into the truth ("ohne einer Erkenntniß des Wahren . . . näher zu kommen"; 512/206). For Jacobi, then, "play" seems to be the *opposite* of science, of real philosophy and of how it should work—and thus nothing of any real value. Or so one would assume.

But truth be told: Jacobi's dichotomy—of real "science" or philosophy on the one hand and "play" on the other—is not as straightforward as it might at first seem. Rather, in his open letter to Fichte, Jacobi is clearly playing with Johann Gottlieb Fichte, the philosopher he most admired. And when one understands the game—or rather the rules of the game—Jacobi here plays by means of his open letter and by means of what can certainly be read as an invective, however philosophically tempered, one will at the same time get a better sense both of his understanding and critique of Fichte's science and of his own sense of play.[3] This will lead to a more general insight into how the epistolary and the epistemic are being negotiated in the late eighteenth and the early nineteenth centuries through modes of rhetorical playing. For heuristic reasons, I will begin by working with a purposefully vague notion of play.[4] It is only through the subsequent reading of Jacobi's open letter to Fichte that a more concrete idea of what play could mean—in this particular context and at the time of Jacobi's letter more generally—will emerge.

WRITING AS PLAY

Now, both Jacobi's concept and his practice of play—his act of writing and addressing an open and obviously polemical letter to his venerated Fichte—can be illuminated by means of his *Strumpf*, of his simile of the sock. For those familiar with Jacobi, the focus on this simile might not seem particularly original. Although Jacobi has long been neglected in scholarship, the simile of the sock is in fact relatively well known.[5] But no one thus far has tried to examine what Jacobi *does* with this simile in a rhetorical and performative sense.[6] Without a doubt, the very object of comparison, the sock, is in itself already witty and playful. And one could easily assume that Jacobi makes fun of Fichte and his *Wissenschaftslehre* by choosing such a, well, ludicrous comparison. Nonetheless, Jacobi's strategy in dealing with Fichte—who was in fact less offended by Jacobi's letter than one might imagine—has yet to be described and understood. Jacobi's rhetorical strategy, and his mode of writing, is quite remarkable. On the one hand, the letter clearly draws on the rhetorical strategies and generic moments of invective, even if in a moderated and modernized fashion.[7] And yet, at one and the same time, Jacobi's invective must be understood as an emphatic affirmation. And vice versa: for any affirmation of Fichte is, at least in Jacobi's letter, at the same time a radical critique. Thus when Fichte expressed his appreciation for Jacobi's letter, it would be wrong to claim that, blinded by his vanity, he had in fact missed the point.[8] Hence, what the following explorations are meant to demonstrate is the ludic performance we see at work in Jacobi's rhetorically sophisticated and at the same time proto-romantic writing.

Inspired by Roland Barthes's notion of "mode of writing," the following reading of Jacobi's letter positions his text both *within* and *outside* or at the unruly margins of the generic and rhetorical conventions of invective and of the open letter as they unfolded in the eighteenth century.[9] For Barthes, the "mode of writing" or *écriture*, as he discusses it in his early *Writing Degree Zero*, designates what is neither "language" nor "style." Language is determined by history, style by the writer's biography and biology. Both are inevitable. Language is open to society, but without the force of change. Style is closed and personal. There is, however, a third dimension that escapes language and style and which, for Barthes (against Sartre), is the only space of both "freedom" and commitment.[10] The relentless struggle with the established conventions becomes apparent or visible only on the level of this *écriture* or mode of writing. For Barthes, the mode of writing thus represents the writer's active commitment, but communicating *beyond* message or content. The mode of writing therefore lies rather in the form of the utterance: tone, ethos, and personal expression, for example, are part of the "ensemble of features" that make up *écriture* for Barthes.[11] And it is precisely this dimension of writing that Jacobi's open letter exposes—and that it exposes as a playground for an open discussion. Of course, Jacobi's letter is not "literature" in the sense of Barthes's *Writing Degree Zero*. But it does exhibit, quite in the sense of the earlier Barthes, what escapes both language and style, conventional rhetoric and self-involved idiosyncrasy, in the way it engages with Fichte's doctrine of science. And it is precisely the idea of "play" that can provide a deeper understanding of how Jacobi's mode of writing inscribes itself in the generic codes of epistolary rhetoric while—as playfully as powerfully—eluding them at the same time.

SCIENCE, PLAY, AND THE SOCK

One of the main reasons Jacobi describes science, *Wissenschaft* in Fichte's sense of the word, as a kind of "play" is to point up one of its essential characteristics, namely, that science, as it appears in Fichte, is not a mode of observation, but a form of action—a doing that is directed at itself and that consummates itself by its own activity. It is, as it were, curved in on itself; and in this curving, it also generates its own object. In this sense, knowledge or cognition, when engaging in science, does not explore external objects, but its own—homemade—edifices of notions, of *Begriffe*: "By fashioning concepts the human spirit only seeks, in all things and from all things, to retrieve itself" ("In Allem und aus Allem sucht der menschliche Geist nur sich selbst, Begriffe bildend, wieder hervor"; 505/198).

Now, in order to illustrate what he, Jacobi, believes to be the true mechanism of this new form of science, of Fichte's idealism, he uses the telling and conspicuous simile of the sock: "In a mischievous moment last winter, in Hamburg, I summed up the result of Fichtean Idealism in a simile. I compared it to a knitted sock" ("In einem muthwilligen Augenblick vorigen Winter zu Hamburg, brachte ich das Resultat des Fichtischen Idealismus in ein Gleichniß. Ich wählte einen Strickstrumpf"; 509/203), Jacobi reports. With these words, Jacobi introduces what will be, by all accounts, an astute discussion of Fichte's philosophy. But despite the evident seriousness with which it is advanced—the argument Jacobi makes by no means takes a back seat to his wit—the image of the sock is clearly designed to change the register. Rarely does Jacobi insert trivial biographical anecdotes into his philosophical expositions; that he does so here ("In a mischievous moment last winter . . .") sets up the analogy, in all its explanatory earnestness, as a kind of playful badinage. But what exactly is this simile meant to demonstrate?

Jacobi loses no time exploiting the potential of his image:

> To form an idea of the origin and constitution of a knitted sock in other than the usual empirical way, one only need undo the end of the knitted web, and let it run off on the thread of the identity of this object-subject. One will then clearly see how this individual thing attained actuality through the mere back-and-forth-movement of the thread, that is, through an incessant restriction of its movement preventing it from following its striving towards the infinite—without empirical intervention or other admixture or adjunct of sorts. (509–510)

> [Um sich eine andere als die gewöhnliche empirische Vorstellung von dem Entstehen und Bestehen eines Strickstrumpfs zu machen, braucht man nur den Schluß des Gewebes aufzulösen, und es an dem Faden der Identität dieses Object-Subjects ablaufen zu laßen. Man sieht deutlich alsdenn, wie dieses Individuum, durch ein bloßes Hin- und herbewegen des Fadens, das ist, durch ein unaufhörliches Einschränken seiner Bewegung, und Verhindern, daß er seinem Streben ins Unendliche hinaus folgte—ohne empirischen Einschlag, oder sonst eine Beymischung oder Zuthat, zur Wirklichkeit gelangte.] (203–204)

The knitted sock is given to our imagination, literally our *Vorstellung*, as a performance and as an experiment—as a kind of performative thought experiment. If one wants to understand what the sock—any sock, that is—really is in its essence, one has to analyze it, one has to unravel it. The unraveling then demonstrates that the process of knowledge or cognition does not rely on any external givens or auxiliary means. It is uniquely concerned with the "back-and-forth-movement of the thread."

> To this sock of mine I give borders, flowers, moon and stars, all kinds of figures, and cognize: how all this is nothing but a product of the productive imagination of the fingers hovering between the I of the thread and the not-I of the needles. Looked at from the *standpoint of truth*, all these figures, along with the being of the sock, are but the one bare thread. Neither from the needles nor from the fingers has anything entered into it. It alone, pure and simple, is all these things, and there is nothing in all of them apart from it. What it is, is nothing but these things, but—together with its movements of reflection on the needles which, by continuing them, it has retained, thereby becoming this determinate individual.
>
> (510)

> [Diesem meinem Strumpfe gebe ich Streifen, Blumen, Sonne, Mond und Sterne, alle möglichen Figuren, und erkenne: wie alles dieses nichts ist, als ein Product der, zwischen dem Ich des Fadens und dem Nicht-Ich der Drähte schwebenden productiven Einbildungskraft der Finger. Alle diese Figuren mit dem Strumpfwesen zusammen, sind, aus dem Standpuncte der Wahrheit betrachtet, der Alleinige nackte Faden. Es ist nichts in ihn gefloßen, weder aus den Dräthen, noch aus den Fingern; Er allein und rein ist jenes Alles, und es ist in Allem jenen nichts außer ihm; Er ist es ganz und gar, nur—Mit *seinen Bewegungen der Reflexion an den Dräthen*, die er, fortsetzend, behalten hat, und dadurch zu diesem bestimmten Individuum geworden ist.]
>
> (204)

As complex as the pattern it produces may be, as much as it may appear to be woven into "infinite manifolds," the thread is nevertheless, in truth, only a thread (510/204). Its real and original identity, once unwound and divested of its coil—and this unwinding is the accomplishment of *Wissenschaft* in the new sense Fichte gives it—is exposed not as threadbare but as a bare thread. The return—the process of unraveling—to the origin makes clear "that that infinite manifold, and manifold infinity, was nothing but an empty weaving of its weaving, and that the one single reality is only itself in its *self-initiated, self-contained, and self-directed activity*" ("daß jene unendliche Mannigfaltigkeit, und mannigfaltige Unendlichkeit, nichts als ein leeres Weben seines Webens war, und das einzige Reale nur er selbst in seinem *Handeln, aus, in und auf sich selbst*"; 510/204). The seemingly infinite manifold and the manifold infinity are revealed to be nothing but a weaving of its weaving; the real is constituted by a literally self-involved activity. To put it differently, nothing from the external world beyond the sock, not even the knitting needle, has had any essential impact on the constitution or appearance of the sock with all its flowers and stars. The sock's pattern is constituted neither by anything external nor even through some kind of modification of the thread. Everything is the thread, or to be more precise, a movement or action (*Handlung*) of the thread. Not only are the flowers and stars nothing in themselves; they cannot even be seen as having been caused by the thread. They *are* nothing at all, but rather only a movement, the movement of the thread.

It would thus seem—to cut the unraveling yarn short—that Jacobi's simile of the sock is no more and no less than a satire: a means of mocking Fichte's extravagant idealism and of exposing to ridicule the self-enclosed and self-involved character of the *Wissenschaftslehre*. The sock's thread demonstrates how any process of analysis that claims to be self-sustaining will always end up demonstrating only itself. Like a cat with a ball of yarn, science as sock, one could say, is at play: at play with its own self- or single-knit conceptual weave.

SERIOUSNESS AT PLAY

The sock would thus be Jacobi's way of showing how Fichte, with his uncompromisingly idealist reformulation of science, goes too far, of *distancing* himself from his open letter's addressee. But it is nevertheless clear that the sock is much more than just this. That it has only a single thread does not mean that it has only a single sense—on the contrary. For what seems to be, and indeed really is the most biting critique and satire is at the same time—the highest praise. The simile is employed in what is clearly a eulogistic if not reverent missive. Jacobi is *as enthusiastic* about Fichte's philosophy and its concept of *Wissenschaft* as he is skeptical of it. But acknowledgment and critique are not simply distributed between the frame (as a form of praise) and the simile (as a form of playful invective); rather, the simile of the sock is itself a tribute—indeed, it is *primarily* a tribute—to Fichte's philosophy. Now, while this claim may sound puzzling or even extravagant, I must at this point ask my readers to simply accept this seemingly unmotivated twist or knot in my remarks—or in the wool I seem to be pulling over their eyes—and to allow me to proceed.

My claim is that Jacobi's simile of the sock exhibits and performs both critique and praise, invective and eulogy, at one and the same time and in one and the same, as it were, discursive substance. For what the metaphorical experiment demonstrates is that Fichte's *Wissenschaftslehre* is in itself both coherent and unavoidable. It is a closed system in which the act of unraveling indeed reveals the inevitability of the act itself. Jacobi fully acknowledges this form of thinking as the highest possible achievement of *Wissenschaft* and the most refined and convincing form of philosophical thinking. This is why Jacobi can simultaneously make a mockery of the *Wissenschaftslehre* by means of his simile while also coming to its defense. Indeed he explicitly imagines a lengthy Fichtean response to his critique that can by no means be rejected out of hand: "Scoff as much as you wish at this pure pleasure in the pure knowledge *of pure knowledge alone*. . . . We don't deny that in it we are blessed" ("Spotte so viel du willst über diese reine Lust am reinen Wißen *allein des reinen Wißens*. . . . Wir läugnen nicht, daß wir in ihm selig sind"; 511/205; emphasis in the original). Jacobi includes himself in the circle of those who adhere to this form of philosophy, which he calls "this lofty love for knowledge—for mere knowing" ("Liebe des Erkenntnißes—blos des Erkennens"; 511/205). This form of *Wissenschaft* is the only one that has reconciled itself to itself. There can thus be no doubt for Jacobi that with Fichte, speculative philosophy has reached, as it were, its ultimate and most distinguished destination. It is for this reason that Jacobi can call Fichte "the true Messiah of speculative reason" (501/194).

This thus means that the simile of the sock is not just playful and witty badinage; it is, rather, also meant in all earnestness. But, of course, and to be sure, the ambiguity does not end there. Rather, it is crucial to understand that within the very mode of earnestness, there is *at once* eulogy and invective.

One gains a better sense for this by all means playful ambiguity if one recalls to mind what the disagreement between Jacobi and Fichte was all about. As is well known, what Jacobi objects to in Fichte's philosophy is that it necessarily leads to nihilism. Followed to its logical consequence, reason itself, rather than an authorized faculty of knowledge, would turn out to be a mere "production of the spirit," a mere "*act-act*" (*That-That*; 507/201). The spirit, the *Geist*, would thus end up as its own self-creator. This is why Jacobi protests that there must be truth, *Wahres*, beyond the weft and warp of *Wissenschaft*. But since there can be no thread leading from *Wissenschaft* to *Wahres*, just as the sock's single thread always only leads to itself, the only way to get around Fichte's speculative idealism would be what Jacobi calls "non-philosophy," *Unphilosophie* or a philosophy of non-knowledge, of *Nichtwissen*. And this can be attained only via a leap, a *Sprung*, a *salto mortale*, a kind of dropped stitch, as it were, opening a gap into the unknown. Hence, Jacobi's critique of Fichte's philosophy is indeed radical.[12] And nevertheless, he still adheres to, remains tied to it. And one could say that the reason for this adherence, this tie or knot, is that the very necessity of the leap Jacobi argues for becomes evident only in the seamless weave of philosophy as *Wisssenschaft*. No philosophy better demonstrates the necessity of non-knowledge than the philosophy that consummates knowledge.[13] For if the highest form of philosophy is a philosophy that is all act, all act-act and ultimately an act of self-consummation, it leaves the philosopher with nothing more to philosophize—save in the form of an endless performance of the same, which is what Jacobi pejoratively calls play, a futile and empty undertaking that takes time and occupies space but doesn't lead anywhere. But for Jacobi, it is only this kind of philosophy that can lead to a philosophical understanding of the need for a non-philosophy. Fichte's *Wissenschaftslehre* and Jacobi's *Unphilosophie* are thus for Jacobi not just intimately linked but also necessarily entwined, *verstrickt*.

This is why Jacobi's sock analogy can function at one and the same time as an acknowledgment of Fichte's achievement while also playing its game with Fichte and the reader.[14] The simile of the sock is both a tribute and, the pun may be excused, a needling, both serious and playful, because Fichte's philosophy does the very serious and very valuable service of providing for its own condition of impossibility. Of course, this condition of impossibility does not prevent it from being carried out or performed endlessly. But precisely in its potential endlessness, it demonstrates its futility. *Spiel* is *Ernst*, turned inside out.

If we now return to the passage with which we began—namely, Jacobi's claim or charge that, thanks to Fichte, the sciences, the *Wißenschaften*, have now become mere *Spiele*, mere games—the passage appears in a new light. What Jacobi *means* by "plays" is already as ambiguous or bivalent as his simile of the sock. For *Spiel* here, while it is clearly meant to be pejorative, is also a matter of the utmost importance, for it has the value of what is unconditional; it signifies a freedom from things that leads the mind to that very act-act, that very *Thathandlung*, that Jacobi too, as much as Fichte, believes to be essential for any philosophical endeavor.

SACRED, PROFANE

Indeed, so much does Jacobi admire Fichte's system that his praise takes on an almost religious character, or rather, the language of eulogy itself becomes literally religious. Fichte is the "Messiah," the *Meßias* of the game called science. This game is "infinite" and "engrossing," it produces a kind of "ecstasy" (*berauschend*; 512/206), and the science in Fichte's sense grants "freedom" (*Freyheit*) and "rescue[s]" (*retten*) nothing less than "selfhood" (505/199). Which brings us, finally, to the question of play and religion, and more particularly, to religion as what is at stake in the game Jacobi is playing with Fichte in his open letter. For it is clear that the *salto mortale* Jacobi stands up for is of the nature of faith and is, for that matter, religious in character.[15]

As is well known, the relationship of religion to play is a key point in play theory, as evidenced, for example, in Jost Trier's theory of play as presented in his groundbreaking 1947 study, titled simply "Spiel." Working etymologically, Trier traces the basic meaning behind a series of semantically related terms for play to the concept of an enclosed space, of *Hegung* (from *hegen*, "to enclose or encircle," for example, within a hedge or fence): "Not 'dance' and 'dancing,' but 'Hegung' and ultimately probably 'fence' and 'fencing in' is the foundational meaning of *spil spilon* [play]."[16] The German word *Hegung* means the simultaneous act of enclosing and nurturing. Fencing off and caring for, enclosing and fostering, surrounding and cultivating: play, *Spiel*, according to Trier, has everything to do with this double act. Terms such as *dance*, *round*, *circle*, *ring*, Trier argues, go back to the action of *Hegung* in which a group of people form a ring and take up places within that enclosed space they themselves make up. Trier goes on to show the essential link between play in this sense and the "sacred," the cordoned-off holy space separated from the profane space in front of it. Play and the sacred are both constituted by *Hegung*. The enclosing of *Hegung* separates something off, which then differs from the space outside. It is now a safe space in which nurturing can take place. By virtue of its productive difference from the outside, it becomes holy.

Now, it is evident that what Jacobi sees in Fichte's *Wissenschaft* is precisely *Spiel* in its specific function as *Hegung*: the sock is, of course, something that envelops or encloses a space; but just as importantly, Jacobi's main point about Fichte's system—both what he praises it for *and* what he objects to—is its self-enclosed nature, its perfect *Hegung*. And it accords with the essential commonality of play and the sacred that Jacobi then exploits his characterization of *Wissenschaft* as play in order to show how Fichte's philosophy takes on the status of a religion. Fichte's *Wissenschaft* is or functions like a new religion—an enveloped sacred realm. Jacobi's own position vis-à-vis this "new" "covenant" (503/196)—to use Jacobi's own vocabulary—is again exquisitely ambivalent: on the one hand, he, Jacobi, is the first to proclaim Fichte "king" among the "Jews of speculative reason" (503/196); on the other, he finds himself incapable, as it were, of joining the ring: "Since I did not belong to the old covenant but remained still uncircumcised, I must abstain from the new one too, out of the same incapacity or stubbornness" (503/196). Hence, on the one hand, Jacobi introduces religious terms in order to carry out a kind of apotheosis of Fichte—he himself proclaims him, "ever more zealously and loudly" (503/196), "King of the Jews" of speculative philosophy. On the other, however, without making much of a leap, one can see here a second and still more pointed aspect of Jacobi's critique: just as Jacobi reproaches Fichte's game of *Wissenschaft* for its nihilism, here, he accuses it of having usurped religion, of having put itself in the place of Christianity. So Jacobi is both inside and outside of Fichte's sock—his *Wissenschaft*, which is also his sect—at one and the same time.

INSIDE OUT

Which returns us to my main point about writing as play in Jacobi's letter. What allows Jacobi to adopt what I have been calling his "ambivalent" attitude toward Fichte is the particular nature of the "game" he plays with him. Whether acknowledging Fichte's leading role in the advent of the new *Wissenschaft* and his status as its messiah, or reproaching him for nihilism and apostasy, Jacobi is as serious as he is playful—he is, thanks to the dynamic of *Spiel*, both at once. But *Spiel* is more here than just a medium of ambivalence. Rather, it is also Jacobi's way of outdoing Fichte, of beating him at his own game. If *Wissenschaft* and religion are both modes of "play," then what Jacobi's letter shows is why it is not possible to simply take up a position *within* either: play is, ultimately, not an enclosure, but—as Trier had already understood—the *act of enclosing*, which is also *the act of opening*, the dance-ring or *Reigen* that constantly plays with its two sides, the inside and the outside, preserving their difference while questioning their opposition. What Fichte seems to have forgotten, Jacobi's game with Fichte shows, is that the sock of science, the *Strumpf* of *Wissenschaft*, can always be turned inside out.

If one now reflects on this further and asks what the inclusion or intrusion of play into philosophy means for our understanding of Jacobi's attitude toward Fichte and his *Wissenschaftslehre*, and at the same time of the relationship of the epistolary to the epistemological circa 1800, one is certainly well advised to take Jacobi's ingenious play with the simile of the sock seriously. For what it teaches the reader (as difficult as it may be to grasp the full significance of Jacobi's epistolary practice) is that any real form of critique can only happen from the inside. Without the enthusiastic embrace of what is ultimately—as it were on its own grounds—rejected, it is impossible to perform *any* criticism at all. Any rejection that happens outside of the knitting would be literally pointless. Jacobi's eulogy, in this sense, is thus not merely rhetorical but entirely sincere. At the same time, of course, the highest form of eulogy for Jacobi is and must be messianic, and this is at the same time when the eulogy turns against itself. It must do so if it doesn't want to become idolatry. Hence by *playfully*—in the new, full meaning of this term that is emerging from this reading of Jacobi—choosing the image of the sock, Jacobi ensures that the eulogy exposes itself as the invective it must also be given that it is the highest form of eulogy. Only by playing, by playing the game Fichte's *Wissenschaftslehre* is denounced to be, by making Fichte's own game operative in an itself playful way, can it become clear that the only commensurate way of dealing with the doctrine of science is play itself. Of course, if one were to go deeper into the texture of Jacobi's open letter, one would soon find that it is itself knit like a sock and that Jacobi exposes his double attitude from the first lines of the letter on. As he makes explicit or as he at least claims, it took him a very long time to write his letter, a letter that is meant as the (obviously expected) response to Fichte's doctrine of science. Jacobi is preparing the ground for his critique, and he does so by knitting his way into the very eulogy of Fichte, the messiah of philosophy, the eulogy that also leads him to revile what he praises. For the reason for his objection is precisely the reason for his accolade. There could be no better way to expose this, of course, in this case very productive double-bind than by using the double-bind of play. A simple invective or satire would certainly have been possible, but the message would have been unidirected and univocal. Very obviously, this is not the attitude the letter is meant to convey. Instead, it is clearly meant to convey a message that incessantly moves between the two poles of seriousness *and* badinage, of eulogy *and* invective. Only through the dynamic vitality of the playful, the incessantly inclusive but also undecisive and undirected movement of the play, can this be achieved.

Now, if one wants to get an insight into the laboratory of writing and the practice of the open letter circa 1800, Jacobi's open letter to Fichte certainly offers an entry of the first order—or one should perhaps say: of the second order. For it offers less a paradigmatic example of the open letter circa 1800 than rather a second-order observation of its very practice. It is not uncommon in the second half of the eighteenth century to begin an open letter with a critique or even an invective that is then tempered by a good portion of praise, or vice versa.[17] This common rhetorical practice is clearly not Jacobi's approach. But by alluding to this common rhetoric, Jacobi puts its practice not only into play but also on display. And it is by means of the simile of the sock that Jacobi can show how any attempt at separating performance from knowledge is doomed to failure—a very Fichtean idea at that. The epistemic, the science of knowing, is never just a set of sentences and doctrines. It always is an activity. But for Jacobi, this activity is also inherently sensual.[18] This is why the epistolary and the epistemic enter into a new relationship in Jacobi's open letter, one that is paradigmatic for his thinking—and one that certainly left its mark on the next generation of the Jena Romantics.[19] For Jacobi, writing an *open* letter still bears the traces of the subjective, of the *closed* intimacy of the personal letter, while at the same time reaching the highest level of philosophical abstraction and the most general form of address.[20] Following the open-closed logic of *Spiel* in Trier's sense, the simile of the sock, in all its sensualness, mediates between the two, the epistolary and the epistemic: the image, taken from the realm of the private and the home, with its connotations of the female and the sensual, is meant to both make palpable and *ex*plain, expose, or unravel the most abstract concept, namely, that of the act-act. Just as it mediates between earnestness and irony or badinage, the letter also mediates between the epistolary and the epistemological, the sensual and the abstract. Of course, were it not for the playfulness of the mediation, Jacobi's strategy of mediation, of openness and closure, would be futile.

END NODE

Far from being just some playful thesis about Jacobi, this reading sheds new light both on Jacobi's letter, the genre of the philosophical open letter circa 1800, and on the notion and practice of play that the letter exemplifies. What one can observe in Jacobi's letter as under a magnifying glass is how it turns the classical rhetoric of the invective against itself. While invective debases an opponent by means of personal insult, Jacobi uses something clearly base, namely, the image of the sock, a household item that one can literally trample underfoot, to showcase the true mechanism of Fichte's doctrine of science.[21] But instead of thereby demeaning its importance or rejecting it, Jacobi brings it to the senses. He makes it palpable, and, yes, at the same time likable and ultimately even admirable. Instead of insulting Fichte's character, which is what the genre of the invective would call for, Jacobi playfully uses the debasing means of the classical insult—and turns it on its head. One could even say that it is at the point of the utmost humiliation of Fichte's philosophy that the disdain turns into praise. The same can be said about the way Jacobi plays with the generic conventions of eulogy. When Jacobi calls Fichte the "Messiah of speculative reason," the solemn panegyric turns against itself, turns into derision, without thereby diminishing the praise. Jacobi's mode of writing pushes the generic conventions of eulogy and invective to their point of indifference, to a point of free play that allows Jacobi to change the terms of philosophical engagement. This is as playful as it is serious.

NOTES

1. It was Gotthold Ephraim Lessing—who in a conversation with Jacobi in 1780 confessed he considered Spinozism to be the only true philosophy—who incited Jacobi to study Spinoza's works more carefully. In 1785, Jacobi published *Concerning the Doctrine of Spinoza in Letters to Herr Moses Mendelssohn*, a treatise in which he developed a substantive critique of any dogmatic system in philosophy and showed that Spinoza's philosophy was mere materialism and would eventually lead to atheism. This earned him the fierce opposition of a number of thinkers, beginning with Moses Mendelssohn. See Kurt Christ, *Jacobi und Mendelssohn: Eine Analyse des Spinozastreits* (Würzburg: Königshausen und Neumann, 1988), Alexander Altmann, "Lessing und Jacobi: Das Gespräch über den Spinozismus," *Lessing Yearbook* 3 (1971): 25–70, and Klaus Hammacher, "Über Friedrich Heinrich Jacobis Beziehungen zu Lessing im Zusammenhang mit dem Streit um Spinoza," in *Lessing und der Kreis seiner Freunde*, ed. Günter Schulz (Heidelberg: Lambert Schneider, 1985), 51–74. For a brief overview of the pantheism controversy, see Jürg Freudiger, "Der Pantheismusstreit: Eine Bestandsaufnahme," *Kriterion—Journal of Philosophy* 5, no. 1 (1993): 39–48. For a more recent and particularly illuminating account, see Ursula Goldenbaum, "The Pantheismusstreit—Milestone or Stumbling Block in the German Reception of Spinoza?" in *Spinoza's Ethics: A Collective Commentary*, ed. Michael Hampe, Ursula Renz, and Robert Schnepf (Leiden: Brill, 2011), 325–350. The first edition of the main writings of the controversy remains one of the best resources for intellectual history and philosophical epistolary practices: see Heinrich Scholz, ed., *Die Hauptschriften zum Pantheismusstreit zwischen Jacobi und Mendelssohn* (Berlin: Reuther & Reichard, 1916). One of the most insightful discussions of the controversy remains Hermann Timm, "Die Bedeutung der Spinozabriefe für die Entwicklung der idealistischen Religionsphilosophie," in *Friedrich Heinrich Jacobi: Philosoph und Literat der Goethezeit*, ed. Klaus Hammacher (Frankfurt am Main: Klostermann, 1971), 35–81. More detailed overviews are given by David Bell, *Spinoza in Germany from 1670 to the Age of Goethe* (London: Institute of Germanic Studies, 1984); Vittorio Morfino, *La Spinoza-Renaissance nella Germania di Fine Settecento* (Milan: Unicopli, 1998); and Sylvain Zac, *Spinoza en Allemagne: Mendelssohn, Lessing et Jacobi* (Paris:

Meridiens Klincksieck, 1989). Friedrich C. Beiser, *The Fate of Reason: German Philosophy from Kant to Fichte* (Cambridge, MA: Harvard University Press, 1987), 61–75, provides a reconstruction which—in Freudiger's apt characterization (39)—reads "like a mystery novel" but in the process exaggerates the insidiousness of the adversaries.

2. Jacobi even explicitly designates his and Fichte's philosophical endeavors as equally invested in "earnestness" (*Ernst*). Friedrich Heinrich Jacobi, "Jacobi to Fichte (1799)," in *Main Philosophical Writings and the Novel "Allwill,"* trans. and ed. George di Giovanni (Montreal: McGill-Queen's University Press, 1994), 505; Friedrich Heinrich Jacobi, *Jacobi an Fichte (1799)*, in *Werke, Gesamtausgabe*, vol. 2, *Schriften zum Transzendentalen Idealismus*, ed. Walter Jaeschke and Irmgard-Maria Piske (Hamburg: Meiner, 2004), 199. References to this text are henceforth in parentheses, giving the page number of the English translation followed by that of the original; the translation has sometimes been modified.

3. The genre of the invective, of course, has its own generic codes and its own history. See note 7 below for further references.

4. For a first orientation, see Angelika Corbineau-Hoffmann, "Spiel," in *Historisches Wörterbuch der Philosophie*, ed. Joachim Ritter and Karlfried Gründer (Basel: Schwabe, 1995), 9:1383–1390, and Tanja Wetzel, "Spiel," in *Ästhetische Grundbegriffe: Historisches Wörterbuch in sieben Bänden*, ed. Karlheinz Barck et al. (Stuttgart: Metzler, 2003), 5:577–618. Particularly helpful in this context are Stefan Deines, "Formen und Funktionen des Spielbegriffs in der Philosophie," in *Spielformen des Selbst: Das Spiel zwischen Subjektivität, Kunst und Alltagspraxis*, ed. Regine Strätling (Bielefeld: transcript, 2012), 23–38; Jörg Neuenfeld, *Alles ist Spiel: Zur Geschichte der Auseinandersetzung mit einer Utopie der Moderne* (Würzburg: Königshausen & Neumann, 2005); and Jürgen Brokoff, "Die Verselbständigung der Poesie als Spiel am Ende des 18. Jahrhunderts und der Spielbegriff bei Johan Huizinga und Jost Trier," in *Literatur als Spiel: Evolutionsbiologische, ästhetische und pädagogische Konzepte*, ed. Thomas Anz and Heinrich Kaulen (Berlin: De Gruyter, 2009), 101–114.

5. Jacobi's sock has been a subject of scholarly interest since at least Alfred Hebeisen, *Friedrich Heinrich Jacobi: Seine Auseinandersetzung mit Spinoza* (Bern: Haupt, 1960).

6. The only exceptions are Klaus Hammacher, "Jacobis Brief 'An Fichte' (1799)," in *Transzendentalphilosophie und Spekulation: Der Streit um die Gestalt einer Ersten Philosophie (1799–1807)*, ed. Walter Jaeschke (Hamburg: Meiner, 1993), 72–84, and Cornelia Ortlieb, *Friedrich Heinrich Jacobi und die Philosophie als Schreibart* (Munich: Fink, 2010), 380–414. However, Hammacher deals with the rhetorical and literary dimensions of Jacobi's simile of the sock only briefly and from the perspective of a historian of philosophy, while Ortlieb focuses on the material and technical dimensions of Jacobi's writing. My approach deliberately deals with the "performative" in the literal sense of what is being "per-formed," that is, what gains form through an acting and working through, namely, in this case, a form of playful and philosophical invective that is at the same time a eulogy. Also, my approach does not strictly distinguish between form and content, procedure and message. The aim of my reading of Jacobi is precisely to make a first attempt to show how an understanding of Jacobi's procedure leads to a better understanding of the message (and vice versa). My approach here is inspired, even if only remotely, by the new discussion on "form" in anglo-saxon scholarship, notably in Caroline Levine, *Forms: Whole, Rhythm, Hierarchy, Network* (Princeton, NJ: Princeton University Press, 2015).

7. See Robert Eisenhauer, *Archeologies of Invective* (New York: Peter Lang, 2007); Rolf Lessenich, "*Ars Disputandi* des Klassizismus 1660–1830: Tradition und Innovation

der *Traditio Classicorum*," in *Streitkultur: Okzidentale Traditionen des Streitens in Literatur, Geschichte und Kunst*, ed. Uwe Baumann et al. (Bonn: Bonn University Press, 2008), 147–161; Uwe Neumann, "Invektive," in *Historisches Wörterbuch der Rhetorik*, ed. Gert Ueding, vol. 3 (Tübingen: DeGruyter, 1996), 549–561; Günter Oesterle, "Das 'Unmanierliche' der Streitschrift: Zum Verhältnis von Polemik und Kritik in Aufklärung und Romantik," in *Kontroversen alte und neue: Akten des VII. Internationalen Germanisten-Kongresses*, vol. 2, *Formen und Formgeschichte des Streitens*, ed. Albrecht Schöne (Tübingen: Niemeyer, 1986), 107–120; Marie Lund, "The Rhetorical Tradition of Invective," in *An Argument on Rhetorical Style* (Aarhus: Aarhus University Press, 2017), 169–173. The essential feature of the rhetorical tradition of the invective is the insult *ad personam*, the denigration and debasement of a person's character. It will become clear that Jacobi, even if his letter inscribes itself partially into this tradition or alludes to it, does not follow these conventions.

8. On Fichte's reaction to Jacobi's letter, see Ives Radrizzani, "Le *Fragment*: Première réponse de Fichte à la *Lettre* de Jacobi," in *Jacobi in Discussione*, ed. Tristana Dini and Salvatore Principe (Milan: Franco Angeli, 2012), 97–104, and, for background, Ives Radrizzani, "Jacobis Auseinandersetzung mit Fichte in den *Denkbüchern*," *Fichte-Studien* 14 (1998): 43–62; Gunnar Hindrichs, "Der Standpunkt des natürlichen Denkens: Fichtes *Bestimmung des Menschen* in der Auseinandersetzung mit der 'Unphilosophie' Jacobis," in *System und Systemkritik: Beiträge zu einem Grundproblem der klassischen deutschen Philosophie*, ed. Birgit Sandkaulen (Würzburg: Königshausen & Neumann, 2006), 109–129; and Walter Jaeschke, "Der Messias der spekulativen Vernunft," in *Kritisches Jahrbuch der Philosophie* 4 (1999): 143–157.

9. Put in a nutshell, for Barthes, the "mode of writing" or *écriture* is, in opposition to a language and a style, the writer's free choice, but as form and not as message. See Roland Barthes, *Writing Degree Zero*, trans. Annette Lavers and Colin Smith (New York: Hill and Wang, 1967), esp. 1–28.

10. See Barthes, *Writing Degree Zero*, 16–23.

11. See Susan Sontag, preface to Barthes, *Writing Degree Zero*, xi–xxv.

12. A particularly illuminating analysis of Jacobi's notion of the *salto* (*Sprung*) and his use of the term "unphilosophy" (*Unphilosophie*) can be found in Birgit Sandkaulen, *Grund und Ursache: Die Vernunftkritik Jacobis* (Munich: Fink, 2000), primarily 11–75.

13. See for a related reading Alberto Iacovacci, "Il doppio grido di Jacobi: Per una rilettura della Lettera a Fichte," in *Jacobi in Discussione*, ed. Tristana Dini and Salvatore Principe (Milan: Franco Angeli, 2012), 83–96.

14. It is not without a certain irony that Fichte, arguably the most earnest even of German philosophers, can be seen as providing the basis for the complete collapse of any stable distinction between earnestness and play. See David Martyn, "Fichtes romantischer Ernst," in *Sprachen der Ironie—Sprachen des Ernstes*, ed. Karl Heinz Bohrer (Frankfurt am Main: Suhrkamp, 2000), 76–90.

15. Remaining aware, of course, of the challenges involved in any simple determination of the term "religious." See Talal Asad, "The Construction of Religion as an Anthropological Category," in *Genealogies of Religion: Discipline and Reasons of Power in Christianity and Islam* (Baltimore: Johns Hopkins University Press, 1993), 27–54. Taking "religion" in the sense not just of faith but also of a certain practice, it begins to make sense to talk about "religion" in this context. It also means to position this approach in contradistinction to Strauss's early but prominent work on Jacobi; see Leo Strauss, "Das Erkenntnisproblem in

der philosophischen Lehre Fr. H. Jacobis," in *Gesammelte Schriften*, vol. 2, *Philosophie und Gesetz—Frühe Schriften*, ed. Heinrich Meier and Wiebke Meier (Stuttgart: Metzler, 1997), 237–292.

16. "Nicht 'Tanz' und 'tanzen', sondern 'Hegung' und letztlich wahrscheinlich 'Zaun' und 'zäunen' ist die Grundbedeutung von *spil spilon*." Jost Trier, "Spiel," *Beiträge zur Geschichte der deutschen Sprache und Literatur* 69 (1947): 451. See also Jost Trier, "Zaun und Mannring," *Beiträge zur Geschichte der deutschen Sprache und Literatur* 66 (1942): 232–264. For an illuminating elaboration on how Trier's theory of play relates to (and is distinct from) the idea of poetry circa 1800, see Jürgen Brokoff, "Die Verselbständigung der Poesie als Spiel am Ende des 18. Jahrhunderts und der Spielbegriff bei Johan Huizinga und Jost Trier," in *Literatur als Spiel: Evolutionsbiologische, ästhetische und pädagogische Konzepte*, ed. Thomas Anz and Heinrich Kaulen (Berlin: De Gruyter, 2009), 101–114. A related but in our context less useful (even if more often discussed) approach to the notion of play and the sacred can be found in Roger Caillois, "Play and the Sacred" [1950], in *Man and the Sacred*, trans. Meyer Barash (Glencoe, IL: Free Press of Glencoe, 1959), 152–162.

17. See Rolf-Bernhard Essig, *Der offene Brief: Geschichte und Funktion einer publizistischen Form von Isokrates bis Günter Grass* (Würzburg: Königshausen & Neumann, 2000); Hans-Dietrich Dahnke, "Wandlungen in Wesen und Funktion öffentlicher literarischer Debatten und Kontroversen zwischen 1780 und 1810," in *Formen und Formgeschichte des Streitens: Der Literaturstreit*, ed. Helmut Koopmann (Tübingen: Niemeyer, 1986), 172–179; Hans-Dietrich Dahnke and Bernd Leistner, eds., *Debatten und Kontroversen. Literarische Auseinandersetzungen in Deutschland am Ende des 18. Jahrhunderts*, 2 vols. (Berlin: Aufbau, 1989); Caspar Hirschi, "Piraten der Gelehrtenrepublik: Die Norm des sachlichen Streits und ihre polemische Funktion," in *Gelehrte Polemik: Intellektuelle Konfliktverschärfungen um 1700*, ed. Kai Bremer and Carlos Spoerhase (Frankfurt am Main: Klostermann, 2011), 176–213; and Ursula Goldenbaum, "Die öffentliche Debatte in der deutschen Aufklärung: Einleitung," in *Appell an das Publikum: Die öffentliche Debatte in der deutschen Aufklärung 1687–1796*, ed. Ursula Goldenbaum (Berlin: Akademie, 2004), 1–118.

18. For an illuminating and helpful discussion of the relationship between "Vernunft" und "Verstand" and what one could call Jacobi's "reason of feeling," see Klaus Hammacher, *Die Philosophie Friedrich Heinrich Jacobis* (Munich: Fink, 1969), 166–184; and for an excellent further elaboration, Birgit Sandkaulen, "'Oder hat Vernunft den Menschen?' Zur Vernunft des Gefühls bei Jacobi," *Zeitschrift für philosophische Forschung* 49, no. 3 (1995): 416–429.

19. This is doubtless also true for Jacobi's potential impact on the "romantic" culture of dispute. For background, see Oesterle, "Das 'Unmanierliche' der Streitschrift."

20. For a helpful exploration of the "epistolary culture" circa 1800 between "the private and the public," see Uwe Hentschel, "'Briefe sind Spiegel der Seelen': Epistolare Kultur des 18. Jahrhunderts zwischen Privatheit und Öffentlichkeit," *Lessing-Yearbook* 33 (2001): 190–194. Further reflections on this topic would need to consider Jacobi's open letter in conjunction with the proliferating self-help literature in the eighteenth century on how to write a good letter, for example, Johann Franz Wagner's much circulated *Anweisung zum Briefschreiben nach dem heutigen Geschmacke*, 2nd ed. (Weimar: Bützow, 1767).

21. See note 7.

Part IV

The Play of Language

CHAPTER NINE

Between Speaking and Listening

Jean Paul's Wordplay

MICHAEL POWERS

IN HIS PEDAGOGICAL TREATISE *Levana; or, the Doctrine of Education* (*Levana oder Erziehlehre*, 1807), Jean Paul stresses the pivotal role of play in childhood learning. Invoking a theme that connects several of his works, he claims that children are best able to develop their individual abilities when parents and educators afford them "play space" (*Spielraum*) to experiment on their own, generally unhampered by externally imposed parameters and guidelines.[1] Only in this way can each child fully realize her or his innate potential, rendering free play critical for the developing subject. In presenting this view, Jean Paul goes so far as to suggest that play not only complements or facilitates learning—as many other pedagogues and scholars assert—but should in fact be considered synonymous with it. This chapter examines the integral connection that Jean Paul establishes between play and learning in *Levana* within the context of his broader interest in the category of play—especially wordplay.

At first glance the acquisition of language and the ability to play with it may seem tangential or secondary to the model of educative play outlined in *Levana*. But as I show in my reading, the conception of play *as* learning that Jean Paul proposes depends on a noninstrumental, poetic notion of wordplay that simultaneously enables and unsettles any simple claims regarding play's didactic utility. Central to such an understanding of wordplay is the paradigmatic opposition between purposive, useful play and autonomous, free play—a dichotomy rehearsed in numerous influential works of the period, chief among them Kant's *Critique of Judgment* (1790) and Schiller's *The Aesthetic Education of Man* (1795). This familiar antinomy acquires a unique bent in Jean Paul's writings insofar as it is shown to be also at play in language. In his pedagogical theory, Jean Paul identifies the existence of a dynamic mode of (word)play at the crux of the child's evolving relationship to the world. Tellingly, however, he does not or cannot fully make sense of this third mode of play at the border of sense and nonsense. By attending closely to his entangled reflections on child development, language, and the imagination, I aim to illuminate the contours of this notion of wordplay that Jean Paul's writings give us to think.

Jean Paul's work has served as a touchstone for several influential theorists of children's play. To name only three, well-known examples, Karl Groos, Sigmund Freud, and Walter Benjamin all directly engage with it in their own respective anthropological, psychoanalytic, and sociocultural studies of play.[2] A language-focused exploration of Jean Paul's educational theory thus promises to open new avenues for understanding not only his own thought but also his intellectual legacy within the field of play theory.

THE STAGES OF CHILDREN'S PLAY: MAKING SENSE OF THE WORLD

Much like the elaborate, digression-filled novels for which Jean Paul is best known (*The Invisible Lodge*, 1793; *Hesperus*, 1795; *Titan*, 1803), *Levana; or, the Doctrine of Education* is a meandering text that touches on a broad span of areas tied to childhood learning. With its sprawling array of sections and subsections, the book-length study can appear disjointed at times, as Jean Paul acknowledges in his prefatory comments.[3] But this apparent disorder is by design. *Levana*, he writes, signals a break from the "usual" attempts, currently in fashion, to construct a "complete system of education."[4] Instead, in keeping with the early German Romantics, he presents the reader not with a system but rather a selection of "fragments" (*Bruchstücke*), as he titles major divisions of the book.[5] It is in view of this fragmentation and rejection of system, which characterizes much of the layout and method of the work, that the section on play first stands out. With uncharacteristic rigor, Jean Paul schematically reinterprets the entire process of childhood learning as an evolution in the child's ability to play.

Jean Paul's ideas concerning the imbrication of children's play and learning belong within a longer genealogy, as he well knew. In the introduction to *Levana*, he cites several contemporary and historical studies on childhood development, singling out one in particular: Jean-Jacques Rousseau's *Émile, or On Education* (1762).[6] He proclaims that "no work compares" with Rousseau's groundbreaking treatise, including his own. It is thus unsurprising that Rousseau, whom Jean Paul venerated so greatly as to inspire his pseudonym, anticipates several of the notable elements from *Levana* in *Émile*.[7] For instance, Rousseau famously proposes that children learn through specific stages. He also tends to aver the importance of free, unstructured learning throughout *Émile*—at least to a certain degree. A tension persists throughout Rousseau's text between giving the child the space to develop on his own and closely supervising or even controlling the child's development. This tension is captured in Rousseau's concept of "well-regulated freedom."[8] Key to Rousseau's complex views on pedagogy and freedom is the capacity of the teacher to work alongside the child by subtly converting what the child perceives as a "game," that is as "easy and voluntary" activity, into an "object of instruction" (148). Rousseau claims that this can be accomplished by "varying [children's] play to render it more pleasant to them without the least constraint ever turning it into work" (148).[9] Although Jean Paul ultimately develops his own versions of these ideas—also fusing them with concepts derived from the many pedagogical studies he consulted—*Levana* can be seen within the context of the educational reforms around 1800 that Rousseau was largely responsible for enacting.[10]

Of Jean Paul's numerous contributions to the theory of play, perhaps his most significant is his stage-based model of play-learning. As play theorist Brian Sutton-Smith has shown, it has become commonplace today across a variety of disciplines to correlate play and progress: "biologists, psychologists, educators and sociologists" generally hold the view that "play is adaptive or contributes to growth, development, and socialization."[11] This attitude—which largely characterizes Jean Paul's own reflections on play—becomes more pronounced in the tendency to tie different forms of play to distinct phases of growth. We find notable examples of such stage-based thinking in Groos's aforementioned anthropological writings, not to mention several later studies focused on play's role on the psyche. Jean Piaget, for instance, develops a stage-based model of cognitive development. A stage-based schema of play also informs Donald Winnicott's psychoanalytic research on child development, which proceeds from the premise that "playing facilitates growth and therefore health."[12] Telling in this regard is Winnicott's claim that "there is a direct development from transitional phenomena to playing, and from playing to shared playing, and from this to cultural experiences" (51). In other words, Winnicott ascribes a different kind of play to almost every phase of growth.

Over a century and a half earlier, Jean Paul provides an uncannily similar vision of play, a vision that serves as a model for such progress-oriented interpretations of stage-based learning. Despite repeated allusions to distinct stages of development from the outset of *Levana*, the discrete phases are only first elucidated nearly a third of the way though the book, in the chapter "Children's Games" ("Spiele der Kinder")—a section that is arguably the conceptual nucleus of the work. There are essentially three main periods of childhood for Jean Paul. In sequence, the child advances from private passive play, to active play with objects, and finally to social play with other individuals. Let us briefly consider these three stages, beginning at their conclusion.

According to Jean Paul, the "first little bond of society is woven" in the "later years" of childhood (157). Initially brought together by an interest in common objects (toys), children enter into a "social contract" as soon as they begin interacting directly with one another. Jean Paul claims that we can recognize "every root and blossom of society" in these collective children's games unstructured by parents or teachers (157). Although such spontaneous social interaction marks the very last phase of childlike experimentation and therefore the outer limit of the schema of learning outlined in *Levana*, this phase well illustrates play's instrumental value. Not only does play serve an important role in introducing young children into society, but it is also crucially implicated in the establishment of the social order (and thus implicitly in the possibility of changing it).[13] As he puts it, for the child who has reached the final phase of childhood, the "play-room" acts as an "entrance into the great world" (157).

The two major phases that one must pass through in corresponding order to reach the state of social, collective play are "theoretical" and "practical" play. Theoretical play occurs during the first years of life, a period in which children are primarily inactive spectators. Jean Paul describes this time as dominated by "games or exertions of the receiving [*empfangenden*], apprehending, learning faculties [*Kraft*]" (151). Innately driven to absorb their surroundings, infant children take in the world, collecting impressions and input. Theoretical play activity flows "from without, working inward," facilitated by the "nerves of sense" (151, translation modified). The body at this stage functions mainly as a site for the passive accruement of information and raw sense data. While the child, it is implied, gradually learns to process what he receives, little other discernible activity occurs during this early mode of play.

This initial period eventually gives way to its opposite, a mode of practical play in which children begin to act upon and shape their external surroundings. Correspondingly, the main "games" that define this next stage indicate the emergence of a diametrically opposed faculty, an "acting, formative power [*Kraft*]" (151). Practical play emanates "from within, working outward" (151, translation modified). The child transforms from a passive recipient into an active agent. Such play occurs not through the "nerves of sense," but rather through what Jean Paul terms the "nerves of motion" (151). The child is no longer an empty gathering site, but rather an embodied subject capable of self-expression, movement, and action.

The opposition between theoretical and practical play seems clear. In the first stage of life, the child's experimental play is generally passive, receptive, and inwardly oriented. In the stage that follows, the child tends to relate to its surroundings in an active, creative, and outwardly oriented manner. Through his choice of words, Jean Paul tacitly aligns these two modes of play with the ancient Greek distinction between *theoria* and *praxis*: on the one hand passive spectatorship, speculation, and contemplation, *theoria*, and on the other hand *praxis*, doing and action that can be said to place theory into practice. Conspicuously missing from this scheme is what Plato and Aristotle identify as the third fundamental type of human activity: *poiesis*—making, producing, bringing forth (also a key term for the early German Romantics, discussed further in the following text). While Jean Paul never mobilizes the precise phrase "poetic play" in *Levana*, a close reading reveals the centrality of poetic creation, and in particular the quintessential poetic medium—language—for the model of playful learning proposed. Jean Paul goes beyond recognizing the crucial role of language as the condition of possibility that subtends and enables the various stages of the ludic. His most forceful intervention, I propose, is the gesture toward a nonpurposive notion of wordplay—developed further in other parts of his oeuvre—that is difficult to assimilate neatly into the otherwise teleological, progress-oriented concept of playful learning advanced throughout *Levana*.

PLAYING WITH WORDS

Although Jean Paul goes into considerable detail in explaining the distinction between theoretical and practical play, he only fleetingly focuses on the transitional space between these two modes. It is here, at the threshold between these two first stages of playful learning that the question of language explicitly enters his analysis. Of the shift from passive to active play, he writes, "it is only at a later period, when, by means of the five acts of the five senses, the knowledge of the outer world is attained, and one word after another gradually liberates [*freispricht*] the mind, that greater freedom produces active play [*Selbstspiel*]" (153). The pivotal turn to active, practical play requires not only the development of the bodily senses—the aforementioned transformation of the "nerves of sense" into "nerves of motion"—but also, importantly, the acquisition of language. "Active play," more accurately translated here as "self-play" (*Selbstspiel*), can occur only once successive words "liberate" or "speak free" (*freisprechen*) the mind.[14] Hence language appears to forge a necessary bridge for the child's newfound, dynamic relation to the external world.

Language's bearing as a key distinguishing factor between theoretical and practical play is also indicated at other places in the text. Jean Paul depicts language as "the gate of the soul," and the dividing border between the "early years" and the "second . . . season of childhood" (75). In the first period of life, the child exists in a "speechless" state of "native innocence . . . unsusceptible of verbal empoisonment," a state of simple "sensuous experience."[15] In a vivid analogy, he emphasizes the difference between theoretical, "sensuous experience" and a linguistically mediated relation to one's surroundings by comparing the gap between the first two stages of child's play to the "boundary line between the monkey and the man" (75). While the monkey, in Jean Paul's reading, reflects a passive and corporeal form of existence—features shared with the child during its "speechless period"—humans (or further developed children in this analogy) exemplify a more advanced state based on the ability to speak (143). Language opens for the child the possibility not only of externalizing his inner thoughts but also of asserting authority over his environment through the colonizing force that attends the act of imposing words onto things. According to Jean Paul, "by the fact of naming, external objects, like islands, are taken possession of, and animals are tamed by accustoming them to answer to a name" (362). Problematically, he suggests that one should strive to foster the hierarchical relationship that language establishes between humans and the world by naming for "the child every object, every sensation, [and] every action" (369). Words are the "finest line-drawer of infinity" (369). Thus by teaching children "defining words," we instruct them to accurately divide and grasp "unlimited nature," which otherwise "stands before a child like a column of quicksilver without a barometric scale" (362).

By reexamining the difference between theoretical and practical play with this focus on language in mind, we gain a new perspective on the model of learning elaborated in *Levana*. At first sight, the gulf that divides passive and active learning appears to correspond to prelinguistic and linguistically mediated ways of relating to the world. Quite literally, theoretical play can be said to demarcate the phase of *infancy*, derived from the Latin *infantia*, meaning the "inability to speak." However, closer attention to Jean Paul's reflections on language throughout *Levana* reveals a more complex understanding of language in his schema.

If the distinction between passive and active play-learning depends on the child's ability to wield language, then what about the transition between these two states? Where do we situate the child who does not yet command language, for whom words have not yet acquired fixed meanings, who is in the process of learning a first language—but for the same reason, is also not quite *outside* of the realm of language? Jean Paul contemplates this question both directly and indirectly at several turns in *Levana*. Altogether these moments depict a different view of language than as an instrument of mastery, gesturing toward the recalcitrant, meaningless underside of language that always abides in communication, but rarely shows or communicates itself.

In a key passage that draws our attention to the liminal space separating theoretical and practical play, Jean Paul writes, "only with words does the child conquer [*erobert*] an inner world opposed to the outer, by which he can set the external universe in motion" (153, translation modified). Once again, language is claimed to establish a relationship of control—the child "conquer[s] an inner world" in the face of an outer one. But the instrumental view of language implied in this diction—seemingly in accord with active, practical play—is undermined by two significant details in the same sentence. First, at the outset the child does not utilize words in order to "conquer" the external world, but rather it is words, language itself, that enable and make visible the distinction between inside and outside, a difference on which language, understood as a mediating tool, hinges. In other words, before language can assume a communicative role, it must first set the ground, call forward, and set into relation that between which it mediates—inside and outside, subject and object, self and other. Intricately connected with this a priori differentiating force is the second detail in the line above that likewise silently announces a more original, noninstrumental relation to language. Jean Paul is careful to write that the child acquires an inner world in opposition to an outer one "with" (*mit*) words and not *through* them. This suggests that the infant child initially acts in unison *with* language, does not yet treat it as a vessel for the transmission of content or meaning.

Jean Paul's own words betray a conflict between two competing notions of language beneath the surface of his thought: a mode of instrumental, communicative language, and language that does not yet mediate between self and other as fully differentiated entities, but instead first calls this difference into being.[16] Further accentuating this transitional space where the child first acts in accordance *with* language before relating to the world *through* it is the depiction of the passage from theoretical to practical play as transpiring in increments: "one word after another *gradually* liberates the mind" (emphasis added).

Although Jean Paul largely leaves this idea of language as an original differentiating force underdeveloped in *Levana*—perhaps because of the difficulty if not impossibility of theorizing this space of indistinction from a position of distinction—he skirts around it throughout, especially in the chapter on games and play.[17] His most explicit attempt at articulating such a notion of language occurs when he speculates on the possibility of a "third class of play" in-between the theoretical and the practical. While he only momentarily touches on this third category—which falls outside of the parameters of the teleological, stage-based model of learning with which he is mainly concerned—he does offer us the following evocative description: it is play "in which the child merely plays the game, does not drive the game nor feel it, that is, where he takes and gives a comfortable form and tone" ("worin das Kind das Spiel nur spielt, nicht treibt, noch fühlt. Nämlich die, wo es behaglich Gestalt und Ton nimmt und gibt"; 152, translation modified).[18] This third type of play is neither active (*treiben*) nor passive (*fühlen*), but rather a mode of play in which the child simultaneously "takes *and* gives" (emphasis added), folding reception and creation into one another in a way that appears to privilege neither side of this dichotomy. Unmotivated by external aims or desires, "the child merely plays the game." The self-enclosed, autonomous character of such play is especially striking in the German where the word for "game" (*Spiel*) and the verb "to play" (*spielen*) derive from the same stem. This leads to the almost tautological phrase, "das Spiel nur spielt"—the child merely plays in this third state of play, no more and no less.

The prime example Jean Paul offers of such a self-reflexive, nonpurposive "game" is children's wordplay. We can observe *mere play* in cases of "joking, of senseless speech" in which children talk not in order to impart their thoughts with others, but simply "in order to have something to say to themselves" ("Scherzen, sinnloses Sprechen, um sich selber etwas vorzusprechen"; 152, translation modified). Before they become tools of communication or carry sense for children, words are simply something to be played *with*. They are sounds to be repeated, groupings of letters that can be rearranged like loose building blocks. In other words, children's wordplay lays bare the meaningless, material substrate of language to which the child is especially attuned, not yet having learned to look past or through it as a self-erasing medium. For the uninitiated child, words carry no metaphysical surplus value of meaning. They are empty. But for children learning to invest signs with meaning, those at the threshold of language (the broad focus of *Levana*), language oscillates fluidly and dynamically between two interconnected poles: language as "senseless" (*sinnlos*), bare physical transport (the invisible underside that always attends signification), and language that conveys a meaning but is "senseless" in a more literal sense, insofar as it depends on the withdrawal, the self-effacement of the sensuous material of language for communication to occur successfully.

In his reading of the Kantian sublime, Paul de Man identifies a similar tension in what he calls the sheer "materiality of the letter."[19] For de Man, such a "materiality" is "devoid of any reflexive or intellectual complication" (83). It precedes the tropological and figurative dimensions of language, and yet is not entirely separate from it as "materiality *of* the letter" (90, emphasis added). This is what makes such a materiality difficult to render "clearly intelligible" through "linguistic terms" (82). Borrowing on this idea, we might consider Jean Paul's comments on the third form of wordplay through the prism of such a reduced notion of language, that is to say, as spontaneous play that occurs on the level of the bare "materiality of the letter"—a mode of wordplay most manifest in the naïve way children utilize words, often testing and pushing the boundaries between sense and nonsense (83).

In a chapter devoted to "truthfulness," Jean Paul expands on the idea that children who are still in the midst of learning to speak often take little heed of the possible meanings implied when they play with language: "During the first five years [children] say neither what is true, nor what is false—they merely talk [*sie reden nur*]. Their talking is thinking aloud; and since the one half of thought is frequently a yes, and the other a no, and both escape them (though not us), they seem to lie when they are merely talking to themselves [*bloß mit sich reden*]. Further: at first they find great pleasure in playing with [*spielen mit*] their new art of speech, and so they often talk nonsense [*Unsinn*] only for the sake of hearing their acquisitions in language [*Sprachkunde*]."[20] Unable to clearly distinguish between such stark binary oppositions as "yes" and "no," "true" and "false," young children "merely talk." The image Jean Paul paints in this passage, however, is not one of absolute indistinguishability. Rather, he also intimates a play-space nestled between distinction and indistinction, a borderland that the child can be seen exploring in its self-dialogue. A parody of successful communicative transmission, the child occupies the positions of listener and speaker both at once in "merely talking" to himself. The scene of communication between two separate entities is transposed onto one fissured site, an individual riven in two by its play *with* language. In other words, Jean Paul offers us a striking example of the sort of linguistically enabled interrelation of self and other alluded to above: the coemergence of an "inner world opposed to an outer" (153). At the same time, he also presents us with an embryonic scene of the child's attempts to use language as a medium of communication—a capacity that evolves as the child matures.

In retracing Jean Paul's scattered reflections on language and the role it plays in child development, it is important to note that he does not consistently or unequivocally endorse raising children from the state of nonsensical wordplay to the meaningful utilization of language (if these two approaches toward language can in fact be held apart, which Jean Paul's reflections on the third form of play begin to call into question). While he does, as we saw above, advocate teaching established words as a necessary step for children prepared to enter the stage of social play (and through it eventually enter the adult sphere, ruled by existing laws and conventions), he also suggests at other points that children greatly benefit from the opportunity to play freely without purpose. The overbearing instructor, he writes, "considers himself the U without which the child's Q cannot be pronounced" (206, translation modified). Rather than allowing for the child's creativity to flourish, such a misguided teacher rushes to the student's aid, directing him at every turn. Returning to a theme already present in his first novel, Jean Paul contends that one only needs to provide young children "play-space" and their internal "light" will "grow of itself" (143).[21] Although learning the names, words, and structures by which adults have ordered the world becomes essential for children entering the social sphere, those who have not yet adopted the established tongue inhabit an arguably more dynamic play-space that precedes—and thus has the potential to undermine—existing linguistic and social constructs.

Jean Paul rarely dwells on the disruptive capacity of wordplay in *Levana*. Instead, the categorizing impulse tends to win out as he unfolds his developmental model, one that appears to depend on quietly absorbing the divergent "third class" of play and the notion of language that it suggests. In the section devoted to "speech and writing," however, we see him assume a different stance in highlighting the ability of children's wordplay to uncover the "living foundation" of language, which too often remains forgotten and concealed beneath the "colorless images of everyday speech" (371). For this reason, he argues that "we may learn to speak" from children and their creative inventions, just as we may "teach them by speaking." To prove his point, he provides several examples of verbal ingenuity directly overheard "from three- and four-year-old children." The majority involve novel compound noun constructions or neologisms that throw new light on an existing link. For instance, one child terms the person who builds beer casks (*Bierfass*) a "beer-casker" (*Bierfässer*); another calls the person who looks through a telescope the "see-through-man" (*Durchsehmann*). In both cases, subject and object mutually define one another, implying not an instrumental relation but a reciprocity between interrelated entities (although Jean Paul himself refrains from stating what precisely these coinages might teach us). Yet another child transforms the word for the animal "bat," literally a "flutter-mouse" in German (*Fledermaus*), into "air-mouse" (*Luftmaus*), a name that Jean Paul deems substantially more fitting (371). Whether we agree with him or not, the larger point seems evident: in inventing new words, or modifying or even misappropriating what exists (catachresis), children infuse life and color into the pale, common terms that adult speakers habitually overlook or take for granted (for example, rarely would a German speaker stop to dwell on the etymological origin and literal sense of the common word *Fledermaus*).

In their wordplay, children gesture toward a dynamic force that inheres within but also fundamentally precedes the fixed signs that compose established language systems. Jean Paul approaches such an understanding of wordplay at numerous points in *Levana*. But he struggles to conceptually grasp this form of wordplay, that is to say, to fix or capture it in his own language and thus to reduce the potential for alterity intimated by wordplay into static, established categories and words. At one point, in what may be seen as one of these attempts to circumscribe the idea of language that children's wordplay exposes, he summons *Poesie*—a crucial term for the early German Romantics that also invokes the missing category that one would expect to see linked to the "third class" of play between the theoretical and the practical.[22] With these different connotations circling, he declares that "play is the first poetry [*Poesie*] of the human being" (152).

While *Poesie* carries a variety of interconnected meanings for the writers associated with the *Frühromantik* (Ludwig Tieck, Novalis, F.W.J. Schelling, Friedrich Schlegel, and his brother August Wilhelm Schlegel), perhaps the most useful conceptualization in view of Jean Paul's mobilization of the term can be found in the writings of Friedrich Schlegel. Schlegel, Frederick Beiser maintains, understands by *Poesie* a basic "creative power in human beings," a power that unites man and nature.[23] We find such an idea of *Poesie* in Schlegel's "Conversation on Poesie" ("Gespräch über die Poesie," 1800), where he paradigmatically describes it as an invisible power (*Kraft*) inside each one of us, a primary force (*Urkraft*) that underlies and forms all other faculties.[24] In unmistakably similar rhetoric, Jean Paul defines the "first" play of *Poesie* as an original force that constitutes "all the powers [*Kräfte*], without imparting a prevailing tendency [*siegende Richtung*] to any one."[25] Jean Paul's word choice allows us to read the force of *Poesie* in contrast to the colonizing power of language discussed above. Without establishing a "prevailing tendency," *Poesie* precedes and thus appears to lie beyond any relation of mastery that such a notion of language would entail. While Jean Paul does not explain any further, as we saw earlier, he also aligns theoretical and practical play with specific powers (*Kräfte*), namely, the receptive (*empfangende*) and formative (*gestaltende*) faculties (151). What might it therefore mean to situate a poetic form of play at the foundation of these two opposed modes of relation?

If theoretical play and practical play are defined by their respective inward and outward orientation, then the play of *Poesie* appears to indicate an attempt to think a radical lack of orientation (*Richtung*)—the midway point from which all directions spring and at which all directions meet. Underlying all the faculties without privileging any one "tendency" or direction (*Richtung*), *Poesie* can be seen as residing in the indistinct yet distinguishing space between inside and outside, play that "takes" and play that "gives" (152). Such an idea hearkens back to the original Greek understanding of *poeisis* as the action of producing or making that brings forth a thing separate from itself, allowing for something different, or perhaps even difference itself to unfold.[26]

Poesie appears to intimate the relational, differential space that language first engenders. However, Jean Paul leaves open the precise relation between *Poesie* and language—a connection that also remains a point of some scholarly debate regarding Schlegel and the other early German Romantics.[27] Jean Paul's refusal or inability to more explicitly define the play of *Poesie* as either inherent in language or anterior to it once again indicates the difficulty in articulating the indistinct, third type of play that he repeatedly approaches by way of several interrelated, if not quite synonymous, terms. Arguably more important than *Poesie* for Jean Paul in this context is the faculty of *fantasy*—the creative imagination—yet another concept that he links with language and the generative third space of play, the threshold region between the developing subject and the world.

THE LANGUAGE OF FANTASY

In *Levana*, Jean Paul notably locates the emergence of the faculty of fantasy (*Phantasie*) in the childhood transition from theoretical to practical play, a transition spurred by language. As the child accrues words, "fantasy begins to move, whose unfledged wings language first plumes" ("es regt sich die Phantasie, deren Flügelknochen erst die Sprache befiedert").[28] By the time he wrote *Levana*, Jean Paul had been developing his ideas on fantasy in writing for over a decade. Perhaps the most fully developed articulation of fantasy in Jean Paul's writings can be found in his study of Romantic theory and art, *School for Aesthetics* (*Vorschule der Ästhetik*, 1804). There he stresses the difference—critical for Kant and his contemporaries—between the *reproductive* and *creative* forms of the imagination.[29] For Jean Paul these mark utterly distinct capacities, what he calls "poetic faculties" (not to be confused with *Poesie*), each deserving of its own name.[30] He uses *Einbildungskraft*, the common German word for the imagination, to designate the reproductive imagination, which he dismisses as little more than an "intensified and more vividly colored memory." Like memory, the reproductive imagination creates based on what once existed, "its images are only fallen leaves wafted from the real world" (28). While the scenes one imagines via the faculty of *Einbildungskraft* may appear more intense than those one simply remembers, they nonetheless lack true creativity. *Einbildungskraft* reconstructs; it does not create something new. In this sense *Einbildungskraft* parallels the passivity of receptive, theoretical play. Although theoretical play centers for Jean Paul on an inward movement facilitated by the senses, and *Einbildungskraft* emphasizes intellectual rather than physical action, both categories stress reception over creation.

To signal the productive imagination, Jean Paul strips *Einbildungskraft* of the prefix *ein* (inward, into) to form *Bildungskraft* (formative, creative power). In an act of linguistic conjuration, he removes three simple letters and in the process discovers *or* creates—it is difficult to say which—the creative imagination. But Jean Paul's search for the right word for the productive imagination does not end there. He introduces a third term, presented as a synonym for *Bildungskraft*: "fantasy" (*Phantasie*), the term he ultimately favors.[31] Fantasy is generative in a different sense than *Einbildungskraft*. If the latter reflects back images "from the inner world into the outer" that there "stiffen into bodies," fantasy infuses its creations, its externalized imaginings, with life (28).

Jean Paul puts fantasy's animating power on display at different points throughout *Levana*. We see it, for example, in the "play talking"

(*Spielsprechen*) of children who enliven "inanimate playthings" through personifying utterances such as "the lights have covered themselves up and gone to bed," "the spring has dressed itself," and "the wind dances."[32] The relation of animating fantasy to language becomes even more explicit in other texts, for instance in the following examination of the operations that define the poet's "black magic"—the processes that imbue poetic creations with life:[33] "In that he makes through metaphor a body [*Körper*] into the shell [*Hülle*] for something intellectual [*Geistig*] (e.g., blossom of science): the poet forces us to see the bodily (here "blossom") more clearly than would happen in a botanical dictionary. And conversely, just as by metaphor he lends higher colors to the bodily through the intellectual, he does the same for the intellectual through the bodily by means of personification" (Jean Paul, Werke, 4:199). In order to make sense of the link presented here between linguistic creation and fantasy, it helps to consider the third place that fantasy occupies for Jean Paul between reception and creation, body and mind. Several years before he began to use "fantasy" to denote solely the productive side of the imagination, Jean Paul reflected at length on the different functions of the imagination (*Phantasie*) in a text titled "On the Natural Magic of the Imagination" ("Über die natürliche Magie der Einbildungskraft," 1795).[34] Anticipating many of the topics around which his investigations of children's play would revolve, he compares the ways the imagination and the senses connect the individual to the world. With regard to the ability to receive or form perceptions, he writes, "the five senses bring forth before my soul a flower garden outside of my head, fantasy one inside of my head; the senses form and paint, fantasy does this as well; they reprint nature with five different plates, fantasy, as a *sensorium commune*, delivers it with one" (195).[35] Through different means and within different spheres, the senses and the imagination (*Phantasie*) are capable of bringing forth iterations of the same object (an external empirical flower garden, and an internal imagined one). In view of this example, Jean Paul enlists Kant to help debunk the idea that the senses and the imagination perform completely separate actions. In the first *Critique*, Kant has "proven" that we do not only "receive" (*empfangen*) through the "nerves of sense," nor solely "create" (*erzeugen*) through the imagination. We deceive ourselves into thinking this to be the case, Jean Paul argues, because the "play-space" (*Spielraum*) of the senses is "narrower than that of fantasy" (195). In other words, the objective limits set by sense perception conflict with the vast play space unleashed by fantasy. We therefore falsely assume that physical sense reception and mental creation mutually exclude one another rather than work together at all times (even if to varying degrees).

Jean Paul's reflections on the complex relation between the imagination and sensation lead him to observe that despite our extraordinary capacity to imagine things that lie beyond the physical realm, our imaginings rarely achieve the same intensity of color or liveliness as sensuous perceptions. But, he notes, there do exist certain instances where the inventions of fantasy blur with reality, where what the imagination creates becomes indistinguishable from what the senses receive. The hallucinatory, fever-stricken subject exemplifies the extreme power of the fantastic imagination to animate to such a degree that it becomes difficult if not impossible to separate sensuous perception from mental construction. In his delusional fever, the sick man infuses the "pale corpse" of an imagined person with so much "spirit of life" (*Lebensgeist*) that the effigy becomes for him as real as a "living person outside of [his] head" (195–196).[36]

Although the pathological hallucinations of the sick man differ in origin from the fantastic creations of the poet mentioned above, the comparison begins to reveal what is at stake for Jean Paul in presenting fantasy's power to animate as also poetic in character: the *interplay* of bare, material sensation (devoid of meaning), and unembodied, immaterial thought. When Jean Paul speaks of metaphor making "a body [*Körper*] into the shell [*Hülle*] for something intellectual," he recasts fantasy as a function of tropological figuration, a poetic (and not transparently communicative) mode of relation. The ability of the poet to create and enliven via fantasy centers on two interlinked figures: metaphor and personification. In inverse manner, both tropes animate by fusing content and form, mind and body to one another. Metaphor breathes spirit and meaning into lifeless matter; and personification renders the intellectual visible, tangible by giving it a shape. Fantasy thus animates in a more forceful, fuller manner than the reproductive imagination through linguistic processes that imbue form with content and vice versa.

One begins to sense a performative concept of language in Jean Paul's explorations of fantasy, of language that does not simply passively transmit what it receives but creates, giving body life. In the section of *Levana* devoted to play, Jean Paul himself describes fantasy's ability to (linguistically) create as "dramatic."[37] "Dramatic fantasy," he writes, occasionally intervenes (*eingreifen*) into children's passive, theoretical play, for example, when simply lying still and looking around a room. Fantasy can then induce children to see "the room now large now small, and themselves alone one moment and in company the next," transforming the gaze and passive sensuous reception into an instance of imaginative creation (151). He also presents other cases where fantasy might intercede: children peering out of a window, lying on the grass, or "watching the employment of their parents." But he saves the most outstanding example for last. He claims that, for children, "listening to a conversation" (*Sprechen-Hören*) can also be "to them a game of this kind" (151). Inaudible between the two words, although visible as a material graphic marker, is a hyphen separating the spoken conversation from the listening child: *Sprechen-Hören*, more appropriately translated as "speaking-listening." Unlike in composite nouns where little ambiguity remains regarding their meaning, in "speaking-listening" it is unclear which word modifies which.[38] Are we dealing here with the passive reception, the listening of spoken words (as the translator would have it)? Or is listening itself a kind of speaking, a "speaking-listening" that fantastically constructs what it receives, or that creates in the very act of receiving? What type of relation or relationality does the hyphen, which unsettles and destabilizes the order and our understanding of the connection between these two words and actions, indicate? Is this play that "takes" or "gives," or is it the "and" in-between them?[39] And if so, what would that mean? A possible answer to such questions may lie in a different set of Jean Paul's reflections on wordplay that highlight his interest in punctuation marks and dashes (*Gedankenstriche*), and the inherent alterity in language that they reveal.

ANAGRAMMATIC W-O-R-D-P-L-A-Y

In *School of Aesthetics*, Jean Paul connects the play of wit to both language and fantasy through the following cryptic analogy: "If wit is the playful *anagram* of nature, then fantasy is its *hieroglyphic alphabet*."[40] He attempts to differentiate the playful, anagrammatic character of wit, which reshuffles what exists like loose letters into order to create new words, from fantasy, which unites both body and form through a synthesizing force that seeks to "totalize everything." For Jean Paul, "wit" (*Witz*) names the ability to reorganize and recombine what exists to form new constellations.[41] Unlike "learned men, whose heads contain nothing but immoveable furniture," those with wit are capable of uprooting what has been established to discover new arrangements or unexpected connections (382–383). Children tend to exhibit inordinate amounts of wit, which Jean Paul argues we should nurture as a part of their ongoing education. Especially following the "severe rule and lesson-time" of math, the "sans-culottish freedom and play-time of wit" acts as a potent antidote (383). Through his evocative choice of the word "sans-culottish," Jean Paul links the free play of wit with revolutionary freedom, and thus with another, more politically inflected tradition of thinking about play (epitomized by Schiller). Although a shift to the political would take us beyond the scope of the current study, it seems important to note that Jean Paul's historical appeal to freedom can be read not only figuratively—in terms of what the *sans-culottes* represented or fought for through their rejection of breeches—but also literally, those simply "without breeches."

In the move from a figurative to a literal reading of this image, the distinction that Jean Paul draws between the play of recombinatory wit and dramatic, fantastic play begins to break down. If wit lays bare, sheds the trappings of custom and convention to reveal the unfixity and the arbitrariness of what has been established, it does so as the literal reading rids itself of the figurative one built upon it. Like a *Vexierbild*, the figurative and literal coexist in dynamic tension, and the same can be said of wit and fantasy. When we exercise our wit, we also forge *new* links through analogies, similes, and other forms of association and thus discover (create?) what did not seem to previously exist. Wit starts to become constructive, although without necessarily resolving the tension between creation and reception in favor of the former.

The tension between these two modes of play becomes strikingly visible in the final text addressed here, a text that brings together play, language, and punctuation marks: *The Life of Fibel* (*Leben Fibels*, 1812).[42] In the fictional novel, Jean Paul investigates and recounts the biography of Fibel, the mysterious author of the *Bienroder Primer*, a well-known A-B-C book for children and a genre that eventually assumes Fibel's own name following the publication of his book (the word for "primer" in German is indeed *Fibel*, on which Jean Paul plays). The story, told from the perspective of a first-person narrator, centers on the discovery and collection of Fibel's vast oeuvre, including at its center his autobiography, which functions as the purported source for the majority of the text. Although the editor-narrator finds parts of the autobiography at the antiquarian bookshop where he first unearths Fibel's writings, many sections of it lie scattered across the world and are now being used for practical purposes (e.g., as wrapping paper or paper bags). Prominently missing is Fibel's account of the period surrounding his most well-known work. By chance the narrator first discovers these pages one day from a child playing with a paper kite.[43] From its inception, the eponymous *Fibel* is presented in the form of play.

Predictably, many of the themes we have seen in Jean Paul's discussions of children's play, fantasy, and language arise in *The Life of Fibel*, particularly in the depiction of Fibel's relation to language. By the time young Fibel begins work on his A-B-C book, the precocious child has already taught himself countless languages, from the ancient to the modern. To everyone's astonishment, he is capable of "reading any book" he is given (398). However, Fibel's so-called reading ability remains bare and superficial: "naturally he did not understand one word of what he read aloud; but, like a poet, the content did not matter to him, but rather only the form" (398). Fibel's parents encourage his interest in language, for example, by gifting him "empty notebooks" for Christmas. Fibel is able to "create more intellectual [*geistig*] nourishment" from these bare white books than the narrator receives from filled ones (387). The force of Fibel's poetic fantasy hinted at in this scene mirrors a case Jean Paul offers in *Levana* of a young girl who sat beside him one day as he was writing, a girl who herself "wrote for a long time with a pen [*Feder*] dipped only in air on an ever-white sheet of paper."[44] Much like the quill or feather (*Feder*) of fantasy through which this child's play takes flight (echoing the "unfledged wings" of fantasy, which "language first plumes"), Fibel's love of language centers on its generative potential (154). The culmination of Fibel's profound interest in language is the A-B-C book project, an attempt to create the "book of all books."[45]

The idea to compose his own primer first comes to Fibel in a vivid dream. In it, a wild rooster roams around carrying the helpless boy on its back, all the while crowing an unintelligible sound. Eventually Fibel deciphers it to be the sound "ha," as in the first part of the word "rooster," *Hahn*. In the dream, however, it becomes evident to him that the sound is meant to signify neither the name of the rooster nor laughter, but rather the "bare ha of the alphabet" (426). In other words, it is the phonetic expression of the letter *h*, which in German sounds like "ha," although the rooster, Fibel notes, might as well have crowed "he" or "hu" since the vowel that makes the letter pronounceable is irrelevant.

Fibel delights in the witty, anagrammatic play space revealed by the "bare" letters of the alphabet. In order to remind the reader of the dynamic fluidity of the alphabet and the storehouse of potential combinations that it holds, he chooses to reprint the alphabet in full at the top of every page—this way the reader may also enjoy the "pleasure of the pure alphabet" not yet arranged into fixed, solid words (429). He further accentuates the bare elements that join together to form language by inserting hyphens (*Teilungsstriche*) between the individual syllables of words, putting on display for both the novice and experienced reader the constitutive parts of which language is assembled (Jean Paul offers as an example the word "dash": *Stri-che*; 430). Fibel's unique method of dismantling words through hyphens leads the narrator to describe him as the creator of the dash (*Gedankenstrich*). The dash, as a marker of both separation and conjunction, symbolizes both mediation and interruption simultaneously, as two sides of the same coin.

At the beginning of *The Invisible Lodge*, Jean Paul provides the following "motto" or epigraph: "Man is the great dash [*Gedankenstrich*] in the book of nature."[46] The emergence of mankind marks a gap or caesura in the continuity of nature, a dividing line (*Strich*) tied to the ability to think (*Gedanken*). As we saw above in the description of language as the force that separates monkey and man, Jean Paul believes that words raise man above nature, allowing for creative intellect to form and detach itself from mere sensuous reception, and in doing so elevate mankind to a higher level, a state of active, practical play. The anthropocentric, instrumentalizing view of language that Jean Paul advances in this context, however, is undercut by the bare wordplay of children, which we see exemplified above all in the example of Fibel. By breaking down words to expose the anagrammatic potential of playing *with* bare, unorganized letters (wit), Fibel uncovers the usually inaudible (hyphenated) play-ground that subtends and enables dynamic wordplay, to which children at the border of language are especially attuned.

Let us end at the beginning, that is to say, at the beginning of language as presented in Fibel's eponymous primer. The narrator makes a startling discovery when he finally finds the original drafts of Fibel's A-B-C book. On the opening page under "A," Fibel did not initially intend to have an ape (*Affe*) "eating an apple" under a picture depicting the same. Instead, he imagined a biblical scene, namely, "Adam" biting into the apple (333). The narrator attributes Fibel's decision, supported by Fibel's own writings, to a question of propriety (*Anstand*). It would have been indecent to depict Adam, who was nude before the fatal bite, as naked; and it would have also posed a pragmatic problem of representation in that this static scene was supposed to mark a point of transition, of change from one state to another—the fall from paradise through the introduction of knowledge and language. The ape poses an easy solution, since he is "decently clothed in his animal fur" both before and after the fall. But beyond offering a practical answer, the ape in its fur also points to a material continuity that underlies the transition from one state of play to another. It is a marker of our distance from an original, bare state but also of our closeness to it. The naked ape, covered in its fur, marks the folding or enmeshment of inside and outside, content and form, signified and signifier. Like the dash marks that render the empty, meaningless space between words visible—space that allows for meanings and words to emerge, to differentiate themselves from one another—the ape at the beginning of Fibel's primer throws into doubt our ability to absolutely transcend a bare, nonsensical playing *with* that always attends and inheres at the base of our communicative use of language. If such nonsensical wordplay, which Jean Paul both acknowledges and dismisses, can teach us anything, then perhaps it is that learning does not occur *through* language, or through stages facilitated by it, but rather *with* it—just as the ape emerges *with*, inseparable from, its fur.

NOTES

1. Jean Paul, *Werke*, ed. Norbert Miller, 6 vols. (Munich: Carl Hanser, 1959–63), 1:143. Unless otherwise noted, all translations from the German are my own. Occasionally, existing English translations have been modified in order to adhere closer to the original.

2. Groos draws on *Levana*, alongside several contemporary studies in evolutionary biology, in his monumental anthropological study *The Play of Man* (1899). Specifically, he points to Jean Paul's understanding of social play as an example of the sort of stage-based "system" that he aims to establish in his own study. See Karl Groos, *The Play of Man* (New York: D. Appleton, 1919), esp. 395–397. From a different perspective, Freud approaches Jean Paul's ideas on play in his book *Jokes and Their Relation to the Unconscious* (1905). In particular, Jean Paul's writings on wit (*Witz*), understood as a form of wordplay, inform Freud's investigation into the psychological functions of jokes. See Sigmund Freud, *The Standard Edition of the Complete Psychological Works of Sigmund Freud*, ed. James Strachey (London: Hogarth, 1953–74), 8:128. Benjamin, meanwhile, was a great admirer of both Jean Paul and *Levana*. One finds several references to the author and this work in Benjamin's writings on toys and play, themes he returns to in several essays, reviews, and literary texts. For more on Freud's and Benjamin's views on play (and their intersections with Jean Paul's thought), see my essay "The Smallest Remainder: Benjamin and Freud on Play," *MLN* 133, no. 3 (2018): 720–742.

3. Interspersed with appendices and divided into a variety of fragments, chapters, and paragraphs, Jean Paul explores topics ranging from general modes of education (religious, moral, physical, royal) to specific child-rearing practices.

4. Jean Paul, *Levana; or, the Doctrine of Education* (London: George Bell & Sons, 1897), 74.

5. For the importance of the fragment for the early German Romantics, as both a literary genre and an aesthetic category, see Philippe Lacoue-Labarthe and Jean-Luc Nancy, "The Fragment: The Fragmentary Exigency," in *The Literary Absolute: The Theory of Literature in German Romanticism*, trans. Philipp Barnard and Cheryl Lester (Albany: State University of New York Press, 1988). While Jean Paul is often aligned with the Jena Romantics, he diverges from them on several points. For an overview of Jean Paul's connection to German Romanticism, see Götz Müller, "Jean Pauls Ästhetik im Kontext der Frühromantik

und des deutschen Idealismus," in *Jean Paul im Kontext: Gesammelte Aufsätze* (Tübingen: Königshausen und Neumann, 1996).

6. Jean Paul, *Levana*, 71.

7. Jean Paul's birth name was Johann Paul Friedrich Richter.

8. Jean-Jacques Rousseau, *Emile or on Education*, trans. Allan Bloom (New York: Basic Books, 1979), 92.

9. For a synopsis of Rousseau's views on this topic, and an attempt to correct the prevailing account of his pedagogy as "romantic noninterventionist" in the image of Fröbel or Pestalozzi, see Eugene O. Iheoma, "Rousseau's Views on Teaching," *Journal of Educational Thought* 31, no. 1 (1997): 69–81.

10. Some of the most prominent authors and pedagogical works referenced in *Levana*, including in the preface to the later, second edition, are Johann Heinrich Pestalozzi's popular ideas on educational reform; Johann Friedrich Herbart's *Allgemeine Pädagogik aus dem Zweck der Erziehung abgeleitet* (1806); Johann Baptist Graser's *Divinität oder das Prinzip der einzig wahren Menschenbildung* (1811); and F.H.C. Schwarz's *Erziehungslehre* (1829).

11. Brian Sutton-Smith, *The Ambiguity of Play* (Cambridge, MA: Harvard University Press, 1997), 6.

12. Donald Woods Winnicott, *Playing and Reality* (New York: Basic Books, 1971), 41.

13. On this point, Jean Paul presages Johan Huizinga's influential argument in *Homo Ludens* (1944) that play is not merely a key part of culture but in fact the force that founds it. According to Huizinga, play exists "before culture itself existed, accompanying and pervading it from the earliest beginnings right up to the phase of civilization we are now living in." Johan Huizinga, *Homo Ludens: A Study of the Play-Element in Culture* (New York: Roy, 1950), 4.

14. Jean Paul uses various terms to describe active play. *Selbstspiel*, which occurs only once, stands out in its suggestive ambiguity. The word conjures ideas of self-determined action, of solipsism, but also potentially of an *interplay* between *self* and *other* that language makes possible.

15. He reaffirms this idea later in *Levana*, stating that during the "first section" of life, the child suffers from a "want of the power of speech" (143).

16. Jean Paul explores the tension between these two dimensions of language more explicitly in other writings. As Paul Fleming shows via Kommerell's influential reading of Jean Paul, we could rephrase this opposition as one between what language "intends" (*das Gemeinte*) and the "gesture of expression" (*Ausdrucksgebärde*). See Paul Fleming, "The Crisis of Art: Max Kommerell and Jean Paul's Gestures," *MLN* 115, no. 3 (2000): 519–543.

17. We find a related understanding of language in Karl Philipp Moritz's short essay, "Yet Another Hypothesis Concerning Moses's Creation" (1784). Like Herder, who considers thought inseparable from language, Moritz argues that the ability to differentiate (*unterscheiden*), perceive, and order the world is inextricably linked with our capacity to name (*benennen*) said world. See Karl Philipp Moritz, "Auch eine Hypothese über die Schöpfungsgeschichte Mosis," in *Werke*, vol. 3, ed. Horst Günther (Frankfurt am Main: Insel Verlag, 1981).

18. For the German, see Jean Paul, *Werke*, 5:602–603.

19. Paul de Man, "Phenomenality and Materiality in Kant," in *Aesthetic Ideology*, ed. Andrzej Warminski (Minneapolis: University of Minnesota Press, 1996), 90.

20. Jean Paul, *Levana*, 332 (translation modified); Jean Paul, *Werke*, 5:791.

21. In *The Invisible Lodge* (1793), Jean Paul describes "playful teaching" (*spielender Unterricht*) as the ideal method of instruction, for play may "awaken a passion" lying dormant within the child. Jean Paul, *Werke*, 1:127.

22. Elsewhere, he mobilizes the related verb "poetise" (*dichten*) to describe the fanciful way children may seem to "lie" when they are in fact engaged in imaginary play. Jean Paul, *Levana*, 333.

23. Frederick C. Beiser, "The Meaning of 'Romantic Poetry,'" in *The Romantic Imperative: The Concept of Early German Romanticism* (Cambridge, MA: Harvard University Press, 2003), 15.

24. Schlegel variously describes *Poesie* as each person's "ownmost essence" (*eigenstes Wesen*), "innermost power" (*innerste Kraft*), and "the invisible primal force of humankind" (*die unsichtbare Urkraft der Menschheit*). Friedrich Schlegel, *Kritische Friedrich-Schlegel-Ausgabe*, ed. Ernst Behler, Jean Jacques Anstett, and Hans Eichner (Munich: Schöningh, 1958), 2:284–285.

25. Jean Paul, *Levana*, 152 (translation modified).

26. For a brief history of the Greek concept of *poiesis* (including the way Kant and the Idealists inherit the term and connect it to the category of play), see Hans Robert Jauss, "Poiesis," *Critical Inquiry* 8, no. 3 (1982), esp. 600.

27. Addressing this relation, Beiser argues that Schlegel's concept of *Poesie* goes beyond a linguistic understanding. Meanwhile, Lacoue-Labarthe and Nancy indirectly assume an opposite stance in framing the overall early German Romantic project as literary in kind.

28. Jean Paul, *Levana*, 153; Jean Paul, *Werke*, 5:604.

29. An overview of these two terms in the philosophical tradition can be found in John Bullitt and Walter Jackson Bate, "Distinctions between Fancy and Imagination in Eighteenth-Century English Criticism," *MLN* 60 (1945): 8–15.

30. Jean Paul, *Horn of Oberon: Jean Paul Richter's School for Aesthetics*, trans. Margaret R. Hale (Detroit: Wayne State University Press, 1973), 28; Jean Paul, *Werke*, 5:47.

31. The translators of *School of Aesthetics* consistently use "imagination" for *Phantasie*, often amending it with the descriptors "productive" or "creative." In order to eschew confusion, I have chosen to use "fantasy" (rather than "fancy") throughout for *Phantasie*.

32. Jean Paul, *Levana*, 153–154.

33. Jean Paul, *Werke*, 4:195.

34. Generally, Jean Paul uses the term "fantasy" in a manner consistent with his later distinction, although at this point he also occasionally uses it to describe the reproductive imagination. For a gloss of this text and its importance for understanding Jean Paul's own method of poetic creation, see Eckart Goebel, *Am Ufer der zweiten Welt: Jean Pauls "Poetische Landschaftsmalerei"* (Tübingen: Stauffenberg, 1999).

35. Although Jean Paul invokes Kant explicitly later in the same passage, the phrase *sensorium commune* indicates a longer tradition reaching back to Aristotle and his idea of the *sensus communis* (in "De Anima"), which postulates that the senses flow together and are coordinated into one via thought (with the help of memory).

36. This can be directly juxtaposed with the images that the reproductive imagination projects, which "stiffen into bodies" immediately upon materializing "from the inner world into the outer." Jean Paul, *Horn of Oberon*, 28.

37. Jean Paul, *Levana*, 151.

38. Approximately a decade after *Levana*, Jean Paul publishes *On the German Double-Words* (*Über die deutschen Doppelwörter*, 1818), a collection of twelve letters detailing the grammatical rules and usages of composite nouns in the German language. The key to compound nouns, he writes, lies in the relation between the "determining word" (*Bestimmwort*) and the "base word" (*Grundwort*). When two words are conjoined (without a hyphen), the latter word forms a base, which the former modifies. One can easily flip the fused words to derive new constructions and corresponding meanings (he gives these untranslatable examples: "Landtrauer in Trauerland, Priesterrock in Rockpriester, Staatsdiener in Dienerstaat, Bundestag in Tagesbund"), but the rule always remains the same—one word modifies another solidifying, base word. The same cannot be said, however, of words connected via hyphens. Jean Paul, *Werke*, 3.2:14–15.

39. Jean Paul, *Levana*, 152.

40. Jean Paul, *Horn of Oberon*, 28.

41. Jean Paul discusses wit in several writings. From *The Invisible Lodge*, through *Introduction to Aesthetics* (*Vorschule der Ästhetik*, 1804), to *Levana*, he repeatedly highlights the aesthetic value of the childlike ability to make witty, innovative connections between seemingly unrelated things. For an instructive passage on wit's relation to children's play, see *Werke* 5:42.

42. For an enlightening reading of this text (which also touches briefly on Jean Paul's conception of play), see Thomas Schestag, "Bibliographie für Jean Paul," *MLN* 113, no. 3 (1998): 465–523.

43. Jean Paul, *Werke*, 6:425.

44. Jean Paul, *Levana*, 155.

45. Jean Paul, *Werke*, 6:427. In the preface, the narrator remarks that he read a primer (*Fibel*) before the Bible (*Bibel*), indicating the precedent of language, of the creative word (370).

46. Jean Paul, *Werke*, 1: frontmatter.

CHAPTER TEN

Authorship, Translation, Play

Schleiermacher's Metalangual Poetics

DAVID MARTYN

FEW TERMS ARE ENTRUSTED with such important discursive functions by the aesthetics and poetics of the Age of Goethe than "play." Neither Kant's revolutionary aesthetic theory, nor Schiller's politicization of Kant's aesthetics, nor the Romantic poetics of Novalis, nor Friedrich Schlegel's theory of irony, nor the hermeneutics of Schleiermacher—to name just a few central references—would have been possible without these authors' signature employment of the term "play" (*Spiel*). So much do aesthetics and poetics rely on this term during this period that one can claim, without any great exaggeration, that aesthetic and poetic theory in the Age of Goethe are as much an aesthetics and poetics of play as they are of that other and much more thoroughly researched cardinal term of the age, namely, "genius."[1] Indeed, even the term "genius" is affected by the age's fondness of play. In the prescriptive poetics of the preceding epoch of the sort exemplified, in Germany, by Johann Christoph Gottsched (1700–66), its most prominent representative, creativity was something that required genius in the sense of "talent," but it was still governed by universally valid rules and principles that furnished objective criteria for the assessment of quality. With thinkers such as Johann Georg Hamann (1730–88), Johann Gottfried Herder (1744–1803), and finally Kant, the creative genius is liberated from any such objective rules, creating a need for a new set of criteria. In Kant in particular, one can clearly observe how the moment at which genius is freed from prescriptive rules goes hand in hand with a new reliance on the concept of play. Having defined "genius" as "a *talent* to produce that for which no determinate rule can be given," Kant specifies that such a talent consists in "an ability to apprehend the swiftly passing *play of the imag-*

ination [*Spiel der Einbildungskraft*] and to bring it together into a concept . . . that is susceptible of being communicated universally."[2] What defines aesthetic experience, for Kant, is nothing less than the pleasure one feels when one's mental faculties are relieved of their usual epistemic function, or in other words: when they are allowed to play. "The faculties of knowledge that are put into a state of play [*ins Spiel gesetzt*]" by the sight of an aesthetically pleasing object, Kant writes, "find themselves in *free play* [sind hierbei in einem *freien Spiele*], since no determinate concept limits them to any certain rule of knowledge."[3] Without the invocation of and new value attached to the concept of play—a word that turns up no fewer than seven times in the key paragraph 9 of the *Critique of Judgment* from which this last quotation is taken—Kant would have no criteria by which to define or ground the judgment of aesthetic and poetic productions. The same could doubtless be shown in many of the other authors of the period.[4]

Like any axiomatic term, "play" is thus a point of vulnerability for the theory that rests on it. It is a term on which the aesthetic and poetic theory of this era comes to rely without any clear definition of what it contains; in short, a blind spot. For by untethering the principle of poetic creativity from prescriptive rules and entrusting it to "free play," the problem arises of how to distinguish ingenious invention from mere license, chaos, or nonsense. How does one draw the line between *free* play in the way the creative genius engages in it to produce original works of exemplary accomplishment, on the one hand, and *mere* play in the sense of fatuous combinations that may be original but of no aesthetic or poetic value at all? Mustn't "play" at some point encounter a limit in order to fulfill its function of providing a distinctive origin for works of aesthetic value? We can expect this cardinal issue to find expression in the double valence of the term "play." On the one hand, "play" is used in a new way to designate the fecund medium of artistic genius; its opposite is then "rule" or "precept." On the other hand, "play" can still be used pejoratively to designate empty and worthless activity, any fruitless or barren use of time; its opposite or contrasting term is then "seriousness" (*Ernst*). How this difference between "play" in the good sense and "play" in the pejorative sense is determined promises to tell us a lot about the dynamics of aesthetic and poetic discourse in this period.

In what follows, I would like to look more closely at how the use of the word "play" can be a symptom of uncontrolled assumptions in this discourse, assumptions which, when exposed, can teach us a good deal about these theories but also about their continuing influence—to the extent, namely, that they are still operative today. My case in point will be the way "play" enters into the conception of creative authorship developed by the Romantic theologian, philosopher, and hermeneutic theorist Friedrich Schleiermacher (1768–1834). Instead of addressing this issue in Schleiermacher's writings where one would tend first to look, namely, in his hermeneutics, I will be approaching it obliquely by choosing what might seem to be an unlikely point of entry: namely, Schleiermacher's famous theory of translation, as presented in his 1813 address to the Berlin Royal Academy of Sciences, "On the Different Methods of Translation." It turns out that in confronting what it means to translate the kind of poetic or creative writing that is at issue in the Romantic theory of authorship, Schleiermacher comes to rely on the term "play" in a highly revealing way—one that betrays one of this theory's least understood, most problematic, and most influential presuppositions.

LANGUALITY

Schleiermacher's theory of authorship, as advanced both in the translation address and in other works, clearly moves within the framework of the new approbation of "play." This is most evident in the text for which Schleiermacher is best known today, the lectures on hermeneutics he held from 1805 until 1833. While "play," for Schleiermacher, is not in itself a sufficient criterion of literary value, it is nevertheless of signal importance for the interpreter of any creative production: "It would be a great mistake," Schleiermacher emphasizes in his hermeneutics, "to banish this free play [*freies Spiel*] from the literary domain."[5] For the task of "psychological interpretation," of the famous "empathy" (*Einfühlung*) into the individuality of the author, can only be carried out by careful study not just of the author's works themselves, since these are subject to objective constraints, but of examples of the author's "freer communication [*freiere Mitteilung*]" (181), in which the author's individuality and the mode of her or his creativity can be better observed. In a word, in order to understand how an author creates, one must observe the author at play. For the truly generative moment in the creative process—"the emergence of the thoughts out of the totality of the individual's life moments" (181)—is always a form of play, "a free play of thoughts that precedes and to a certain degree prepares for artistic production" ("ein freies Spiel der Gedanken, welches der künstlerischen Produktion in gewissem Grade vorbereitend vorausgeht"; 180). The same emphasis on play as the root of creativity is in evidence in the *Aesthetics*, where Schleiermacher locates the source of artworks in the domain of "free play" and defines art as "play in opposition to work and business."[6]

But while Schleiermacher echoes Kant and Schiller in his emphasis on free play as the source of artistic production, there is another element in Schleiermacher's theory that clearly limits or relativizes the influence of "free play." This other element is *language*, that is, the specific (national) language in which the author writes. "Every speech"—that is, every concrete use of language, such as a written work—"presupposes a given language," postulates Schleiermacher at the beginning of the *Hermeneutics*. He then explains: "The individual is conditioned in his thinking through the (common) language and can only think thoughts that already have an expression for them in his language."[7] And since all languages are different in the way they articulate and combine related ideas, this means that, even in the work of the most original and creative author, what is expressed can in fact be seen as expressive not just of the author's originality, but of the particular spirit or genius of the author's language: "If we objectify language, we find that all acts of speech are only a manner in which the language in its particular nature comes into appearance, and each individual is only a place in which the language appears; this is why, when reading eminent authors, we direct our attention to their language" (78). Hence, authorship is a process in which two forces collide: on the one hand, the *free play* of thoughts, rooted in the totality of the author's life; and, on the other, the influence of the language in which the author expresses them. But "collision" should not be understood negatively: as he makes clear in the *Hermeneutics*, what Schleiermacher has in mind is a kind of mutual enrichment. The author's language—the language into which they are born[8]—modifies the author's thinking; but the author, too, modifies the language into which they are born (see 79). Author and language are two "individuals" (80); original or creative authorship arises from the interplay between them. The result is a theory that can, on the one hand, exploit the potential of the concept of play to account for the source of artistic creativity without relying on the notion of rules, while, on the other hand, imposing a limit on it in the form of the givenness of a specific language to which the author's play is subject.

Given the central role of language in Schleiermacher's theory of authorship, we can expect that where there is a sustained focus on the issue of language identity and individuality, this aspect of authorship will assume a new importance. And such is indeed the case in Schleiermacher's theory of translation, where as a matter of course Schleiermacher must confront languages in the plural, in their difference and thus also in their distinguishing identity. Written in just two days, from June 21 to June 23 of 1813, and presented on June 24, Schleiermacher's "On the Different Methods of Translation" is by far the most influential treatise on translation to emerge from the Romantic movement in Germany.[9] Its signature achievement is to have moved beyond the hitherto central but overly simple distinction of translation theory between free and literal translation with his new distinction between two "methods," commonly glossed as "domesticating" and "foreignizing" (on which more anon).[10] As important, Schleiermacher grounds his theory of translation *within* his elaborate theory of authorship and of understanding, clearly distinguishing between two different tasks, depending on the nature of the text to be rendered. Business communications, travel descriptions, newspaper reports, court minutes, and similar documents are suitable only for the more mechanical work of what Schleiermacher refers to as "interpreting" (*Dolmetschen*), a term more commonly used for the simultaneous translation of spoken communications but which Schleiermacher extends to include the written translation of any text the primary function of which is to provide an impersonal record or description of extra-linguistic objects or events. The term "translation" (*Übersetzung, Übertragung*) Schleiermacher reserves for the task of rendering "those spiritual products of art and science in which everything comes down to the free characteristic combinatory faculty of the author, on the one hand, and the spirit of the language, with its characteristic system of ways of seeing, of capturing the nuances of mood, on the other, while the object no longer exercises any dominion at all but is rather dominated by thought and mind or indeed is only brought into being with and is only present in the composition of the work."[11] The *translator* in Schleiermacher's strict sense of the term deals exclusively with the works of creative or original authorship in his special sense: works that are the products, on the one hand, of "the free combinatory faculty of the author"—in other words, of "free play"—and, on the other, of the spirit of the author's "language" (*der Geist der Sprache*), with which his or her creative play, his or her signature character or identity, enters into a mutually beneficial competition. The difference between the work of *interpretation* (*Dolmetschen*) and that of translation (*Übersetzung*) is thus categorical:[12] whereas the interpreter has a single purpose in mind, to render a specific *content*, the translator has a double task: the translator must render, first, the *author's* characteristic way of seeing and expressing things; and, second, the characteristic way of seeing and expressing things that is peculiar to that author's *language*. Translation, in other words, does not just translate or transfer *from* one language *to* another, it also has the task of representing, in the language of the translation, another language. It is in this sense that we find Schleiermacher speaking of "representing" (*Darstellen*) not just *what* the language of the author conveys, but the very "spirit of the language" itself.[13] If a creative work is always a cross-section, as it were, of authorial play with the character of the author's language, then the translator cannot just translate the *author*; the translator must also translate the very language—say, Attic Greek or classical Latin—in which the author writes. The translator must render language difference, and hence language identity, itself.

Needless to say, this considerably complicates the task of the translator, to the point of making it a near impossibility. (At one point, Schleiermacher wonders aloud whether the whole business of translation is not "a fool's errand" ["ein thörichtes Unternehmen"; 72/45].) Schleiermacher offers two possible approaches to this impossible task, neither of them entirely satisfactory:

> Either the translator leaves the author where he is, as much as possible, and moves the reader toward him; or he leaves the reader where he is and moves the author toward him.
>
> (74/47)

How exactly we are to understand this famous distinction, often characterized as that between the "foreignizing" and the "domesticating" method of translation, is best grasped by focusing on the metaphors Schleiermacher relies on: translation, for Schleiermacher, is here described as a kind of *transport*—the literal sense of *Über-setzen*—or displacement in which one or the other of the parties, the author of the original and the reader of the translation, is made to move across the border between two discrete languages.[14] It is a matter, we could say, of language *transgression*, taking this term in its literal sense of a "stepping across." Importantly (though this is seldom recognized), the depiction of the movement in the two methods is not symmetrical: in the description of the first method, the stipulation "as much as possible" (*möglichst*) implies that the author is in fact *not* left entirely where he is, but is obliged to move somewhat, while the reader is transported to the intermediate place the author has been moved to; both parties are in movement.[15] In the description of the second method, there is no such limiting stipulation. Here, the author is transported to the reader, who need not move at all. This difference is made explicit in Schleiermacher's further remarks, in which the first method is explained as one in which "the two parties meet at an intermediate point," while in the second, "one party must himself go to meet the other" (74–75/48).[16]

Now, there are two ways to move across a language divide: either in the act of reading, namely, when one reads a text in a language other than one's own; or in the act of writing, when one writes in a language other than one's own. Somewhat surprisingly, *both* modes of language transgression make an appearance in Schleiermacher's further descriptions of *each* of the two methods of translation—a circumstance that does not make it any easier to sort out what Schleiermacher has in mind with his famously difficult distinction. In the description of the first method, we are told that what the translator does is to afford her reader the impression that the translator herself, equipped with her knowledge of the language of the original, has formed of the work when reading it in the original. Here, the transgression that is imagined at the basis of translation is that of *reading* across the language divide: the reader of the translation is to experience what it is like to *read* in a language other than one's own, such as Latin. We are then told that such a translation will be perfect in its kind "when one can say that, had the author learned German as well as the translator had learned Latin, he would not have translated his originally Latin work any differently from the way the translator has in fact translated it" (74/48). Here, the transgression that is imagined at the basis of translation is that of *writing* across the language divide: the translation must be written *as though the author had translated it into a language other than his own*, into a "learned" language, that is, a language acquired only through formal instruction. In the description of the second method, the two kinds of transgression, in reading and in writing, are invoked somewhat differently. We are told first that the method consists in rendering the author "not as he would have *translated* [his original work], but as he would have *originally written* it in German as a German" (74/48, italics added). Here, the transgression that is imagined is one that occurs in the act of writing, but with a crucial difference: instead of imagining the writer translating her work into a *learned* language, as in the first method, she is imagined writing in the language of the translation *as though it were her own*; the envisioned writing, in other words, is (as) mother-tongue writing. Schleiermacher then goes on to say that such a translation will be perfect "when one can affirm that, had the German readers all been transformed into knowers and contemporaries of the author, the work itself would have been to them as the translation is to them now that the author has transformed [*verwandelt*] himself into a German" (74/48). Here, the imagined transgres-

Table 10.1 Schleiermacher's Two Methods of Translation

	Method 1: Transportive	Method 2: Transformative
Process	Translation reproduces the experience of reading the work in the (learned) language of the original: *reading* across languages.	Translation produces what the author would have written had the author spoken the reader's language *as her or his native tongue*: *writing* across languages.
Movement	Reader is transported to the "midway point" that is occupied by the translator.	Author, as though transformed into a language compatriot of the reader, is transported to the reader.
Mark of perfection	Translation reads as though the author had translated the work into the (learned) language of the reader: *writing* across languages.	Translation reads as though the readers had been transformed into experts and contemporaries of the author: *reading* across languages.

sion occurs in the act of reading: the German readers *read* the work, for example, of classical Latin, as though they were themselves Romans. But here again, the reading that is envisioned is not that of a *learned* language, as in the first method, but as that of one's own mother-tongue. Accordingly, the language transgression that the second method entails is not, in fact, depicted as a kind of *transport*, but explicitly as a *transformation* (*Verwandlung*, and later also *Umwandlung*). There has been a crucial shift in the metaphor. Instead of glossing the two methods as "foreignizing" and "domesticating"—terms that occur nowhere in Schleiermacher's characterization of them[17]—we would remain closer to Schleiermacher's descriptions if we called them *transportive* and *transformative*, respectively. We can then schematize the two methods as shown in table 10.1. It is clear why the two methods become so hard to keep apart: the *process* of method one is virtually identical to the *mark of perfection* of method 2: both involve reading across languages; and the *mark of perfection* of method 1 is very close to the *process* of method 2: both involve the author writing across languages. In effect, the two methods are close to mirror images. The essential distinction is that in method 1, language difference is always in evidence: the translation reads as though one were reading a *foreign* language; the transport brings the reader to a midway point *between* two languages. In method 2, language difference is made to disappear as though by magic: the translation reads as though author and reader were both speaking the same, native language; the transport is so complete as to utterly transform reader and author, erasing all trace of the origin at the point of destination. In method 1, *two* languages are constantly present: both the reading and the imagined writing of the author are multilingual affairs; the reader has the constant impression that she or he is reading in a language other than his or her own.[18] In method 2, only one language is present.

Given the way Schleiermacher has set up his central opposition, it is not hard to see why he should end up favoring the transportive method over the transformative one—or rather, and this is just one of the most striking oddities about the address, rejecting the transformative method altogether. "Indeed it might be said," Schleiermacher finally reveals after extended explanations of the two methods, "that the aim of rendering the text as the author would have written it originally in the language of the translation is not just unattainable, but is by its very nature null and void" (82/60). In effect, Schleiermacher has set up the transformative method as a kind of straw man. Whereas the transportive method is based on an actual, concrete experience, namely, that of reading the work in a language one has learned later in life, such that the reading is constantly accompanied by the impression of foreignness, of language "transgression" in our sense, the second is envisioned in terms of a fantastic transformation of substances, a kind of alchemy in which the author is literally remade as a language compatriot of the reader. Indeed, the language of the fantastic is very much in evidence in Schleiermacher's descriptions of the transformative method. He describes it as "an evil and magic art, like that of being someone's double" ("frevelhafte und magische Kunst wie das Doppeltgehen"; 84/64), as "a new, as-it-were chemical process" ("einen neuen, gleichsam chemischen Prozess"; 82/60), as an attempt to conjure the author into the immediate proximity of the reader "as if by magic" ("den fremden Verfasser in seine unmittelbare Gegenwart hinzuzaubern"; 81/58). Its goal is not just unattainable but internally incoherent, a kind of nonsense fantasy or chimera—and, as we shall see in a moment, something on the level of "mere play" in the pejorative sense. For in effect, an author who has been transformed, for example, from a first-century Roman into a nineteenth-century German will not be the same author at all, and the work such a *Doppelgänger* might have produced, even if this could be realized, will not afford the reader an experience that is in any way equivalent to what the first-century contemporaries of the author, who are themselves in thought and habit utterly unlike the nineteenth-century readers of the translation, experienced in reading the original.[19] In view of this, one wonders why Schleiermacher takes up the second method at all. There seems to be some ulterior motive at work.

And this ulterior motive can be discerned without much difficulty, although readers of the address have rarely, to my knowledge, identified it: it is to *preserve the notion of language difference and language identity on which Schleiermacher's entire theory of creative authorship rests*. For in fact, contrary to Schleiermacher's stated intentions, what his address accomplishes is not just to show how writing *beyond* language identity, beyond the plurality of distinct languages, is possible, but indeed how any creative writing worthy of the name is *always* a form of language transgression. It is impossible to write creatively *in* any one language. In other words, what Schleiermacher offers us in his address, very much despite himself, is a theory of literature as something that is "outside of (any one) language." His theory thus puts into question the element Schleiermacher had relied on to *limit* the element of play in his theory of authorship—the productive constraint provided by the "givenness" of the specific language in which the author writes. Instead of depicting creative authorship as what emerges from the productive "play" of two opposing but mutually enriching forces, namely, the individuality of the author and the constraints of his or her language, what Schleiermacher's address ends up advancing is an insight into the necessarily language-transgressive nature of authorship or into what one might call its *metalanguality*.

METALANGUALITY

This word—monstrous, as will become clear, for good reason—derives from a translation of a neologism Robert Stockhammer coined some years ago in his work on writing "across" languages, that is, writing in a language other than one's "own." Under the term *Sprachigkeit*, Stockhammer understands the "consciousness of the fact that the linguistic medium is always a single language."[20] One does not write or speak simply in "language," but always in *a* language; texts are not only *lingual* (in the medium of *Sprache überhaupt*, language in general), not only "sprach*lich*," but, as texts that are, for example, English (*englischsprachig*), French (*französischsprachig*), or Russian (*russischsprachig*), they are also all "sprach*ig*": *langual*. With this word, which yokes the French term *langue*, in Saussure's technical sense of a specific (national) language, to an English suffix, I propose to designate, following Stockhammer's use of *sprachig*, the character or quality of belonging to a specific language, to language as one-among-many.

Now, as we have seen, a key tenet of Schleiermacher's theory of authorship is that all texts are *langual* in this sense: as stated in the *Hermeneutics*, every text or speech "presupposes a given language."[21] In fact, however, it is evident that not all texts remain comfortably within the confines of any given language. Indeed, this is something that follows directly from Schleiermacher's own theory of authorship. Transgressing their belonging to any specific *langue*, transgressing, that is, what had served to limit the "free play" of their individual creations, the products of true authorship in Schleiermacher's sense are all, in effect, "metalangual." This, at least, as we will presently see, is what Schleiermacher's translation address ends up showing, intentions notwithstanding. And it shows this on multiple fronts.

First, on a most basic level, the metalanguality of all creative authorship follows from the principle of the ubiquity of translation with which Schleiermacher begins his address. Translation, Schleiermacher announces right at the start, is not just something that occurs between the languages of the various regions of the world, or between ancient and modern languages, but even *within* "the domain of *one* language": "For not only are the dialects spoken by different tribes belonging to the same nation, and the different stages of the same language or dialect in different centuries, different languages in the strict sense of the word, not infrequently requiring a complete translation between them: moreover even contemporaries who are not separated by dialects, but merely belonging to different classes which are not often linked through social intercourse and are far apart in education, often can understand one another only by means of a similar mediation" (68/38). The differences of dialect, of historical change, of sociolect explode the unity of what we think of as *a* language: the texts and speeches, the words that we say and write are not in a language, but in a variant of a language and are in need of translation to be properly understood. Of course, one might then say that, if not the "language," then the variant—the dialect, the sociolect, the specific stage in the language's historical development—is what constitutes the unity in which texts are written and understood. But Schleiermacher makes clear that the splintering of language is in fact without limit:

> Are we indeed not often required to translate the speech of another for ourselves, even if he is totally our equal but possesses a different frame of mind or feeling? For when we feel that the same words would, in our mouth, have a totally different sense, or at least have a stronger weight here and a weaker impact there than in his, and that, if we wanted to express the same things he meant, we would

> make use of totally different words and locutions, according to our nature—it seems, if we define this feeling more closely, and as it becomes a thought for us, that we translate. Indeed, we must sometimes even translate our own words after a while, when we want to make them really our own again.
>
> (68/38–39)

If the need for translation extends into every interlocution, indeed into one's own self-understanding—if not even an *idiolect* can stand as a clearly defined, stable unity—then *no* use of language, no *parole*, can ever be said to occur *in* a defined "language" or even a variant of one.

Such is the first indication that, for the Schleiermacher of the translation essay, despite his stated axiom, no speech or text "presupposes a given language." But it is not just the internal diversity of language that leads to this consequence. Rather, and more fundamentally, the consequence follows from the very nature of what it means to speak or write anything other than the most mundane utterances destined to be forgotten the minute they are said. For while it is true, on the one hand, that "every man is in the power of the language he speaks, and all his thinking is a product thereof," it is also true that "every freely thinking, mentally self-employed human being shapes his own language" (71/43). "It is the living power of the individual which creates new forms by means of the plastic material of language. . . . It might even be said that a person deserves to be heard beyond his immediate environment only to the extent to which he influences language" (71/43–44). A language, in other words, is not *given*, but is rather plastic, and any significant use of it will change it. This is still more the case with the exceptional works of scholarship and art that are worthy of translation. "Every exceptional mind . . . works and exercises influence on the language, and his works must therefore contain a part of its history. . . . Any sufficiently knowledgeable reader who reads such a work in the original cannot help feeling its influence on the language" (76–77/52). The paradox Schleiermacher outlines both in the *Hermeneutics* and in the translation address, namely, that the author is "under the power" of her language, but also leaves her imprint on it, remains incomprehensible unless one gives up the notion *both* of creative genius as independent of the influence of her language *and* on the notion that a language is in any sense set or given.[22] It is precisely the concept of language *transgression*, as it emerges from the translation address, that names this paradox. To speak or to write is not to speak or write *in* a language, but to transgress that language; and a language is its own transgression.

But the essay does not merely provide an abstract statement of this paradox; it also unfolds it in ways that allow us to see concretely what it means and how our experience of different languages and different texts substantiates it. The key here is the notion that the task of the translator is to afford the reader with the experience, within her own language, of reading the text in another language. What is meant by this is not simply that the reader be given "the merely indeterminate sense that what he is reading sounds not quite native" (80/57). The translation should not just sound unidiomatic or odd in a merely negative sense. Rather, it should sound "like something different, yet definite" ("nach etwas bestimmtem anderem"), so that the reader is provided with a "sense, if only a distant one, of the original language itself" (80/57). She should be able, for example, to "distinguish"—on the basis merely of the translations, their language and style, themselves—"works of Greek origin from those of Latin origin, those of Italian origin from those of Spanish origin" (80/57). But that is not all. Since the original is not simply "in" Greek, Latin, Italian, or Spanish but also changes or transgresses these languages, the translation should afford the reader "the ability to sense and gradually to distinctly grasp not just the spirit of the language, but also the peculiar spirit of the author in his work" (80/57). The translation, in other words, should allow the reader to grasp the characteristic way in which a specific author and a specific work of that author transgress a specific language. Needless to say, this is a tall order; and for it to be possible at all, certain conditions need to be met. For one, the language into which the foreign work is to be translated must be of a specific nature. Namely: Languages are not all the same sort of thing. There are what Schleiermacher calls "bonded languages" (*gebundene Sprachen*), those that "lie caught in the too-narrow confines of a classical expression" (79/56). These are not suited to translation in Schleiermacher's sense, for in them, any deviation from the norm will of necessity read like a mistake; and faults cannot be combined to give a sense of a specific *character* of foreign language or author. Against these, there are the "freer languages" (*freiere Sprachen*; 80/56) in which deviations and innovations are more easily tolerated, "so that, when these are accumulated, under certain conditions a specific character can emerge" (80/56).[23] In our terms: not all languages are equally *langual* (*sprachig*). Some languages—the "bonded" ones—are more set, more clearly delineated, correspond more closely to the concept of "a" language in the sense of *langue*. The "freer languages," by contrast, are more fluid in their identity; their borders are porous, they are less resistant to foreign influence, less determinate in their status as *langue*. These are those that are capable of rendering foreign works. But the "flexibility" (*Biegsamkeit*; 81/58) of the language is not in itself sufficient to allow for translation. If the reader is to develop a sense for the character of the different languages from which works are translated, and for the impact of specific authors on these languages, this cannot be achieved through the translation of a few individual works and authors. Rather, what is called for is nothing less than a kind of wholesale importation of the literatures of the world:

> This way of translating thus calls for a large-scale process, a transplantation of whole literatures into a language, and it makes sense and is of value only to a nation that has the definite inclination to appropriate what is foreign.
>
> (80)

> [Daher erfordert diese Art zu übersezen durchaus ein Verfahren im großen, ein Verpflanzen ganzer Litteraturen in eine Sprache, und hat auch nur Sinn und Werth unter einem Volk welches entschiedene Neigung hat sich das fremde anzueignen.]
>
> (57)

Translation, in short, cannot be seen in isolation, as a task to be carried out between given "languages," as something one does with individual works. Nor is it simply a matter, as has sometimes been said,[24] of creating a special kind of "translationese," a language of transport, as it were, between given languages, for the purposes of "representing the foreign" in the "mother tongue" (79/56). Rather, translation can only be seen in the context of a comprehensive cultural politics, one that would fundamentally alter our understanding of how reading and writing are related to what we think of as "languages." Schleiermacher's translation address has long been seen as propagating a program of world literature or *Weltliteratur*.[25] What has not been seen is the way this project explodes the notion not just of national literatures but of the various languages as the media of literature, and at the same time allows us to imagine what this means. If writing is never something that occurs in a language, but transgresses it; and if understanding, too, as Schleiermacher insists at the beginning of his address, is never something that occurs neatly within the limits of a single language, but is always a translation that moves across languages, then the medium of literature is never "a given language" but precisely language's transgression. The language of (world) literature, in other words, is always a kind of *translationese*.[26]

And if languages can be more or less "bonded" or "free," if languality is subject to differences of degree, as Schleiermacher's typology of language suggests, then we cannot help envisioning what it would mean—at the far end of the cultural-political development Schleiermacher imagines, of the "transplantation" of "whole literatures" into a "language"—for the medium of literature to emancipate itself from the constraints of any particular *langue*. To imagine, that is, what it would mean for creative authorship to be seen as a form of *play* in a more radical sense than Schleiermacher himself would want to attach to that word.

COSMOLANGUALITY

For it is more than evident that Schleiermacher does his best to resist this conclusion. Even while the address *begins* by proclaiming translation to be a universal aspect of all reading and writing, even of one's own enunciations—a tenet that already does away with the notion that two interlocutors ever speak, read, or write the "same" language—and even though, in the course of the address, Schleiermacher develops a concept of authorship from which it follows that no (significant) writing is ever simply "in" a language, Schleiermacher clearly sees himself as holding to the axiom that "every speech presupposes a given language." The discursive means he most employs to uphold this axiom is a gesture of exclusion: the exclusion, namely, of what today might be called the "translingual": the author (or reader) who has dissolved all ties to his mother tongue. This figure, while clearly marginal for Schleiermacher, haunts the translation address, turning up at multiple points and clearly playing a key if unacknowledged role in Schleiermacher's efforts to establish a methodology of translation. Schleiermacher himself calls attention to this, offering at one point an apology—"But we have dealt with what is strange at too great length, and it must have seemed as if we have been talking about writing in foreign languages instead of translating from them" (85/64)—only to return immediately, apology notwithstanding, to the topic he claims not to have wanted to address, namely, writing in a language that is not one's own.

Indeed, the figure of the translingual is at the crux of Schleiermacher's discussion of both of the different methods of translation. In providing the reader with the experience she would have could she read the work in the original, there is, Schleiermacher insists, one kind of reading across languages that may *not* be emulated by the translation, namely, that of a reader for whom the language of the original has lost all foreignness. It is at this point that the figure of the translingual makes his first appearance in the address. He appears in two guises. First, as a *miracle* or *wonder of nature*: "Let us think of such wonders of the sort nature produces every so often, as if to show that it is also capable of destroying the barriers of nationality [*Volksthümlichkeit*] in isolated cases: People who feel such a peculiar kinship with a foreign existence that they completely live and think in a foreign language and its products, and while they are totally occupied with a foreign world they let their own language and their own world become totally foreign" (75–76/50). The translingual is a wonder of nature because he has transgressed the "barriers of nationality"—passed beyond his belonging to a specific people and a specific language. The first characterization of the translingual is thus that of a *traitor*. To this is then added the characterization of the translingual as a kind of cosmopolitan: "Or let us think of such people who are destined to represent, as it were, the faculty of language in its full compass, and to whom all languages, to the extent they have acquired them at all, are fully the same and fit like a glove" (76/50–51). Here, the translingual is one who has not simply transgressed, but transcended the givenness of specific languages. Such a person might be understood as moving within what Walter Benjamin, in "The Task of the Translator," calls "pure language" (*die reine Sprache*): that language which every given language falls short of, and which is attainable only in the "totality of their mutually complementary intentions" ("Allheit ihrer einander ergänzenden Intentionen").[27] Schleiermacher loses no time, having introduced into his address these cosmopolitans of languages who transcend all languality, in ruling them out of bounds—outside the field of fair play—as far as translation is concerned: "These people have reached a point at which the value of translation becomes nil, for since there is not even the slightest influence of the mother tongue in their perception of foreign works, and since they by no means become conscious of their understanding in their mother tongue but are immediately and totally at home in the original language itself, they also do not feel any incommensurability between their thinking and the language in which they read; it is therefore obvious that no translation can reach or portray their understanding" (76/51).

Given the heights to which Schleiermacher has raised the task of the translator, who must not only transgress her language by representing another language in it but also render the author's transgression of the language of the original, it is unclear why, in fact, the goal of translation should not be the kind of understanding Schleiermacher envisions here.[28] Indeed, a practice of reading and writing in which the difference between languages ceased to play any appreciable role might in fact seem *more* attainable than the elaborate construction Schleiermacher sets up for his first (and only true) method of translation.

The miraculous, treacherous figure of the translingual makes a second appearance later in the essay, and again, the figure of the translingual is invoked only in order to exclude it—and along with it the entire transformative method of translation. The method that would dissolve the bond between an author and her language in order to render her as though she had originally composed the work in the language of the translation is "null and void," Schleiermacher insists, because every author is what she is by virtue of the language in which she learned to think and to speak. Author and language are not separable:

> Whoever acknowledges the shaping power of language, as it is one with the peculiar character of a nation, must concede that every most excellent human being has acquired his knowledge, as well as the possibility of expressing it, in and through language and that no one therefore adheres to his languages mechanically, as if he were strapped into it, to use a superficial simile, and that no one could change languages in his thinking as he pleases, the way one can easily change a span of horses and replace it with another; rather everyone produces original work in his mother tongue only, so that the question cannot even be raised of how he would have written his works in another language.
>
> (82/60)

The transformation that is imagined as providing a basis for the transformative method is excluded as nonsensical: to change one's language is to change one's being; the author of an original written in another language is simply not the same author. "Can anyone . . . want to sever a man from the language he was born into, and think that a man, or even just his train of thought, could be one and the same in two languages?" Schleiermacher asks rhetorically (82/60). An author cannot be separated from his language and remain the same author; this being the case, it follows, for Schleiermacher, that "everyone produces original work in his mother tongue only" (82/60). There is no such thing as a translingual author in Schleiermacher's sense of "authorship." Therefore, the transformative method of translation, which would take the translingual author as its model, is not just unattainable; it is not even a coherent idea, not even imaginable.

At this point Schleiermacher devotes over four pages—some 10 percent of the address, and this is not counting the earlier passages devoted to the same topic—to several variants of translingual authorship, all with the intent of showing either why they can't exist or why they are not original authorship and hence fall out of the domain of translation in Schleiermacher's sense, or why they are immoral, monstrous, and "contrary to all rules and order" (85/64). The result is, as with the earlier remarks devoted to translingual reading, a strikingly detailed description of what writing beyond languality is or could be. We hear of "the ability to write in languages other than one's native tongue, indeed even to philosophize in them and to write poetry in them" (82/61); of early modern authors for whom "Latin was more of a mother tongue than the vernaculars" (83/61); of "our great king," Friedrich II of Prussia, who "received all his finer and higher thoughts in a foreign language" (83/61), namely, French; of courtiers and diplomats who, when making pleasant conversation in foreign languages, are able to "speak with the same excellence in many tongues" and to "think in all these languages with the same ease" (83/62); of "the writing of Latin or French" in order "to produce as well in a foreign language as in one's own and with the same originality" (84/64–65); of "production in a foreign language" that is guided by "remembrance of a certain writer or even of the style of a certain period, which represents a general person" (E 84–85/64); of an author who "has formally become a deserter to his mother tongue and given himself to another" (85/64); of someone who, by rendering authors as they would have written in any number of languages, foreign both to the author and to the translator, has shown himself to be "a master of the difficult and almost impossible art of dissolving the spirits of languages into each other" (87/68). Along the way, we have been told that "a man is in a certain sense educated and a citizen of the world [*Weltbürger*] only through his knowledge of various languages" (84/63). To be sure, Schleiermacher enters into a discussion of all these variants of translingual authorship for the sole purpose of denying their possibility or worth. But the point is that, in describing them at such length and in such detail, Schleiermacher does no more and no less than to provide a map not simply of translingualism, but of meta- and cosmolangualism: of writing not just outside the mother tongue, but beyond belonging to *any langue*, any language as "one among many."

In his gloss on Schleiermacher's rejection of the transformative method, Antoine Berman points out that it "negates the profound relation that connects the author to his own language." He continues: "This theory is at once the negation of other mother tongues and the negation of one's own mother tongue—it is the negation *of the very idea of a mother tongue.*"[29] Berman is clearly capturing Schleiermacher's intent when he sees this as reason to reject any such translation as "inauthentic." But we are also free to reclaim what both Schleiermacher and Berman intend to exclude, namely, writing that would negate the very idea of a mother tongue, for a metalangual poetics: as a paradigm of what authorship beyond language belonging might mean.

PLAY

Having thus provided something of a blueprint for what metalangual literature might be, it is small wonder that Schleiermacher devotes considerable energy to putting the metalangual genius, as it were, back into its bottle—to undoing or disqualifying all of the possibilities of metalangual reading and writing he has been envisioning. And it is here that play reenters the argumentation, or more particularly: the double valence of "play," which Schleiermacher exploits in order to reestablish the monolingual paradigm in the theory of authorship.

First, we are told that translingual production—specifically, as exemplified by the conversation of courtiers and diplomats—is "neither the sacred seriousness of language nor its beautiful well-measured play" ("weder der heilige Ernst der Sprache, noch das schöne wohlgemessene Spiel derselben"; 83/62). Here, "play" is used in the same positive valence that we find in Schleiermacher's theory of creative authorship. It names that mysterious source to which all original artistic or philosophical production can be traced, the element that distinguishes true art and science from mere imitation or repetition of what has long since been seen or thought. By saying that translingual production is *neither* sacred seriousness *nor* well-measured play, Schleiermacher *aligns* play with seriousness in order to exclude translingual production from any kind of original authorship. Play, hand-in-hand with seriousness, is the distinguishing characteristic of true artistic and philosophical value.

But scarcely has he disqualified translingual production for *lacking* the element of (serious) "play," Schleiermacher hastens to disqualify it as a form of "*mere*" play. The practice of writing in a foreign language with the object of producing works that are as original and as good as those one can produce in one's own language is nothing more than "a refined mimic game [*Spiel*] with which to while away the hours pleasantly in the outer courts of scholarship and art" ("ein feines mimisches Spiel, womit man sich höchstens in den Vorhöfen der Wissenschaft und Kunst die Zeit anmuthig vertreibt"; 64/84).

From this point on, Schleiermacher will not cease to employ both the term and the semantics of "play" pejoratively to dispel the visions of translingual and metalangual authorship he has conjured up. A translation that renders the work as the author would have written it originally in the language of the translation "can be fully enjoyed *only as a game* [*nur als Spiel*]" (85/65, emphasis added); no one who has "even the slightest respect for philosophical endeavors can allow himself to be drawn into so loose a game [*Spiel*]" (86/66); such an endeavor, when forced to shuttle between translation and imitation, "cruelly bounces the reader back and forth like a ball between the foreign world and his own" (86/67); it is no more than "an artificial and elegant game [*Spiel*]" (87/68) or, worse still, a "tempting and somewhat dangerous game" ["ein[] reizende[s] und etwas gefährliche[s] Spiel"] (88/68). The same word Schleiermacher relies on to distinguish original authorship, he relies on as well to discount writing beyond the mother tongue.

This is more than a mere coincidence. Rather, the uncontrolled, double valence of "play" points toward a central blind spot in the Romantic theory of creative authorship as exemplified in authors such as Kant, Schiller, and Schleiermacher. Defining creative authorship as a form of *play* makes the redefinition of authorship in the new framework of original genius possible. But it also opens the door to all kinds of productivity that these authors were intent on excluding. In Schleiermacher's case, what is excluded is the possibility of writing works of creative genius in a language other than that into which one was born.

This is a view that Schleiermacher shares with many other thinkers from at least the age of Herder up to the current era: it seems natural, even today, to suppose that creative authorship is something that normally or even almost exclusively occurs in a *specific* language, in the language into which one was born. But it is precisely where this view is being most forcefully advanced—and the vehemence with which Schleiermacher rejects translingual authorship in his translation address is extraordinary if not unparalleled—that it is also most forcefully refuted. What the reliance on one and the same word, "play," in order both to distinguish and to exclude shows us is that this exclusion cannot in fact be carried out. Despite his best efforts, Schleiermacher finds himself played by "play" in his translation address. If we are to take the use of "play" in the Age of Goethe at its word, then we must move beyond the moral distinction between "serious" play and "mere" play, between play as the fecund emancipation from rules and precepts—play as genius—and play as worthless, empty, sterile, the moral dichotomy that the discourse of the epoch relies on to control what it has invented. Contrary to what authors such as Schleiermacher do, we must accept play in all its valences. In the case of the translation address, the result is a much more radically playful vision of authorship than Schleiermacher himself recognized: the vision of original authorship as something that occurs not just outside of one's mother tongue but outside of any identifiable language at all.

NOTES

1. For an overview of the function of "play" in the Age of Goethe, see Tanja Wetzel, "Spiel," in *Ästhetische Grundbegriffe: Historisches Wörterbuch in sieben Bänden*, ed. Karlheinz Barck et al. (Stuttgart: Metzler, 2003), 5:577–618.

2. Immanuel Kant, *Kritik der Urteilskraft*, ed. Karl Vorländer (Hamburg: Meiner, 1924; repr. 1974), 161 (sec. 46); ibid., 172 (sec. 49), my emphasis. Here as elsewhere, unless otherwise noted, the translation is mine.

3. Kant, *Kritik der Urteilskraft*, 55 (sec. 9), my emphasis. For an excellent disquisition on the function of the concept of "play" in Kant's aesthetics, see Michel Chaouli, *Thinking with Kant's "Critique of Judgment"* (Cambridge, MA: Harvard University Press, 2017), 122–124, 130–136.

4. On the dynamics of "play" in its symbiotic relationship with "seriousness" in the fragments of Friedrich Schlegel, see David Martyn, "Fichtes romantischer Ernst," in *Sprachen der Ironie—Sprachen des Ernstes*, ed. Karl Heinz Bohrer (Frankfurt am Main: Suhrkamp, 2000), 76–90.

5. Friedrich Schleiermacher, *Hermeneutik und Kritik*, ed. Manfred Frank (Frankfurt am Main: Suhrkamp, 1977), 180.

6. Friedrich Schleiermacher, *Ästhetik (1819/25)*, ed. Thomas Lehnerer (Hamburg: Meiner, 1984), 16, 26.

7. Schleiermacher, *Hermeneutik und Kritik*, 78.

8. Schleiermacher speaks explicitly of the "innateness of language" ("die Angeborenheit der Sprache") in *Hermeneutik und Kritik*, 79.

9. For astute critical acknowledgments of the address's accomplishments and influence, see especially Antoine Berman, *The Experience of the Foreign: Culture and Translation in Romantic Germany*, trans. S. Heyvaert (Albany: State University of New York Press, 1992), 141–152, originally published as *L'épreuve de l'étranger: Culture et traduction dans l'Allemagne romantique* (Paris: Gallimard, 1984; repr., Collection Tel, 1995); and Susan Bernofsky, *Foreign Words: Translator-Authors in the Age of Goethe* (Detroit: Wayne State University Press, 2005), 25–31.

10. See Teresa Seruya and José Miranda Justo's introduction to *Rereading Schleiermacher: Translation, Cognition and Culture* (Heidelberg: Springer, 2016), xix.

11. Friedrich Schleiermacher, "On the Different Methods of Translating," trans. André Lefevere, in *Translating Literature: The German Tradition from Luther to Rosenzweig*, trans. and ed. André Lefevere (Assen, The Netherlands: Van Gorcum, 1977), 66; Schleiermacher, "Ueber die verschiedenen Methoden des Uebersezens," in *Das Problem des Übersetzens*, ed. Hans Joachim Störig (Stuttgart: Henry Goverts, 1963), 41. References to Schleier-

macher's translation address henceforth give the page number of Lefevere's English translation followed by that of this edition of the original; the translation has frequently been modified. See also the other translations and editions referenced in the bibliography.

12. Of course, as Schleiermacher makes clear (69/40), most texts will be mixed in character, containing both impersonal rendering of fact and characteristic expression of an author. This means that in practice, for the most part neither task will be exercised to the full exclusion of the other. But this circumstance does nothing to alter the strict opposition of the two underlying principles.

13. We hear, for example, of the need for the "spirit of the original language" to be "represented" (*dargestellt*) in the translation (73/46), or of the task of "representing" (*darstellen*), in one's mother tongue, what is foreign to it (79/56).

14. For a view of how this metaphor leads to unresolved problems in Schleiermacher's address, see Kirsten Malmkjær, "Schleiermacher's Metaphor," in *Friedrich Schleiermacher and the Question of Translation*, ed. Larisa Cercel and Adriana Şerban (Berlin: De Gruyter, 2015), 185–196.

15. Hence, the numerous readers of Schleiermacher's address who fault it for absolutizing the opposition between the two methods and disregarding the possibility of a middle ground typically miss the asymmetry of Schleiermacher's opposition, according to which the second method *is* the one that occupies a middle ground. See, for example, Anthony Pym, "Schleiermacher and the Problem of Blendlinge," *Translation and Literature* 4 (1995): 5–30. For an attempt to situate Schleiermacher's dichotomy in the history of binary typologies of translation, see Josefine Kitzbichler, "From Jerome to Schleiermacher? Translation Methods and the Irrationality of Languages," in *Rereading Schleiermacher: Translation, Cognition and Culture*, ed. Teresa Seruya and José Miranda Justo (Heidelberg: Springer, 2016), 27–40.

16. The passage from which these two quotations are taken has caused readers of the translation address no end of trouble. Douglas Robinson wonders if Schleiermacher is not here introducing a *third* method of translating beyond the other two. Robinson, *Schleiermacher's Icoses: Social Ecologies of the Different Methods of Translating* (Bucharest: Zeta Books, 2013), 63. But this would make the passage in question directly contradict the very claim that it is meant to show, namely, "that there cannot be a third method . . . over and above these two" (74/48). It makes much more sense to understand the passage as a clarifying development of the asymmetry already marked in the one-sided stipulation "as much as possible" in the initial introduction of the dichotomy (which Robinson suppresses; see *Schleiermacher's Icoses*, 236). Method 1 simulates the experience of reading the original as a foreign language, thus bringing the reader to the same midway point occupied by the translator; method 2 simulates the composition of the original in the language of the reader, thus leaving the reader where he is. Robinson's book-length analytical critique of the translation address, from which he derives his concept of social ecologies or "icoses," brings out many important issues elided by other readers; it is unfortunate that the paraphrases he extracts from this analysis do not always help to grasp the deeper point of Schleiermacher's analogies and distinctions.

17. It is true that Schleiermacher speaks of the first method retaining the "tone of the foreign" (79/56), but there is no indication that he sees this as its essence. And nowhere is there talk of "domesticating."

18. Hence, the reading experience that method 1 strives to provide is specifically described as that of the "dilettante and devotee [*Liebhaber und Kenner*], the type of reader who is familiar with the foreign language while it yet always remains foreign to him" and who remains "conscious of the difference between that language and his mother tongue, even where he enjoys the beauty of a foreign work in total peace" (51/76).

19. The situation might have been different had Schleiermacher taken the simpler route of distinguishing the two methods symmetrically, by describing the first as language transgression in reading (the translation renders the reading of the original in a learned language) and the second in terms of language transgression in writing (the translation renders the writing of the original in a learned language). But as it stands, *both* of these are cast as variants or aspects of the same method, of method 1. It is this very asymmetry that makes Schleiermacher's dichotomy so productive.

20. See Susan Arndt, Dirk Naguschewski, and Robert Stockhammer's introduction to *Exophonie: Anders-Sprachigkeit (in) der Literatur* (Berlin: Kadmos, 2007), 26. Stockhammer elaborates further on this term—which he had earlier introduced in a 2003 lecture—in "Zur Konversion von Sprachigkeit in Sprachlichkeit (langagification des langues) in Goethes *Wilhelm Meister*-Romanen," *Critical Multilingualism Studies* 5, no. 3 (2017): 13–31. It should be emphasized that Arndt, Naguschewski, and Stockhammer are very much aware, even as they introduce the term *Sprachigkeit* to designate the consciousness that one speaks and writes in *one* language among many, that the very concept of *a* language is untenable. See their introduction, 25.

21. *Hermeneutik und Kritik*, 78.

22. It is symptomatic that the first point here is frequently made in criticism of Schleiermacher, while the second is routinely missed. Hence, in a frequently cited analysis of Schleiermacher's address, Lawrence Venuti pointedly rejects Schleiermacher's reliance on a "transcendental subject" who "shapes his own language," but he explicitly affirms the way Schleiermacher acknowledges the "determinate nature of language" as the "shaping force" of subjects. See his *The Translator's Invisibility: A History of Translation* (London: Routledge, 1995), 115. One reader who has very effectively problematized Schleiermacher's reliance on a monolingual paradigm in the translation address is Daniel Weidner, "Frevelhafte Doppelgänger und sprachbildende Kraft: Zur Wiederkehr der Anderssprachigkeit in Schleiermachers Hermeneutik," in *Exophonie: Anders-Sprachigkeit (in) der Literatur*, ed. Susan Arndt, Dirk Naguschewski, and Robert Stockhammer (Berlin: Kadmos, 2007), 229–247.

23. The model of the bonded language is clearly French, whereas German represents for Schleiermacher the type of the freer language; German is thus the ideal language of translation. See Berman, *Experience of the Foreign*, 148–149.

24. This is, for example, the main critique directed by Lefevere against Schleiermacher's preferred method of translating. See his *Translating Literature: The German Tradition from Luther to Rosenzweig*, ed. and trans. André Lefevere (Assen, The Netherlands: Van Gorcum, 1977), 67.

25. See Andreas Huyssen, *Die frühromantische Konzeption von Übersetzung und Aneignung: Studien zur frühromantischen Utopie einer deutschen Weltliteratur* (Zurich: Atlantis Verlag, 1969), 67–68. Broadly speaking, readers of the translation address have split into two camps regarding its cultural-political implications. On the one extreme, there are those such as Lawrence Venuti, who see the essay as propagating a nationalistic and ethnocentric program (*Translator's Invisibility*, 107). At the other end of the spectrum is Antoine Ber-

man's treatment, which finds in Schleiermacher's "foreignizing" method a potent antidote to the ethnocentric closure that translation most frequently exercises (*Experience of the Foreign*, 141–153). More recently, Hélène Quiniou has criticized the "foreignizing" paradigm as developed by Schleiermacher, and as it is construed by Berman, as a kind of integrative universalism that uses the detour of the Other only to reinforce and enrich the identity of the Self. See "From Friedrich Schleiermacher to Homi K. Bhabha: Foreignizing Translation from Above or from Below?" in *Rereading Schleiermacher: Translation, Cognition and Culture*, ed. Teresa Seruya and José Miranda Justo (Heidelberg: Springer, 2016), 79–88. The present reading places emphasis not on any nationalistic or ethnocentric appropriation, reappropriation, or co-optation of the foreign that may be entailed in translation, but on the construction of the "foreign" itself in Schleiermacher's essentialization of the mother tongue, while showing at the same time how the translation address moves beyond such essentializing identity constructions despite Schleiermacher's own intentions. I concur with Berman that the address provides us with a powerful antidote to ethnocentrism, but precisely not with its paradigm of "foreignizing" translation, but rather with the third term that Schleiermacher is at such pains to exclude from all consideration—namely, those positions, on which more anon, for which the entire distinction between domestic and foreign, own and other, cease to apply.

26. As can be gleaned from the concept of world literature that emerges from Robert Stockhammer, "Das Schon-Übersetzte: Auch eine Theorie der Weltliteratur," *Poetica* 41, no. 3/4 (2009): 257–291.

27. Walter Benjamin, "Die Aufgabe des Übersetzers," in *Gesammelte Schriften*, vol. 4, bk. 1, ed. Tillman Rexroth (Frankfurt am Main: Suhrkamp, 1991), 13.

28. A conclusion also arrived at by Robinson (*Schleiermacher's Icoses*, 128–130) for somewhat different reasons. What Robinson sees as "sloppy thinking" (130) is better read as symptomatic of Schleiermacher's desire to hold on to the notion of the mother tongue and of languages as distinct idioms. Schleiermacher's conclusion that "no translation can reach or portray" the reading experience of someone for whom the original has lost all foreignness indeed only follows if we assume that translations, by definition, must entail some kind of language transgression, that language difference must be in some sense "present" in anything that deserves to be called "translation." More to the point, however, it only follows if we assume there *is* language difference at all: if languages are domains that one either can remain within *or* can pass between. What appears here, in the illogic of Schleiermacher's exclusion, is precisely the possibility that this presumption is false: the possibility, that is, that remaining "within" a language and passing between them are not as different as one might assume.

29. Berman, *Experience of the Foreign*, 147; trans. modified. See Berman, *L'épreuve de l'étranger*, 236.

CHAPTER ELEVEN

Playing with Words in Early German Romanticism

BRIAN TUCKER

THE IDEA OF PLAY occupies an interesting place, if not an especially prominent one, in early German Romanticism. Friedrich Schlegel describes play, for instance, as the opposite of earnestness or seriousness, and Schlegel's essay on Goethe's *Wilhelm Meister's Apprenticeship*, widely regarded as an exemplary piece of Romantic literary criticism, relies on the tension between the playful and the serious to explicate the novel's structure.[1] In fact, turning to the novel's final volume, Schlegel closes his review with the synoptic statement, "It is as if everything up to now has been an ingenious, interesting game [*Spiel*], and as if it were now becoming earnest [*Ernst*]" (2:146). Schlegel presents the intellectual game carried out in the first three parts as essential to the novel's aim, in that it prepares the way for the serious work of the concluding volume. Moreover, the inability to distinguish between earnest and playful forms of expression plays a crucial role in the delineations of Romantic irony and incomprehensibility.

In various contexts, then, one perceives a general notion of play in early German Romanticism. One finds in these Romantic references to play, however, little that strikes one as distinctive or rigorously thought through. In other words, play does not appear as one of those original, generative concepts, such as *Fragment* or *Witz*, that define Romanticism's view of poetics and criticism. The occurrences of play in the writings of the *Athenaeum* period seem rather like an offshoot of the broader discourse of play around 1800. In the wake of Kantian aesthetics and Schiller's reflections on the play drive, "play" constitutes part of the critical philosophical discourse within which Romantic authors situate themselves and to which they respond.

And yet, in addition to this general notion of play, there is a more specific form of play that lies much closer to the center of the Romantic project—namely, wordplay. In early German Romantic reflections on language, literature, translation, and criticism, "wordplay" is a recurring term that develops a largely underacknowledged degree of technical specificity. Indeed, playing with words, or the play of language itself, forms the basis of Romantic poetry. Novalis, for example, writes in his brief reflection on language, entitled "Monologue," "Matters of speaking and writing are a crazy [*närrische*] thing; true dialogue is merely a play of words [*ein bloßes Wortspiel*]."[2] Here, Novalis uses the figure of wordplay to characterize conversation, speaking, and writing—to define language itself. Much like Friedrich Schiller raises play to the defining quality of the human, Novalis makes wordplay a touchstone of poetic language.[3] His point is that although people assume language to be an indexical instrument that exists to denote its referents, in reality it is a game played for its own sake, concerned primarily with itself.[4] Wordplay also operates in Romantic reflections on literature and poetry, for instance in Friedrich Schlegel's history of modern poetry (3:27) and in August Wilhelm Schlegel's lectures on dramatic literature.[5]

In instances such as these, Romantic writers develop wordplay as a particular and particularly important form of literary language. Friedrich Schlegel, in addition to pointing out examples of wordplay in Spanish poetry, goes on in 1802 to make programmatic statements such as, "The primordial [*ursprüngliche*] form of poetry is wordplay" (16:428). This is a remarkable pronouncement that situates wordplay at the very heart of poetic production. One should not mistake the reference to "primordial form," with its sense of *Ursprung* or origin, for an indication that Schlegel means to sequester wordplay in poetry's ancient history, as a primeval form from which modern poetics has evolved. Quite the contrary, Schlegel casts wordplay as both originary and au courant. Another note from around 1800 declares, for example, that "*Tieck's* poems are, according to their form, *wordplays*, and that is the foundation of romantic poetry" (16:327).[6] Taken together, Schlegel's statements assert that wordplay constitutes both the original form of poetry and the basis of Romantic poetry.

According to Schlegel, we should be able to explore wordplay as a pillar of Romantic poetics, as a term that deserves as much scrutiny as irony, wit, or fragment. Despite Schlegel's statements, however, wordplay has remained largely overshadowed by other critical terms and thus undertheorized in the secondary (or perhaps better, tertiary) literature. In what follows, I aim to address this gap by tracing the role of wordplay in early German Romanticism, by drawing out the relationship between wordplay and wit, and by showing that play is an important category within Romantic conceptions of language and poetics. Among critical terms, wordplay also has the advantage of bridging the gap between literary theory and poetic practice. That is, Schlegel's statements not only describe wordplay as a fundamentally important poetic category; they also point the reader to Tieck's poetry, which in his view exemplifies the Romantic understanding of wordplay. The present chapter takes Schlegel's pronouncements at their word. Through close readings of two poems by Tieck, it documents the formal principle of wordplay at work (or at play) in Romantic poetry and recasts the notion of *Poesie*, as conceived by the Jena Romantics, through a particular conception of words at play.

Wordplay enters the Romantic critical purview primarily through the study and translation of foreign-language literature, in particular via August Wilhelm Schlegel's work on Shakespeare. In his lectures, Schlegel's reflections on instances of wordplay in Shakespeare lead him to consider the nature and function of wordplay more generally. He attributes the widespread predilection for wordplay to something fundamental in the human relationship to language. Within the human psyche, Schlegel says, there exists a deep-seated desire that "language should use sound to represent sensuously [*sinnlich*] its signified objects" (6:133). The passage describes a desire for an ideal—perhaps primeval—onomatopoeic language, in which each word's sound would suggest by resemblance the thing to which it refers. But Schlegel notes that this desire is at odds with the reality of modern language and communication. Because human language is overwhelmingly composed of arbitrary signs whose relation to their referents is entirely conventional, one feels as a rule no meaningful connection between sound and sense. Within this wilderness of arbitrary signification, occurrences of wordplay stand out as happy coincidences that reveal the promise of a deeper connection between sound and meaning. In those instances when sound imitates sense, Schlegel writes, "a lively and excited imagination thus throws itself gladly upon corresponding sounds in order to evoke once again in the individual instance the lost similarity between word and thing" (6:133–134). Wordplay, then, reveals the traces of a prior form of language, a different means of signification. It opens a window onto a Golden Age of language, in which signifying sounds were concrete and unspoiled, rather than deracinated and arbitrary.

As evidence for this view of linguistic evolution, Schlegel points to children and to simple, undeveloped cultures. "Particularly children, as well as nations of the most basic customs, display a marked proclivity for wordplay [*Wortspielen*] because in these cases the correct ideas about derivation and word families have not yet developed" (6:134). Employing a version of ontogeny-replicates-phylogeny thinking, Schlegel means to say that one finds a more robust engagement with wordplay and the musical side of language in earlier stages of human development—that is, in children and in so-called primitive cultures. Leopold Wurth, in his late nineteenth-century study of wordplay in Shakespeare, makes a similar point, writing, "The further the development of a people [*Volkes*], like that of an individual, progresses, the more the musical moment in language gives way to the conceptual, and the less often one plays with sounds."[7] In both cases, wordplay represents the remnant of a prior, innocent, and idealized stage of language, one in which words provided an immediate and more meaningful connection to the world. Both authors thus view the evolution of language as entailing a loss, or at least a trade-off: as children grow up, as civilizations develop, their musical, concrete sense of language gives way to a more abstract, conceptual form of language. The coincidence of sound and sense retreats to the realm of poetry and instances of wordplay.

When August Wilhelm and Friedrich Schlegel use the term "wordplay," they have in mind a specific poetic-linguistic structure that was theorized in the Romantic era. August Bernhardi, linguist, brother-in-law to Tieck, and contributor to the *Athenaeum* and *Europa*, includes in the second, or "applied," volume of his grammar, *Theory of Language*, a discussion of wordplay that comes to provide a canonical definition for Romantic writers. Here Bernhardi defines wordplay as "the linkage of two linguistic spheres [*Sprachsphären*] that sound alike, such that a particular consideration of their meaning comes about," and he asserts that wordplay thus constitutes "*the fundamental figure* of all the other musical-poetic linguistic figures."[8] One hears the resonance between Bernhardi's definition and the Schlegels' interest in wordplay. First, the idea that wordplay is a fundamental figure from which other figures are derived accords with Friedrich Schlegel's dictum that wordplay represents an originary poetic form. Second, like both Schlegels, Bernhardi too emphasizes a certain relation between sound and sense, between the musical and the conceptual. Wordplay, in this conception, is a form of phonetic play—of homophones and phonetic correspondences—but it should not be seen as standing in opposition to the work of meaning and denotation, to the conceptual function of language. Rather, wordplay is a certain kind of phonetic play that also does significant work. Its phonetic correspondences reveal otherwise unseen connections among words and cast their meaning in a new light. Of course, the idea that hidden connections and esoteric truths could be embedded in a natural language is a typically Romantic view, and Bernhardi's *Theory of Language* gives voice to it: "If we view language as a mirror and image of ourselves, then the idea immediately suggests itself that there is a secret bond between the two [between the sensual and nonsensual world] that language expresses."[9] In the absence of a primeval, natural language, wordplay represents instances where language can give sensuous expression to abstract, nonsensuous meaning.

Bernhardi goes on to write, "Wordplay is the *wit* [*Witz*] *of language*, and no one can doubt its excellence unless one is completely ignorant of what wit is and means."[10] The passage does two things at once: it seeks both to link wordplay, through wit, to the critical discourse of early Romanticism and to rebut a critical discourse that would disparage or even dismiss the relevance of wordplay and wit. First, why the skepticism with regard to wordplay? Bernhardi could be referring here to a general sense in eighteenth-century German aesthetics that wordplay was a figure unworthy of serious attention. Johann Christoph Gottsched, in his 1730 *Essay toward a Critical Poetics*, denounces wordplay. Though plays on words used to be widely admired, Gottsched writes, they have become "in our times rather laughable."[11] One feels a lingering sense of skepticism in Johann Christoph Adelung's late eighteenth-century *Dictionary*, when he defines wordplay as "an occupation with words and their meanings that aims merely for amusement." He writes that wordplay occurs in a more narrow sense, "when words and their meanings are set against each other merely for amusement, without achieving a truth that is pertinent on its own."[12] Adelung's entry repeatedly stresses that wordplay aims "merely" to amuse or entertain.[13] Words and meanings get crammed together, but their juxtaposition in wordplay does not achieve its own substance, relevance, or truth. This is precisely the sort of attitude that Bernhardi means to correct by linking wordplay and wit.

When Bernhardi characterizes wordplay as the linguistic form of wit, he embeds wordplay in the core terminology of German Romanticism. Wit, in its Romantic usage, refers to a synthetic or combinatory mental faculty, the ability to find similarity among things that appear to be essentially different in kind, to uncover hidden relations among unrelated things. Wit in this sense is like quick wit, a sudden revelation or epiphany, something that occurs to the mind without conscious effort or reflection. In one of the

Athenäum fragments, Friedrich Schlegel writes, "Some witty ideas [*witzige Einfälle*] are like the unexpected reunion of two friendly thoughts after a long separation" (2:171, A 37). Schlegel casts wit as an illuminating realization that brings together disparate thoughts and reveals their subtle affinity. Philippe Lacoue-Labarthe and Jean-Luc Nancy, who include Bernhardi's *Theory of Language* in their analysis of Romantic *Witz*, write of this fragment, "The essence of the 'sudden idea' consists in its being a synthesis of thoughts."[14] This idea of a startling, unexpected reunion also captures the essence of wordplay for Bernhardi and August Wilhelm Schlegel. Wordplay effects similarly surprising syntheses in language, through phonetic correspondences that bring thoughts together in an unexpected way. In unpublished notes from around 1800, Friedrich Schlegel also equates wordplay with various forms of *Witz*, describing it variously as "musical wit" and "grammatical wit" (16:162, 180). Wordplay represents a momentary return to that ideal of natural language, a reunion of sound and sense that briefly overcomes their long-standing separation in modern language.

Another of Schlegel's fragments states, "Wit is the appearance, the external lightning bolt [*Blitz*] of the imagination" (2:258, I 26), and Bernhardi echoes that sentiment in his discussion: "wit is the lightning bolt that illuminates a single point in the whole and lets the identity within the particular emerge."[15] Here, too, wit is sudden, illuminating, and revelatory. It mediates between the whole and the part and lays bare the deep homogeneity that lies buried under apparent heterogeneity. It is important to keep in mind that Bernhardi is not out to elucidate the nature of wit in these pages; the discussion of wit is, rather, instrumental to analogize and explicate the nature of wordplay. Because, for Bernhardi, wordplay represents the operations of wit within language, he sees it as a combinatorial phonetics in which related sounds reflect obscure relations among the things to which they refer.[16] This operation is evident in the cited passage in the rhyme between *Blitz* and *Witz*, which makes plain the kind of illuminating combinations that wordplay can bring about. Through wordplay, Bernhardi concludes, "allusions [*Andeutungen*] can be brought forward that are possible only through this medium, and that, like music, flow physically through the ear and into the mind."[17] Wordplay, in other words, is not simply a waste of time or a cheap form of amusement. Its combinations provide an inkling or insinuation—Tieck's word of choice for this phenomenon would be *Ahnung*—of truths that would otherwise be inexpressible.

Although it was published between 1801 and 1803, after the peak years of the *Athenaeum*, Bernhardi's *Theory of Language* was taken seriously and exerted an influence on early German Romantic authors. Indeed, August Wilhelm Schlegel reviewed the two volumes in the journal *Europa* in 1803, praising Bernhardi's book as a breakthrough, a philosophically informed work that applies the insights of Idealism to developing a theory of the nature and structure of language.[18] And a recounting of Bernhardi's view of wordplay forms the centerpiece of the review. Schlegel cannot resist quoting the section on wordplay at length, a quotation that runs for over a page and by itself constitutes more than 10 percent of Schlegel's review. He justifies the lengthy quotation by saying that "the main passage about wordplay . . . affords us a great view onto the domain of philosophy as well as poetry."[19] For our present purposes, the most pertinent issue is the poetic function of wordplay, the way in which the analysis of wordplay could provide an insight into the nature of Romantic poetry. Schlegel's review already opens a window onto the nexus of wordplay and poetic form: both rely on and make use of the musical dimension of language. Schlegel, for instance, praises Bernhardi's *Theory of Language* because, "rhyme, along with everything related to it, is linked to wordplay and derived from it in a very perceptive way."[20] In other words, the strength and originality of Bernhardi's take on rhyme—as well as assonance and alliteration—lie in the linkage it establishes between wordplay and the musical side of poetry. In fact, the book casts rhyme as originating and descending from wordplay, which makes sense from the Romantic perspective that sees wordplay as the remnant of a primeval, natural language.

The connection between wordplay, rhyme, and the sound of language is a point on which Romantic writers agree. Alongside August Wilhelm Schlegel and Bernhardi, Friedrich Schlegel, too, emphasizes the similarities between wordplay and rhyme. In notes written between 1797 and 1800, Schlegel refers to the sixteenth-century poet Johann Fischart as a *locus classicus* for "arabesque wordplays": in his works "one sees clearly the affinity between rhyme and wordplay" (16:198). The affinity Schlegel points to recalls Bernhardi's definition of wordplay and its insistence on linguistic spheres that sound alike. Both rhyme and wordplay are formal features that intertwine sound and sense, that use homophonic play to suggest unexpected semantic relationships. This is why Schlegel calls wordplay "musical wit" (16:162), and why he says of wordplays that "they must be *musical* to be good" (16:180). The prominence of musicality in the discussion of wordplay perhaps offers a clue as to how Schlegel could characterize wordplay as the foundation of Romantic poetry. Romantic poems are based on the nature of wordplay to the extent that they use sound, the musical dimension of language, to hark back to a more immediate form of sensuous representation in language.

At this point, it will be instructive to turn from the abstract discussion of wordplay and Romantic poetry to concrete examples. If wordplay is indeed critical to the project and structure of Romantic poetry, and if, as Friedrich Schlegel asserts, Tieck's works exemplify that relationship, then one should be able to observe the operations of wordplay in his poems. The goal here resembles what Manfred Frank undertakes in his analysis of Tieck's poetry in the collection of lectures *Introduction to Early Romantic Aesthetics*. Having parsed at length the *concept* of Romantic irony, Frank turns late in his lectures to trying to observe the workings of irony in literary praxis. He focuses in particular on a series of songs from the *Magelone* cycle and explores the ways "in which the poem allows itself to be understood as an illustration of Romantic irony."[21] In what ways do Tieck's poems also illustrate the Romantic notion of wordplay? Are they indeed constructed according to the model of wordplay?

The first poem to consider in this context is "Sicherheit," meaning "security" or "certainty." Written in 1795, the poem first appeared without title in Tieck's dramatic fairy tale *Bluebeard*. I cite it here in both English and German, so that the sound of original wording will be apparent:

> Delighted is he who on the faithful's breast
> In full love rests,
> No sorrow comes to disturb the pleasure,
> The fire only burns brighter.
>
> No shifting, no wavering,
> Back to tranquil happiness
> Flee all thoughts
> Of faraway places.
>
> And more fondly and anxiously
> Mouth presses to mouth,
> More dearly and longer:
> From hour to hour
> Tighter and closer
> Grows the sweet bond.
>
> [Beglückt, wer an des Treuen Brust
> In voller Liebe ruht,

Kein Kummer naht und stört die Lust,
Nur heller brennt die Glut.

Kein Wechsel, kein Wanken,
Zum ruhigen Glück
Fliehn alle Gedanken
Der Ferne zurück.

Und lieber und bänger
Drückt Mund sich an Mund,
So inn'ger, so länger:
Von Stunde zu Stund
Beschränkter und enger
Der liebliche Bund.][22]

All the early Romantic writers on wordplay draw attention to the relationship between form and content, sound and sense. In the poem's original context, in *Bluebeard*, the characters Anne and Agnes trade songs. After Anne delivers this song, Agnes comments on it, saying, "That's one of those songs that's easier to sing than to understand" (6:416). On the one hand, Agnes asserts—counterintuitively—that the role of listener in this instance is more demanding than the role of performer. But on the other, if singing is easier than understanding, then the poem's sound takes precedence over its meaning.

This poem might be easier to sing than understand because it seems that Tieck's primary concern in the final stanza is to craft an intricately woven network of repeated and rhyming syllables. The sound "und" alone accounts for eight syllables in the final stanza, almost a fourth of its thirty-three total syllables. Moreover, only three of those instances are standard rhymes at the end of a line; the rest occur inside the lines, through repetition and conjunctions. (Note, in contrast, that the "und" sound occurs only once in the other two stanzas, in line three.) In addition, *-er*, used mostly in comparative forms, makes up seven syllables, and sounds of *äng/k* or *eng* add another four syllables. Taken together, this means that nineteen of the stanza's thirty-three syllables represent only three sounds. Or put another way, Tieck devotes over half of the final stanza to this pattern of repeating syllables. He chooses the majority of his words to create a sound effect that carries rhyming and repetition far into his lines. No wonder this poem is easier to sing than to understand: these words were chosen primarily for the sound of the signifier and only secondarily for the meaning they denote.

The poem thus illustrates the operations of wordplay within literary praxis. The final stanza is structured primarily along the lines of phonetic correspondence, and its form is based on the playful use of certain sounds. But the point of wordplay, according to Bernhardi's understanding, is not simply a free play of signifiers, one in which playing with sounds becomes an end in itself. Rather, the aural correspondence in wordplay also serves a semantic function in that it draws attention to a particular and more essential relationship. This attempt to reflect a deeper sense is what differentiates wordplay and the poem "Sicherheit" from the poetics of nonsense or incoherence that Winfried Menninghaus has identified in Tieck's early works such as *Bluebeard*.[23] In this poem that describes a unification, a process of two becoming like one, the phonetic correspondences gradually become more tightly intertwined. Apart from the alliteration of "Kein Kummer" in line three, the first stanza contains little in the way of phonetic play. The second stanza, picking up the repetition of *kein* from stanza one, amplifies the patterns of phonetic correspondence with alliteration on the consonants *W* and *G*. And in the final stanza, the sound of language becomes another kind of content. In particular, Tieck structures this final stanza as a series of pairs that reflect the basic pairing the poem describes: two mouths, two hours, and in the first, third, and fifth lines, two coupled attributes. It is fitting that, in its last line, the series of coupled elements finally gives way to what binds them together: "the sweet bond [*Bund*]." At the same time, it is not as if this unification appears only in the concluding line. By the time one arrives at the last line, the *Bund* simply names the *-und* sound that has been connecting the pairs throughout the last stanza. This word *Bund* itself exemplifies the interplay of sound and sense in wordplay: it is fitting that the German word for "bond" sounds so much like the conjunction *und*, since the bond is essentially a means to conjoin two parts. As intimacy grows and the two press their lips together, the sound of their conjunction, their *Bund*, travels between them, from mouth to mouth, from *Mund* to *Mund*.

There are a couple of summarizing points to make here. First, Tieck's poem not only illustrates Friedrich Schlegel's statements on the role of wordplay in Romantic poetry, it also accords with August Wilhelm Schlegel's reflections on wordplay in his lectures on Shakespeare. One will recall that Schlegel locates the fondness for wordplay in a residual desire for natural language and sensuous expression, a language in which a word's sound would resemble its referent in some meaningful way. Tieck's poem accomplishes that in a limited way: it takes an abstract idea—intimacy, say, close human association or a deepening bond—and it gives the idea sensuous expression through the sound of its language. If the poem's central theme is a deepening or tightening association between two people, one can hear that development through the course of the poem, through its gradual tightening or weaving together of phonetic associations. Second, this poem also exemplifies the affinity of wordplay and rhyme that has been remarked upon by Bernhardi and both Schlegels. Indeed, much of the poem's effect comes about by allowing the aural correspondences of rhyme to move deeper into the lines, through repetition, alliteration, assonance, and internal rhyme. Rhyming involves a linkage of sounds within the parameters of the poem's sense. But Tieck's poem takes the operation of rhyme a good deal further and tips the balance of that relationship so that sound predominates. In this instance, the intertwining and repetition of syllables performs the sense of intimacy that the poem's words describe. The poem thus delivers a pristine illustration of what Friedrich Schlegel would call "musical wit," of wordplays that attend as much to the "musical moment" in language as to its conceptual function.[24]

While "Sicherheit" illustrates nicely the relationship between rhyme and wordplay, as well as wordplay's joining of sound and sense, it does not deliver as strong an example of how wordplay could operate as a formal poetic principle. That is, although the poem certainly plays with the sound of language, especially in its final stanza, it is less clear that the poem as a whole—beyond its last stanza—is structured according to wordplay, that it bears out Friedrich Schlegel's observation that "*Tieck's* poems are, according to their form, *wordplays*" (16:327). The early Romantics cite numerous examples of poems and dramatic works that play on words, but the radical originality of Tieck's poetry, in Schlegel's view, is that it does not just *employ* wordplay; it *is* wordplay.

On this point, we can turn to a second example, the poem "Neuer Sinn" ("New Sense"), drawn from the cycle of songs in Tieck's *Liebesgeschichte der schönen Magelone* (*Romance of the Fair Magelone*). The poem occurs at the story's central turning point, when Peter decides to escape from his service to the Sultan and his daughter and to sail back to Europe in a small boat. But the entire poem is structured as an extended wordplay. Close analysis of "Neuer Sinn" shows that the poem is at least as concerned with recycling the tropes of Goethe's 1789 poem "Auf dem See" ("On the Lake") as it is with advancing the love story of Peter and Magelone. Indeed, reading the two poems side by side reveals much of the imagery in the *Magelone* songs to be a playful allusion to Goethe's work.[25]

Goethe wrote a first draft of "Auf dem See" in his travel journal in 1775, following an outing on Lake Zurich. The first published version of the poem, which appeared in 1789, begins,

And fresh nourishment, new blood
I suck from a world so free;
Nature, how gracious and how good,
Her breast she gives to me.
The ripples buoying up our boat
Keep rhythm to the oars,
And mountains up to heaven float
In cloud to meet our course.[26]

[Und frische Nahrung, neues Blut
Saug' ich aus freier Welt;
Wie ist Natur so hold und gut,
Die mich am Busen hält!
Die Welle wieget unsern Kahn
Im Rudertakt hinauf,
Und Berge, wolkig himmelan,
Begegnen unserm Lauf.][27]

There are numerous parallels between Goethe's "Auf dem See" and Tieck's "Neuer Sinn," and some of the overlap undoubtedly derives from the poems' similar settings. Both depict men sailing in small boats, far removed from the objects of their affection.[28] Tieck, for instance, similarly sets Peter in a "small rowboat [*Kahn*]" (6:279) or "a small boat" (6:289). And as he drifts farther from shore, the narrative emphasizes the sound of the boat on the water: "the waves barely rippled, and the beat of the oars [*Ruderschlag*] rung out through the lonely silence" (6:290). The reference here to the oars' beat echoes the musicality of the oars' cadence (*Rudertakt*) in Goethe's poem.

In various ways, Tieck's narrative establishes a setting that resembles that of Goethe's poem. But the playful similarities extend far beyond the narrative context and into the poem itself. "Neuer Sinn" reads in its entirety:

How bright and fresh my spirit lifts
All fear remains behind,
My breast aspires with newfound courage,
A new desire awakes.

The stars reflect upon the sea,
And golden gleams the tide.—
I once ran lurching to and fro
And was not bad, not good.

But dragged down by
Doubts and wavering spirits,
Oh carry me, you rocking waves,
Back to my longed-for home.

There, in the dear, dusky distance,
My native songs are calling,
From each and every star
She gazes down with a gentle eye.

Level yourself, you trusty wave,
Lead me down distant paths
To that beloved doorstep,
Toward my happiness at last!

[Wie froh und frisch mein Sinn sich hebt,
Zurückbleibt alles Bangen,
Die Brust mit neuem Mute strebt,
Erwacht ein neu Verlangen.

Die Sterne spiegeln sich im Meer,
Und golden glänzt die Flut.—
Ich rannte taumelnd hin und her
Und war nicht schlimm, nicht gut.

Doch niedergezogen
Sind Zweifel und wankender Sinn,
O tragt mich, ihr schaukelnden Wogen,
Zur längst ersehnten Heimat hin.

In lieber dämmernder Ferne,
Dort rufen einheimische Lieder,
Aus jeglichem Sterne
Blickt sie mit sanftem Auge nieder.

Ebne dich, du treue Welle,
Führe mich auf fernen Wegen

Zu der vielgeliebten Schwelle,
Endlich meinem Glück entgegen!]
(6:291)

Looking only at the first stanza of Goethe's "Auf dem See," one sees that Tieck's song reproduces the scene of the small boat on the water, the focus on the oar's cadence, and the lyrical "I" that extols the feeling of a new beginning. The descriptive language is similar, with both works using the adjectives "fresh," "new," and "good." And the image of rocking waves (*wieget* in Goethe, *schaukelnd* in Tieck) recurs as well.

More importantly, though, Tieck's poem also follows the structure and line of thought of "Auf dem See." Goethe's second stanza breaks emphatically from the sentiment of the first:

Eyes, my eyes, why abject now?
Golden dreams, are you returning?
Dream, though gold, away with you:
Life is here and loving too.[29]

[Aug', mein Aug', was sinkst du nieder?
Goldne Träume, kommt ihr wieder?
Weg, du Traum, so gold du bist:
Hier auch Lieb' und Leben ist.][30]

Rising spirits are deflated, and the lyric subject suffers a momentary crisis of confidence. One notes that the *Magelone* cycle has already repurposed Goethe's imagery of the sinking gaze, the eyes compared to stars, and their golden reflection on the water's surface. In chapter 8, for instance, the poem "Erinnerung" ("Memory") includes the lines,

Everything sounded again in my heart,
My eyes sank down . . .
Like a pair of stars
The eyes sparkled, the cheeks
Rocked her golden hair.

[Alles klang im Herzen wieder
Meine Blicke sanken nieder . . .
Wie ein Sternenpaar

Glänzten die Augen, die Wangen
Wiegten das goldene Haar.]

(6:270)

Golden, glittering, rocking, the falling gaze, and the figure of eyes as stars—it is as if Tieck takes the elements of Goethe's poem like a set of building blocks with which he playfully constructs his own stanza.[31]

In "Auf dem See," the shift in mood—from reveling in nature's embrace to yearning for something more—is abrupt, and Goethe emphasizes the change in tone through changes in meter and rhyme pattern. In stanza one, the lines are consistently composed in iambic meter, with alternating rhymes on stressed final syllables. The second stanza provides a counterpart to all those patterns. Composed in trochaic meter, which reverses the iambs, it consists of rhyming couplets, with the first pair ending on unstressed syllables.[32] Goethe thus employs poetic form to underscore the shift in mood from the first to the second stanza.

"Neuer Sinn" does something similar. Here the abrupt shift in mood occurs in the third stanza, where Goethe's image of the gaze sinking down (*niedersinken*) is echoed by the idea of being dragged down (*niedergezogen*). Here, too, at the poem's midpoint, the lyric subject must pass through a negative moment of doubt and uncertainty. And here, too, the poem stresses the contrast in tone not only through the introductory particle "But" ("*Doch*") but also through a metrical change. Up to this point, Tieck's poem has been written without exception in iambic meter with alternating rhymes. When the middle stanza introduces this new sentiment of doubt and faltering indecision, however, it also introduces a new metrical element. Its first three lines all insert one or two dactylic feet among the iambs, which is to say, these lines include more unstressed syllables than the established metrical pattern would lead one to expect. In sum, Tieck's poem, like Goethe's, uses metrical variation to reflect variation in mood.

Manfred Frank, analyzing songs from the *Magelone* cycle, also notes their frequent changes in metrical pattern. He takes this as a sign that Tieck's compositions begin from the principle of formal variation rather than from the desire to convey any particular content. He writes of these poems, "In general, one observes . . . that the only citable rule is that of maximal variation in metrical feet and of the most sudden successive contrasts."[33] Frank is right to point out the recurrent formal changes and contrasts in these poems, but in the case of "Neuer Sinn," at least, there is another principle at work. That is, Tieck introduces metrical variations in the poem not only for the sake of variation itself but also to emulate the metrical shifts that accompany the line of thought in Goethe's "Auf dem See." It is true that the middle stanza in Tieck's poem does not precisely mirror the metrical change in Goethe's—where Goethe turns from iambic to trochaic meter, Tieck inserts dactylic feet into iambic lines. Yet Tieck's change resembles the metrical pattern that occurs in the final stanza of "Auf dem See." In lines such as "Auf der Welle blinken / Tausend *schwebende* Sterne" ("Over the ripples twinkling / Star on *hovering* star"),[34] one notices the dactyl set between two trochaic feet. This metrical pattern occurs in the second, fourth, sixth, and eighth lines of the last stanza. If these two poems use changes in meter to indicate changes in the subject's attitude or outlook, Tieck's poem also uses metrical variation to underscore its relationship to another poem. It is not only that lines such as "Die Sterne spiegeln sich im Meer / Und golden glänzt die Flut" ("The stars reflect upon the sea / And golden gleams the tide") reproduce the imagery of Goethe's "Auf dem See"; subsequent lines also take up and reproduce the metrical patterns in Goethe's poem.

In these various ways, Tieck's poem recycles the setting, the imagery, and the metrical variation of "Auf dem See." It thus serves two purposes at the same time. On the one hand, the song has to make sense coming from Peter in this moment in the story. It conveys his newfound resolve as he seeks to find his way back to Magelone. On the other, though, the poem's language is also chosen with regard to its aural dimension, to the connections that it evokes by sounding in many ways similar to Goethe's poem. In this sense, the poem's title "Neuer Sinn" plays on words to encapsulate the operations of the poem at large.[35] It suggests, through the semantic ambiguity of "Sinn" or "sense," both sides of the poem's function. The title signifies, first, the poem's position and function in the romance story. Peter sings this song to express a "new sense" of purpose and optimism; his mind is made up, his spirit resolute. Rather than tarry with Sulima in the Sultan's pleasure gardens, he will attempt to cross the sea and return to his homeland. On one level, then, "Neuer Sinn" simply names Peter's new frame of mind at the story's main turning point.

But "Sinn" also has a specific semantic register as the "meaning" or the "sense" behind an utterance, so that the poem's "New Sense" or "New Meaning" can refer not only to the protagonist's state of mind but also to the way in which the poem disassembles "Auf dem See" only to reconfigure its elements to create a new meaning. After all, despite the figural and formal parallels, the lyric subjects in the two poems arrive at radically different conclusions. Whereas the subject in Goethe's poem opts for the here and now, affirming the suitability of his present location ("Hier auch Lieb' und Leben ist"), Peter's "wavering spirit" has to do precisely with the attractions of his present location. Just as Goethe's lyrical subject resolves to seek happiness where he is, so Tieck's subject resolves to seek happiness in his distant homeland. On this level, the title names a different kind of wordplay—not the conjunction of particular words through phonetic correspondence, as in the case of rhyme and assonance, but the intertextual conjunction of different linguistic spheres (*Sprachsphären*, in Bernhardi's definition) through the appropriation of imagery, meter, and stylistic details. Tieck's poem is consonant with Goethe's "Auf dem See." One might even say that it "rhymes" with Goethe's poem, because it seems designed to evoke figural, phonetic, and formal similarities with Goethe's work. It thus delivers a more thoroughgoing illustration of a poem that could be understood, following Schlegel, as a wordplay according to its form, a poem whose primary compositional principle is play with established poetic elements.[36]

Novalis compares language to wordplay for the same reason that he compares it to mathematical formulae—"they play only with themselves, express nothing but their wonderful nature, and it is precisely for that reason that they are so expressive—this is precisely why the strange play of relationships among things is reflected in them."[37] In its playfulness and self-referentiality, language turns away from representational expression and comes instead to reflect the network of relationships in nature. Edgar Landgraf, making a similar point, describes how Novalis's text exchanges representation for emulation: "Poetic language does not speak about things, [Novalis] claims. But in its liberal play with itself, it comes to imitate nature."[38] So it is with language as wordplay, and so it is with poetry as wordplay. Tieck's "Neuer Sinn" is a poem concerned primarily with other poetry, a poem that plays with another poem. What looks like a dialogue between prose and poetry, between text and reader, is actually more a monologue of poetry talking to itself.

I realize, of course, that arguments about literary allusion face a high evidentiary bar, that the evidence for allusion can often seem inconclusive, or merely incidental. Some readers might remain unpersuaded by the correspondences I have tried to lay out between Tieck's and Goethe's poems. One might object, that is, that Tieck's poem is not really a playful allusion to another author's work, that the parallels are better explained as the derivative by-product of genre poetry, or the overuse of a narrow set of tired poetic images. But Tieck's narrative explicitly encourages a reading that remains alert to allusion and the play of words. For instance, encountering voices from a distant, unknown source runs as a leitmotif through the story. Early on, before Peter meets Magelone, the narrator says, "It was as if distant voices were calling indistinctly through the woods, he wanted to follow" (6:249). This notion of perceiving—in nature, in the self, in art—a strange language that is simultaneously meaningful and enigmatic is a well-established Romantic topos. Through allusion and wordplay, Tieck weaves a distant voice into his text and allows it to call, indistinctly, through the structure and imagery of his poems. And this leitmotif that frames the songs encourages the reader to follow that barely audible voice, to trace it to its source. Later, when Peter is beginning his escape in the boat, the narrator prefaces the poem "Neuer Sinn" by saying of the waves' "melodic murmuring" that it "sounded like a song in a foreign [*fremder*] language, whose sense [*Sinn*] one could nevertheless divine" (6:290). To perceive the wordplay of Tieck's poems, the reader too must be attentive to their musical dimension, their "melodic murmuring," and to the presence within the poem of language that is *fremd*, other, foreign, or belonging to someone else.

Moreover, the entire story is framed, in the *Phantasus*, by a dialogue about the merits of literary adaptation. Tieck, of course, did not invent the love story of Peter and Magelone; he adapted material that he drew from a French romance that was translated into German in the sixteenth century. As soon as the character Friedrich finishes reading his modern version of the romance, the other characters begin discussing to what extent an author can borrow from and revise an original work.[39] Their conversation grapples with the relationship of an adaptation to its original. Auguste, for instance, defends Friedrich's use of an existing story, saying, "But if it were completely forbidden . . . to revise old, familiar stories according to one's whim, as one sees fit, and to prepare them to our taste, then we would undoubtedly lose a great deal" (6:301). Or as Tieck himself puts it in a preface to an 1828 edition, the characters in the epilogue "discuss the extent to which the new narrator distorts the sense [*Sinn*] of the poem and modernizes its pure simplicity with alterations and additions" (6:1307). In other words, the epilogue's debate revolves around one main question: does the process of adaptation result merely in a distorted sense of the original or rather in a new sense?

Whereas the epilogue treats this question discursively, the song "Neuer Sinn" treats it playfully, poetically, and performatively. *The Romance of the Fair Magelone* is a literary adaptation that reflects—in typically Romantic fashion—on its own status as adaptation. And within this self-reflexive adaptation that is simultaneously about the nature and exigencies of adaptation, the poems themselves play out processes of adaptive borrowing and recycling. The playful, allusive borrowing of "Neuer Sinn" is thus not just play, but also work; the poem does real work within the context of the romance as a product of adaptation. It demonstrates the productive (poetic) potential of adaptation, the way in which borrowing and reassembling can generate new meaning out of recycled elements. The successful results are evident in August Wilhelm Schlegel's praise for the poems. He writes in his *Magelone* review, "I don't know who among us besides Goethe could have written songs like these." Schlegel goes on to assert that the *Magelone* romance shows that Tieck "did not take his model [Goethe] in a one-sided way, nor follow him without his own independent appropriation [*selbständige Aneignung*]" (cited in Tieck, 6:1316). These passages speak to the general tone and style of Tieck's work, but the above analysis demonstrates that Schlegel's judgments characterize the *Magelone* more thoroughly even than Schlegel perhaps intended. It is high praise indeed to say that no one besides Goethe could have written these poems—but there is also a good reason for that comparison lurking in the background. Goethe is the only other author who could have written this kind of poem, because he's the other author who *did write* this kind of poem. His voice, his melody, is what one hears murmuring or calling indistinctly through the thicket of Tieck's verses. And it is precisely this ambivalent process of appropriation (*Aneignung*, in Schlegel's words)—of adoption, adaptation, of making something one's own—that Tieck explores through every section of the *Magelone* romance. The model of appropriation that the text suggests only comes into focus through the medium of wordplay.

Both poems by Tieck show how wordplay operates not only in theoretical reflections on language and literature but also in the production of Romantic literature itself. Though I have focused here on but two examples, one begins to sense how wordplay could indeed constitute a foundation for Romantic poetry. For the early German Romantics, Shakespeare provided a towering literary model, and one of the things that Romantic criticism explores and takes seriously in Shakespeare is his fondness for wordplay. In part through their reading of Shakespeare, the Romantics come to see playing with words as a constitutive element of poetry and an aspect of literary language that had been undervalued by the normative aesthetics of the eighteenth century. And they value wordplay for the way in which its turn away from the conceptual, representational function of language allows unforeseen connections to emerge. Though it goes well beyond the scope of this essay, the readings carried out here suggest that the scholarship on German Romanticism would do well to take the Romantic critical interest in Shakespeare as a template for its own investigations. In other words, contemporary readers of German Romanticism should approach its literary corpus with an eye as keenly attuned to the operations of wordplay as the German Romantics were in their study of Shakespeare and other poetic traditions. For wordplay is the technical mechanism through which wit enters language; it is the poetic equivalent of the witty idea that suddenly occurs to the mind. The Romantics thus see wordplay as a form of play that is not *merely* play. Its ability to layer a register of allusion, insinuation, and adumbration (*Andeutung*) onto language, its power to convey insights that would otherwise be ineffable—this allows wordplay to bridge the divide between the playful and the earnest, between *Spiel* and *Ernst*. In Romantic literature, wordplay is play with a serious purpose—reflecting the play of relationships in the world itself. By reading for wordplay in German Romanticism, one traces the partial and limited ways in which its literary production aims to recoup a natural language and its promise of sensuous expression.

NOTES

1. Friedrich Schlegel, *Kritische Friedrich-Schlegel-Ausgabe*, ed. Ernst Behler, Jean Jacques Anstett, and Hans Eichner (Munich: Schöningh, 1958), 2:245, A 419. Further references to the *Kritische Friedrich-Schlegel-Ausgabe* will be given parenthetically with volume and page number. All translations, unless otherwise noted in the works cited, are my own.

2. Novalis (Friedrich von Hardenberg), *Schriften: Die Werke Friedrich von Hardenbergs*, ed. Paul Kluckhohn and Richard Samuel, 6 vols. (Stuttgart: Kohlhammer, 1960–65), 2:672.

3. See Friedrich Schiller, *On the Aesthetic Education of Man in a Series of Letters*, ed. and trans. Elizabeth Wilkinson and L. A. Willoughby (Oxford: Oxford University Press, 1982), 106–107.

4. The juxtaposition of wordplay and the foolish might also perform its own sort of self-reflexive linguistic play. August Wilhelm Schlegel's translation of Shakespeare's *The Merchant of Venice* renders the line from Lorenzo, "How every fool can play upon the word!" as "Wie jeder Narr mit den Worten spielen kann!" and further, "The fool hath planted in his memory an army of good words" as "Der Narr hat ins Gedächtnis sich ein Heer Wortspiele eingeprägt." Shakespeare, *The Complete Works of Shakespeare*, ed. David Bevington (New York: HarperCollins, 1992), 3.5, 204–205; Shakespeare, *William Shakspere's sämtliche Dramatische Werke*, trans. August Wilhelm Schlegel et al., 3 vols. (Leipzig: Reclam, 1882), 3.5, 3:274. (References are to act and scene, followed by volume and page number.) In addition to saying something definitive about language, Novalis's passage also playfully recycles the language of wordplay.

5. August Wilhelm Schlegel, *Kritische Schriften und Briefe*, ed. Edgar Lohner, 5 vols. (Stuttgart: Kohlhammer, 1962–66), 6:118. Further references to this edition will be given parenthetically with volume and page number.

6. I cite this same passage in an essay on wordplay in Tieck's early prose. For examples of wordplay in "Der blonde Eckbert" and *William Lovell*, see Brian Tucker, *Reading Riddles: Rhetorics of Obscurity from Romanticism to Freud* (Lewisburg, PA: Bucknell University Press, 2011), 78–106.

7. Leopold Wurth, *Das Wortspiel bei Shakspere* (Vienna: Wilhelm Braumüller, 1895), 3–4.

8. August Bernhardi, *Sprachlehre*, 2 vols. (Hildesheim: Georg Olms Verlag, 1973), 2:395.

9. Bernhardi, *Sprachlehre*, 2:11.

10. Bernhardi, *Sprachlehre*, 2:395.

11. Johann Christoph Gottsched, *Versuch einer critischen Dichtkunst* (Leipzig: Breitkopf, 1730), 207.

12. Johann Christoph Adelung, *Grammatisch-kritisches Wörterbuch der hochdeutschen Mundart* (Vienna: Bauer, 1811), 4:1616.

13. It's worth pointing out that Kant differentiates wit and judgment along similar lines, writing, "The activity of comparative wit is more like play; but that of judgment is more like business." Immanuel Kant, *Anthropology from a Pragmatic Point of View*, trans. and ed. Robert B. Louden (Cambridge: Cambridge University Press, 2006), 116 [221]. On wit and judgment in the eighteenth century, see Stanley Corngold, "Wit and Judgment; or, Lessing and Kant," in *Complex Pleasure: Forms of Feeling in German Literature* (Stanford, CA: Stanford University Press, 1998), 27–47, and more recently, Erica Weitzman, *Irony's Antics: Walser, Kafka, Roth and the German Comic Tradition* (Evanston, IL: Northwestern University Press, 2015), 28–34.

14. Philippe Lacoue-Labarthe and Jean-Luc Nancy, *The Literary Absolute: The Theory of Literature in German Romanticism*, trans. Philip Barnard and Cheryl Lester (Albany: State University of New York Press, 1988), 52.

15. Bernhardi, *Sprachlehre*, 2:397.

16. On the pairing *Blitz-Witz*, see Lacoue-Labarthe and Nancy, *Literary Absolute*, 53.

17. Bernhardi, *Sprachlehre*, 2:397.

18. August Wilhelm Schlegel, "Ankündigung: *Sprachlehre* von A.F. Bernhardi," *Europa: Eine Zeitschrift* 2, no. 1 (1803): 193.

19. Schlegel, "Ankündigung," 200.

20. Schlegel, "Ankündigung," 200.

21. Manfred Frank, *Einführung in die frühromantische Ästhetik* (Frankfurt am Main: Suhrkamp, 1989), 412.

22. Ludwig Tieck, *Schriften in zwölf Bänden*, ed. Manfred Frank et al., 12 vols. (Frankfurt am Main: Deutscher Klassiker Verlag, 1985–), 6:22. Further references to Tieck's *Schriften* will be given parenthetically.

23. Winfried Menninghaus, *In Praise of Nonsense: Kant and Bluebeard*, trans. Henry Pickford (Stanford, CA: Stanford University Press, 1999), 38.

24. See Wurth, *Das Wortspiel*, 4.

25. Of course, at its etymological core, allusion is by nature playful. The Latin elements *ad-* and *ludere* suggest a sense of playing toward something, evocative here in the sense that Tieck's *Magelone* poems are "playing their way toward" Goethe.

26. Johann Wolfgang von Goethe, *Selected Poems*, ed. Christopher Middleton, trans. Michael Hamburger et al. (Princeton, NJ: Princeton University Press, 1994), 41. Translation by Christopher Middleton.

27. Goethe, *Werke*, ed. Erich Trunz (Hamburger Ausgabe), 14 vols. (Hamburg: Wegner, 1952–64), 1:102.

28. Whereas Peter clearly pines for Magelone, Goethe's poem requires more autobiographical background. It is said that Goethe undertook the trip to Switzerland to remove himself from his relationship with Lili Schönemann. See Erich Trunz's notes in Goethe, *Werke*, 1:458–461.

29. Goethe, *Selected Poems*, 41.

30. Goethe, *Werke*, 1:102.

31. Joseph von Eichendorff provides another example of this sort of wordplay, in which the citation and iterative reapplication of a limited set of images, idioms, and metaphors is raised to a creative principle. Theodor Adorno remarks on this principle in a radio address. Like Tieck, "Eichendorff achieves the most extraordinary effects with a stock of images that must have been threadbare even in his day." Adorno, *Notes to Literature*, ed. Rolf Tiedemann, trans. Shierry Weber Nicholsen (New York: Columbia University Press, 1991), 1:66.

32. Frauke Berndt and Claudia Maienborn discuss this metrical variation in a rhetorical analysis of "Auf dem See," "The Sucking Subject: Structural Ambiguities of Goethe's 'Auf dem See' in Literary and Linguistic Perspective," *Goethe Yearbook* 20 (2013):103–106.

33. Frank, *Einführung*, 389.

34. Goethe, *Werke*, 1:102. *Selected Poems*, 41. Italics mine.

35. The songs in the *Romance of the Fair Magelone* are untitled; the titles first appear in later collections. See Tieck, *Schriften*, 7:70, and the commentary, *Schriften*, 7:598.

36. One might note here the proximity of the Romantic conception of wordplay to certain definitions of metaphor. Much like the Romantics conceive of wordplay as the linkage of two disparate linguistic spheres, David Wellbery argues, for example, "that metaphors should be thought of as relationships between systems." For more on metaphor as "a game that consists of discovering (or inventing) the rules that it follows," see David Wellbery, "Übertragen: Metapher und Metonymie," in *Literaturwissenschaft—Einführung in ein Sprachspiel*, ed. Heinrich Bosse and Ursula Renner (Freiburg im Breisgau: Rombach, 1999), 146.

37. Novalis, *Schriften*, 2:672.

38. Edgar Landgraf, "Comprehending Romantic Incomprehensibility: A Systems-Theoretical Perspective on Early German Romanticism," *MLN* 121, no. 3 (2006): 599. Andrew Bowie puts it in slightly different terms, writing, "Language whose propositional aspect is not its most significant attribute therefore takes on a higher status than language which determinately refers to things in the world." Bowie, *From Romanticism to Critical Theory: The Philosophy of German Literary Theory* (London: Routledge, 1997), 68.

39. Incidentally, issues of adaptation also constitute a key point in August Wilhelm Schlegel's *Magelone* review in the *Athenaeum*, and much of the epilogue reads like an intradiegetic reflection on extradiegetic critique. See Manfred Frank's commentary in Tieck, *Schriften*, 6:1308.

ACKNOWLEDGMENTS

We would like to thank the series editor, Karin Schutjer, for her engagement with, and support of, this project from its earliest stages. We would also like to thank the two outside readers for their insightful commentary and suggestions. Ellen Lohman copyedited the final manuscript with exacting care, and we are grateful to her, to the editorial team at Bucknell University Press, and to Gregory Hyman for his attentiveness as production editor. Keven Berland, our indexer, truly took the time to engage closely with each contribution in our volume. Many of the chapters in this volume were first presented as papers at a panel series at the German Studies Association Convention in 2016, and we would like to thank the Goethe Society of North America for sponsoring this series. Our sincere thanks to Dean of Faculty Jonathan Chenette of Vassar College for the funds (from the Tatlock Endowed Fund for Strategic Faculty Support) to license the cover art, and to Bridgman Images for the right to reproduce the painting *Gamblers in the Foyer* (also known as *Gamblers in the Ridotto*) by Johann Heinrich Tischbein (1722–89). We would also like to thank Bowling Green State University and Vassar College for funding the indexing of this volume.

BIBLIOGRAPHY

Adelung, Johann Christoph. *Grammatisch-kritisches Wörterbuch der hochdeutschen Mundart.* Vienna: Bauer, 1811.

Adorno, Theodor W. *Notes to Literature*. Edited by Rolf Tiedemann. Translated by Shierry Weber Nicholsen. European Perspectives. New York: Columbia University Press, 1991.

Allen, Ann Taylor. "Spiritual Motherhood: German Feminists and the Kindergarten Movement." *History of Education Quarterly* 22, no. 3 (Autumn 1982): 319–339.

———. *The Transatlantic Kindergarten: Education and Women's Movements in Germany and the United States*. New York: Oxford University Press, 2017.

Allert, Beate. "Pluralisierung der Ringe oder Ringverlust? Lessings Beitrag zur Metaphorisierung und/oder Politisierung der Sprache." In *Streitkultur: Strategien des Überzeugens im Werk Lessings; Referate der Internationalen Lessing-Tagung der Albert-Ludwigs-Universität Freiburg und der Lessing Society an der University of Cincinnati, Ohio/USA vom 22. bis 24. Mai 1991 in Freiburg im Breisgau*, edited by Wolfram Mauser and Günter Saße, 113–120. Tübingen: Niemeyer, 1993.

Allison, Henry. *Kant's Theory of Taste: A Reading of the "Critique of Aesthetic Judgment."* Cambridge: Cambridge University Press, 2001.

Altmann, Alexander. "Lessing und Jacobi: Das Gespräch über den Spinozismus." *Lessing Yearbook* 3 (1971): 25–70.

Alxinger, Johann Baptist Edler von, ed. *Nuditäten oder Fantasien auf der Venus-Geige*. Reprint edition. Leipzig: Nationales Druckhaus, 1985.

Anz, Thomas, and Heinrich Kaulen, eds. *Literatur als Spiel: Evolutionsbiologische, ästhetische und pädagogische Konzepte*. Berlin: De Gruyter, 2009.

Appadurai, Arjun. Introduction to *The Social Life of Things: Commodities in Cultural Perspective*. Edited by Arjun Appadurai. Cambridge: Cambridge University Press, 1988.

———, ed. *The Social Life of Things: Commodities in Cultural Perspective.* Cambridge: Cambridge University Press, 1988.

Arndt, Susan, Dirk Naguschewski, and Robert Stockhammer, eds. *Exophonie: Anders-Sprachigkeit (in) der Literatur.* Berlin: Kadmos, 2007.

Asad, Talal. "The Construction of Religion as an Anthropological Category." In *Genealogies of Religion: Discipline and Reasons of Power in Christianity and Islam*, 27–54. Baltimore: Johns Hopkins University Press, 1993.

———. *Genealogies of Religion: Discipline and Reasons of Power in Christianity and Islam.* Baltimore: Johns Hopkins University Press, 1993.

Assmann, Aleida. *Erinnerungsräume: Formen und Wandlungen des kulturellen Gedächtnisses.* Munich: C. H. Beck, 1999.

Auslander, Leora. "Beyond Words." *American Historical Review* 10, no. 4 (October 2005): 1015–1045.

Austermann, Simone. *Die "Allgemeine Revision": Pädagogische Theorieentwicklung im 18. Jahrhundert.* Bad Heilbrunn: Julius Klinkhardt, 2010.

Baker, David. *The Schooled Society: The Educational Transformation of Global Culture.* Stanford, CA: Stanford University Press, 2014.

Bakhtin, Mikhail. *Rabelais and His World.* Translated by Hélène Iswolsky. Bloomington: Indiana University Press, 1984.

Barck, Karlheinz, and Martin Fontius, eds. *Ästhetische Grundbegriffe: Historisches Wörterbuch in sieben Bänden.* Stuttgart: Metzler, 2000–2005.

Barthes, Roland. *Writing Degree Zero* [1967]. Translated by Annette Lavers and Colin Smith. New York: Hill and Wang, 2009.

Basile, Giambattista. *The Tale of Tales, or Entertainment for Little Ones.* Translated by Nancy L. Canepa. New York: Penguin Books, 2016.

Bateson, Gregory. "Metalogue: About Games and Being Serious." In *Steps to an Ecology of Mind: Collected Essays in Anthropology, Psychiatry, Evolution, and Epistemology*, 24–30. Northvale, NJ: Jason Aronson, 1987.

———. *Steps to an Ecology of Mind: Collected Essays in Anthropology, Psychiatry, Evolution, and Epistemology.* Northvale, NJ: Jason Aronson, 1987.

———. "A Theory of Play and Fantasy." In *Steps to an Ecology of Mind: Collected Essays in Anthropology, Psychiatry, Evolution, and Epistemology*, 183–198. Northvale, NJ: Jason Aronson, 1987.

Baumann, Uwe, Arnold Becker, and Astrid Steiner-Weber, eds. *Streitkultur: Okzidentale Traditionen des Streitens in Literatur, Geschichte und Kunst.* Bonn: Bonn University Press, 2008.

Baumgarten, Alexander Gottlieb. *Ästhetik.* Edited by Dagmar Mirbach. Hamburg: Meiner, 2007.

Becker-Cantorino, Barbara. "Witch and Infanticide: Imaging the Female in *Faust I*." *Goethe Yearbook* 7 (1994): 1–22.

Beetz, Manfred, and Hans-Joachim Kertscher, eds. *Anakreontische Aufklärung.* Tübingen: Niemeyer, 2005.

Beiser, Frederick C. *The Fate of Reason: German Philosophy from Kant to Fichte.* Cambridge, MA: Harvard University Press, 1987.

———. "The Meaning of 'Romantic Poetry.'" In *The Romantic Imperative: The Concept of Early German Romanticism*, 6–22. Cambridge, MA: Harvard University Press, 2003.

———. *The Romantic Imperative: The Concept of Early German Romanticism.* Cambridge, MA: Harvard University Press, 2003.

———. *Schiller as Philosopher: A Re-Examination.* Oxford: Clarendon, 2005.

Bell, David. *Spinoza in Germany from 1670 to the Age of Goethe.* London: Institute of Germanic Studies, 1984.

Benjamin, Walter. "Altes Spielzeug: Zur Spielzeugausstellung des Märkischen Museums." In *Gesammelte Schriften*, edited by Rolf Tiedemann and Hermann Schweppenhäuser. Vol. 4, bk. 1, edited by Tillman Rexroth, 511–515. Frankfurt am Main: Suhrkamp, 1991.

———. "The Cultural History of Toys." In *Selected Writings*, vol. 2, *1927–1934*, edited by Michael W. Jennings, Howard Eiland, and Gary Smith, translated by Rodney Livingstone, Anna Bostock, Ben Brewster, Edmund Jephcott, Thomas Y. Levin, Kingsley Shorter, Knut Tarnowski, Jerolf Wikoff, and Harry Zohn, 113–116. Cambridge, MA: Harvard University Press, 1999.

———. "Die Aufgabe des Übersetzers." In *Gesammelte Schriften*, edited by Rolf Tiedemann and Hermann Schweppenhäuser. Vol. 4, bk. 1, edited by Tillman Rexroth, 9–21. Frankfurt am Main: Suhrkamp, 1991.

———. *Gesammelte Schriften*. Edited by Rolf Tiedemann and Hermann Schweppenhäuser. Frankfurt am Main: Surkamp, 1991. First published 1972–1989.

———. "Kulturgeschichte des Spielzeuges." In *Gesammelte Schriften*, edited by Rolf Tiedemann and Hermann Schweppenhäuser. Vol. 3, edited by Hella Tiedemann-Bartels, 113–117. Frankfurt am Main: Suhrkamp, 1991.

———. "Marginal Notes on a Monumental Work." In *Selected Writings*, vol. 2, *1927–1934*, edited by Michael W. Jennings, Howard Eiland, and Gary Smith, translated by Rodney Livingstone, Anna Bostock, Ben Brewster, Edmund Jephcott, Thomas Y. Levin, Kingsley Shorter, Knut Tarnowski, Jerolf Wikoff, and Harry Zohn, 117–121. Cambridge, MA: Harvard University Press, 1999.

———. "Randbemerkungen zu einem Monumentalwerk." In *Gesammelte Schriften*, edited by Rolf Tiedemann and Hermann Schweppenhäuser. Vol. 3, edited by Hella Tiedemann-Bartels, 127–132. Frankfurt am Main: Suhrkamp, 1991.

———. *Selected Writings*. Vol. 2, *1927–1934*, edited by Michael W. Jennings, Howard Eiland, and Gary Smith, translated by Rodney Livingstone, Anna Bostock, Ben Brewster, Edmund Jephcott, Thomas Y. Levin, Kingsley Shorter, Knut Tarnowski, Jerolf Wikoff, and Harry Zohn. Cambridge, MA: Harvard University Press, 1999.

———. *Selected Writings*. Vol. 4, *1938–1940*, edited by Howard Eiland and Michael W. Jennings. Cambridge, MA: Belknap Press, 2003.

———. "The Toy Exhibition at the Märkisches Museum." In *Selected Writings*, vol. 2, *1927–1934*, edited by Michael W. Jennings, Howard Eiland, and Gary Smith, translated by Rodney Livingstone, Anna Bostock, Ben Brewster, Edmund Jephcott, Thomas Y. Levin, Kingsley Shorter, Knut Tarnowski, Jerolf Wikoff, and Harry Zohn, 98–102. Cambridge, MA: Harvard University Press, 1999.

Berman, Antoine. *The Experience of the Foreign: Culture and Translation in Romantic Germany*. Translated by S. Heyvaert. Albany: State University of New York Press, 1992. Originally published as *L'épreuve de l'étranger: Culture et traduction dans l'Allemagne romantique*. Paris: Gallimard, 1984. Repr., Collection Tel, 1995.

Berndt, Frauke. *Poema / Gedicht: Die epistemische Konfiguration der Literatur um 1750*. Berlin: De Gruyter, 2011.

Berndt, Frauke, and Claudia Maienborn. "The Sucking Subject: Structural Ambiguities of Goethe's 'Auf dem See' in Literary and Linguistic Perspective." *Goethe Yearbook* 20 (2013): 91–115.

Bernhardi, August. *Sprachlehre*. 2 vols. Hildesheim: Georg Olms Verlag, 1973.

Bernofsky, Susan. *Foreign Words: Translator-Authors in the Age of Goethe*. Detroit: Wayne State University Press, 2005.

Berns, Jörg Jochen, and Wolfgang Neuber, eds. *Ars memorativa: Zur kulturgeschichtlichen Bedeutung der Gedächtniskunst 1400–1750*. Tübingen: Niemeyer, 1993.

Bertaux, Pierre. *Gar schöne Spiele spiel' ich mit dir! Zu Goethes Spieltrieb*. Frankfurt am Main: Insel, 1986.

Bischoff, Cäcilia. *Masterpieces of the Picture Gallery: A Brief Guide to the Kunsthistorisches Museum*. Vienna: Kunsthistorisches Museum, 2010.

Blod, Gabriele. *"Lebensmärchen": Goethes "Dichtung und Wahrheit" als poetischer und poetologischer Text*. Würzburg: Königshausen & Neumann, 2003.

Boethius. *The Theological Tractates: The Consolation of Philosophy*. Translated by H. F. Stewart, E. K. Rand, and S. J. Tester. Cambridge, MA: Harvard University Press, 1973.

Böhm, Elisabeth. "Epoche Machen: Goethes Konstruktion der Weimarer Klassik zwischen 1786 und 1796." PhD diss., University of Bayreuth, 2010.

Böhme, Gernot. *Kants "Kritik der Urteilskraft" in neuer Sicht*. Frankfurt am Main: Suhrkamp, 1999.

Bohnenkamp, Anne, and Matías Martínez, eds. *Geistiger Handelsverkehr: Komparatistische Aspekte der Goethezeit*. Göttingen: Wallstein, 2008.

Bohrer, Karl Heinz, ed. *Sprachen der Ironie—Sprachen des Ernstes*. Frankfurt am Main: Suhrkamp, 2000.

Bosse, Heinrich, and Ursula Renner, eds. *Literaturwissenschaft—Einführung in ein Sprachspiel*. Freiburg im Breisgau: Rombach, 1999.

Bovenschen, Silvia. *Die imaginierte Weiblichkeit: Exemplarische Untersuchungen zu kulturgeschichtlichen und literarischen Präsentationsformen des Weiblichen*. Frankfurt am Main: Suhrkamp, 2003.

Bowie, Andrew. *From Romanticism to Critical Theory: The Philosophy of German Literary Theory*. London: Routledge, 1997.

Bremer, Kai, and Carlos Spoerhase, eds. *Gelehrte Polemik: Intellektuelle Konfliktverschärfungen um 1700*. Frankfurt am Main: Klostermann, 2011.

Brodsky, Claudia. "'Judgment' and the Genesis of What We Lack: 'Schema,' 'Poetry,' and the 'Monogram of the Imagination' in Kant." *Eighteenth Century* 51, no. 3 (2010): 317–340.

Brokoff, Jürgen. "Die Verselbständigung der Poesie als Spiel am Ende des 18. Jahrhunderts und der Spielbegriff bei Johan Huizinga und Jost Trier." In *Literatur als Spiel: Evolutionsbiologische, ästhetische und pädagogische Konzepte*, edited by Thomas Anz and Heinrich Kaulen, 101–114. Berlin: De Gruyter, 2009.

Brown, Jane K. *Goethe's Allegories of Identity*. Philadelphia: University of Pennsylvania Press, 2014.

Browne, Richard J., and M. C. Davis. "Goethe and the Yo-Yo." *Modern Language Quarterly* 14, no. 1 (March 1953): 98–101.

Bullitt, John, and Walter Jackson Bate. "Distinctions between Fancy and Imagination in Eighteenth-Century English Criticism." *MLN* 60 (1945): 8–15.

Butzer, Günter. "Höllenfahrt ohne Auferstehung: Die Unterweltsreise als Narrativ katastrophischen Erinnerns." In *Katastrophe und Gedächtnis*, edited by Thomas Klinkert and Günter Oesterle, 167–190. Berlin: De Gruyter, 2013.

Caillois, Roger. *Man and the Sacred*. Translated by Meyer Barash. Glencoe, IL: Free Press of Glencoe, 1959.

———. "Play and the Sacred" [1950]. In *Man and the Sacred*, translated by Meyer Barash, 152–162. Glencoe, IL: Free Press of Glencoe, 1959.

Campe, Johann Heinrich, ed. *Allgemeine Revision des gesammten Schul- und Erziehungswesens*. Hamburg: Bohn, 1785–92.

Campe, Rüdiger. *The Game of Probability: Literature and Calculation from Pascal to Kleist*. Translated by Ellwood H. Wiggins. Stanford, CA: Stanford University Press, 2012.

Cercel, Larisa, and Adriana Şerban, eds. *Friedrich Schleiermacher and the Question of Translation*. Berlin: De Gruyter, 2015.

Chaouli, Michel. *Thinking with Kant's "Critique of Judgment."* Cambridge, MA: Harvard University Press, 2017.

Chapman, Rachel. "A Case Study of Gendered Play in Preschools: How Early Childhood Educators' Perceptions of Gender Influence Children's Play." *Early Childhood Development and Care* 186, no. 8 (2016): 1271–1284.

Christ, Kurt. *Jacobi und Mendelssohn: Eine Analyse des Spinozastreits*. Würzburg: Königshausen und Neumann, 1988.

Cicero, Marcus Tullius. *De oratore*. 2nd ed. Cambridge, MA: Harvard University Press, 1967.

Colebrook, Claire. "The Context of Humanism." *New Literary History* 42, no. 4 (Autumn 2011): 701–718.

Corbineau-Hoffmann, Angelika. "Spiel." In *Historisches Wörterbuch der Philosophie*, edited by Joachim Ritter and Karlfried Gründer, vol. 9, 1383–1390. Basel: Schwabe, 1995.

Corngold, Stanley. *Complex Pleasure: Forms of Feeling in German Literature*. Stanford, CA: Stanford University Press, 1998.

———. "Wit and Judgment; or, Lessing and Kant." In *Complex Pleasure: Forms of Feeling in German Literature*, 27–47. Stanford, CA: Stanford University Press, 1998.

Cousin, Victor. *Rapport sur l'état de l'Instruction Publique dans quelques pays de l'Allemagne et particulièrement en Prusse*. Paris: Imprimerie royale, 1832.

Dahnke, Hans-Dietrich. "Wandlungen in Wesen und Funktion öffentlicher literarischer Debatten und Kontroversen zwischen 1780 und 1810." In *Formen und Formgeschichte des Streitens: Der Literaturstreit*, edited by Helmut Koopmann, 172–179. Tübingen: Niemeyer, 1986.

Dahnke, Hans-Dietrich, and Bernd Leistner, eds. *Debatten und Kontroversen: Literarische Auseinandersetzungen in Deutschland am Ende des 18. Jahrhunderts*. 2 vols. Berlin: Aufbau, 1989.

Dante Alighieri. *Inferno*. Translated by Robert Hollander and Jean Hollander. New York: Anchor Books, 2002.

———. *La divina commedia*. Edited by Giorgio Petrocchi. Turin: Einaudi, 1975.

———. *Paradiso*. Translated by Robert Hollander and Jean Hollander. London: Doubleday, 2007.

———. *Purgatorio*. Translated by Jean Hollander and Robert Hollander. London: Doubleday, 2003.

Das Goethe-Schiller Denkmal in San Francisco, California: Erinnerungen an den "Deutschen Tag" der California Midwinter International Exposition 1894, an das "Goethe Schiller Fest" 1895 und an die "Enthüllung des Denkmals im Golden Gate Park 1901." San Francisco: C. Leidecker, 1901.

De Lisi, Richard. "Piaget's Sympathetic but Unromantic Account of Children's Play." In *The Handbook of the Study of Play*, vol. 1, edited by James E. Johnson, Scott G. Eberle, and Thomas S. Henricks, 227–238. New York: Rowman & Littlefield, 2015.

de Man, Paul. *Aesthetic Ideology*. Edited by Andrzej Warminski. Minneapolis: University of Minnesota Press, 1996.

———. "Kant and Schiller." In *Aesthetic Ideology*, edited by Andrzej Warminski, 129–162. Minneapolis: University of Minnesota Press, 1996.

———. "Phenomenality and Materiality in Kant." In *Aesthetic Ideology*, edited by Andrzej Warminski, 70–90. Minneapolis: University of Minnesota Press, 1996.

Deines, Stefan. "Formen und Funktionen des Spielbegriffs in der Philosophie." In *Spielformen des Selbst: Das Spiel zwischen Subjektivität, Kunst und Alltagspraxis*, edited by Regine Strätling, 23–38. Bielefeld: transcript, 2012.

Deleuze, Gilles. *Kant's Critical Philosophy*. Translated by Hugh Tomlinson and Barbara Habberjam. Minneapolis: University of Minnesota Press, 1984 [1963].

deMause, Lloyd. "The Evolution of Childhood." In *The History of Childhood*, edited by Lloyd deMause, 1–73. New York: Psychohistory Press, 1974.

———, ed. *The History of Childhood*. New York: Psychohistory Press, 1974.

———. Preface to *The History of Childhood*, edited by Lloyd deMause. New York: Psychohistory Press, 1974.

Derrida, Jacques. "Structure, Sign, and Play in the Discourse of the Human Sciences." In *Writing and Difference*, translated by Alan Bass, 278–294. Chicago: University of Chicago Press, 1978 [1967].

———. *Writing and Difference*. Translated by Alan Bass. Chicago: University of Chicago Press, 1978.

Dini, Tristana, and Salvatore Principe, eds. *Jacobi in Discussione*. Milan: Franco Angeli, 2012.

Direk, Zeynep, and Leonard Lawlor, eds. *A Companion to Derrida*. Chichester, West Sussex: Wiley Blackwell, 2014.

Donovan, Tristan. *It's All a Game: The History of Board Games from Monopoly to Settlers of Catan*. New York: Thomas Dunne Books, 2017.

Eisenhauer, Robert. *Archeologies of Invective*. New York: Peter Lang, 2007.

Essig, Rolf-Bernhard. *Der offene Brief: Geschichte und Funktion einer publizistischen Form von Isokrates bis Günter Grass*. Würzburg: Königshausen & Neumann, 2000.

Ewers, Hans-Heino. Introduction to *Kinder- und Jugendliteratur der Romantik: Eine Textsammlung*, 7–58. Edited by Hans-Heino Ewers. Stuttgart: Reclam, 1984.

———, ed. *Kinder- und Jugendliteratur der Romantik: Eine Textsammlung*. Stuttgart: Reclam, 1984.

Faull, Katherine M., ed. *Masculinity, Senses, Spirit*. Lewisburg, PA: Bucknell University Press, 2011.

Fischer, Gerhard, and Bernhard Greiner, eds. *The Play within the Play: The Performance of Meta-theatre and Self-reflection*. Amsterdam: Rodopi, 2007.

Flax, Neil M. "Goethe's *Faust II* and the Experimental Theater of His Time." *Comparative Literature* 31, no. 2 (1979): 154–166.

Fleming, Paul. "The Crisis of Art: Max Kommerell and Jean Paul's Gestures." *MLN* 115, no. 3 (2000): 519–543.

———. "Forgetting—*Faust*: Adorno and Kommerell." In *Adorno and Literature*, edited by Nigel Mapp, 133–144. London: Continuum, 2006.

Förster, Eckart. *Die 25 Jahre der Philosophie*. Frankfurt am Main: Klostermann, 2012.

Frank, Manfred. *Einführung in die frühromantische Ästhetik*. Frankfurt am Main: Suhrkamp, 1989.

Freud, Sigmund. *Beyond the Pleasure Principle*. Vol. 18 of *The Complete Psychological Works of Sigmund Freud*, translated and edited by James Strachey. New York: W. W. Norton, 1976.

———. *The Standard Edition of the Complete Psychological Works of Sigmund Freud*. Vol. 8, edited by James Strachey. London: Hogarth, 1953–74.

Freudenfeld, Regina. *Gedächtnis-Zeichen: Mnemologie in der deutschen und französischen Aufklärung*. Tübingen: Narr, 1996.

Freudiger, Jürg. "Der Pantheismusstreit: Eine Bestandsaufnahme." *Kriterion—Journal of Philosophy* 5, no. 1 (1993): 39–48.

Fröbel, Friedrich. *The Education of Man*. Translated by W. N. Hailmann. Mineola, NY: Dover, 2005. First published 1898 by D. Appleton (New York).

———. *Die Menschenerziehung, die Erziehungs-, Unterrichts-, und Lehrkunst, angestrebt in der allgemeinen deutschen Erziehungsanstalt zu Keilhau*. Keilhau: Verlag der allgemeinen deutschen Erziehungsanstalt, 1826.

———. *Die Pädagogik des Kindergartens: Gedanken Friedrich Fröbel's über das Spiel und die Spielgegenstände des Kindes*. Vol. 2 of *Friedrich Fröbel's gesammelte pädagogische Schriften*, edited by Wichard Lange. Berlin: Th. Chr. Fr. Enslin, 1862.

———. *Friedrich Fröbel's Pedagogics of the Kindergarten*. Translated by Josephine Jarvis. New York: D. Appleton, 1895.

———. *The Student's Froebel*. Adapted by William H. Herford, introduced by Professor M. E. Sadler. London: Sir Isaac Pitman & Sons, 1916.

———. *Ueber deutsche Erziehung überhaupt, und über das allgemeine Deutsche der Erziehungsanstalt in Keilhau insbesondere*. Rudolstadt: Hofbuchhandlung, 1822.

Gailus, Andreas. "Of Beautiful and Dismembered Bodies: Art as Social Discipline in Schiller's *On the Aesthetic Education of Man*." In *Impure Reason: Dialectic of Enlightenment in Germany*, edited by Daniel W. Wilson and Robert C. Holub, 146–165. Detroit, MI: Wayne State University Press, 1993.

Geitz, Henry, Jürgen Heideking, and Jürgen Herbst, eds. *German Influences on Education in the United States to 1917*. Cambridge: Cambridge University Press, 1995.

Gersdorff, Dagmar von. *Goethes Enkel: Walther, Wolfgang und Alma*. Frankfurt am Main: Insel Verlag, 2008.

Giese, Peter Christian. "Glück, Fortüne und Happy Ending in Lessings *Minna von Barnhelm*." *Lessing Yearbook* XVIII (1986): 21–46.

Gillis, John R. "Epilogue: The Islanding of Children—Reshaping the Mythical Landscapes of Childhood." In *Designing Modern Childhood: History, Space and the Material Culture of Children*, edited by Marta Gutman and Ning de Coninck-Smith, 316–330. New Brunswick, NJ: Rutgers University Press, 2008.

Gisbertz, Anna-Katharina, ed. *Stimmung: Zur Wiederkehr einer ästhetischen Kategorie*. Munich: Fink, 2011.

Gleim, Friedrich Wilhelm. *Sämmtliche Schriften*. Leipzig: Gräff, 1802.

Goebel, Eckart. *Am Ufer der zweiten Welt: Jean Pauls "Poetische Landschaftsmalerei."* Tübingen: Stauffenberg, 1999.

Goethe, Catharina Elisabeth. *Die Briefe der Frau Rath Goethe*. Edited by Albert Köster. Frankfurt am Main: Insel, 1969.

Goethe, Johann Wolfgang von. *Dichtung und Wahrheit*. Vol. 8 of *Werkausgabe in zehn Bänden*. Cologne: Könemann, 1998.

———. *Erotic Poems*. Translated by David Luke, introduction by Hans Rudolf Vaget. Oxford: Oxford University Press, 1988.

———. *Faust I & II*. Edited by David E. Wellbery. Translated by Stuart Atkins. Princeton, NJ: Princeton University Press, 2014.

———. *Faust-Dichtungen*. Edited by Ulrich Gaier. 3 vols. Stuttgart: Reclam, 1999.

———. "Frauenrollen auf dem römischen Theater durch Männer gespielt." *Der deutsche Merkur* (November 1778): 97–103.

———. *From My Life: Poetry and Truth*. Parts One to Three. Translated by Robert Heitner and edited by Thomas P. Saine and Jeffrey L. Sammons. Vol. 4 of *Goethe's Collected Works*, edited by Victor Lange, Eric A. Blackall, and Cyrus Hamlin. New York: Suhrkamp, 1983.

———. *Goethes Ehe in Briefen*. Edited by Hans Gerhard Gräf. 2nd ed. Frankfurt am Main: Rütten & Loening, 1922.

———. *Sämtliche Werke: Briefe, Tagebücher und Gespräche*. Edited by Friedmar Apel, Hendrik Birus, Anne Bohnenkamp, Dieter Borchmeyer, Hans-Georg Dewitz, Karl Eibl, Wolf von Engelhardt, Gerhard Femmel, Horst Fleig, Harald Fricke, Wilhelm Große, Walter Hettche, Herbert Jaumann, Dorothea Kuhn, Petra Maisak, Christoph Michel, Klaus-Detlef Müller, Gerhard Neumann, Norbert Oellers, Wolfgang Proß, Hartmut Reinhardt, Dorothea Schäfer-Weiss, Gerhard Schmid, Irmtraud Schmid, Albrecht Schöne, Rose Unterberger, Wilhelm Voßkamp, Manfred Wenzel, and Waltraud Wiethölter. Frankfurt am Main: Deutscher Klassiker Verlag, 1985–2013. [=FA]

———. *Selected Poems*. Edited by Christopher Middleton. Translated by Michael Hamburger, David Luke, Christopher Middleton, John Frederick Nims, and Vernon Watkins. Princeton, NJ: Princeton University Press, 1994.

———. *Truth and Poetry: From My Own Life, Books I.–XX*. Translated by John Oxenford. London: George Bell and Sons, 1897.

———. *Werke*. Edited by Erich Trunz. Hamburger Ausgabe. 14 vols. Hamburg: Wegner, 1952–64.

———. *Wilhelm Meister's Apprenticeship*. Translated and edited by Eric A. Blackall in cooperation with Victor Lange. Vol. 9 of *Goethe's Collected Works*, edited by Victor Lange, Eric A. Blackall, and Cyrus Hamlin. New York: Suhrkamp, 1983.

Goetsch, Paul, ed. *Lesen und Schreiben im 17. und 18. Jahrhundert: Studien zu ihrer Bewertung in Deutschland, England, Frankreich*. Tübingen: Narr, 1994.

Goldenbaum, Ursula, ed. *Appell an das Publikum: Die öffentliche Debatte in der deutschen Aufklärung 1687–1796*. Berlin: Akademie, 2004.

———. "Die öffentliche Debatte in der deutschen Aufklärung: Einleitung." In *Appell an das Publikum: Die öffentliche Debatte in der deutschen Aufklärung 1687–1796*, edited by Ursula Goldenbaum, 1–118. Berlin: Akademie, 2004.

———. "The Pantheismusstreit—Milestone or Stumbling Block in the German Reception of Spinoza?" In *Spinoza's Ethics: A Collective Commentary*, edited by Michael Hampe, Ursula Renz, and Robert Schnepf, 325–350. Leiden: Brill, 2011.

Goldmann, Stefan. "Statt Totenklage Gedächtnis: Zur Erfindung der Mnemotechnik durch Simonides von Keos." *Poetica* 21 (1989): 43–66.

Göres, Jörn. "Goethes Verhältnis zur Topik." *Goethe-Jahrbuch* 26 (1964): 144–180.

Goto-Jones, Chris. "The Secret Life of Yo-Yos." *Atlantic*, April 9, 2015. https://www.theatlantic.com/technology/archive/2015/04/the-yo-yo-effect/389868/.

Gottsched, Johann Christoph. *Versuch einer critischen Dichtkunst*. Leipzig: Breitkopf, 1730.

Greiner, Bernhard. "Streitkultur des Als Ob: Komödie als transzendentale Bedingung des Streitens in *Minna von Barnhelm*." In *Streitkultur: Strategien des Überzeugens im Werk Lessings; Referate der Internationalen Lessing-Tagung der Albert-Ludwigs-Universität Freiburg und der Lessing Society an der University of Cincinnati, Ohio/USA vom 22. bis 24. Mai 1991 in Freiburg im Breisgau*, edited by Wolfram Mauser and Günter Saße, 247–257. Tübingen: Niemeyer, 1993.

Grimm, Jacob, and Wilhelm Grimm. "Preface to Volume I of the First Edition of *Children's Stories and Household Tales*." In *The Annotated Brothers Grimm*, translated and edited by Maria Tatar, 401–407. New York: W. W. Norton, 2004.

Gröber, Karl. *Children's Toys of Bygone Days: A History of Playthings of All Peoples from Prehistoric Times to the XIXth Century*. Translated by Philip Hereford. New York: Frederick A. Stokes, 1928.

Groos, Karl. *The Play of Man*. Translated with the author's cooperation by Elizabeth L. Baldwin. New York: D. Appleton, 1919.

Grunert, Frank. "Die Marginalisierung des Gedächtnisses und die Kreativität der Erinnerung. Zur Gedächtnistheorie der deutschen Aufklärungsphilosophie." In *Erinnerung, Gedächtnis, Wissen: Studien zur kulturwissenschaftlichen Gedächtnisforschung*, edited by Günter Oesterle, 29–51. Göttingen: Vandenhoeck & Ruprecht, 2005.

———. "Erinnerung als Kreation: Zur Gedächtnistheorie von Christian Wolff und der Wolff-Schule." In *Christian Wolff und die europäische Aufklärung: Akten des 1. Internationalen Christian-Wolff-Kongresses, Halle (Saale), 4.–8. April 2004*, edited by Jürgen Stolzenberg and Oliver-Pierre Rudolph, 391–404. Hildesheim: Olms, 2007.

"Guillotine as Toy for Children in 1793: Goethe's Mother Refused to Buy Machine for Youth." *San Francisco Call*, February 7, 1910.

Gutman, Marta, and Ning de Coninck-Smith, eds. *Designing Modern Childhood: History, Space and the Material Culture of Children*. New Brunswick, NJ: Rutgers University Press, 2008.

Habermas, Jürgen. *The Philosophical Discourse of Modernity: Twelve Lectures*. Translated by Frederick G. Lawrence. Cambridge, MA: MIT Press, 1987.

———. *The Theory of Communicative Action*. Translated by Thomas McCarthy. Vol. 1, *Reason and the Rationalization of Society*. Boston: Beacon, 1985.

Hamann, Johann Georg. *Sokratische Denkwürdigkeiten: Aesthetica in nuce*. Edited by Sven-Aage Jœrgensen. Stuttgart: Reclam, 1998.

Hamlin, David D. *Work and Play: The Production and Consumption of Toys in Germany, 1870–1914*. Ann Arbor: University of Michigan Press, 2007.

Hammacher, Klaus. *Die Philosophie Friedrich Heinrich Jacobis*. Munich: Fink, 1969.

———, ed. *Friedrich Heinrich Jacobi: Philosoph und Literat der Goethezeit*. Frankfurt am Main: Klostermann, 1971.

———. "Jacobis Brief 'An Fichte' (1799)." In *Transzendentalphilosophie und Spekulation: Der Streit um die Gestalt einer Ersten Philosophie (1799–1807)*, edited by Walter Jaeschke, 72–84. Hamburg: Meiner, 1993.

———. "Über Friedrich Heinrich Jacobis Beziehungen zu Lessing im Zusammenhang mit dem Streit um Spinoza." In *Lessing und der Kreis seiner Freunde*, edited by Günter Schulz, 51–74. Heidelberg: Lambert Schneider, 1985.

Hampe, Michael, Ursula Renz, and Robert Schnepf, eds. *Spinoza's Ethics: A Collective Commentary*. Leiden: Brill, 2011.

Hanschmann, Alexander Bruno. *Friedrich Fröbel: Die Entwickelung seiner Erziehungsidee in seinem Leben*. Eisenach: J. Bacmeister, 1874.

Haraway, Donna. "A Cyborg Manifesto: Science, Technology, and Socialist-Feminism in the Late 20th Century." *International Handbook of Virtual Learning Environments*, edited by Joel Weiss, Jason Nolan, Jeremy Hunsinger, and Peter Trifonas, 117–158. Dordrecht, Netherlands: Springer, 2006. Previously published as "Manifesto for Cyborgs: Science, Technology, and Socialist Feminism in the 1980s," *Socialist Review*, no. 80 (1985): 65–108.

———. *When Species Meet*. Minneapolis: University of Minnesota Press, 2007.

Haye, Thomas. "Die Invektive als poetische Gattung—Überlegungen zu einer wenig bekannten Tradition des lateinischen Mittelalters." *Eranos* 106 (2012): 25–41.

Hebeisen, Alfred. *Friedrich Heinrich Jacobi: Seine Auseinandersetzung mit Spinoza*. Bern: Haupt, 1960.

Heidemann, Ingeborg. *Der Begriff des Spieles und das ästhetische Weltbild in der Philosophie der Gegenwart*. Berlin: De Gruyter, 1968.

Heidsieck, Arnold. *G. E. Lessing: Nathan der Weise / Die Erziehung des Menschengeschlechts*. Strasbourg: PU de Strasbourg, 2000.

———. "Lessings Vorstellung von Offenbarung." In *G. E. Lessing: Nathan der Weise / Die Erziehung des Menschengeschlechts*, 27–39. Strasbourg: PU de Strasbourg, 2000.

Heiland, Helmut. *Die Spielpädagogik Friedrich Fröbels*. Vol. 5 of *Beiträge zur Fröbelforschung*. Hildesheim: Olms, 1998.

Henrich, Dieter. *Aesthetic Judgment and the Moral Image of the World: Studies in Kant*. Stanford, CA: Stanford University Press, 1992.

Henricks, Thomas S. "Classic Theories of Play." In *The Handbook of the Study of Play*, edited by James E. Johnson, Scott G. Eberle, Thomas S. Henricks, and David Kuschner, vol. 1, 163–180. New York: Rowman & Littlefield, 2015.

———. *Play and the Human Condition*. Urbana: University of Illinois Press, 2015.

Hentschel, Uwe. "'Briefe sind Spiegel der Seelen': Epistolare Kultur des 18. Jahrhunderts zwischen Privatheit und Öffentlichkeit." *Lessing-Yearbook* 33 (2001): 183–195.

Hermanns, William. *Einstein and the Poet: In Search of the Cosmic Man*. Brookline Village, MA: Branden, 1983.

Hexter, Ralph. "Poetic Reclamation and Goethe's *Venetian Epigrams*." *MLN* 96, no. 3 (1981): 526–555.

Hilgers, Philipp von. *War Games: A History of War on Paper*. Translated by Ross Benjamin. Cambridge, MA: MIT Press, 2012.

Hindrichs, Gunnar. "Der Standpunkt des natürlichen Denkens: Fichtes *Bestimmung des Menschen* in der Auseinandersetzung mit der 'Unphilosophie' Jacobis." In *System und Systemkritik: Beiträge zu einem Grundproblem der klassischen deutschen Philosophie*, edited by Birgit Sandkaulen, 109–129. Würzburg: Königshausen & Neumann, 2006.

Hinske, Norbert, ed. *Zentren der Aufklärung I: Halle; Aufklärung und Pietismus*. Heidelberg: Schneider, 1989.

Hirschi, Caspar. "Piraten der Gelehrtenrepublik: Die Norm des sachlichen Streits und ihre polemische Funktion." In *Gelehrte Polemik: Intellektuelle Konfliktverschärfungen um*

1700, edited by Kai Bremer and Carlos Spoerhase, 176–213. Frankfurt am Main: Klostermann, 2011.

Hogarth, William. *The Analysis of Beauty*. London: John Reeves, 1753.

Huhn, Tom. *Imitation and Society: The Persistence of Mimesis in the Aesthetics of Burke, Hogarth, and Kant*. University Park: Penn State University Press, 2004.

Huizinga, Johan. *Homo Ludens: A Study of the Play-Element in Culture*. New York: Roy, 1950.

———. *Homo Ludens: Vom Ursprung der Kultur im Spiel*. Hamburg: Rowohlt, 1969.

Huyssen, Andreas. *Die frühromantische Konzeption von Übersetzung und Aneignung: Studien zur frühromantischen Utopie einer deutschen Weltliteratur*. Zurich: Atlantis Verlag, 1969.

Iacovacci, Alberto. "Il doppio grido di Jacobi: Per una rilettura della Lettera a Fichte." In *Jacobi in Discussione*, edited by Tristana Dini and Salvatore Principe, 83–96. Milan: Franco Angeli, 2012.

Iheoma, Eugene O. "Rousseau's Views on Teaching." *Journal of Educational Thought* 31, no. 1 (1997): 69–81.

Iser, Wolfgang. *Das Fiktive und das Imaginäre: Perspektiven literarischer Anthropologie*. Frankfurt am Main: Suhrkamp, 1993.

Jacobi, Friedrich Heinrich. *Jacobi an Fichte (1799)*. In *Werke: Gesamtausgabe*. Vol. 2, *Schriften zum Transzendentalen Idealismus*, edited by Walter Jaeschke and Irmgard-Maria Piske, 191–260. Hamburg: Meiner, 2004.

———. "Jacobi to Fichte (1799)." In *Main Philosophical Writings and the Novel "Allwill,"* translated and edited by George di Giovanni, 497–536. Montreal: McGill-Queen's University Press, 1994.

———. *Main Philosophical Writings and the Novel "Allwill."* Translated and edited by George di Giovanni. Montreal: McGill-Queen's University Press, 1994.

———. *Werke: Gesamtausgabe*. Vol. 2, *Schriften zum Transzendentalen Idealismus*, edited by Walter Jaeschke and Irmgard-Maria Piske. Hamburg: Meiner, 2004.

Jacobi, Johann Georg, ed. *Iris: Vierteljahrsschrift für Frauenzimmer*. Berlin: Haude & Spener, 1774–1776.

Jaeger, Michael. *Fausts Kolonie: Goethes kritische Phänomenologie der Moderne*. Würzburg: Königshausen & Neumann, 2004.

Jaeschke, Walter. "Der Messias der spekulativen Vernunft." *Kritisches Jahrbuch der Philosophie* 4 (1999): 143–157.

———, ed. *Transzendentalphilosophie und Spekulation: Der Streit um die Gestalt einer Ersten Philosophie (1799–1807)*. Hamburg: Meiner, 1993.

Jagoda, Patrick. "Gamification and Other Forms of Play." *Boundary 2* 40, no. 2 (2013): 113–144.

Jameson, Fredric. *The Political Unconscious: Narrative as a Socially Symbolic Act*. Ithaca, NY: Cornell University Press, 1981.

Jaumann, Herbert. "Memoria in der Auseinandersetzung zwischen *érudition* und *science* im 17. Jahrhundert." In *Ars memorativa: Zur kulturgeschichtlichen Bedeutung der Gedächtniskunst 1400–1750*, edited by Jörg Jochen Berns and Wolfgang Neuber, 286–296. Tübingen: Niemeyer, 1993.

Jauss, Hans Robert. "Poiesis." *Critical Inquiry* 8, no. 3 (1982): 591–608.

Johnson, James E. Introduction to *The Handbook of the Study of Play*, edited by James E. Johnson, Scott G. Eberle, Thomas S. Henricks, and David Kuschner, xi–xiii. New York: Rowman & Littlefield, 2015.

Johnson, James E., Scott G. Eberle, Thomas S. Henricks, and David Kuschner, eds. *The Handbook of the Study of Play*. 2 vols. New York: Rowman & Littlefield, 2015.

Kant, Immanuel. *Anthropology from a Pragmatic Point of View*. Translated and edited by Robert B. Louden. Cambridge: Cambridge University Press, 2006.

———. *Critique of Judgement*. Translated and analytical indexes by James Creed Meredith. Oxford: Oxford University Press, 1973.

———. *Critique of the Power of Judgment*. Translated by Paul Guyer and Eric Matthews. Edited by Paul Guyer. Cambridge: Cambridge University Press, 2000.

———. *The Educational Theory of Immanuel Kant*. Translated and edited by Edward Franklin Buchner. Philadelphia: J. B. Lippincott, 1904.

———. *Groundwork of the Metaphysics of Morals*. Translated by Mary Gregor. Cambridge: Cambridge University Press, 1998.

———. *Kant's gesammelte Schriften*. Vol. 9. Berlin: De Gruyter, 1923.

———. *Kritik der Urteilskraft*. Edited by Karl Vorländer. Hamburg: Meiner, 1924; reprint, 1974.

———. *Über Pädagogik*. Edited by Friedrich Theodor Rink. Königsberg: Friedrich Nicolovius, 1803.

———. "Über Pädagogik." In *Kant's gesammelte Schriften*. Vol. 9. Berlin: De Gruyter, 1923.

———. *Werkausgabe in zehn Bänden*. Edited by Wilhelm Weischedel. Frankfurt am Main: Suhrkamp, 1974. [=WA]

Kayser, Wolfgang. "Goethe und das Spiel." In *Kunst und Spiel: Fünf Goethe-Studien*, 30–46. Göttingen: Vandenhoeck & Ruprecht, 1961.

———. *Kunst und Spiel: Fünf Goethe-Studien*, 30–46. Göttingen: Vandenhoeck & Ruprecht, 1961.

Kesserling, Thomas. "The Mind's Staircase Revisited." In *The Cambridge Companion to Piaget*, edited by Ulrich Müller, Jeremy I. M. Carpendale, and Leslie Smith, 372–399. Cambridge: Cambridge University Press, 2009.

Kettelkamp, Gilbert Clarence. "Jean Paul and His Relationship to the Pedagogical Theories of His Day." Abstract, PhD diss., University of Illinois, Urbana, 1941.

Key, Ellen. *A Century of the Child*. Translated from German version by Frances Maro, reviewed by the author. New York: G. P. Putnam and Sons, Knickerbocker Press, 1909.

Kimmich, Dorothea. "Auf der Suche nach dem ganzen Menschen: Die künstlichen Paradiese epikureischen Glücks im Rokoko." In *Anakreontische Aufklärung*, edited by Manfred Beetz and Hans-Joachim Kertscher, 77–91. Tübingen: Niemeyer, 2005.

Kittler, Friedrich A. *Dichter—Mutter—Kind*, 19–45. Munich: Fink, 1991.

———. *Discourse Networks 1800 / 1900*. Translated by Michael Metteer and Chris Cullens. Stanford, CA: Stanford University Press, 1990.

———. "Lessing: 'Erziehung ist Offenbarung.'" In *Dichter—Mutter—Kind*, 19–45. Munich: Fink, 1991.

Kitzbichler, Josefine. "From Jerome to Schleiermacher? Translation Methods and the Irrationality of Languages." In *Rereading Schleiermacher: Translation, Cognition and Culture*, edited by Teresa Seruya and José Miranda Justo, 27–40. Heidelberg: Springer, 2016.

Kladderadatsch: Humoristisch-satirisches Wochenblatt. No. 36, September 7, 1891.

Klass, Perri. "Breaking Gender Stereotypes in the Toy Box." *New York Times*, February 5, 2018. https://www.nytimes.com/2018/02/05/well/family/gender-stereotypes-children-toys.html.

Klinkert, Thomas, and Günter Oesterle, eds. *Katastrophe und Gedächtnis*. Berlin: De Gruyter, 2013.

Klopstock, Friedrich Gottlieb. *Ausgewählte Werke*. Edited by Karl August Schleiden. Munich: Hanser, 1962.

Knodt, Eva M. *"Negative Philosophie" und dialogische Kritik: Zur Struktur poetischer Theorie bei Lessing und Herder*. Tübingen: Niemeyer, 1988.

Kohl, Katrin, and Kevin F. Hilliard, eds. *Klopstock an der Grenze der Epochen*. Berlin: De Gruyter, 1995.

Kohlmeyer, Otto. *Die Pädagogische Provinz in "Wilhelm Meisters Wanderjahren": Ein Beitrag zur Pädagogik Goethes*. Langensalza: Julius Beltz, 1923.

Kommerell, Max. *Geist und Buchstabe der Dichtung: Goethe, Schiller, Kleist, Hölderlin*. 4th ed. Frankfurt am Main: V. Klostermann, 1956.

Koopmann, Helmut, ed. *Formen und Formgeschichte des Streitens: Der Literaturstreit*. Tübingen: Niemeyer, 1986.

Koschorke, Albrecht. "Die Verschriftlichung der Liebe und ihre empfindsamen Folgen: Zu Modellen erotischer Autorschaft bei Gleim, Lessing und Klopstock." In *Lesen und Schreiben im 17. und 18. Jahrhundert: Studien zu ihrer Bewertung in Deutschland, England, Frankreich*, edited by Paul Goetsch, 251–264. Tübingen: Narr, 1994.

Kraß, Andreas, and Alexandra Tischel, eds. *Bündnis und Begehren: Ein Symposium über die Liebe*. Berlin: Erich Schmidt, 2002.

Kühme, Dorothea. *Bürger und Spiel: Gesellschaftsspiele im deutschen Bürgertum zwischen 1750 und 1850*. Frankfurt am Main: Campus Verlag, 1997.

Lacoue-Labarthe, Philippe, and Jean-Luc Nancy. "The Fragment: The Fragmentary Exigency." In *The Literary Absolute: The Theory of Literature in German Romanticism*, translated by Philipp Barnard and Cheryl Lester, 39–58. Albany: State University of New York Press, 1988.

———. *The Literary Absolute: The Theory of Literature in German Romanticism*. Translated by Philip Barnard and Cheryl Lester. Albany: State University of New York Press, 1988.

Landfester, Ulrike. "Das Zittern der Rose: Versuch über Metapher, Geschlecht und Begehren in der deutschen Liebeslyrik." In *Bündnis und Begehren: Ein Symposium über die Liebe*, edited by Andreas Kraß and Alexandra Tischel, 35–63. Berlin: Erich Schmidt, 2002.

Landgraf, Edgar. "Comprehending Romantic Incomprehensibility: A Systems-Theoretical Perspective on Early German Romanticism." *MLN* 121, no. 3 (2006): 592–616.

———. *Improvisation as Art: Conceptual Challenges, Historical Perspectives*. New York: Continuum, 2011.

———. "Romantic Love and the Enlightenment: From Gallantry and Seduction to Authenticity and Self-Validation." *German Quarterly* 77, no. 1 (Winter 2004): 29–46.

———. "*Werther*'s Sentimental Narcissism: Consciousness, Communication, and the Origin of the Modern Psyche." In *The Self as Muse: Narcissism and Creativity in the German Imagination, 1750–1830*, edited by Alexander Mathäs, 114–133. Lewisburg, PA: Bucknell University Press, 2011.

Lange, Horst. "Betting on Providence: Gambling in Lessing's *Minna von Barnhelm*." *Colloquia Germanica* 41, no. 1 (2008): 1–9.

———. "Goethe's Strategy of Self-Censorship: The Case of the *Venezianische Epigramme*." *Monatshefte* 91, no. 2 (1999): 224–240.

Lauer, Gerhard, ed. *Das Erdbeben von Lissabon und der Katastrophendiskurs im 18. Jahrhundert*. Göttingen: Wallstein, 2008.

Lefevere, André, ed. and trans. *Translating Literature: The German Tradition from Luther to Rosenzweig*. Assen, The Netherlands: Van Gorcum, 1977.

Lempa, Heikki. "Techniques of Epicurean Masculinity: The Play Method in German Education, 1774–1820." In *Masculinity, Senses, Spirit*, edited by Katherine M. Faull, 81–106. Lewisburg, PA: Bucknell University Press, 2011.

Lessenich, Rolf. "*Ars Disputandi* des Klassizismus 1660–1830: Tradition und Innovation der *Traditio Classicorum*." In *Streitkultur: Okzidentale Traditionen des Streitens in Literatur, Geschichte und Kunst*, edited by Uwe Baumann, Arnold Becker, and Astrid Steiner-Weber, 147–161. Bonn: Bonn University Press, 2008.

Lessing, Gotthold Ephraim. *Ernst and Falk: Conversations for the Freemasons*. Translated by William L. Zwiebel. In *Nathan the Wise, Minna von Barnhelm, and Other Plays and Writings*, edited by Peter Demetz, foreword by Hannah Arendt, 277–306. New York: Continuum, 1991.

———. *Minna von Barnhelm*. Translated by Kenneth J. Northcott. In *Nathan the Wise, Minna von Barnhelm, and Other Plays and Writings*, edited by Peter Demetz, foreword by Hannah Arendt, 1–74. New York: Continuum, 1991.

———. *Nathan the Wise*. Translated by Bayard Quincy Morgan. In *Nathan the Wise, Minna von Barnhelm, and Other Plays and Writings*, edited by Peter Demetz, foreword by Hannah Arendt, 173–275. New York: Continuum, 1991.

———. *Nathan the Wise, Minna von Barnhelm, and Other Plays and Writings*. Edited by Peter Demetz, foreword by Hannah Arendt. New York: Continuum, 1991.

———. *Werke und Briefe in 12 Bänden*. Edited by Wilfried Barner, Klaus Bohnen, Gunter E. Grimm, Helmuth Kiesel, Arno Schilson, Jürgen Stenzel, and Conrad Wiedemann. Frankfurt am Main: Deutscher Klassiker Verlag, 1984.

Leventhal, Robert S. *The Disciplines of Interpretation: Lessing, Herder, Schlegel and Hermeneutics in Germany, 1750–1800*. Berlin: De Gruyter, 1994.

Levine, Caroline. *Forms: Whole, Rhythm, Hierarchy, Network*. Princeton, NJ: Princeton University Press, 2015.

Lloyd, Clive L. *Napoleonic and American Prisoners of War, 1756–1816*. Woodbridge, Suffolk: Antique Collectors Club, 2007.

Louden, Robert B. "'Not a Slow *Reform*, but a Swift *Revolution*': Kant and Basedow on the Need to Transform Education." In *Kant and Education: Interpretations and Commentary*, edited by Klas Roth and Chris W. Surprenant, 39–54. New York: Routledge, 2012.

Luhmann, Niklas. *Gesellschaftsstruktur und Semantik: Studien zur Wissenssoziologie der modernen Gesellschaft*. 2 vols. Frankfurt am Main: Suhrkamp, 1993.

———. "Theoriesubstitution in der Erziehungswissenschaft: Von der Philanthropie zum Neuhumanismus." In *Gesellschaftsstruktur und Semantik: Studien zur Wissenssoziologie der modernen Gesellschaft*, vol. 2, 105–194. Frankfurt am Main: Suhrkamp, 1993.

Lund, Marie. *An Argument on Rhetorical Style*. Aarhus: Aarhus University Press, 2017.

———. "The Rhetorical Tradition of Invective." In *An Argument on Rhetorical Style*, 169–173. Aarhus: Aarhus University Press, 2017.

Luserke, Matthias. "*O vis superba formae!* Über die Basia-Gedichte des Johannes Sekundus (1511–1536) und ihr Nachspiel bei Goethe." In *Literatur und Kultur des Rokoko*, edited by Matthias Luserke, Reiner Marx, and Reiner Wild, 9–32. Göttingen: Vandenhoek & Rupprecht, 2001.

Luserke, Matthias, Reiner Marx, and Reiner Wild, eds. *Literatur und Kultur des Rokoko*. Göttingen: Vandenhoek & Rupprecht, 2001.

Malmkjær, Kirsten. "Schleiermacher's Metaphor." In *Friedrich Schleiermacher and the Question of Translation*, edited by Larisa Cercel and Adriana Şerban, 185–196. Berlin: De Gruyter, 2015.

Mann, Horace. *Report of an Educational Tour in Germany, and Parts of Great Britain and Ireland*. London: Simpkin, Marshall, 1846.

Mapp, Nigel, ed. *Adorno and Literature*. London: Continuum, 2006.

Marchart, Oliver. *Post-Foundational Political Thought: Political Difference in Nancy, Lefort, Badiou and Laclau*. Edinburgh: Edinburgh University Press, 2007.

Marcuse, Herbert. *Eros and Civilization: A Philosophical Inquiry into Freud*. Boston: Beacon, 1955.

Marenholtz-Bülow, Bertha von. *Erinnerungen an Friedrich Fröbel*. Vol. 1 of *Gesammelte Beiträge zum Verständniß der Fröbel'schen Erziehungsidee*. Kassel: Georg H. Wigand, 1876.

———. *How Kindergarten Came to America: Friedrich Froebel's Radical Vision of Early Childhood Education*. Translated by Mrs. Horace Mann. New York: New Press, 2007.

Martini, Fritz. *Lustspiele—und das Lustspiel*. Stuttgart: Ernst Klett, 1974.

Martyn, David. "Fichtes romantischer Ernst." In *Sprachen der Ironie—Sprachen des Ernstes*, edited by Karl Heinz Bohrer, 76–90. Frankfurt am Main: Suhrkamp, 2000.

———. *Sublime Failures: The Ethics of Kant and Sade*. Detroit: Wayne State University Press, 2003.

Mathäs, Alexander. *Narcissism and Paranoia in the Age of Goethe*. Newark: University of Delaware Press, 2008.

———, ed. *The Self as Muse: Narcissism and Creativity in the German Imagination, 1750–1830*. Lewisburg, PA: Bucknell University Press, 2011.

Matthews, Gareth, and Amy Mullin. "The Philosophy of Childhood." In *The Stanford Encyclopedia of Philosophy* (Spring 2015 Edition), edited by Edward N. Zalta. https://plato.stanford.edu/archives/spr2015/entries/childhood/.

Matussek, Peter. "*Faust II*—die Tragödie der Gedächtniskultur." In *Peter Stein inszeniert Faust von Johann Wolfgang Goethe: Das Programmbuch Faust I und II*, edited by Roswitha Schieb and Anna Haas, 291–296. Cologne: DuMont, 2000.

Mauser, Wolfram, and Günter Saße, eds. *Streitkultur: Strategien des Überzeugens im Werk Lessings: Referate der Internationalen Lessing-Tagung der Albert-Ludwigs-Universität Freiburg und der Lessing Society an der University of Cincinnati, Ohio/USA vom 22. bis 24. Mai 1991 in Freiburg im Breisgau*. Tübingen: Niemeyer, 1993.

McClellan, Marjorie L. "Hunting for Everyday History Theme 1: Toys and Games." In *Hunting for Everyday History: Local and Regional Organizations*. Wright State University CORE Scholar, 2003. https://corescholar.libraries.wright.edu/cgi/viewcontent.cgi?article=1001&context=hunting.

McClure, George. *Parlour Games and the Public Life of Women in Renaissance Italy*. Toronto: University of Toronto Press, 2013.

Meier, Georg Friedrich. *Frühe Schriften zur ästhetischen Erziehung der Deutschen in drei Teilen, Teil 2: Der "kleine Dichterkrieg" zwischen Halle und Leipzig.* Edited by Hans-Joachim Kertscher and Günter Schenk. Halle: Hallescher Verlag, 2000.

———. *Frühe Schriften zur ästhetischen Erziehung der Deutschen in drei Teilen, Teil 3: Philosophische Ästhetik—Literaturtheorie—neue deutsche Literatur.* Edited by Hans-Joachim Kertscher and Günter Schenk. Halle: Hallescher Verlag, 2002.

———. *Gedancken von Schertzen.* Halle: Hemmerde, 1754.

Menninghaus, Winfried. *In Praise of Nonsense: Kant and Bluebeard.* Translated by Henry Pickford. Stanford, CA: Stanford University Press, 1999.

Michel, Christoph. *Goethe: Sein Leben in Bildern und Texten.* Frankfurt am Main: Insel Verlag, 1998.

Miller, J. Hillis. "Derrida and de Man: Two Rhetorics of Deconstruction." In *A Companion to Derrida*, edited by Zeynep Direk and Leonard Lawlor, 345–361. Chichester, West Sussex: Wiley Blackwell, 2014.

Moretti, Franco. *Modern Epic: The World-System from Goethe to García Márquez.* London: Verso, 1996.

———. *Signs Taken for Wonders: Essays in the Sociology of Literary Forms.* Translated by Susan Fischer, David Forgacs and David Miller. New York: Verso, 1983.

Morfino, Vittorio. *La Spinoza-Renaissance nella Germania di Fine Settecento.* Milan: Unicopli, 1998.

Moritz, Karl Philipp, "Auch eine Hypothese über die Schöpfungsgeschichte Mosis." In *Werke.* Vol. 3, edited by Horst Günther, 787–792. Frankfurt am Main: Insel Verlag, 1981.

———. *Werke.* 3 vols. Edited by Horst Günther. Frankfurt am Main: Insel Verlag, 1981.

Moser, Christian, and Regine Strätling, eds. *Sich selbst aufs Spiel setzen: Spiel als Technik und Medium von Subjektivierung.* Paderborn: Fink, 2016.

———. "Sich selbst aufs Spiel setzen: Überlegungen zur Einführung." In *Sich selbst aufs Spiel setzen: Spiel als Technik und Medium von Subjektivierung*, edited by Christian Moser and Regine Strätling, 9–27. Paderborn: Fink, 2016.

Mücke, Dorothea von. "Spiel und Glück in Lessings *Minna von Barnhelm oder das Soldatenglück.*" In *Sich Selbst aufs Spiel setzen: Spiel als Technik und Medium von Subjektivierung*, edited by Christian Moser and Regine Strätling, 51–66. Paderborn: Wilhelm Fink, 2016.

Müller, Götz. *Jean Paul im Kontext: Gesammelte Aufsätze.* Tübingen: Königshausen und Neumann, 1996.

———. "Jean Pauls Ästhetik im Kontext der Frühromantik und des deutschen Idealismus." In *Jean Paul im Kontext: Gesammelte Aufsätze*, 63–77. Tübingen: Königshausen und Neumann, 1996.

Müller, Ulrich, Jeremy I. M. Carpendale, and Leslie Smith, eds. *The Cambridge Companion to Piaget.* Cambridge: Cambridge University Press, 2009.

Neuenfeld, Jörg. *Alles ist Spiel: Zur Geschichte der Auseinandersetzung mit einer Utopie der Moderne.* Würzburg: Königshausen & Neumann, 2005.

Neumann, Uwe. "Invektive." In *Historisches Wörterbuch der Rhetorik*, edited by Gert Ueding, vol. 3, 549–561. Tübingen: De Gruyter, 1996.

Niethammer, Friedrich Immanuel. *Der Streit des Philanthropinismus und Humanismus in der Theorie des Erziehungs-Unterrichts unserer Zeit.* Jena: Friedrich Frommann, 1808.

Novalis [Friedrich von Hardenberg]. *Schriften: Die Werke Friedrich von Hardenbergs*. Edited by Paul Kluckhohn and Richard Samuel. 6 vols. Stuttgart: Kohlhammer, 1960–65.

Oesterle, Günter. "Das 'Unmanierliche' der Streitschrift: Zum Verhältnis von Polemik und Kritik in Aufklärung und Romantik." In *Kontroversen alte und neue: Akten des VII. Internationalen Germanisten-Kongresses*. Vol. 2, *Formen und Formgeschichte des Streitens*, edited by Albrecht Schöne, 107–120. Tübingen: Niemeyer, 1986.

———, ed. *Erinnerung, Gedächtnis, Wissen: Studien zur kulturwissenschaftlichen Gedächtnisforschung*. Göttingen: Vandenhoeck & Ruprecht, 2005.

Oliver, Valerie. "History of the Yo-Yo." Museum of Yo-Yo History. yoyomuseum.com /museum_view.php?action=profiles&subaction=yoyo. Accessed June 7, 2019.

Ortlieb, Cornelia. *Friedrich Heinrich Jacobi und die Philosophie als Schreibart*. Munich: Fink, 2010.

Oswald, Stephan. *Früchte einer großen Stadt—Goethes "Venezianische Epigramme."* Heidelberg: Winter, 2014.

Overhoff, Jürgen. ". . . aber mit Lust!" *Die Zeit*, April 10, 2003. http://www.zeit.de/2003 /16/A-Basedow.

Paul, Jean [Johann Paul Friedrich Richter]. *Horn of Oberon: Jean Paul Richter's School for Aesthetics*. Translated by Margaret R. Hale. Detroit: Wayne State University Press, 1973.

———. *Levana; or, the Doctrine of Education*. London: George Bell & Sons, 1897.

———. *Werke*. Edited by Norbert Miller. 6 vols. Munich: Carl Hanser, 1959–63.

Pestalozzi, (Johann) Heinrich. "Die Methode: Eine Denkschrift Pestalozzi's." In *Allgemeine Monatschrift für Erziehung und Unterricht*, vol. 9, edited by J. P. Rossel, 66–80, 161–174. Aachen, 1828.

———. *How Gertrude Teaches Her Children: An Attempt to Help Mothers to Teach Their Own Children and an Account of the Method*. Edited by Ebenezer Cooke and translated by Lucy E. Holland and Frances C. Turner. Syracuse, NY: C. W. Bardeen, 1898.

———. *Wie Gertrud ihre Kinder lehrt, ein Versuch den Müttern Anleitung zu geben, ihre Kinder selbst zu unterrichten*. Bern: Heinrich Gess, 1801.

Pfau, Thomas. "The Appearance of *Stimmung*: Play as Virtual Rationality." In *Stimmung: Zur Wiederkehr einer ästhetischen Kategorie*, edited by Anna-Katharina Gisbertz, 95–111. Munich: Fink, 2011.

———. "*Bildungsspiele*: Vicissitudes of Socialization in *Wilhelm Meister's Apprenticeship*." *European Romantic Review* 21, no. 5 (October 2010): 567–587.

Piaget, Jean. *Insights and Illusions of Philosophy*. Translated by Wolfe Mays. New York: World, 1971.

———. *Judgment and Reasoning in the Child*. Translated by Marjorie Warden. Paterson, NJ: Littlefield, Adams, 1964.

———. *The Language and Thought of the Child*. Translated by Marjorie and Ruth Gabain. London: Routledge, 2002.

———. *The Moral Judgment of the Child*. Translated by Marjorie Gabain. New York: Free Press Paperbacks, 1997.

———. *Play, Dreams and Imitation in Childhood*. Translated by C. Gattegno and F. M. Hodgson. New York: W. W. Norton, 1962.

———. "Response to Brian Sutton-Smith." *Psychological Review* 73, no. 1 (1966): 111–112.

Powers, Michael. "The Smallest Remainder: Benjamin and Freud on Play." *MLN* 133, no. 3 (2018): 720–742.

Prelinger, Catherine M. *Charity, Challenge, and Change: Religious Dimensions of the Mid-Nineteenth-Century Women's Movement in Germany*. Westport, CT: Greenwood, 1987.

Pym, Anthony. "Schleiermacher and the Problem of Blendlinge." *Translation and Literature* 4 (1995): 5–30.

Quiniou, Hélène. "From Friedrich Schleiermacher to Homi K. Bhabha: Foreignizing Translation from Above or from Below?" In *Rereading Schleiermacher: Translation, Cognition and Culture*, edited by Teresa Seruya and José Miranda Justo, 79–88. Heidelberg: Springer, 2016.

Radrizzani, Ives. "Jacobis Auseinandersetzung mit Fichte in den *Denkbüchern*." *Fichte-Studien* 14 (1998): 43–62.

———. "Le *Fragment*. Première réponse de Fichte à la *Lettre* de Jacobi." In *Jacobi in Discussione*, edited by Tristana Dini and Salvatore Principe, 97–104. Milan: Franco Angeli, 2012.

Rak, Michele. "Logic of Fairies." *Romanic Review* 99, no. 3–4 (May–November 2008): 297–316.

Rehwinkel, Kerstin. "Kopflos, aber lebendig? Konkurrierende Körperkonzepte in der Debatte um den Tod durch Enthauptung im ausgehenden 18. Jahrhundert." In *Körper mit Geschichte: Der menschliche Körper als Ort der Selbst- und Weltdeutung*, edited by Clemens Wischermann and Stefan Haas, 151–171. Stuttgart: Franz Steiner Verlag, 2000.

Rennie, Nicholas. "Hier wird's Eräugnis: Performativität und Ende in Goethes *Faust*." In *Geistiger Handelsverkehr: Komparatistische Aspekte der Goethezeit*, edited by Anne Bohnenkamp and Matías Martínez, 395–410. Göttingen: Wallstein, 2008.

———. *Speculating on the Moment: The Poetics of Time and Recurrence in Goethe, Leopardi and Nietzsche*. Göttingen: Wallstein, 2005.

Richardson, Ruth Drucilla, ed. *Friedrich Schleiermacher's Toward a Theory of Sociable Conduct and Essays on Its Intellectual-Cultural Context*. Lewiston: Edwin Mellen, 1995.

Richter, Karl. "Die Legitimierung der Sexualität in Gedichten des Rokoko." In *Anakreontische Aufklärung*, edited by Manfred Beetz and Hans-Joachim Kertscher, 63–77. Tübingen: Niemeyer, 2005.

Ricœur, Paul. *Time and Narrative*. Translated by Kathleen McLaughlin and David Pellauer. 3 vols. Chicago: University of Chicago Press, 1990.

Rinke, Alfons. *Friedrich Fröbels philosophische Entwicklung unter dem Einfluß der Romantik*. Langensalza: Hermann Beyer & Söhne, 1935.

Ritter, Joachim, and Karlfried Gründer, eds. *Historisches Wörterbuch der Philosophie*. Vol. 9. Basel: Schwabe, 1995.

Robinson, Douglas. *Schleiermacher's Icoses: Social Ecologies of the Different Methods of Translating*. Bucharest: Zeta Books, 2013.

———, ed. *Western Translation Theory from Herodotus to Nietzsche*. Manchester, UK: St. Jerome, 1997.

Rönne, Ludwig von. *Das Unterrichtswesen des preußischen Staates*. Berlin: Veit & Comp., 1855.

Rossel, J. P. *Allgemeine Monatschrift für Erziehung und Unterricht*. Vol. 9. Aachen, 1828.

Roth, Klas, and Chris W. Surprenant, eds. *Kant and Education: Interpretations and Commentary*. New York: Routledge, 2012.

Rousseau, Jean-Jacques. *Emile or on Education*. Translated by Allan Bloom. New York: Basic Books, 1979.

Russell, Wendy, and Emily Ryall. "Philosophizing Play." In *The Handbook of the Study of Play*, edited by James E. Johnson, Scott G. Eberle, Thomas S. Henricks, and David Kuschner, vol. 2, 139–162. New York: Rowman & Littlefield, 2015.

Sadigh, Parvin. "Killerspiele schaden doch." 1. November 2006, 13:00 Uhr. Aktualisiert am 18. April 2008, 5:56 Uhr. *ZEIT* online. https://www.zeit.de/online/2006/49/computerspiele-gewalt-psychologie. Accessed June 7, 2019.

Salen, Katie, and Eric Zimmermann, eds. *The Game Design Reader: A Rules of Play Anthology*. Cambridge, MA: MIT Press, 2006.

Sandkaulen, Birgit. *Grund und Ursache: Die Vernunftkritik Jacobis*. Munich: Fink, 2000.

———. "'Oder hat Vernunft den Menschen?' Zur Vernunft des Gefühls bei Jacobi." *Zeitschrift für philosophische Forschung* 49, no. 3 (1995): 416–429.

———, ed. *System und Systemkritik: Beiträge zu einem Grundproblem der klassischen deutschen Philosophie*. Würzburg: Königshausen & Neumann, 2006.

Sanislo, Teresa. "Models of Manliness and Femininity: The Physical Culture of the Enlightenment and Early National Movement in Germany, 1770–1819." PhD diss., University of Michigan, 2001.

Schanze, Helmut. *Goethes Dramatik: Theater der Erinnerung*. Theatron: Studien zur Geschichte und Theorie der dramatischen Künste 4. Tübingen: Niemeyer, 1989.

Scherer, Heinrich. *Die Pädagogik als Wissenschaft von Pestalozzi bis zur Gegenwart*. Leipzig: Friedrich Brandstetter, 1907.

Schestag, Thomas. "Bibliographie für Jean Paul." *MLN* 113, no. 3 (1998): 465–523.

Scheuer, Hans Jürgen. *Manier und Urphänomen: Lektüren zur Relation von Erkenntnis und Darstellung in Goethes Poetologie der "geprägten Form."* Würzburg: Königshausen & Neumann, 1996.

Schieb, Roswitha, and Anna Haas, eds. *Peter Stein inszeniert Faust von Johann Wolfgang Goethe: Das Programmbuch Faust I und II*. Cologne: DuMont, 2000.

Schiller, Friedrich. "Briefe zur ästhetischen Erziehung des Menschen." *Schillers Werke: Nationalausgabe*. Edited by Julius Petersen, Hermann Schneider, Liselotte Blumenthal, Benno von Wiese, Norbert Oellers, and Siegfried Seidel. Vol. 20, *Philosophische Schriften I*. Weimar: Bölhaus, 1962.

———. *On the Aesthetic Education of Man in a Series of Letters*. Translated by Elizabeth M. Wilkinson and L. A. Willoughby. Oxford: Clarendon, 1982.

———. *On the Aesthetic Education of Man in a Series of Letters*. Translated and introduced by Reginald Snell. New Haven, CT: Yale University Press, 1954.

———. *Sämtliche Werke*. Edited by Gerhard Fricke and Herbert G. Göpfert. Munich: Hanser, 1962.

———. *Schillers Sämmtliche Werke*. Vol. 4. Stuttgart: J. G. Cotta'sche Buchhandlung, 1879.

———. *Schillers Werke: Nationalausgabe*. Edited by Julius Petersen, Hermann Schneider, Liselotte Blumenthal, Benno von Wiese, Norbert Oellers, and Siegfried Seidel. Weimar: Bölhaus, 1943–.

———. *Über die ästhetische Erziehung des Menschen in einer Reihe von Briefen*. Stuttgart: Reclam, 1965.

Schings, Hans-Jürgen. *Der mitleidigste Mensch ist der beste Mensch: Poetik des Mitleids von Lessing bis Büchner*. Munich: Beck, 1980.

Schlaffer, Heinz. *Musa iocosa: Gattungspoetik und Gattungsgeschichte der erotischen Dichtung in Deutschland*. Stuttgart: Metzler, 1971.

Schlegel, August Wilhelm. "Ankündigung: *Sprachlehre* von A.F. Bernhardi." *Europa: Eine Zeitschrift* 2, no. 1 (1803): 193–204.

———. *Kritische Schriften und Briefe*. Edited by Edgar Lohner. 5 vols. Stuttgart: Kohlhammer, 1962–66.

Schlegel, Friedrich. *Kritische Friedrich-Schlegel-Ausgabe*. Edited by Ernst Behler, Jean Jacques Anstett, and Hans Eichner. Munich: Schöningh, 1958–.

Schleiermacher, Friedrich. *Ästhetik (1819/25)*. Edited by Thomas Lehnerer. Hamburg: Meiner, 1984.

———. *Erziehungslehre: Aus Schleiermacher's handschriftlichem Nachlasse und nachgeschriebenen Vorlesungen*. In *Friedrich Schleiermacher's Sämmtliche Werke*, Abteilung 3, vol. 9, edited by C. Platz. Berlin: G. Reimer, 1846ff.

———. *Friedrich Schleiermacher's Sämmtliche Werke*. Abteilung 3, vol. 9. Edited by C. Platz. Berlin: G. Reimer, 1846ff.

———. "Gelegentliche Gedanken über Universitäten im deutschen Sinn: Anhang über eine neu zu errichtende Universität." In *Friedrich Schleiermacher's Sämmtliche Werke*, Abteilung 3, vol. 1, edited by C. Platz, 602–616. Berlin: G. Reimer, 1846ff.

———. *Hermeneutik und Kritik*. Edited by Manfred Frank. Frankfurt am Main: Suhrkamp, 1977.

———. *Kritische Gesamtausgabe*. Part I, *Schriften und Entwürfe*. Vol. 11, *Akademievorträge*. Edited by Martin Rößler. Berlin: De Gruyter, 2002.

———. *Occasional Thoughts on Universities in the German Sense: With an Appendix Regarding a University Soon to Be Established*. Translated by Terrence Tice and Edwina Lawler. Lewiston, NY: Edwin Mellen, 1991.

———. "On the Different Methods of Translating." In *Translating Literature: The German Tradition from Luther to Rosenzweig*, translated and edited by André Lefevere, 66–89. Assen, The Netherlands: Van Gorcum, 1977.

———. "On the Different Methods of Translating." Translated by Douglas Robinson. In *Western Translation Theory from Herodotus to Nietzsche*, edited by Douglas Robinson, 225–238. Manchester, UK: St. Jerome, 1997.

———. "On the Different Methods of Translating." Translated by Susan Bernofsky. In *The Translation Studies Reader*, edited by Lawrence Venuti, 43–63. London: Routledge, 2000; 3rd ed., 2012.

———. "Toward a Theory of Sociable Conduct." Translated by Jeffrey Hoover. In *Friedrich Schleiermacher's Toward a Theory of Sociable Conduct and Essays on Its Intellectual-Cultural Context*, edited by Ruth Drucilla Richardson, 20–39. Lewiston, NY: Edwin Mellen, 1995.

———. "Über die verschiedenen Methoden des Übersetzens." In *Kritische Gesamtausgabe*. Part I, *Schriften und Entwürfe*. Vol. 11, *Akademievorträge*, edited by Martin Rößler, 65–94. Berlin: De Gruyter, 2002.

———. "Ueber die verschiedenen Methoden des Uebersezens." In *Das Problem des Übersetzens*, edited by Hans Joachim Störig, 38–70. Stuttgart: Henry Goverts, 1963.

Schleunes, Karl. *Schooling and Society: The Politics of Education in Prussia and Bavaria, 1750–1900*. Providence, RI: Berg, 1989.

Schneider, Helmut J., ed. *Idyllen der Deutschen*. Frankfurt am Main: Insel, 1981.

———. "Playing Tragedy: Detaching Tragedy from Itself in Classical Drama from Lessing to Büchner." In *The Play within the Play: The Performance of Meta-theatre and Self-reflection*, edited by Gerhard Fischer and Bernhard Greiner, 237–247. Amsterdam: Rodopi, 2007.

———. "Schenken und Tauschen: Bemerkungen zu einer Grundfigur der Lessingschen Dramatik." In *Streitkultur: Strategien des Überzeugens im Werk Lessings; Referate der Internationalen Lessing-Tagung der Albert-Ludwigs-Universität Freiburg und der Lessing Society an der University of Cincinnati, Ohio/USA vom 22. bis 24. Mai 1991 in Freiburg im Breisgau*, edited by Wolfram Mauser and Günter Saße, 462–471. Tübingen: Niemeyer, 1993.

Schneider, Steffen. *Archivpoetik: Die Funktion des Wissens in Goethes "Faust II."* Tübingen: Niemeyer, 2005.

Scholz, Heinrich, ed. *Die Hauptschriften zum Pantheismusstreit zwischen Jacobi und Mendelssohn*. Berlin: Reuther & Reichard, 1916.

Schöne, Albrecht, ed. *Kontroversen alte und neue: Akten des VII. Internationalen Germanisten-Kongresses*. Vol. 2, *Formen und Formgeschichte des Streitens*. Tübingen: Niemeyer, 1986.

Schreiber, Elliott. *The Topography of Modernity: Karl Philipp Moritz and the Space of Autonomy*. Ithaca, NY: Cornell University Press and Cornell University Library, 2012.

———. "The Virtue of Play: Games and Stories for Children in Three Pedagogical Texts of the Enlightenment." *Eighteenth-Century Studies* (forthcoming).

Schulz, Günter, ed. *Lessing und der Kreis seiner Freunde*. Heidelberg: Lambert Schneider, 1985.

Seruya, Teresa, and José Miranda Justo, eds. *Rereading Schleiermacher: Translation, Cognition and Culture*. Heidelberg: Springer, 2016.

Shakespeare, William. *The Complete Works of Shakespeare*. Edited by David Bevington. New York: HarperCollins, 1992.

———. *William Shakspere's sämtliche Dramatische Werke*. Translated by August Wilhelm Schlegel, O. Benda, Johann Heinrich Voss, and Max Leopold Moltke. 3 vols. Leipzig: Reclam, 1882.

Shifrin, Donald, Ari Brown, David Hill, Laura Jana, and Susan K. Flinn. "Growing up Digital: Media Research Symposium." American Academy of Pediatrics, October 1, 2015. https://www.aap.org/en-us/Documents/digital_media_symposium_proceedings.pdf.

Simon, Ralf. "Nathans Argumentationsverfahren: Konsequenzen der Fiktionalisierung von Theorie in Lessings Drama *Nathan der Weise*." *Deutsche Vierteljahrsschrift für Literaturwissenschaft und Geistesgeschichte* 65, no. 4 (December 1991): 609–635.

Simpson, Patricia Anne. *The Erotics of War in German Romanticism*. Lewisburg, PA: Bucknell University Press, 2006.

Smith, Dana. "This Is What Candy Crush Saga Does to Your Brain." *Guardian*, April 1, 2014. https://www.theguardian.com/science/blog/2014/apr/01/candy-crush-saga-app-brain.

Smith, Gary, and Hinderk M. Emrich, eds. *Vom Nutzen des Vergessens*. Berlin: Akademie-Verlag, 1996.

Sontag, Susan. Preface to *Writing Degree Zero* by Roland Barthes [1967]. Translated by Annette Lavers and Colin Smith. New York: Hill and Wang, 2009.

Spariosu, Mihai I. *Dionysus Reborn: Play and the Aesthetic Dimension in Modern Philosophical and Scientific Discourse*. Ithaca, NY: Cornell University Press, 1989.

Stockhammer, Robert. "Das Schon-Übersetzte: Auch eine Theorie der Weltliteratur." *Poetica* 41, no. 3/4 (2009): 257–291.

———. "Zur Konversion von Sprachigkeit in Sprachlichkeit (langagification des langues) in Goethes *Wilhelm Meister*-Romanen." *Critical Multilingualism Studies* 5, no. 3 (2017): 13–31.

Störig, Hans Joachim, ed. *Das Problem des Übersetzens*. Stuttgart: Henry Goverts, 1963.

Strätling, Regine, ed. *Spielformen des Selbst: Das Spiel zwischen Subjektivität, Kunst und Alltagspraxis*. Bielefeld: transcript, 2012.

Strauss, Leo. "Das Erkenntnisproblem in der philosophischen Lehre Fr. H. Jacobis." In *Philosophie und Gesetz—Frühe Schriften*, edited by Heinrich Meier and Wiebke Meier, 237–292. Vol. 2 of *Gesammelte Schriften*. Stuttgart: Metzler, 1997.

———. *Gesammelte Schriften*. Vol. 2, *Philosophie und Gesetz—Frühe Schriften*, edited by Heinrich Meier and Wiebke Meier. Stuttgart: Metzler, 1997.

Strauss, Thomas. *Frühe Spielwelten zur Belehrung und Unterhaltung: Die Spielwarenkataloge von Peter Friedrich Catel (1747–1791) und Georg Hieronimus Bestelmeier (1764–1829)*. Hochwald: Librum, 2015.

Suruya, Teresa, and José Miranda Justo, eds. *Rereading Schleiermacher: Translation, Cognition and Culture*. Heidelberg: Springer, 2016.

Sutton-Smith, Brian. *The Ambiguity of Play*. Cambridge, MA: Harvard University Press, 1997.

———. "Piaget on Play: A Critique." *Psychological Review*, no. 1 (1966): 104–110.

———. "Play and Ambiguity." In *The Game Design Reader: A Rules of Play Anthology*, edited by Katie Salen and Eric Zimmermann, 296–313. Cambridge, MA: MIT Press, 2006.

———. "Play Theory: A Personal Journey and New Thoughts." *American Journal of Play* 1, no. 1 (Summer 2008): 80–123.

Szondi, Peter. "Friedrich Schlegel and Romantic Irony, with Some Remarks on Tieck's Comedies." In *On Textual Understanding and Other Essays*, translated by Harvey Mendelsohn, 57–73. Minneapolis: University of Minnesota Press, 1986.

———. *On Textual Understanding and Other Essays*. Translated by Harvey Mendelsohn. Minneapolis: University of Minnesota Press, 1986.

Tatar, Maria, ed. and trans. *The Annotated Brothers Grimm*. New York: W. W. Norton, 2004.

Tieck, Ludwig. *Schriften in zwölf Bänden*. Edited by Manfred Frank, Paul Gerhard Klussmann, Ernst Ribbat, Uwe Schweikert, and Wulf Segebrecht, 12 vols. Frankfurt am Main: Deutscher Klassiker Verlag, 1985–.

Till, Dietmar. *Transformationen der Rhetorik: Untersuchungen zum Wandel der Rhetoriktheorie im 17. und 18. Jahrhundert*. Berlin: De Gruyter, 2004.

Timm, Hermann. "Die Bedeutung der Spinozabriefe für die Entwicklung der idealistischen Religionsphilosophie." In *Friedrich Heinrich Jacobi: Philosoph und Literat der Goethezeit*, edited by Klaus Hammacher, 35–81. Frankfurt am Main: Klostermann, 1971.

Torner, Evan, Aaron Trammell, and Emma Leigh Waldron. "Reinventing Analog Game Studies." *Analog Game Studies* 1, no. 1 (August 1, 2014). http://analoggamestudies.org/2014/08/reinventing-analog-game-studies/.

Trier, Jost. "Spiel." *Beiträge zur Geschichte der deutschen Sprache und Literatur* 69 (1947): 419–462.

———. "Zaun und Mannring." *Beiträge zur Geschichte der deutschen Sprache und Literatur* 66 (1942): 232–264.

Trop, Gabriel. *Poetry as a Way of Life: Aesthetics and Askesis in the German Eighteenth Century.* Evanston, IL: Northwestern University Press, 2015.

Tucker, Brian. *Reading Riddles: Rhetorics of Obscurity from Romanticism to Freud.* Lewisburg, PA: Bucknell University Press, 2011.

Ueding, Gert, Gregor Kalivoda, Walter Jens, Wilfried Barner, and Ole Kazich, eds. *Historisches Wörterbuch der Rhetorik.* 12 vols. Tübingen: De Gruyter, 1992–2015.

Uz, Johann Peter. *Saemmtliche Poetische Werke.* Vienna: von Trattnern, 1769.

Venuti, Lawrence, ed. *The Translation Studies Reader.* London: Routledge, 2000; 3rd ed., 2012.

———. *The Translator's Invisibility: A History of Translation.* London: Routledge, 1995.

Verweyen, Theodor. "'Halle, die Hochburg des Pietismus, die Wiege der Anakreontik': Über das Konfliktpotential der anakreontischen Poesie als Kunst der 'sinnlichen Erkenntnis.'" In *Zentren der Aufklärung I: Halle; Aufklärung und Pietismus*, edited by Norbert Hinske, 209–238. Heidelberg: Schneider, 1989.

Vygotsky, L. S. *Mind in Society: The Development of Higher Psychological Processes.* Edited by Michael Cole, Vera John-Steiner, Sylvia Scribner, and Ellen Souberman. Cambridge, MA: Harvard University Press, 1978.

———. "The Role of Play in Development." In *Mind in Society: The Development of Higher Psychological Processes*, edited by Michael Cole, Vera John-Steiner, Sylvia Scribner, and Ellen Souberman, 92–104. Cambridge, MA: Harvard University Press, 1978.

Wachter, Alexander. *Das Spiel in der Ästhetik: Zu Kants "Kritik der Urteilskraft."* Berlin: De Gruyter, 2006.

Wagner, Johann Franz. *Anweisung zum Briefschreiben nach dem heutigen Geschmacke.* 2nd ed. Weimar: Bützow, 1767.

Warminski, Andrzej. "Returns of the Sublime: Positing and Performative in Kant, Fichte, and Schiller." *MLN* 116, no. 5 (December 2001): 964–978.

Weber-Kellermann, Ingeborg. *Die Kinderstube.* Frankfurt am Main: Insel, 1991.

———. *Die Kindheit: Eine Kulturgeschichte.* Frankfurt am Main: Insel, 1997.

———. *Die Kindheit: Kleidung und Wohnen, Arbeit und Spiel: Eine Kulturgeschichte.* Frankfurt am Main: Insel, 1979.

Weidner, Daniel. "Frevelhafte Doppelgänger und sprachbildende Kraft: Zur Wiederkehr der Anderssprachigkeit in Schleiermachers Hermeneutik." In *Exophonie: Anders-Sprachigkeit (in) der Literatur*, edited by Susan Arndt, Dirk Naguschewski, and Robert Stockhammer, 229–247. Berlin: Kadmos, 2007.

Weimar, Klaus. "Das Wandeln des Wortlosen in der Sprache des Gedichts." In *Klopstock an der Grenze der Epochen*, edited by Katrin Kohl and Kevin F. Hilliard, 33–45. Berlin: De Gruyter, 1995.

Weinrich, Harald. "Dante und Faust." In *Vom Nutzen des Vergessens*, edited by Gary Smith and Hinderk M. Emrich, 105–132. Berlin: Akademie-Verlag, 1996.

———. *Lethe: The Art and Critique of Forgetting*. Ithaca, NY: Cornell University Press, 2004.

Weiss, Joel, Jason Nolan, Jeremy Hunsinger, and Peter Trifonas, eds. *International Handbook of Virtual Learning Environments*. Dordrecht, Netherlands: Springer, 2006.

Weitzman, Erica. *Irony's Antics: Walser, Kafka, Roth and the German Comic Tradition*. Evanston, IL: Northwestern University Press, 2015.

Wellbery, David E. *Lessing's Laocoon: Semiotics and Aesthetics in the Age of Reason*. Cambridge: Cambridge University Press, 1984.

———. *The Specular Moment: Goethe's Early Lyric and the Beginnings of Romanticism*. Stanford, CA: Stanford University Press, 1996.

———. "Übertragen: Metapher und Metonymie." In *Literaturwissenschaft—Einführung in ein Sprachspiel*, edited by Heinrich Bosse and Ursula Renner, 139–155. Freiburg im Breisgau: Rombach, 1999.

Wetzel, Tanja. "Spiel." In *Ästhetische Grundbegriffe: Historisches Wörterbuch in sieben Bänden*, edited by Karlheinz Barck and Martin Fontius, vol. 5, 577–618. Stuttgart: Metzler, 2003.

Wijman, Tom. "Mobile Revenues Account for More than 50% of the Global Games Market as It Reaches $137.9 Billion in 2018." *Newzoo*, April 30, 2018. https://newzoo.com/insights/articles/global-games-market-reaches-137-9-billion-in-2018-mobile-games-take-half/.

Wild, Reiner. *Goethes klassische Lyrik*. Stuttgart: Metzler, 1999.

Wilson, W. Daniel, *Das Goethe-Tabu: Protest und Menschenrechte im klassischen Weimar*. Munich: Deutscher Taschenbuchverlag, 1999.

———. "Goethe's Writings as Minister of State in Saxe-Weimar and Eisenach." *Goethe Yearbook* 22 (2015): 261–266.

Wilson, W. Daniel, and Robert C. Holub, eds. *Impure Reason: Dialectic of Enlightenment in Germany*. Detroit: Wayne State University Press, 1993.

Winnicott, Donald Woods. *Playing and Reality*. New York: Basic Books, 1971.

Wischermann, Clemens, and Stefan Haas, eds. *Körper mit Geschichte: Der menschliche Körper als Ort der Selbst- und Weltdeutung*. Stuttgart: Franz Steiner Verlag, 2000.

Wood, Kelli. "'Balls on Walls, Feet on Streets': Subversive Play in Grand Ducal Florence." *Renaissance Studies* 32, no. 3 (2018): 365–387.

———. "Chancing It: Print, Play, and Gambling Games in the Sixteenth Century." *Art History* 42, no. 3 (2019): 450–481.

World Health Organization. "Gaming Disorder. Online Q&A." September 2018. https://www.who.int/features/qa/gaming-disorder/en/.

Wurth, Leopold. *Das Wortspiel bei Shakspere*. Vienna: Wilhelm Braumüller, 1895.

Yates, Frances Amelia. *The Art of Memory*. Chicago: University of Chicago Press, 1966.

Yogman, Michael, Andrew Garner, Jeffrey Hutchinson, Kathy Hirsh-Pasek, Roberta Michnick Golinkoff; AAP Committee on Psychosocial Aspects of Child and Family Health, AAP Council on Communications and Media. "The Power of Play: A Pediatric Role in Enhancing Development in Children." *Pediatrics* 142, no. 3 (September 2018). http://pediatrics.aappublications.org/content/pediatrics/142/3/e20182058.full.pdf.

Zac, Sylvain. *Spinoza en Allemagne: Mendelssohn, Lessing et Jacobi*. Paris: Meridiens Klincksieck, 1989.

Zalta, Edward N., ed. *The Stanford Encyclopedia of Philosophy* (Spring 2015 Edition). https://plato.stanford.edu/.

Zammito, John. *The Genesis of Kant's "Critique of Judgment."* Chicago: Chicago University Press, 1992.

Zamosky, Lisa. "Toy Guns: Do They Lead to Real-Life Violence?" *WebMD*, December 1, 2011. https://www.webmd.com/parenting/features/toy-guns-do-they-lead-real-life-violence#1.

Zeh, Christian. "Bericht über die Fröbelsche Erziehungsanstalt zu Keilhau: An das hochfürstliche Consistorium zu Schwarzburg-Rudolstadt." *Isis von Oken* 2, no. 7 (1825): 779–784.

Zeuch, Ulrike. "Goethes Sinngebung des Erdbebens von Lissabon: Zur Funktion der Seismos-Episode im *Faust II.*" In *Das Erdbeben von Lissabon und der Katastrophendiskurs im 18. Jahrhundert*, edited by Gerhard Lauer, 173–187. Göttingen: Wallstein, 2008.

NOTES ON CONTRIBUTORS

CHRISTIANE FREY is an Alexander-von-Humboldt senior research fellow at the Humboldt Universität zu Berlin and taught at Princeton University, the University of Chicago, and, most recently, as associate professor, at New York University. Her research focuses on seventeenth- and eighteenth-century German literature and the history of knowledge in the European context. Her recent publications include *Laune: Poetiken der Selbstsorge von Montaigne bis Tieck* (Fink, 2016) and the coedited volume *Zu einer Poetik des Seriellen* (diaphanes, 2016). A coedited volume on *Säkularisierung: Grundlagentexte zur Theoriegeschichte* has recently been published (Suhrkamp, 2020), and she is the author of articles on topics ranging from "The Art of Observing the Small" to "The Semiotics of Crisis" and "Proportion and Mood in Kant's Aesthetic Theory." Current research projects include "The Time in Parenthesis: Constellations between Shakespeare and Gryphius" and "Micrologies of Knowledge and Narration."

SAMUEL HEIDEPRIEM is a Tsinghua-Michigan postdoctoral fellow in the Institute for World Literatures and Cultures at Tsinghua University in Beijing. He received his PhD from the Department of Germanic Languages and Literatures at the University of Michigan in 2017. His research focuses on political theory, intellectual history, and literary and media studies. He has published in the *Goethe Yearbook*, and is currently at work on a monograph, *The Politics of Writing*, which analyzes the role of written and print media in the construction of political ideology from the mid-eighteenth century to the present.

EDGAR LANDGRAF is professor of German at Bowling Green State University (Ohio). His research interests include German literature, aesthetics, and philosophy from the Enlightenment to today as well as critical improvisation studies, performance studies, systems theory, and theories of posthumanism. Recent publications include articles on improvisation, Goethe, Kant, Kleist, Nietzsche, and Johannes Müller. His book *Improvisation as Art: Conceptual Challenges, Historical Perspectives* was published in 2011 with Continuum (reissued as paperback by Bloomsbury in 2014). His anthology *Posthumanism in the Age of Humanism: Mind, Matter, and the Life Sciences After Kant*, coedited with Gabriel Trop and Leif Weatherby, appeared in October 2018. He is currently working on a monograph on Nietzsche's posthumanism.

DAVID MARTYN is professor of German studies at Macalester College. His research interests are eighteenth- and early nineteenth-century German literature and philosophy and theories of secularization. He is the author of *Sublime Failures: The Ethics of Kant and Sade* (Wayne State University Press, 2003), and a critical edition of Moses Mendelssohn's *Jerusalem*. Recent articles include a critical essay for the new Norton Anthologies edition of Goethe's *Werther*; a survey of the history of the "sublime" for Harvard University Press's forthcoming *Keywords in German Aesthetics*; and an article on Jewish secularization for a recent volume on Moses Mendelssohn in the *Text + Kritik* series. He is currently completing *Literatur als Zweitsprache von Leibniz bis Tawada: Ansätze zu einer Archeologie der Sprachigkeit* (under contract with the Fink Verlag).

IAN F. MCNEELY is professor of history and department head of German and Scandinavian at the University of Oregon. His publications include two books on nineteenth-century Germany, *The Emancipation of Writing: German Civil Society in the Making, 1790s–1820s* and *"Medicine on a Grand Scale": Rudolf Virchow, Liberalism, and the Public Health*, in addition to *Reinventing Knowledge: From Alexandria to the Internet* and articles on the Renaissance academies, Wilhelm von Humboldt's global linguistics, and the Viennese intellectual-turned-American management guru Peter Drucker. His current work focuses on the origins of the neoliberal university in the late twentieth century.

MICHAEL POWERS is visiting assistant professor of German studies at Kalamazoo College. His research interests include literary theory, visual culture, media studies, and intersections of art, politics, and philosophy. He has published on Goethe, Benjamin, Freud, and Merleau-Ponty in journals including *MLN* and *The German Quarterly*, and his current book project centers on the writings of Walter Benjamin.

NICHOLAS RENNIE is associate professor of German and an affiliate in comparative literature at Rutgers University. As a Humboldt Fellow, he has undertaken research at the Free University Berlin and the Ludwig-Maximilians-University Munich, where he also taught. Author of *Speculating on the Moment: The Poetics of Time and Recurrence in Goethe, Leopardi, and Nietzsche* (Wallstein, 2005), he has published articles on these writers as well as on Molière, Lessing, and Benjamin. His research focuses on literature of the Enlightenment and the Age of Goethe, aesthetics and intellectual history from the eighteenth century to the present, and theories of drama. He is currently working on a book project tentatively titled *Gotthold Ephraim Lessing and the Eighteenth-Century Reinvention of Memory.*

ELLIOTT SCHREIBER is associate professor of German studies at Vassar College, where he also serves as departmental chair. His monograph, *The Topography of Modernity: Karl Philipp Moritz and the Space of Autonomy*, appeared with Cornell in 2012. He has recently coedited a special section of the Goethe Yearbook on "The Poetics of Space in the *Goethezeit*." He has published several articles on the European fairy tale in the eighteenth and nineteenth centuries, and is currently at work on a book titled *Toy Stories: Fairy Tales, Toys, and the Discovery of Imaginative Play in Germany around 1800.*

PATRICIA ANNE SIMPSON is a professor and chairperson of modern languages and literatures at the University of Nebraska. Her monograph, *Reimagining the European Family: Cultures of Immigration* (Palgrave, 2013), examines the effects of recent patterns of immigration on the representation of the family in Europe. Author of *Cultures of Violence in the New German Street* (Rowman & Littlefield, 2012) and *The Erotics of War in German Romanticism* (Bucknell University Press, 2006), Simpson has also coedited several volumes on the literature, religion, and visual cultures in the Age of Goethe. Most recently, the coedited volume *Digital Media Strategies of the Far Right in Europe and the United States* appeared (Lexington Books, 2015); this work led to a further project on the European far right and the refugee crisis (special issue of *German Politics and Society*). Project Director and Principal Investigator for a US Department of Education Title VI Undergraduate International Studies and Foreign Languages grant (UISFL, 2008–2010), recipient of the Goethe Society of North America's Essay Prize (2014), the Meritorious Research Award from MSU (2015), and the Cox Family Award for Creative Scholarship and Teaching (2016), Simpson is currently working on a coauthored book chapter, "German Is the New Green? Language, Environmentalism, and Cultural Competence" for a planned MLA volume, *Foreign Language Teaching and the Environment: Theory, Curricula, Institutional Structures*. In addition, Simpson is completing a book-length study on the play world and childhood in transatlantic modernity.

BRIAN TUCKER is professor of German at Wabash College. His research interests center on German-language literature and intellectual history of the long nineteenth century. He is the author of *Reading Riddles: Rhetorics of Obscurity from Romanticism to Freud* (Bucknell University Press, 2011) and the coeditor of *Fontane in the Twenty-First Century* (Camden House, 2019). He is currently working on a monograph on irony and avowal in Fontane's works.

CHRISTIAN P. WEBER is an associate professor of German at Florida State University. Weber's monograph *Die Logik der Lyrik: Goethes Phänomenologie des Geistes in Gedichten* argues that Goethe's early "hymns of genius" perform as a poetic whole a thorough critique of the imagination that complements Kant's *Critique of Judgment* and rivals Hegel's *Phenomenology of Spirit*. He is currently working on a sequel that examines Goethe's later poetry on the same trajectory. Another book-length project investigates the formative powers of biopolitical metaphors (for example "grafting," "elective affinities," "self-generation") as cultural life-models for the organization of national identities and institutions.

INDEX

Note: Page numbers in italics denote figures.